MISHLEI

A MODERN COMMENTARY
ON PROVERBS

by
LEONARD S. KRAVITZ
and
KERRY M. OLITZKY

UAHC PRESS
NEW YORK, NEW YORK

Library of Congress Cataloging-in-Publication Data

Kravitz, Leonard S.
  Mishlei: a modern commentary on Proverbs / Leonard S. Kravitz and Kerry M. Olitzky.
    p. cm.
  Includes bibliographical references and index.
  ISBN 0-8074-0757-7 (pbk.: alk. paper)
  1. Bible. O.T. Proverbs—Commentaries. I. Olitzky, Kerry M. II. Title.

BS1465.53 K73 2002
223'.7077—dc21

                                                                    2002071974

The authors gratefully acknowledge the following for permission to reprint previously published material:

KTAV PUBLISHING HOUSE, INC.: Excerpts from *A Jewish Mourner's Handbook*
by Ron H. Isaacs and Kerry M. Olitzky. Reprinted by permission of KTAV Publishing House.

Typesetting: El Ot Ltd., Tel Aviv
This book is printed on acid-free paper.
Copyright © 2002 by UAHC Press
Manufactured in the United States of America
10 9 8 7 6 5 4 3 2 1

For Rabbi Bennett Miller

Acknowledgments

This volume represents the ongoing work of two colleagues, friends who have taught one another in their struggle over the content and context of Jewish life. On a regular basis, we have studied sacred text and argued about the veracity of its message for contemporary Jews. Whatever position we have taken in these pages and elsewhere, it is always "for the sake of heaven." While we taught in adjacent classrooms in the past, our work has now taken us to different places to teach. But our passion for sacred literature and its ability to enlighten us as it illumines our path in the world keeps us close together. For the opportunity to work with one another and to continue to drink from the wells of our tradition, we are profoundly grateful. We pray that we may be able to teach to others what we have learned from one another.

While this book contains the words of many who have discovered the wisdom of our tradition in their lives, it is important to note the contribution to the field and to this book of W. Gunther Plaut's *The Book of Proverbs: A Commentary,* published by the Union of American Hebrew Congregations in 1961. Plaut's insights are scattered throughout this volume.

We want to thank the staff of the UAHC Press for its continual support and encouragement in helping us to provide easily accessible vehicles that allow our people to reclaim the texts and own them. In particular we would like to thank Ken Gesser, Stuart Benick, Rick Abrams, Liane Broido, Benjamin David, and Debra Hirsch Corman. We express our deep appreciation to our former student and colleague Rabbi Hara Person. This book would not have been possible without her keen attention to detail and her special sensitivity to the way primary texts can speak to adults.

We thank our families for continuing on the journey with us and for providing us with a firm foundation so that we might reach higher and deeper at the same time.

Leonard S. Kravitz
Kerry ("Shia") Olitzky
Chanukah 5761

Contents

Contents

Introduction

Seichel, the Yiddish word for "common sense that emerges from reflection" best describes the content of the Book of Proverbs. Of all the books of the Bible, Proverbs more than any other deals with the an understanding of the world and an approach to life that comes from reflections based on human experience. Unlike the Torah or the Prophets, Proverbs does not deal with the sacred obligations of mitzvot, commandments. Rather, it focuses on everyday wisdom. Although it is attributed to King Solomon, it reflects the broader wisdom literature of the ancient Near East.

Because this book is different from the rest of the Bible, words like "wisdom," "instruction," "understanding," and the like will have different meanings as they are used here. Later Rabbinic Judaism understood these terms specifically in light of the mitzvah system, which it had created. For example, "wisdom" was understood by the Rabbis to mean "Torah." Thus, the appeal to "understand" was an appeal to study Torah for understanding. Just as the Rabbis understood the text through the prism of their own experience, we present the Book of Proverbs as it reflects the experience of the postmodern North American Jewish community. What does Proverbs mean to me, today?

We read the text looking for its literal meaning. We tried to understand its difficulties and sifted through rabbinic and medieval commentaries for guidance. Among the classical commentators available for study, we have made primary use of the works of Rashi, Abraham ibn Ezra, and Gersonides. They represent three different perspectives on the text and on Jewish life. We have also often added the perspective of Maimonides and insights culled from the interpretative Aramaic translation of the Bible known as the *Targum.* As a result, we intend to provide a new translation and commentary in a modern idiom, familiar to our readers. This approach will make the text and its wisdom readily available to all who would turn its pages. Along the way, we have added our own comments, those that emerge from the depth of own experience. These will further help us to understand the spiritual meaning of the text so that it can shed divine light on our daily lives.

We must acknowledge that there is some tension in the translation of the text and its commentary as we strive to be true to the original text, while simultaneously being sensitive to the context in which the author is writing and the often insensitive view taken toward women, as well as the gender specificity of the author's God-language. In many cases, we have allowed the author to speak in a personal voice, offering an apology and explanation for that voice in the commentary that follows individual verses. At other times, we have provided a contemporary filter for the author's words, editing out those items that may tend to exclude some readers and thereby rob them of the opportunity to gain from the wisdom and moral directives of the text. Our own individual disagreement over such a compromised approach often emerges in this work, reflecting the similarly polar perspectives taken by members of our postmodern Jewish community.

When it is necessary, and when it is inappropriate to interpret the text in a more politically correct way, it is our hope that readers will transcend the literal expression of the text as we have so that we may all benefit from its profound insight.

The Commentators

Judaism forms the soul of the Jewish people. This soul emerged from its books. First came the books of the Torah, then the books of the Prophets, and then the Writings. Then came those texts that developed from these primary sources: the Mishnah and *Tosefta,* the two forms of the Talmud (Babylonian and Jerusalem), the various midrashim, the commentaries, and the legal codes. This ongoing proliferation of books was the direct result of that people's reading and reflecting on its base literature. It is that reading and reflecting that created the people's soul: Judaism. We are indeed the people of the book! In order for individuals to read these books with greater facility, commentators arose, reading the various texts with the lens of their particular time and interest.

In this volume, we have selected three primary commentators with whose guidance we have come to better understand the text: Rashi, Abraham ibn Ezra, and Gersonides (also known as Ralbag). Rashi, who lived in Troyes (1040–1105), is generally considered the greatest commentator of all times. He commented on the entire Bible and the entire Babylonian Talmud. As a master of the rabbinic tradition, Rashi brought to bear the insights of the Rabbis in his interpretation of the verses of Proverbs, as well as a very good sense of the literal meaning of particular verses.

Abraham ibn Ezra (1089–1164) wrote his commentaries while traveling in Mantua, in Rome, and in London, as well as perhaps in the Land of Israel. Looking at the biblical texts with a critical eye, he hinted that the Torah text contained various strands and strata. Thus he may be considered one of the originators of what has come to be called higher criticism. He approached the text of Proverbs to understand what the writer of the book meant and not, as Rashi did, to have it mean what rabbinic tradition would have it mean.

Ralbag, Rabbi Levi ben Gershom or Gersonides (1288–1344) of Bagnols, reflects the high point of philosophical involvement in Judaism. A mathematician and astronomer, a philosopher and a talmudist, Gersonides may also have had a university degree, as is suggested in his title Maestre Leo. He wrote supercommentaries (that is, commentaries on commentaries) on Averroës' commentaries on Artistotle. His treatise on the astrolabe, as a precursor to the sextant, which he invented, was translated into Latin at the direction of Pope Clement VI. He wrote a commentary on the Torah and on Job, Song of Songs, and Ecclesiastes, as well as on Proverbs. His philosophical masterpiece was *Milchamot HaShem* (The Wars of the Lord). Even so, there is a kind of midrashic quality to his commentary on Proverbs. Just as Rashi read the rabbinic tradition into the text, Gersonides read philosophy into the text. The characters discussed by the writer of Proverbs will turn out, in Gersonides' commentary, to elucidate some of the Aristotelian notions of his time.

The disparate views of these three commentators suggest an important lesson for all of us. Each reader brings him- or herself into the reading of the text. In doing so, each individual reflects his or her own concerns and ideas about the world. A text lives because its readers can find meaning in it, as well as bring meaning to it.

CHAPTER ONE

א:א מִשְׁלֵי שְׁלֹמֹה בֶן־דָּוִד מֶלֶךְ יִשְׂרָאֵל:

1:1 THE PROVERBS OF SOLOMON, SON OF DAVID, KING OF ISRAEL

As we do, our ancestors attributed intellectual creations to persons in authority. While most of us are aware that the president of the United States generally does not write his own speeches, we quote them as if he did. It was the same way in ancient times. Even though much of the Book of Proverbs finds its parallel in what is known as the "wisdom literature of the ancient Near East," and other authors are mentioned such as Agur and Lemuel (take a look at Proverbs 30:1; 31:1), the entire collection of Proverbs is attributed to King Solomon. This is fitting, because elsewhere in the Bible (I Kings 3), Solomon is described as a unique king: he asked for the divine gift of wisdom and received it.

א:ב לָדַעַת חָכְמָה וּמוּסָר לְהָבִין אִמְרֵי בִינָה:

1:2 TO KNOW WISDOM AND DISCIPLINE, TO FULLY GRASP THE WORDS OF UNDERSTANDING

"Discipline" (in Hebrew, *musar*) is a word that is derived from the root *y-s-r* (reprove, chastise, teach). It suggests a kind of learning that comes with pain. While it does suggest antiquated methods of instruction, it also offers us a simple lesson: experience can be a pain-producing teacher. "To fully grasp the words of understanding" is an attempt to translate *l'havin imrei vinah,* literally "to understand understanding." After the title of this proverb, the author announces the purpose of the book: wisdom is sought, and life is the teacher. Thus, Proverbs takes the experience of many and makes it available to the reader.

א:ג לָקַחַת מוּסַר הַשְׂכֵּל צֶדֶק וּמִשְׁפָּט וּמֵישָׁרִים:

1:3 TO LEARN FROM DISCIPLINE [AND THUS TO UNDERSTAND] RIGHTEOUSNESS, JUDGMENT, AND CORRECT BEHAVIOR

This time, *musar* is joined with the word *haskeil,* "insight." Experience has taught us, especially those of us who have had the blessing of raising children, that "chastisement" does not always work. Those who endure physical punishment learn nothing more than to beat others. Thus, *musar haskeil* is the kind of discipline that brings understanding. While the words that follow (*tzedek, mishpat,* and *meisharim*) may seem like synonyms, an alternative translation might read: "[and thus to understand] what is right, what is legal, and what is fair." The author of Proverbs is making an appeal to use human sensibility to determine what is right, legal, and fair. Of course, our own experience tells us that it is easier to determine what is legal than what is right or fair.

אָ:ד לָתֵת לִפְתָאיִם* עָרְמָה לְנַעַר דַּעַת וּמְזִמָּה: יתיר א'

1:4 TO GIVE SHREWDNESS TO FOOLS AND PURPOSEFUL KNOWLEDGE TO THE YOUNG

The writer wants to persuade the reader to deal with the reality of the real world, not necessarily as it ought to be. Therefore, *ormah* (shrewdness or cunning) is, at times, more important than moral virtue. This is the same word used, in a different form, when the Torah tells the story of the serpent in the Garden of Eden. *Ormah* is something that fools need, especially the kind of fool that is described later in the Book of Proverbs (14:15), the one who believes everything. The fool is contrasted with the *arum,* the one who knows where he or she is going in the world. Fools are not the same as those who are young (*naar*). The former believe too much; the latter know too little. Wisdom will give the young the information that is needed and the instruction as to how to use it. By chance, the German word for "fool," *narr,* came into Yiddish and added the nuance of foolish to our understanding of the word "young."

אָ:ה יִשְׁמַע חָכָם וְיוֹסֵף לֶקַח וְנָבוֹן תַּחְבֻּלוֹת יִקְנֶה:

1:5 LET A WISE PERSON HEAR AND THAT PERSON WILL GAIN INSIGHT. THUS, ONE WHO UNDERSTANDS WILL ATTAIN LEADERSHIP;

Wisdom speaks to those who are wise and full of understanding, just as it does to those who are ignorant or foolish. Wisdom increases what each individual has, each according to the depth of the individual. Through the application of wisdom, the learned can understand more than they have studied. And those who *truly* understand will be able to lead society. We will again see the word for "leadership," *tachbulot,* in Proverbs 11:14 "Where there is no guidance [*tachbulot*], the people will fall." In later Hebrew usage, the word means "schemes" or "devices," connotations that are no longer as morally neutral.

It seems clear that wisdom literature was written for those in a leadership group, a kind of "how-to" manual for those destined for power. As such, it calls the reader to reflect on his or her experience, as well as the experience of others. This seems to be the meaning of the next verse.

אִ:ו לְהָבִין מָשָׁל וּמְלִיצָה דִּבְרֵי חֲכָמִים וְחִידֹתָם:

1:6 To understand a proverb and an apothegm, even the words of the wise and their riddles.

A proverb captures the experience of an entire people. It assumes that experiences are repetitive, and so learning about it in the past will give the reader fair warning about what to expect in the future. The Hebrew *m'litzah* may mean either "a mocking statement" or "a figurative statement," depending on how one traces its origin. The English word "apothegm," while not the most common, refers to a sharply pointed aphorism and thereby combines both meanings of the Hebrew.

In the ancient and medieval periods, being "wise" meant that the individual understood that information was to be conveyed in a somewhat guarded manner. Hence, "riddles" may be a vehicle that wise people use to provide information to one group while simultaneously providing disinformation to another. Even Plato, the Greek philosopher, who lived at a time not much later than the time period in which the Book of Proverbs was probably compiled, suggested that rulers were permitted to lie for the sake of the public good (*Republic*, Book III). It is clear that the nature of this book varies from the mitzvah system that animates the rest of the Bible—as the Rabbis see it. The agenda of the "wise" was different than that of priest or prophet, and certainly rabbi. Unlike such figures, the "wise" utilized and even depended on riddles.

אִ:ז יִרְאַת יְהֹוָה רֵאשִׁית דָּעַת חָכְמָה וּמוּסָר אֱוִילִים בָּזוּ:

1:7 The fear of *Adonai* is the beginning of knowledge, while fools scorn wisdom and discipline.

This verse has become the motto for the entire Book of Proverbs. In a significant way, it offers this book legitimacy from the perspective of Rabbinic Judaism. However, what "the fear of *Adonai*" actually means depends on the particular individual (or theologian) reflecting on that particular verse. Gersonides (1288–1344), a medieval philosopher, understood the words to refer to ethical virtues that were the necessary preliminaries to the intellectual virtues. Self-control, even for the philosophers, comes before the acquisition of knowledge.

If there are any villains in this entire book, they are the "fools," those who will not learn and, even worse, disregard the techniques for learning (as they are described in the Book of Proverbs). Study is a discipline. Learning is a process. For most people, there are no shortcuts to wisdom.

שְׁמַע בְּנִי מוּסַר אָבִיךָ וְאַל־תִּטֹּשׁ תּוֹרַת אִמֶּךָ: א:ח

1:8 MY CHILD, ATTEND TO YOUR FATHER'S DISCIPLINE; DON'T LET YOUR MOTHER'S TEACHING SLIP AWAY

As usual, the writer's choice of words is instructive. The way the author combines words in a startling way forces the reader to reflect on the text. *Sh'ma,* can mean "hear" or "obey" or "listen." Here, however, it is better understood as "pay attention." When *musar* is translated as "discipline," as we have chosen to do, a kind of instruction that is usually delivered verbally, *sh'ma* as "attend" suggests that the listener must concentrate and apply what is being heard, as well as reflect on it. Similarly, *musar avicha* (your father's discipline) is contrasted with *torat imecha* (your mother's teaching). The former is associated with physical chastisement, the classic approach of men; *torah*, on the other hand, is associated with speech. It is assumed that mothers approach their children in this manner. The root *n-t-sh* essentially means "to lay out, stretch out, give up." Here the verb has the sense of "allowing something to slip out of one's grasp." If you as the reader seek wisdom, suggests the writer, then reflect on the lessons that parents give to children—and not just what your own parents may have taught you.

In keeping with the evolving role of women in our society, we have taken the liberty of translating the first word of this verse as "my child." Some will argue that it literally means "my son" and reflects the role of women in ancient society—and in some remaining contemporary societies. Since this is a dynamic text, we have chosen to shape the entire translation in such a way as to make it inclusive (and not gender-specific), as we believe that its original intent was to speak to the entire Jewish community.

כִּי לִוְיַת חֵן הֵם לְרֹאשֶׁךָ וַעֲנָקִים לְגַרְגְּרֹתֶיךָ: א:ט

1:9 FOR THEY WILL BE A GRACEFUL GARLAND FOR YOUR HEAD AND CHAINS FOR YOUR NECK.

The writer suggests that the effects of wisdom are perceptible to others. The person who gains wisdom will demonstrate that wisdom in his or her attitude toward others. It will affect his or her entire demeanor. The garland and the necklace are more than elements of beauty. They indicate particular status. Thus, wisdom becomes an adornment of sorts, the kind that is reserved for those whose status is elevated.

בְּנִי אִם־יְפַתּוּךָ חַטָּאִים אַל־תֹּבֵא: א:י

1:10 MY CHILD, SHOULD SINNERS ENTICE YOU, DON'T BE SO WILLING.

A hazard of belonging to a group of smart young people to whom ethical instruction is presented as a matter of prudence is that some in the group may get the idea that

4

they are smart enough to get away with things that others, who are not as smart, will not. We see it in our own lives, particularly in what has come to be called "white-collar crimes," no matter how small or large the offense. Thus, while it may be obvious to some, most people have to be reminded. The specific vocalization of the Hebrew suggests that these "sinners" may not be occasional transgressors. Rather, these are habitual sinners whose sins have become such common practice that they no longer see them as such. The warning thus takes on an added meaning. It is particularly because smart young people are attractive recruits for the corrupt among us that they are warned not to go along with them.

אִא אִם־יֹאמְרוּ לְכָה אִתָּנוּ נֶאֶרְבָה לְדָם נִצְפְּנָה לְנָקִי חִנָּם׃

1:11 If they tell you, come along with us, we will lie in wait to shed blood; for no reason, we will ambush the innocent.

If you think that you are smart enough to get away with anything, you may even think that you are smart enough to get away with murder, as well. Therefore, the author wants to teach wisdom to those who have the capacity to be wise but first warns them not to be snared by their own intelligence. The author uses an extreme example in order to emphasize the point. The author recognizes that most people do not live in the extremes; our lives are not black or white. We live in the middle, in the gray area, where the verse is equally instructive.

אִיב נִבְלָעֵם כִּשְׁאוֹל חַיִּים וּתְמִימִים כְּיוֹרְדֵי בוֹר׃

1:12 Into the grave alive, that is how we'll swallow them; yes, the innocent going down into the pit.

From modern criminology we learn what the author of Proverbs has already taught us. Criminals often fantasize about the acts they have yet to perform, the crimes yet to be done.

אִיג כָּל־הוֹן יָקָר נִמְצָא נְמַלֵּא בָתֵּינוּ שָׁלָל׃

1:13 All the wealth we will find; we will fill our houses with "good stuff."

For many, murder for money makes more sense than does murder for pleasure. In this verse, the writer imagines the words evildoers would use to convince the bright and presumably innocent young person. The corrupt person assumes that if the pleasure of murder is not a sufficient inducement to evil, then its resulting profit may be. The money will afford us the luxury of buying opulent things for our homes.

א:יד גּוֹרָלְךָ תַּפִּיל בְּתוֹכֵנוּ כִּיס אֶחָד יִהְיֶה לְכֻלָּנוּ:

1:14 CAST YOUR LOT WITH US; WE WILL HAVE ONE PURSE.

This is a further inducement. If the young person joins the group—even though he or she may be new to crime—he or she will still share the profits equally with the more seasoned criminals in the group.

א:טו בְּנִי אַל־תֵּלֵךְ בְּדֶרֶךְ אִתָּם מְנַע רַגְלְךָ מִנְּתִיבָתָם:

1:15 MY FRIEND, DON'T GO THEIR WAY; KEEP YOUR FOOT
FROM THEIR PATH.

As all journeys begin with a first step, so the way to evil begins with the first act. Once set on the way of criminal behavior, it is difficult to turn back. So don't take that first step.

א:טז כִּי רַגְלֵיהֶם לָרַע יָרוּצוּ וִימַהֲרוּ לִשְׁפָּךְ־דָּם:

1:16 THEIR FEET RUN TO DO EVIL; THEY ARE IN A HURRY
TO SHED BLOOD.

Since Proverbs is a book that teaches a special kind of reflective thinking, the writer suggests that evildoing is impulsive behavior. Not only does such behavior cause crime, it also brings on punishment, as the next verse suggests.

א:יז כִּי־חִנָּם מְזֹרָה הָרָשֶׁת בְּעֵינֵי כָל־בַּעַל כָּנָף:
א:יח וְהֵם לְדָמָם יֶאֱרֹבוּ יִצְפְּנוּ לְנַפְשֹׁתָם:

1:17 NO BIRD THINKS THAT THE NET IS SPREAD FOR IT.
1:18 SO THOSE WHO LIE IN WAIT TO SHED BLOOD AMBUSH
THEMSELVES.

Sooner or later, one way or another, those who commit murder suffer for their offense. Hence, let no one think that he or she is smart enough to get away with murder and escape retribution. It is not that criminals do things because they want to get caught, as some modern theories on criminal behavior suggest. Rather, it is the act itself that becomes the trap in which they will be snared.

א:יט כֵּן אָרְחוֹת כָּל־בֹּצֵעַ בָּצַע אֶת־נֶפֶשׁ בְּעָלָיו יִקָּח:

1:19 THIS IS THE WAY IT IS. THE ONE WHO ALWAYS TAKES
ONE'S OWN CUT ENDS UP TAKING ONE'S OWN LIFE.

"Botzei-a batza," literally "making a cut," comes to mean to "make a profit." The
reader is warned against the notion that one can continually seek more and more
without paying for it in some way. Again, the notion of prudence assumes a certain
restraint in all activities including seeking a profit.

א:כ חָכְמוֹת בַּחוּץ תָּרֹנָּה בָּרְחֹבוֹת תִּתֵּן קוֹלָהּ:

1:20 OUT IN THE OPEN, WISDOM CRIES OUT; IN THE
STREETS, SHE PROJECTS HER VOICE.

Wisdom is not something that is hidden. Unlike a woman, the classic personification
of wisdom according to the author, wisdom is not bound by some expectation of
modesty. Wisdom is out where people can learn it. It is available wherever people
find themselves.

א:כא בְּרֹאשׁ הֹמִיּוֹת תִּקְרָא בְּפִתְחֵי שְׁעָרִים בָּעִיר אֲמָרֶיהָ תֹאמֵר:

1:21 WHERE THE NOISY STREETS MEET, SHE CALLS; WHERE
THE CITY GATES OPEN, SHE SPEAKS HER WORDS.

Since wisdom can be found wherever one encounters people, it follows naturally that
wisdom is the distillation of human experience. The writer is conveying to a new
generation of readers the insights that he or she has been taught by the past. Like
most mottos, slogans, and folk sayings, proverbs (whether as this biblical book or any
general collection of wise, folksy aphorisms) assume a certain continuity with life. It is
as if one can derive instruction from the past precisely because the future will mimic
it. What has happened before will happen again. The young person living in the
present may imagine a future that is different from the past. But the older person who
has lived longer knows that the future will echo the past. As the writer of Ecclesiastes
knew, the writer of Proverbs knows as well: "There is nothing new under the sun"
(Ecclesiastes 1:9).

א:כב עַד־מָתַי פְּתָיִם תְּאֵהֲבוּ פֶתִי וְלֵצִים לָצוֹן חָמְדוּ לָהֶם וּכְסִילִים יִשְׂנְאוּ־דָעַת:

1:22 FOOLS, HOW LONG WILL YOU LOVE FOLLY? HOW LONG
WILL MOCKERS TAKE PLEASURE IN MOCKING? HOW
LONG WILL THE STUPID HATE KNOWLEDGE?

Since Proverbs teaches prudence, evil is seen more as folly than as sin. The author suggests that pursuing evil is blindness to what is ultimately foolishness and stupidity. One may mock at the lessons of past experience. Nonetheless, those lessons are valid.

א:כג תָּשׁוּבוּ לְתוֹכַחְתִּי הִנֵּה אַבִּיעָה לָכֶם רוּחִי אוֹדִיעָה דְבָרַי אֶתְכֶם:

1:23 IF YOU TURN TO MY REPROOF, I WILL POUR MY SPIRIT
TO YOU; I WILL MAKE KNOWN MY WORDS TO YOU.

Continuing the personification of wisdom, which the writer adopts throughout the book, wisdom calls out to those who will listen. If they have made mistakes in the past, they can turn from these mistakes in the future (what the Rabbis will later call *t'shuvah*). They can learn anew how to live. But the fools who do not listen will remain fools. Thus, the text continues.

א:כד יַעַן קָרָאתִי וַתְּמָאֵנוּ נָטִיתִי* יָדִי וְאֵין מַקְשִׁיב: יחסר "את"

1:24 I DID CALL YOU BUT YOU REFUSED; I STRETCHED OUT
MY HAND, BUT NO ONE WAS LISTENING.

Wisdom has tried and will continue to try. Yet human experience continues to evince folly, as it has since the creation of humankind. One is reminded of the oft-quoted remark of the philosopher Santyana: "What we learn from history is that we learn nothing from history." Looking back at the past, one can see where things might have been different *if* only people had taken the time to think. That pause might have been enough to change the course of human history.

א:כה וַתִּפְרְעוּ כָל־עֲצָתִי וְתוֹכַחְתִּי לֹא אֲבִיתֶם:

1:25 YOU HAVE NULLIFIED MY ADVICE AND REJECTED MY
REPROACH

Wisdom itself complains that it has attempted to correct the mistakes that people make. However, such correction works only if people will listen to wisdom and take its instruction to heart. But people in the past and in the present have not done so. And there is no indication that people in the future will do so either. Yet, fools bereft of wisdom will eventually pay for their folly, as is demonstrated in the next verse.

א:כו גַּם־אֲנִי בְּאֵידְכֶם אֶשְׂחָק אֶלְעַג בְּבֹא פַחְדְּכֶם:

1:26 WHEN CALAMITY COMES, I WILL LAUGH; WHEN WHAT
YOU FEAR HAPPENS TO YOU, THEN I WILL SMIRK

Speaking for wisdom, the author's human nature comes through the text. It is as if to
say, "You didn't listen, although I warned you. You had the chance to do the right
thing, but you kept doing wrong anyway. I told you what would happen, but you
didn't listen to me. Now that you have to pay for the consequences, don't come
crying to me. I am going to enjoy the show!"

א:כז בְּבֹא כשאוה כְשׁוֹאָה פַּחְדְּכֶם וְאֵידְכֶם כְּסוּפָה יֶאֱתֶה בְּבֹא עֲלֵיכֶם
צָרָה וְצוּקָה:

1:27 WHEN LIKE A STORM WHAT YOU FEAR ARRIVES, WHEN
LIKE A WHIRLWIND DISASTER COMES, WHEN TROUBLE
AND WORRY GET TO YOU.

The Hebrew word *shoah*—here translated as "storm"—has become familiar to the
reader as the Hebrew word taken to singularly mean *the* Holocaust. By using such a
strong word, the writer of Proverbs makes the point that the very anticipation of
disaster intensifies its horror. What happens to fools is a consequence of their folly:
not paying attention to the accumulated experience of wisdom. When trouble comes,
it is too late to get smart. Wisdom warns ahead of time. Wisdom, personified,
responds in the next verse.

א:כח אָז יִקְרָאֻנְנִי וְלֹא אֶעֱנֶה יְשַׁחֲרֻנְנִי וְלֹא יִמְצָאֻנְנִי:

1:28 WHEN YOU CALL ME, I WON'T ANSWER; WHEN YOU
SEARCH FOR ME, YOU WON'T FIND ME.

The point of the Book of Proverbs is to gain insight before it is too late. Don't try to do
so afterwards.

א:כט תַּחַת כִּי־שָׂנְאוּ דָעַת וְיִרְאַת יְהֹוָה לֹא בָחָרוּ:

1:29 BECAUSE THEY HATED KNOWLEDGE AND DID NOT
CHOOSE THE FEAR OF *ADONAI.*

Knowledge is presented as "fear of *Adonai.*" Elsewhere in this chapter (1:7) "fear of
Adonai" is considered the beginning of knowledge, and in the Book of Job (28:28) it
is suggested as the beginning of wisdom. The "fear of God" is presented as the basic
morality that binds all persons (Genesis 20:11). Those who have been doomed by
their own foolishness cannot complain that they did not have the information that

would have saved them. They knew what was considered to be "good," and they rejected it nonetheless. Thus, the writer, speaking for wisdom, continues.

א:ל לֹא־אָבוּ לַעֲצָתִי נָאֲצוּ כָּל־תּוֹכַחְתִּי:

1:30 THEY DID NOT WANT MY ADVICE; THEY TREATED MY
REPROACH WITH CONTEMPT.

Even when they were warned, they rejected the warning. *They* knew better, and they are going to pay for it.

א:לא וְיֹאכְלוּ מִפְּרִי דַרְכָּם וּמִמֹּעֲצֹתֵיהֶם יִשְׂבָּעוּ:

1:31 THEY ARE GOING TO EAT THE FRUIT OF THEIR WAY AND
BE SATIATED WITH THEIR SCHEMES.

Using the familiar text *v'achalta v'savata*, "You shall eat and be satisfied" (Deuteronomy 6:11; 8:10; 11:15), which has entered *Birkat HaMazon* (Blessing after Meals), suggests sarcastically that the wicked will suffer the results of their own wickedness. They will harvest what they planted. They will eat and be filled with the results of their nefarious plans. The evil they planned for others will come down instead on their own heads.

א:לב כִּי מְשׁוּבַת פְּתָיִם תַּהַרְגֵם וְשַׁלְוַת כְּסִילִים תְּאַבְּדֵם:

1:32 THE MISCHIEF OF FOOLS WILL SLAY THEM, AND THE
EASE OF DOLTS WILL DESTROY THEM.

The way of wisdom assumes that what is gained from human experience reflects the real order of the world. As certainly as things fall, so stupidity and foolishness injure. And at all times, they kill. Those who pay them no regard, who imagine that by ignoring consequences they can feel at ease, will discover—to their horror—the punishment for their folly.

א:לג וְשֹׁמֵעַ לִי יִשְׁכָּן־בֶּטַח וְשַׁאֲנַן מִפַּחַד רָעָה:

1:33 THE ONE WHO LISTENS TO ME WILL DWELL IN SECURITY
AND BE AT REST, FEARING NO EVIL.

As a concluding statement, the writer reminds the reader that the one who follows the advice of wisdom will be at ease. Those who do not will never find ease. There is a great difference in the consequences faced by those who follow wisdom and those who chase after folly.

Wisdom Literature

What distinguishes wisdom literature from other genres of sacred literature is that its source is human experience rather than divine revelation. Its focus is on learning from an encounter with the world of the everyday. Thus, there is also a reflective quality to wisdom literature. Once one does something, one learns from it after reflecting on the experience. Unlike the Torah, which concentrates on mitzvot (as sacred obligations, divinely revealed), wisdom literature applauds discernment that is either personally achieved or learned from others. However, this distinction is intentionally blurred by the Rabbis when they equate wisdom with Torah. Thus, they read wisdom literature as if its writer, particularly in the biblical canon, is really talking about the Torah. In doing so, even wisdom literature finds its source in God.

Levi ben Gershom, also Known as Gersonides (1288–1344)

Like many commentators who are known by acronyms, Levi ben Gershom (Gersonides) was known as Ralbag. He was well-known for his work as a mathematician, astronomer, and philosophical commentator of the Bible. He also authored *Wars of the Lord* (a philosophical treatise) and a commentary on the Torah, as well as commentaries on Proverbs, Song of Songs, and Job. As a commentator, he extracted the ethical, religious, and philosophical teachings of the text, calling them *to-alot* or *to-aliyot*. In his large commentary he attempted to reconstruct Jewish law based on nine medieval principles of logic, which he substituted for the well-known hermeneutics of his rabbinic colleagues. His proof for the existence of God is based on the orderliness of the world rather than on God as prime mover, which was favored by the followers of Aristotle.

Fear of God

Yirat Elohim may be translated as "fear of God" or "reverence for God." The Talmud uses the term interchangeably with *yirat shamayim,* using heaven, *shamayim,* as a euphemism for God. Sometimes the term is confused with "fear of sin" *(yirat cheit)*—which is really the fear of the consequences of sin. Some scholars argue that there is really no difference between fear and reverence: our *reverence* for God emerges from our *fear* of God. Thus, we follow the Jewish path that God has set out for us (as interpreted by the Rabbis through Jewish tradition) because we are afraid of the consequences meted out by the Deity. However, reverence for God is a component of the covenantal relationship between the individual and the Deity that is contextualized as the experience at Sinai.

11

Birkat HaMazon *(Blessing after Meals)*

Birkat HaMazon, literally "the blessing for a portion [of food]," which emphasizes the sacred character of the meal, is considered to be the core liturgy of the home, although it is customary to say it wherever meals are eaten. However, *Birkat HaMazon* is to be recited only at the conclusion of a meal that includes bread. A shorter form of grace is recommended if bread was not eaten or if you are in a hurry. The earliest text of *Birkat HaMazon* is rather short. Rabbis added to it in the geonic and medieval periods; these additions probably reflected personal preferences. The geonic period takes its name from the leader of the academy, the *gaon,* who thereby served as community leader. The section known as *HaRachaman* (the Merciful One), because of the way each line begins, may reflect the suffering Jews experienced in the Middle Ages.

The Rabbis infer the instruction for grace from the following biblical verse: "You should eat and be satisfied and bless *Adonai* your God for the good land that God has given you" (Deuteronomy 8:10). *Birkat HaMazon* consists of four main blessings. The first blessing thanks God for providing food for all living creatures. The second blessing thanks God for the "good land," the redemption from Egyptian slavery, the covenant of circumcision, and the Torah. The third blessing asks God to have mercy on Israel. In addition, it asks God to restore the Temple and the sovereignty of David, one of the reasons it is left out in some Reform congregations. It includes a plea that God may always sustain and support Israel. A fourth blessing thanks God for divine goodness and includes a prayer that God may fulfill specific desires. Some suggest that this fourth blessing was added after the destruction of Betar (135 C.E.). Located southwest of Jerusalem, Betar was the last Israelite stronghold during the rebellion against Rome. However, Louis Finkelstein (1895–1991) argues that it may date back to the Hadrianic persecutions, approximately 132–135 C.E., corresponding to the Bar Kochba rebellion. During this period, the Roman government forbade the Jewish people from practicing many Jewish rituals, customs, and ceremonies and prevented rabbis from teaching. This fourth blessing is followed by several petitions that were originally designed to suit individual needs but, like many liturgical creations, became standardized. Among Sephardic Jews there are fifteen of these individual petitions, while Ashkenazi Jews include only nine.

On weekdays, *Birkat HaMazon* is preceded by the recitation of Psalm 137, but this practice is not widely observed. The custom of reciting Psalm 126 prior to *Birkat HaMazon* on the Sabbath and the Festivals is more common. When three or more eat together, one traditionally summons the others to say grace using a traditional formula of invitation. This formula, known as the *zimun,* is altered slightly among Sephardic Jews. While the Talmud suggests that as the number of people who eat together increases, the *zimun* should become more elaborate, this practice is not widely followed. However, it is a modern practice to add the word *Elohim* (God) to the *zimun* when there is at least a minyan (of ten people) saying *Birkat HaMazon.* This probably reflects community meals that often took place on the Sabbath.

K'tiv *and* K'rei

These are technical terms referring to the way the text is written *(k'tiv)* and the way it is suggested to be read *(k'rei)*. This distinction was a compromise suggested by the Masoretes, who wanted the text to be read and interpreted correctly without changing the text itself. For this reason, certain words appear in the text twice in a row, once smaller and without vowels *(k'tiv)* and once with vowels *(k'rei)*.

GLEANINGS

The Gate of Understanding

As you stand at the entrance to the heavenly Gate of Understanding, you are entering the final path of the mind. In this gate you will receive insights to help you understand, define, organize, and pattern your life. All the wisdom you have received through imagination, memory, sensation, and experience you will now weave into a comprehensible tapestry of forms and colors that can significantly change the foundation of how you think and act. Now is the time for illuminating your intention, asserting your wisdom, and bringing new concepts into your life in practical, meaningful ways.

The kabbalists describe the relationship between wisdom, understanding, and knowledge as one that is imbued with the tender beauty and miracle of fertilization, incubation, and conception. In wisdom a thought is conceived, and in understanding it is born. Understanding corresponds to logic in the world and the rational part of your mind. The wisdom that was fertilized in the intuitive part of your mind now penetrates and impregnates its rational part. Wisdom unites with understanding in order to birth knowledge. Understanding, like the womb, incubates the wisdom of the past and bears its fruit in the knowledge of the future. Knowledge is the fruit that wisdom and understanding have produced.

Shoni Labowitz, *Miraculous Living: A Guided Journey in Kabbalah through the Ten Gates of the Tree of Life* (New York: Simon & Schuster, 1996), 87

The Religious Mind

The religious mind is a bound mind *(religare*—to bind). It is bound to a coordinate and from this binding up, from its anchoring, it derives principles. It cannot "travel now and pay later." It is not free, because it is maintained in covenantal relationship. The religious mind realizes that the archetypal relationship of the soul with God was misplaced when it was projected on a father of flesh and blood; when an all-too-human father cannot quite manage to personify the values he demands, the religious mind displaces this projection and manages to focus it on Him, the Father who first fashioned the need for this projection.

The religious mind has opted for seeing all anxiety as the "echo that daily radiates from Mount Horeb calling 'Return, ye wayward children.'" It is impossible to still this anxiety, which is the carrier wave of His Voice, with sensuous consolation. The religious mind is not responsible to a pleasure principle. It is responsible to God. Thus it must seek its solution within the matrix of Torah. Often the religious mind is misunderstood by the secular. The secular mind cannot see in the word *Torah*—direction—a prime coordinate for shaping the chaos, but only a legislation that compounds man's chaos by piling a huge amount of new debris in his path.

Zalman Schachter-Shalomi, *Paradigm Shift: From the Jewish Renewal Teachings of Reb Zalman Schachter-Shalomi,* ed. Ellen Singer (Northvale, N.J.: Jason Aronson, 1993), 96–97

Wisdom and Understanding

We used to live in a society that valued things like wisdom and understanding, saw them as the basis for true happiness and peace. They were acquired slowly, through a lifetime of experience, and only by precious few individuals. Today, we tell our children to be happy by acquiring degrees, power, material wealth, and love. The former values are internal, and once acquired can never be taken away; the latter are external, based on others and on things over which we can have little control. We spend our lives pleasing others so that we can acquire all those things outside of us, and then drive ourselves crazy trying to hold on to them. But it rarely works. And we lose it all.

...Understanding is not some intellectual pursuit. Some people believe that if they take enough courses and acquire the right degrees, they will have understanding at the end. That is not the way it works. And the path of faith, the spiritual journey, while it has to be aided by our intellect to help us sort out the wheat from the chaff, is not the result of intellectual processes. In fact, without faith, without letting go of our self-dependence, without reliance on God, we will never come to any real understanding of the world or our place in it. When confronted with the Torah for the very first time, our people said, *"na'aseh v'nishmah"*/"We will do, and then we will understand." Understanding is the reward of faith. It comes from our willingness to go forward on this journey. It comes from our religious doing.

Terry Bookman, *The Busy Soul: Ten-Minute Spiritual Workouts Drawn from Jewish Tradition* (New York: Perigee Books, 1999), 186–87

The Nature of Women

Duality manifests in all things, but in nothing is this two-foldness more plainly seen than in woman's nature.

The weaker sex physically, it is the stronger spiritually, it having been said that religion were impossible without woman. And yet the freedom of the human soul has been apparently effected by man. I say apparently effected, for experience has demonstrated, and history records, that one element possessed by woman has made her the great moral, the great motif force of the world, though she be, as all great forces are, a silence force.

It may be true that sin came into the world because of the disobedience of the first woman, but woman has long since atoned for it by her loving faith, her blind trust in the Unknown. Down through the ages, traditional and historical, she has come to us the symbol of faith and freedom, of loyalty and love.

From the beginning, she sought knowledge; perceive, it does not say wisdom, but knowledge; and this was at the expense of an Eden. She lost Eden, but she gained that wisdom which has made sure of man's immortality.

She walked upon thorns, she bled; but so sincerely repentant was she, so firmly rooted had become her faith in the Almighty, that no amount of suffering, no change of time and circumstance, could destroy it. With repentance something had sprung up, and blossomed in her being, an imperishable flower, beautiful, fragrant, making the world bright and sweet.

This flower twined itself round man, its odors refreshed and strengthened him; its essence healed him when wounded, and nerved him on to gallant and noble deeds. It is the breath of life in him, and he must needs be careful of its clinging stems, its tender leaves, for they are rooted in a woman's heart.

Ray Frank, "Woman in the Synagogue (1893)," in Four Centuries of Jewish Women's Spirituality—
A Sourcebook, ed. Ellen M. Umansky and Dianne Ashton (Boston: Beacon Press, 1992), 130;
originally published in Papers of the Jewish Woman's Congress
(Philadelphia: Jewish Publication Society of America, 1894), 8, 52–65

The Human Dimension

Judaism sees human beings as the measure of all things. We have mixed within us the varied and contradictory characteristics of all creation. Judaism does not look on human beings as essentially sinful. *Original sin,* the view of classical Christianity since Paul and Augustine, seems to condemn us to lose the game before we begin. In this view, all human beings are born sinners, and only unearned grace can save them. In the Jewish tradition, each of us writes his or her own personal moral slate. We do not begin life with an unpayable debt. At each moment we make a moral choice. Our lives are the sum of our actions, tempered by our intention, limited by our endowments, ennobled by our faith.

David J. Wolpe, Why Be Jewish? (New York: Henry Holt and Company, 1995), 16

On Leaders and Leadership

Leadership is an internal quality. Leadership is not a totally separate quality, nor are leaders separate from ordinary people. In that sense, all humans can be leaders. Certain people become leaders when they take certain personal qualities (which all people possess) and raise them to a higher level; then they move ahead and serve as a model (or avant-garde, if you will) for the rest of the people.

Let me draw an analogy: the definition of the *gibor* (hero) in Pirke Avot. "Who is strong? The one who self-controls." The definition plays off a paradox. The strength described is not the obvious physical force and power. Rather, the Mishnah takes a particular quality that all humans have—self-restraint—and says that the person who practices it at a more intense level—who attains self-control—is a hero. Similarly, the intensity factor enables the individual to serve as a focal point or leader for others....

In the case of the Jews, leadership grows out of the function of the Jewish people. The people Israel is the avant-garde of humanity. In turn, Jewish leaders are people who serve as models, teachers, and co-workers at a higher intensity level for their fellow Jews. The quality of vision is particularly needed, for the leader must remind people of the covenantal task that, after all, is directed over generations and centuries. Since there has always been a gap between current reality and the messianic end goal, it is critical that decisions reflect some thrust toward narrowing the distance. Therefore, the dream must in some way guide the daily decisions. There is a constant need for someone to mediate the gap; the leader must remind people that the effort is needed and assert that the results will make the effort worthwhile. Ultimately, the leader is defined as being someone who, either by example, by taking responsibility, or by helping the community deal with a crisis, opportunity, or challenge, has made a difference in the outcome.

Irving (Yitz) Greenberg, *Living in the Image of God: Jewish Teachings to Perfect the World. Conversations with Irving Greenberg as Conducted by Shalom Freedman* (Northvale, N.J.: Jason Aronson, 1998), 197–99

Women's Teachings

Women...tend to lead by the power of persuasion—if only because we are so penalized for giving anything that resembles an order. In the long run, persuasion is the only kind of power that honors the power of others. What we value most in a leader is the ability to posit a vision of what could be—for without a vision of change, there can be none—and to phrase it in an inspirational and persuasive way that brings people together, that resolves conflict instead of creating it.

Men and women alike prefer leadership that guides and persuades by hope, rather than rules and dictates by fear. Like prayer and other forms of thought that provide an organizing principle for reality, hope is a form of planning. This means that the future vision we put forth must be a positive one, for it is also a self-fulfilling prophecy. Why would we want to perpetuate a chain of destruction? I see in women leaders today a great concentration of hope—and that is a very precious commodity for us all.

Men tend to be rebellious in youth, and become more conservative as they grow older. Women tend to be conservative in youth—when we haven't yet experienced the injustices of the labor force; of childrearing, which men don't yet share equally (to put it mildly); and of the double standard of aging. Only after having some of those experiences, as we grow older, do we tend to become more active and rebellious on our own behalf. Since life expectancy has increased in industrialized countries by thirty years since 1900, we now have a lot more time to rebel—and to lead.

Gloria Steinem, "Women and Leadership," in *Lifecycles*, vol. 2, *Jewish Women on Biblical Themes in Contemporary Life*, ed. Debra Orenstein and Jane Rachel Litman (Woodstock, Vt.: Jewish Lights Publishing, 1997), 304–05

CHAPTER TWO

ב:א בְּנִי אִם־תִּקַּח אֲמָרָי וּמִצְוֹתַי תִּצְפֹּן אִתָּךְ:

2:1 MY YOUNG FRIEND, IF YOU TAKE MY WORDS AND IF YOU WILL STORE MY COMMANDMENTS WITH YOU

The chapter begins with "my boy," which we have rendered as "my young friend." The writer could have said (and may have implied) "my girl" as well, an endearing, somewhat patronizing posture inclined to the young—the intended readership. This phrase "my boy" emerges throughout the text, and while the words do not say so explicitly, we mean them to be inclusive of both men and women, hence "my young friend." Two different aspects of moral instruction are now suggested: words and behaviors. The ideas that wisdom proclaims (that is, the accumulated experience of the past) should be reflected upon. The behaviors that could emerge as a result are to be kept as possibilities to be acted upon. The Hebrew root *tz-f-n* (to store) could mean "to hide" or "to treasure." The root clearly underlies the modern Hebrew word *matzpun* (conscience). Thus, the use of the verb suggests that the ethical act must be reflected upon. The implementation of this verse prepares the reader for the verse that follows.

ב:ב לְהַקְשִׁיב לַחָכְמָה אָזְנֶךָ תַּטֶּה לִבְּךָ לַתְּבוּנָה:

2:2 LET YOUR EAR INCLINE TO WISDOM AND YOUR MIND TO COMPREHENSION

For the biblical writer, the mind was located in the heart. Thus, the author of Proverbs uses the Hebrew word *libcha* (your heart) to refer to the locus of wisdom in the body. The kind of wisdom for ethical instruction envisioned in the Book of Proverbs can only be imparted in a personal way, face-to-face. First the ear and then the mind. The student is instructed to listen carefully and then reflect on what he or she has heard.

ב:ג כִּי אִם לַבִּינָה תִקְרָא לַתְּבוּנָה תִּתֵּן קוֹלֶךָ:

2:3 IF YOU CALL FOR UNDERSTANDING AND SHOUT FOR COMPREHENSION

This verse presents a change in direction in the process of ethical instruction. The previous verse suggested an answer given by the teacher. Conversely, this verse suggests the question asked by the student. In the mind of the writer, the student is calling aloud for the teacher to help him or her to understand. And when the student does not get immediate help, he or she begins to shout out for help. The Hebrew expresses it as *titein kolecha,* literally "gives your voice," which is idiomatically understood to mean "to shout."

ב:ד אִם־תְּבַקְשֶׁנָּה כַכָּסֶף וְכַמַּטְמוֹנִים תַּחְפְּשֶׂנָּה:

2:4 IF YOU SEEK IT LIKE SILVER AND SEARCH FOR IT LIKE A
HIDDEN TREASURE

It is unclear whether *kesef* (silver) refers to precious metal or to coins and thus should be translated as "money." In either case, *kesef* is what is sought. At all times, in all places, there is a fascination with *matmonim* (hidden treasure). Whether *kesef* or *matmonim,* what is sought is not what was created by the seeker. So wisdom, which is worth even more, is not something that the individual invented but gets from a study of what other human beings have learned about life over a period of time.

ב:ה אָז תָּבִין יִרְאַת יְהוָֹה וְדַעַת אֱלֹהִים תִּמְצָא:

2:5 THEN YOU WILL UNDERSTAND THE FEAR OF *ADONAI*
AND YOU WILL FIND THE KNOWLEDGE OF GOD.

If the individual will expend the effort, then he or she will be able to acquire wisdom. That's all it takes. This wisdom is of the highest kind: fear of *Adonai* and knowledge of God. Both terms conceal a paradox. They suggest information that is passed on by revelation from the Deity to humans. However, Proverbs—as a book and as a genre of literature—implies information developed by human beings and passed down to human beings by instruction from one generation to another. It is the very use of the terms "fear of *Adonai*" and "knowledge of God" that raises the level of wisdom from the human to the Divine and thereby sanctions it.

ב:ו כִּי־יְהוָֹה יִתֵּן חָכְמָה מִפִּיו דַּעַת וּתְבוּנָה:

2:6 FOR *ADONAI* GIVES WISDOM, FROM GOD'S MOUTH
COMES KNOWLEDGE AND UNDERSTANDING.

This verse continues the process of making "wisdom" literature acceptable. The reader, who previously may have thought that God gave only Torah and commandments, now learns that God also gave "wisdom" and "understanding." What is new—wisdom and understanding—has now been sanctified through its identification with the old—Torah.

ב:ז וְצָפַן לַיְשָׁרִים תּוּשִׁיָּה מָגֵן לְהֹלְכֵי תֹם:

2:7 GOD WILL STORE SUCCESS FOR THE UPRIGHT AND WILL
BE A SHIELD FOR THOSE WHO INNOCENTLY GO ABOUT.

Tushiyah, a word used both in Proverbs and in Job, is difficult to translate. While the recommended translation is as "success, good result," other meanings include "sound wisdom" and "prudence." It might be argued that "success" best fits the context, for the one who follows the dictates of wisdom will be able to apply that wisdom and succeed.

ב:ח לִנְצֹר אָרְחוֹת מִשְׁפָּט וְדֶרֶךְ חֲסִידָו יִשְׁמֹר:

2:8 GOD WILL GUARD THE PATHS OF JUSTICE AND WILL
WATCH THE WAY OF GOD'S PIOUS ONES.

In a monumental study of the word, Rabbi Nelson Glueck defines *chesed* as "steadfast love." It follows, therefore, that a *chasid* is a person who practices such love. Thus, *chasidav* refers to those persons who serve God through acts of *chesed*. In that sense, they belong to God. We have translated *chasidav* as "pious ones." Again, note that the follower of wisdom has been promised specific results.

ב:ט אָז תָּבִין צֶדֶק וּמִשְׁפָּט וּמֵישָׁרִים כָּל־מַעְגַּל־טוֹב:

2:9 YOU WILL THEN UNDERSTAND RIGHTEOUSNESS AND
JUSTICE AND ALSO EQUITY AND EVERY GOOD TRACK.

In this verse the writer has probably presented us with a play on words. *Meisharim*, translated as "equity," comes from the root *y-sh-r* (straight) and can mean "in a straight way," as is used in Proverbs 23:31 and Song of Songs 7:10. *Magal* (track or path) comes from the root *agul*, "to go in a circle." Thus, the promise of wisdom implies not only that you will understand what righteousness ultimately is and how to put it into practice as justice but that you will be able to know without a doubt what is appropriate (straight) and what is inappropriate (bent) in human actions.

ב:י כִּי־תָבוֹא חָכְמָה בְלִבֶּךָ וְדַעַת לְנַפְשְׁךָ יִנְעָם:

2:10 FOR WHEN WISDOM COMES INTO YOUR HEART AND
KNOWLEDGE GIVES PLEASURE TO YOUR SOUL

This verse is dependent on the next for the fulfillment of its promise: you will enjoy what wisdom provides, and even more than that.

ב:יא מְזִמָּה תִּשְׁמֹר עָלֶיךָ תְּבוּנָה תִנְצְרֶכָּה:

2:11 PRUDENCE WILL WATCH OVER YOU AND COMPREHENSION WILL GUARD YOU

"M'zimah" is a neutral term. It can mean either a plan that is good or a plan that is evil. It might also be translated as "scheme." What seems meant here is that planning for the future provides its own protection. Whether we would call such a plan a "scheme" or a "project" is determined primarily by its intended outcome. Since we are trumpeting the importance of prior planning, "prudence" appears to be the best translation for this passage.

ב:יב לְהַצִּילְךָ מִדֶּרֶךְ רָע מֵאִישׁ מְדַבֵּר תַּהְפֻּכוֹת:

2:12 TO DELIVER YOU FROM AN EVIL PATH, FROM PEOPLE WHO SPEAK OF PERVERSE NOTIONS

"Perversity" *(tah'puchot)*, from the Hebrew root *h-f-ch* (turn over), is taken by classical commentators Rashi and Abraham ibn Ezra to refer to those ideas that might turn individuals away from their traditional beliefs and routine behaviors. Although the Book of Proverbs generally challenges traditional beliefs and behaviors because of its prudential outlook, the writer feels compelled to warn those who might carry the notion of mere prudence too far. Since wisdom literature was specifically directed to those who were expected to become part of the ruling elite, it was important to teach them that the measure of their self-control would be seen as an indicator of their ability to control others. Flagrant misbehavior by those who rule is not much of an incentive for good behavior by those who are ruled.

ב:יג הַעֹזְבִים אָרְחוֹת יֹשֶׁר לָלֶכֶת בְּדַרְכֵי־חֹשֶׁךְ:

2:13 WHO LEAVE THE WAYS THAT ARE RIGHT TO WALK IN PATHS THAT ARE DARK

The writer points out the stupidity of the wicked. Although they know what is right, they are still intent on pursuing what is wrong. The writer of Proverbs compares the wicked to those who move on a journey from the route that will bring them to their destination to a path that is so dark that they can't find their bearings. As a result, they stumble and fall.

ב:יד הַשְּׂמֵחִים לַעֲשׂוֹת רָע יָגִילוּ בְּתַהְפֻּכוֹת רָע:

2:14 WHO ARE HAPPY TO DO WRONG AND WHO REJOICE IN THE PERVERSITY OF EVIL

The experience of human history has taught us that evil is appealing. It is attractive. Were it not attractive to many, it might be easily defeated. We are all tempted by it.

That is why the Rabbis identified these evil drives or urges as the *yetzer hara*, the inclination to do evil. The writer further notes—as similarly evinced in human history—that those who do evil rejoice in their wrongdoing and boast about it.

ב:טו אֲשֶׁר אָרְחֹתֵיהֶם עִקְּשִׁים וּנְלוֹזִים בְּמַעְגְּלוֹתָם:

2:15 WHOSE WAYS ARE TWISTED AND WHO ARE CORRUPT IN
THEIR PATHS.

This imagery is common in many languages and cultures. Evil people follow crooked paths. Good people follow straight paths.

ב:טז לְהַצִּילְךָ מֵאִשָּׁה זָרָה מִנָּכְרִיָּה אֲמָרֶיהָ הֶחֱלִיקָה:

2:16 TO SAVE YOU FROM A STRANGER, FROM A FOREIGNER
WHO USES SEDUCTIVE WORDS

While the dominant language is male-biased, as was the dominant culture of the time, it is clear that the sentiment can be similarly expressed from the perspective of women, as well. It may be politically incorrect to say so according to contemporary social mores, but the author nonetheless understands that we are at times more attracted to people outside of our own community than to those who live within its borders. Couched in words of warning to the male readers of his words, the author of Proverbs reminds women in their peer group to be modest and virtuous by suggesting that those who are outside the peer group are immodest and promiscuous. It is precisely that kind of profiling that makes these "foreign women [and men]" so alluring. Thus, the reader must be very cautious in interacting with them. While we might be careful to soften his message to make it palatable to the modern reader, we would surely extend his words to include female readers as well.

ב:יז הַעֹזֶבֶת אַלּוּף נְעוּרֶיהָ וְאֶת־בְּרִית אֱלֹהֶיהָ שָׁכֵחָה:

2:17 SHE WHO FORSAKES THE SPOUSE OF HER YOUTH AND
HAS FORGOTTEN THE COVENANT OF HER GOD.

The writer wants to make sure to paint a repugnant picture of foreign women. Not only are they guilty of adultery, but they are also blamed for apostasy. This connection between sexual temptation and "lapsed religiosity" can be found elsewhere in the Bible. See the story of the daughters of Moab, Cozbi, Zimri, and Pinchas (Numbers 25:1–18).

ב:יח כִּי שָׁחָה אֶל־מָוֶת בֵּיתָהּ וְאֶל־רְפָאִים מַעְגְּלֹתֶיהָ:

2:18 INDEED, HER HOUSE SLIDES DOWN TO DEATH, HER
TRACKS TO THE DEAD.

R'faim, translated as "the dead," may refer to the spirits of the dead who inhabit specific places in the netherworld. The message of warning intensifies with each passing verse by further denigrating "foreigners." The path to this person's house is on the way to the grave. Each step you take in that direction (adultery, apostasy) will lead you to your own death.

ב:יט כָּל־בָּאֶיהָ לֹא יְשׁוּבוּן וְלֹא־יַשִּׂיגוּ אָרְחוֹת חַיִּים:

2:19 THOSE WHO COME TO HER NEVER RETURN; THEY
·NEVER REGAIN THEIR WAY OF LIFE.

As in colloquial English, the term *bo el* (come to) may also mean sexual intercourse. Reading the verse like this—as does Ibn Ezra—allows for the translation "those who make love to her will never turn from their evil way and may never again find the spiritual way." The teacher of this text, the writer of Proverbs, here warns us that illicit sex will be habit-forming; it will constantly degrade those who are involved with it.

ב:כ לְמַעַן תֵּלֵךְ בְּדֶרֶךְ טוֹבִים וְאָרְחוֹת צַדִּיקִים תִּשְׁמֹר:

2:20 YOU SHOULD WALK ON THE PATH OF GOOD PEOPLE
AND YOU SHOULD KEEP THE WAYS OF THE RIGHTEOUS.

To keep the student from sexual sin, the teacher of wisdom denigrates the lewd and licentious who might tempt the student, but praises all those who are good and righteous. They will serve as role models for the student. Since modeling may not be enough to persuade the student, in the following verse the teacher adds that virtue has its own reward.

ב:כא כִּי־יְשָׁרִים יִשְׁכְּנוּ־אָרֶץ וּתְמִימִים יִוָּתְרוּ בָהּ:

2:21 THOSE WHO ARE UPRIGHT WILL DWELL ON THE EARTH.
THOSE WHO ARE PERFECT WILL REMAIN ON IT.

It seems counterintuitive, but for Rashi, "the earth" is the "world-to-come." The righteous will remain *on* it when the wicked go down to *Geihinom* (to hell).

ב:כב וּרְשָׁעִים מֵאֶרֶץ יִכָּרֵתוּ וּבוֹגְדִים יִסְּחוּ מִמֶּנָּה:

2:22 THE WICKED WILL BE CUT OFF FROM THE EARTH, AND
THE TREACHEROUS WILL BE RIPPED OUT OF IT.

Like infertile seeds planted in barren earth, the wicked will not take root in the earth. Were those seeds even to take root, they would be ripped out of their beds. Similarly, the wicked will have no future in this world. This chapter concludes with the message that permeates the entire book: Folly will be punished. Wisdom will be rewarded.

Rashi (1040–1105)

Rashi is an acronym for Rabbi Solomon Yitzchak ben Isaac, French Bible exegete and great biblical and talmudic commentator. His style is simple and concise, and his objective is to present the direct literal meaning of the text. Most of his commentary is not his own. Instead, he applied his encyclopedic knowledge of Jewish tradition to the text under scrutiny, citing relevant texts and contexts. His commentaries on the Bible and on the Talmud have become universally popular.

Abraham ibn Ezra (1089–1164)

Abraham ibn Ezra was a famous Spanish Jewish grammarian and Bible exegete. His Bible commentaries were based on linguistic and factual examinations of the text and even included hints that foreshadow the modern approach of biblical criticism.

Yetzer Hara, Yetzer Hatov

The Rabbis identified two complementary sets of drives that coexist in each person. One set of drives, which may be classified as libidinal drives or urges and include sex, hunger, and the like, are grouped under the term *yetzer hara* (the inclination to evil). While these drives are not evil in themselves, left unchecked, they may lead the individual to evil. For example, while the sexual drive may lead the individual to procreate, it can also lead to lust and illicit sexual behavior. The hunger drive will lead the individual to nourishing the body with food, but it can also lead to obesity. The *yetzer hara* is kept in balance by *yetzer hatov,* the inclination to do good, even as the *yetzer hatov* must be kept in balance by *yetzer hara.* According to this understanding, individuals who may want to give *tzedakah,* for example, run the risk of placing themselves or their family in jeopardy should they give all their money to charitable causes.

Heaven and Hell

During the period of the Second Temple, there appears to be a brief discussion about the immortality of the soul, as can be seen in the Books of the Maccabees. While there are a variety of opinions expressed about the end of life, immortality, and "heaven and hell" in the Talmud and midrash, they are not presented in any kind of system. Rabbinic doctrine emphasizes the existence of a world-to-come because it is in that world (and not necessarily our own) that the person will be resurrected and the righteous will be rewarded while the wicked are punished. According to the Babylonian Talmud (*Shabbat* 152a), after a person dies, the soul leaves the body but retains a temporary relationship with it for twelve months until the body has fully disintegrated. Some say that the righteous go to paradise *(Gan Eden)* and the wicked go to hell *(Geihinom)* after this period. It is rather unclear what the state of the soul is during this period of time. During the messianic period of redemption, the soul will be returned to the body as the individual is resurrected. The messianic redemption is both politically and physically utopian. At the end of the period of redemption, it is in the world-to-come where the righteous sit in the blissful presence of the Divine.

Rabbi Nelson Glueck (1900–1971)

A world renowned biblical archaeologist, Rabbi Nelson Glueck was president of Hebrew Union College and oversaw its merger with the Jewish Institute of Religion in 1950. Glueck was known for his mapping of Transjordan and the archaeological sites found there. As a result of his knowledge of the area, the OSS employed his services during World War II in mapping out an escape route for the Allied forces should Rommel's Africa Corps be successful. His doctoral dissertation on the word *chesed* is considered an important linguistic resource.

Sexuality and Sex

In the well-known story of Adam and Eve in the Torah, the primal pair are first depicted as being naked and unashamed (Genesis 2:25). However, there is no mention of sexual activity. Nevertheless, in the rabbinic mind, since Adam and Eve were created as young adults, about twenty years old, being naked and alone led to what one might expect (*B'reishit Rabbah* 14:7). Since they were involved in sexual activity, the serpent desired Eve upon seeing her, say the Rabbis in another midrash (*B'reishit Rabbah* 18:10). The whole story of the fruit of the forbidden tree and sin starts with an act of voyeurism. One Rabbi even thought that sin was like a kind of venereal disease, that the serpent had intercourse with Eve and infected her and her descendants. Revelation at Sinai had removed the disease from the people of Israel. Those who had not received revelation were still infected (*Yalkut Shimoni, B'reishit* 29).

Sex and sin are linked together in one chapter of the Torah. We hear about the Children of Israel sinning with the daughters of Moab. As the Rabbis retell the story in the midrash, sex was used as an inducement to idolatry (*B'midbar Rabbah* 20:23 and *Tanchuma, Balak* 18). The would-be sinner would unconsciously worship pagan gods. The Cozbi-Zimri affair (Numbers 25:6ff.) presented the problem of sexual activity with Midianite women, something that touched Moses as well. By executing the two sinners, the priest Pinchas supposedly assuaged divine wrath from the people of Israel.

GLEANINGS

Man Becomes the Snake

Here is the lesson. A man who doesn't know how to nurture (and make connections) becomes the Snake. A woman who doesn't know how to judge (and allow independence) is Lilith, one who smothers her lovers and children. Real men and real women are blends. Human life is a Likert scale: Lilith is on one end and the Snake is on the other. Adam and Eve are in the middle, struggling with finding the right balance. It's not easy to be a person—a man who is not in control can easily "kill" or drive everyone away through aggression. Smothering is every woman's nightmare. If she doesn't know when to let go, she "kills" or drives others away by holding things too close. But men can go overboard and strangle their loved ones with affection, and women can find their anger and go on the attack. Every soul or psyche that is attempting to drive a human being through life's obstacle course faces not only the hazards (of which there are plenty), but also the endless struggle to maintain internal balance.

Joel Lurie Grishaver, *The Bonding of Isaac: Stories and Essays about Gender and Jewish Spirituality*
(Los Angeles: The Alef Design Group, 1997), 44

Wisdom

We live in a time and place that does not really value wisdom. We value power, money, youth and good looks, physical prowess. Our heroes are actors, rock stars, and athletes. We may still pay lip service to wisdom, but in truth we will admire someone who is clever or smart, someone who can solve problems or be creative, but not someone who is really wise.

... [In a former time] if one had wisdom, one had everything, or at least everything that mattered. Wisdom comes from age, from experience, from a deeper kind of knowing. Wisdom requires a rich spiritual reservoir, an internal calm, acceptance, and compassion. One who is wise relates easily and comfortably with others and the world, sees to the core of the matter, looks into our souls. Wisdom cannot be purchased or learned; rather, it is acquired or gifted after a lifetime of seeking.

Terry Bookman, *The Busy Soul: Ten-Minute Spiritual Workouts Drawn from Jewish Tradition*
(New York: Perigee Books, 1999), 190–91

Doing Justly

According to Rabbi Israel [Salanter, the founder of the *Musar* movement] each of us is subject to divine command. Each of us is called upon to act in certain ways, both ritually and morally, that aid in our struggle to perfect our character. The ideal Jew is humble when it comes to matters of self and magnanimous in dealing with others. The ideal Jew takes little thought of his or her material success while seeing to the material well-being of others. The ideal Jew takes little notice of the psychological foibles of others but is forever seeking to correct his or her own misguided thinking. The ideal Jew is always aware of the challenge of living a life in line with the highest ideals of Torah and tradition, while compassionate toward those who fail to live up to those ideals. The words that describe the ideal Jew are joyous, compassionate, loving, affectionate, passionate, eager, helpful, and sweet.

Rami Shapiro, "Doing Justly: Fostering Ethical Living Through *Musar*," in *Worlds of Jewish Prayer: A Festschrift in Honor of Rabbi Zalman M. Schachter-Shalomi*, ed. Shohama Harris Wiener and Jonathan Omer-Man (Northvale, N.J.: Jason Aronson, 1994), 160

The Journey

Physical death is certain.

There is "a time to be born, and a time to die" (Ecclesiastes 3:2).

But the spiritual mysteries of life and death are only mysteries when they are clouded by the limitations of earthbound existence and earthbound knowledge.

For at its deepest and most hidden place, each God-created transcendent soul—each human being—knows its origins, its pathways, and its destinations:

From God.

To God.

In the light of God.

The circle is never-ending. The circle continues still.

"Blessed are you in your coming in. Blessed are you in your going out. Blessed are you in your coming in. Blessed are you in your Going out. Blessed are you . . ." (after Deuteronomy 28:6).

Wayne Dosick, *Living Judaism: The Complete Guide to Jewish Belief, Tradition, and Practice* (San Francisco: HarperSanFrancisco, 1995), 322

CHAPTER THREE

ג:א בְּנִי תּוֹרָתִי אַל־תִּשְׁכָּח וּמִצְוֹתַי יִצֹּר לִבֶּךָ:

3:1 MY YOUNG FRIEND, DON'T FORGET MY INSTRUCTION
AND LET YOUR HEART KEEP MY COMMANDMENTS

It is important to note that this book, devoted to prudential knowledge, found in the
genre of wisdom literature, uses the Hebrew word *torati,* "my instruction," literally
"my Torah," and the Hebrew word *mitzvotai,* "my commandments." Since these
words have been elevated to a sacred plain by their use in the Torah and in tradition,
by associating his words with the revealed tradition, the writer raises his own work to
a sacred level.

ג:ב כִּי אֹרֶךְ יָמִים וּשְׁנוֹת חַיִּים וְשָׁלוֹם יוֹסִיפוּ לָךְ:

3:2 THEY WILL INCREASE THE LENGTH OF YOUR DAYS, THE
YEARS OF YOUR LIFE, AND YOUR SERENITY.

Shalom, generally rendered as "peace," also has a wider meaning that includes
wholeness and tranquility. It implies a balanced state. The writer of Proverbs promises
the reader that wisdom guarantees serenity.

ג:ג חֶסֶד וֶאֱמֶת אַל־יַעַזְבֻךָ קָשְׁרֵם עַל־גַּרְגְּרוֹתֶיךָ כָּתְבֵם עַל־לוּחַ לִבֶּךָ:

3:3 DON'T LET STEADFAST LOVE AND TRUTH LEAVE YOU.
TIE THEM AROUND YOUR NECK, WRITE THEM ON THE
TABLET OF YOUR HEART.

As we learned in 2:8, Rabbi Nelson Glueck translates *chesed* as "steadfast love."
Chesed v'emet (true steadfast love) has come to be a cultural construct to refer to
caring for the deceased in Jewish tradition. This is the only kind of *true* steadfast love,
since this act of kindness can never be repaid. In a previous verse (1:9), the writer
referred to the instruction of parents as an ornament around the neck. Thus, the result
of such instruction would be visible in the actions of the child. Here the writer
suggests that if, with your actions, you demonstrate the importance of kindness and
faithfulness, it is as if those virtues were suspended around your neck. Since the writer
of Proverbs believed the heart to be the place of the mind (as does the Bible in
general), to inscribe these ideas on the tablets of the heart means to retain these
notions within one's mind.

ג:ד וּמְצָא־חֵן וְשֵׂכֶל־טוֹב בְּעֵינֵי אֱלֹהִים וְאָדָם:

3:4 THUS YOU WILL FIND GRACE AND PROPER
UNDERSTANDING IN THE EYES OF GOD AND
HUMANKIND.

Grace and proper understanding will be the result of one's manifestation of love and truth. People will respond to such actions.

ג:ה בְּטַח אֶל־יְהֹוָה בְּכָל־לִבֶּךָ וְאֶל־בִּינָתְךָ אַל־תִּשָּׁעֵן:

3:5 TRUST *ADONAI* WITH ALL YOUR HEART AND DON'T
DEPEND ON YOUR OWN UNDERSTANDING.

One might wonder how this statement relates to previous verses, as well as those that follow. While trust in God is important, this literature emphasizes that wisdom emerges from one's own understanding. Rashi interprets "trust *Adonai*" as hiring a teacher from whom one can learn. His view is a reflection of rabbinic tradition that suggests that the will of God may be learned from a teacher. According to the midrashic tradition, when Rebekah went "to seek of *Adonai*" (Genesis 25:22), she went to the rabbinical academy of Shem and Ever.

ג:ו בְּכָל־דְּרָכֶיךָ דָעֵהוּ וְהוּא יְיַשֵּׁר אֹרְחֹתֶיךָ:

3:6 KEEP GOD IN MIND WHEREVER YOU GO, FOR GOD WILL
MAKE ALL YOUR WAYS STRAIGHT.

The first part of this verse may be translated literally "Know God in all your paths." The second half of the verse suggests that just as a traveler would like the road to be straight so that one may arrive at one's destination more easily, an individual hopes that God will remove the twists and turns of life's path so that the individual might be able to achieve everything for which he or she hopes.

ג:ז אַל־תְּהִי חָכָם בְּעֵינֶיךָ יְרָא אֶת־יְהֹוָה וְסוּר מֵרָע:

3:7 DON'T BE TOO SMART IN YOUR OWN SIGHT; FEAR
ADONAI AND TURN AWAY FROM EVIL.

There is always the temptation for the wise person to become a "wise guy," one who is "too smart for his [or her] own good." Such a person can never really become smart. Fear of God, however constructed, suggests a source by which an individual may gauge his or her actions.

ג:ח רְפְאוּת תְּהִי לְשָׁרֶךָ וְשִׁקּוּי לְעַצְמוֹתֶיךָ:

3:8 IT WILL BE MEDICINE FOR YOUR BODY AND
REFRESHMENT FOR YOUR BONES.

Although a common translation for *shorecha* is "your navel," the Greek translation of the Bible, the Septuagint, uses the phrase "your body" *(tow sowmati)*. This implies *b'sarcha* (your flesh) in Hebrew. *Shikui* (drink) thus may be translated as "marrow." What is suggested here is that wisdom will provide both instruction for the mind and healing for the body.

ג:ט כַּבֵּד אֶת־יְהוָֹה מֵהוֹנֶךָ וּמֵרֵאשִׁית כָּל־תְּבוּאָתֶךָ:

3:9 HONOR *ADONAI* WITH YOUR WEALTH, AND WITH THE
FIRST AND BEST PART OF YOUR HARVEST

We have learned that wisdom brings intellectual success and physical well-being. The power of wisdom is extended now to include financial success. The wise are advised to repay the Source of all wisdom with the best that they have.

ג:י וְיִמָּלְאוּ אֲסָמֶיךָ שָׂבָע וְתִירוֹשׁ יְקָבֶיךָ יִפְרֹצוּ:

3:10 SO THAT YOUR BARNS MAY BE FILLED WITH PLENTY AND
YOUR VATS OVERFLOW WITH WINE.

When a work is devoted to the kind of wisdom that can be attained on the basis of past experience, there is a problem trying to figure out what that leaves for God to do. The answer is presented in the previous two verses: "If you serve God, you succeed." Success is measured in economic rewards. While we may debate the veracity of such an approach, the author of this text implies that failure should be taken as both a test and a lesson. This idea provides us with the foundation for the verse that follows.

ג:יא מוּסַר יְהוָֹה בְּנִי אַל־תִּמְאָס וְאַל־תָּקֹץ בְּתוֹכַחְתּוֹ:

3:11 MY YOUNG FRIEND, DON'T REJECT THE CHASTENING
OF *ADONAI.* DON'T LOATHE GOD'S REPROOF.

The notion that we should embrace suffering carries with it the idea that ultimately there will be a payoff. Eventually, the individual will succeed.

ג:יב כִּי אֶת אֲשֶׁר יֶאֱהַב יְהֹוָה יוֹכִיחַ וּכְאָב אֶת־בֵּן יִרְצֶה:

3:12 FOR *ADONAI* REPROVES THE ONE THAT IS LOVED JUST
AS A PARENT MIGHT [DO] WITH A BELOVED CHILD.

This is the idea of *yisurim shel ahavah* (chastisements of love), which became an element of traditional theodicy. Undeserved suffering was viewed as a test of the sufferer. By embracing the suffering without questioning, the sufferers demonstrate their love for God. Just as children mature, they might come to understand past acts of parental discipline as manifestations of parental love—however unpleasant and unwelcome at the time such acts were administered—so a mature person would ultimately realize that suffering that brings such insight is a manifestation of divine love.

ג:יג אַשְׁרֵי אָדָם מָצָא חָכְמָה וְאָדָם יָפִיק תְּבוּנָה:

3:13 HAPPY IS THE ONE WHO HAS FOUND WISDOM, THE ONE
WHO ATTAINS UNDERSTANDING.

"Happy" implies simple joy and easy access to it. The process of acquiring wisdom and understanding is the goal of the Book of Proverbs. This process is neither as easy nor as automatic as the term "happy" might imply. Nevertheless, the one who succeeds at it will indeed be "happy."

ג:יד כִּי טוֹב סַחְרָהּ מִסְּחַר־כָּסֶף וּמֵחָרוּץ תְּבוּאָתָהּ:

3:14 FOR MORE PROFIT CAN BE REALIZED FROM IT THAN
FROM SILVER AND MORE GAIN THAN FROM GOLD.

Once again, we are reminded that wisdom literature is the product of daily living. Real life, the kind that makes up the everyday, is based on business.

ג:טו יְקָרָה הִיא מפניים מִפְּנִינִים וְכָל־חֲפָצֶיךָ לֹא יִשְׁווּ־בָהּ:

3:15 IT IS MORE VALUABLE THAN CORALS; NOTHING YOU
DESIRE CAN COMPARE TO IT.

Trade in precious and semiprecious stones is one of the most ancient forms of business. In the *Targum*, "pearls" is used for *p'ninim*. Other translators use the word "rubies" or "pearls of coral." Whatever the precise meaning, precious stones have an intrinsic value in the marketplace. They remain valuable because they can be easily transported. This is particularly important to those whose status in society is marginal. If you are not sure that you can remain where you are with security and have to be prepared to move at any time, then precious stones are a good investment. However, knowledge is a better investment. Knowledge—and the wisdom derived from it—can be transported even more easily. As a result, the emphasis on learning throughout Jewish history was also a reflection of the uncertainty of Jewish life. Possessions could be lost, but if you were able to retain learning, then you had a chance. This approach has changed greatly since the emergence of the North American Jewish community and the establishment of the modern State of Israel.

ג:טז אֹרֶךְ יָמִים בִּימִינָהּ בִּשְׂמֹאולָהּ* עֹשֶׁר וְכָבוֹד: ‏ מלא ו׳

3:16 LONG LIFE IS IN WISDOM'S RIGHT HAND, WEALTH AND HONOR IN ITS LEFT HAND.

As is the case in many other verses in this text, wisdom is personified here. Because *chochmah* is a feminine noun, the phrase is actually "in *her* right hand" and "in *her* left hand." The rewards of long life, wealth, and honor are not guaranteed with wisdom, but they are heartfelt yearnings.

ג:יז דְּרָכֶיהָ דַרְכֵי־נֹעַם וְכָל־נְתִיבוֹתֶיהָ שָׁלוֹם:

3:17 HER [WISDOM'S] WAYS ARE PLEASANT, AND ALL HER PATHS ARE PEACE.

This verse and the next are used in liturgy, particularly when the Torah is returned to the ark following its reading.

ג:יח עֵץ־חַיִּים הִיא לַמַּחֲזִיקִים בָּהּ וְתֹמְכֶיהָ מְאֻשָּׁר:

3:18 IT IS A TREE OF LIFE TO THOSE WHO HOLD IT FAST, AND ALL WHO CLING TO IT FIND HAPPINESS.

In this verse, familiar to many because of its role in liturgy, a subtle shift has occurred. In the Book of Proverbs, wisdom offers life and happiness to the individual. By associating it with the Torah, as the Rabbis did by assigning these verses to the concluding part of the service in which the Torah is read, wisdom is shifted from the experience of the world to a relationship with the Divine. Thus, it is nearly impossible to read this text without the echoes of revelation reverberating in the soul of the reader.

ג:יט יְהֹוָה בְּחָכְמָה יָסַד־אָרֶץ כּוֹנֵן שָׁמַיִם בִּתְבוּנָה:

3:19 WITH WISDOM *ADONAI* ESTABLISHED THE EARTH; WITH UNDERSTANDING GOD SET UP THE HEAVENS.

In the midrash (*B'reishit Rabbah* 1:2), the Rabbis transformed wisdom and associated it with the Torah by suggesting that God used the Torah as a blueprint for the world in much the same way as an architect uses plans to erect a building. The text that supported this notion, what is called a "prooftext," is Proverbs 8:22, which has wisdom saying, "God acquired me as the first of the way." Thus, wisdom became Torah, and Torah became the plan of the universe. The notion of wisdom as a plan for the universe has a parallel in the Greek idea of *logos*. This idea resurfaces in a different form in the first verse of the Gospel of John.

ג:כ בְּדַעְתּוֹ תְּהוֹמוֹת נִבְקָעוּ וּשְׁחָקִים יִרְעֲפוּ־טָל:

3:20 THROUGH GOD'S KNOWLEDGE, THE DEPTHS BURST APART AND THE CLOUDS DRIP DEW.

For the author of Genesis (7:11), the "depths" are the primordial waters beneath the earth. For the writer of Proverbs, all natural phenomena follow a natural plan that reflects divine wisdom. The medieval commentator Abraham ibn Ezra suggests that the splitting of the "depths" provided water for animals and birds.

ג:כא בְּנִי אַל־יָלֻזוּ מֵעֵינֶיךָ נְצֹר תֻּשִׁיָּה וּמְזִמָּה:

3:21 MY YOUNG FRIEND, DON'T LOSE SIGHT OF THEM. MAINTAIN PRUDENCE AND PURPOSE.

It would seem that "them" refers to the aforementioned "wisdom" and "knowledge." As we suggested in the translation of verse 1:4, here we translate *m'zimah* as "purpose." Similarly, as we suggested in 2:7, *tushiyah* may be translated as "prudence." It seems that the author of Proverbs is telling the reader to keep the order of nature in mind as an indicator of the role that wisdom and reason play in the world and in life.

ג:כב וְיִהְיוּ חַיִּים לְנַפְשֶׁךָ וְחֵן לְגַרְגְּרֹתֶיךָ:

3:22 THEY WILL ADD LIFE TO YOUR SOUL AND GRACE TO YOUR NECK.

The promise of wisdom is the enhancement of life. Moreover, as is indicated in verse 1:9, one's possession of wisdom and knowledge will be easily discerned by others. Wisdom and knowledge make their mark on the individual both inside and out.

ג:כג אָז תֵּלֵךְ לָבֶטַח דַּרְכֶּךָ וְרַגְלְךָ לֹא תִגּוֹף:

3:23 THEN YOU CAN CONFIDENTLY GO ON YOUR WAY; YOU
WON'T EVEN STUMBLE.

When you possess wisdom and knowledge, you can go forward toward your goal without having to worry about details, just as a traveler can proceed toward his or her destination without having to look down to avoid stumbling over an obstacle (literally, "hit your foot").

ג:כד אִם־תִּשְׁכַּב לֹא־תִפְחָד וְשָׁכַבְתָּ וְעָרְבָה שְׁנָתֶךָ:

3:24 DON'T BE AFRAID WHEN YOU LIE DOWN, FOR WHEN
YOU DO, YOUR SLEEP WILL BE PLEASANT.

Not only will wisdom protect the individual during the day, but it will also do so at night. The author promises that wisdom, like pious belief, will protect its possessor.

ג:כה אַל־תִּירָא מִפַּחַד פִּתְאֹם וּמִשֹּׁאַת רְשָׁעִים כִּי תָבֹא:

3:25 SUDDEN TERROR WON'T FRIGHTEN YOU, NOR THE
DEVASTATION BY THE WICKED, SHOULD IT COME.

As is promised, wisdom will bring serenity. Terrible things may occur. The wicked will do evil. Here the author promises that, nonetheless, the possession of wisdom will allay any fear that the reader may have.

ג:כו כִּי־יְהֹוָה יִהְיֶה בְכִסְלֶךָ וְשָׁמַר רַגְלְךָ מִלָּכֶד:

3:26 FOR *ADONAI* WILL GIVE YOU CONFIDENCE AND KEEP
YOUR FOOT FROM TRIPPING.

In this verse, we move from our dependence on wisdom to our dependence on God. This is a necessary pious remark in a book that is devoted to prudential wisdom.

ג:כז אַל־תִּמְנַע־טוֹב מִבְּעָלָיו בִּהְיוֹת לְאֵל ידיך יָדְךָ לַעֲשׂוֹת:

3:27 DON'T HOLD BACK FROM DOING GOOD TO THOSE
WHO ARE DESERVING, WHEN YOU HAVE THE POWER
TO DO IT.

We translate the word *mibaalav* as "[from] those who are deserving," while it literally means "from those who possess it," or from its owners. These people do not yet possess the good that is promised. Here the instruction is given to the wise to do good as well as to anticipate that good will be directed to them. This "promised good" may be a rather simple act, as we see in the next verse.

ג:כח אַל־תֹּאמַר לרעיך לְרֵעֲךָ לֵךְ וָשׁוּב וּמָחָר אֶתֵּן וְיֵשׁ אִתָּךְ:

3:28 DON'T SAY TO YOUR NEIGHBOR, WHEN YOU'VE GOT
WHAT HE [OR SHE] WANTS, "COME BACK TOMORROW
AND I WILL GIVE IT TO YOU."

Why make your neighbors struggle for something that you can easily give them?
Because the author of Proverbs seems to understand human nature and our proclivity
toward haughty acts, he wants to remind us that being smart is no reason to take
advantage of others or to be unconcerned about them.

ג:כט אַל־תַּחֲרֹשׁ עַל־רֵעֲךָ רָעָה וְהוּא־יוֹשֵׁב לָבֶטַח אִתָּךְ:

3:29 DON'T PLOT EVIL AGAINST YOUR TRUSTING NEIGHBOR
WHILE HE [OR SHE] IS LIVING WITH YOU.

Being smart may lead to being clever. Being clever may lead you to think that you can
get away with doing anything you want. You may even be able to harm people
without getting caught. Such clever people, however, are generally smart enough not
to take on those who are powerful, recognizing that the powerful generally look out
for themselves. The "mark" is usually someone who is not powerful and is usually
very trusting. Acknowledging who reads Proverbs, the writer warns us not to take
advantage of those who trust us.

ג:ל אַל־תרוב תָּרִיב עִם־אָדָם חִנָּם אִם־לֹא גְמָלְךָ רָעָה:

3:30 DON'T QUARREL WITH ANYONE WITHOUT REASON,
[PARTICULARLY] IF THAT PERSON HAS NOT HARMED
YOU.

This warning is delivered to the kind of individuals who the author anticipates will
read the book: just because you are smart enough to do it—and even get away with
it—*don't!* If you think that your intellectual prowess allows you to do whatever you
want, think again.

ג:לא אַל־תְּקַנֵּא בְּאִישׁ חָמָס וְאַל־תִּבְחַר בְּכָל־דְּרָכָיו:

3:31 DON'T BE JEALOUS OF THE VIOLENT PERSON, AND
DON'T FOLLOW HIS [OR HER] WAYS.

Here the warning shifts from intelligence to "tough guys." The one who has used
intelligence as a tool will find that a move from words to violence is difficult
and dangerous.

ג:לב כִּי תוֹעֲבַת יְהֹוָה נָלוֹז וְאֶת־יְשָׁרִים סוֹדוֹ:

3:32 THE CORRUPT ARE AN ABOMINATION TO *ADONAI*. THE
SECRET COUNSEL OF GOD ARE THE UPRIGHT.

We are warned once again. Immoral behavior is not only unwise; it is also wicked in
the eyes God.

ג:לג מְאֵרַת יְהֹוָה בְּבֵית רָשָׁע וּנְוֵה צַדִּיקִים יְבָרֵךְ:

3:33 THE CURSE OF *ADONAI* IS IN THE HOUSE OF THE
WICKED, WHILE THE HOME OF THE RIGHTEOUS IS
BLESSED.

By invoking God's judgment on the wicked and the righteous, the writer has moved
the theme of the Book of Proverbs from prudence to virtue.

ג:לד אִם־לַלֵּצִים הוּא יָלִיץ ולעניים וְלַעֲנָוִים יִתֶּן־חֵן:

3:34 GOD MAKES FUN OF THE MOCKERS AND GIVES GRACE
TO THE HUMBLE.

Mockery is seen as a threat to an ethical system, because those who engage in it
express a contempt for virtue. So the writer of Proverbs, in making a statement as
fact, is here expressing the hope that God will punish those who make a mockery out
of ethics.

ג:לה כָּבוֹד חֲכָמִים יִנְחָלוּ וּכְסִילִים מֵרִים קָלוֹן:

3:35 THE WISE WILL INHERIT HONOR. THE FOOLISH WILL
CARRY OFF SHAME.

In this verse, the author returns to the contrast between "wise" and "foolish,"
pairing them with "righteous" and "wicked." Just as the writer moved from moral
judgment ("righteous" and "wicked") to intellectual judgment, he moves to what
might be named a secular evaluation of human acts. Honor and shame are the
result of what people do to one another. For some, "honor" is granted. To others,
"shame" is delivered.

Shem and Ever

Shem was the eldest son of the biblical Noah. In the episode of Noah's drunkenness, he appears as the most sensitive of the three brothers. Shem is thus blessed and is listed in Genesis 10 as the father of five sons who had twenty-one descendants. Since most of these descendants had little to do with Israelite history, the connection between Shem and Abraham as "the ancestor of all the descendants of Ever" is important. The detailed lineage of Shem through Ever (his great-grandson) is continued in Genesis 11 (verses 10–26) and concludes with the birth of Abraham. In the *aggadah*, Shem's importance is inflated simply because of his role as a primary ancestor of the people of Israel.

Since the Rabbis considered Torah institutions to exist prior to the revelation at Sinai, they identified the tents of Shem as a rabbinical academy of sorts and named Ever as the head of its rabbinical court *(av beit din)* (*B'reishit Rabbah* 63:7; *Yalkut Shimoni, Toldot* 25). Students of Torah will be privileged to study in the heavenly courts of Shem and Ever, as well, continues the midrash in another source (Babylonian Talmud, *Avodah Zarah* 36b; *Makot* 23b).

Yisurim shel Ahavah *(Chastisements of Love)*

Yisurim may refer to either physical or spiritual suffering that is inexplicable and unmerited. While most people argue that the classic example comes from the Book of Job, Rabbi Arthur Green suggests that it emerges from the generation of the Bar Kochba rebellion (132–135 C.E.). In Hebrew this period is called the "generation of destruction" *(doro shel shmad)*. In the Ashkenazi version of the Yom Kippur service, the deaths of ten rabbinic martyrs are tearfully recalled each year. Thus, Rabbi Akiva, the most well-known figure in this group, has become the classic example of the Jewish martyr. He called his suffering *yisurim shel ahavah* (sufferings of love).

This idea may mean that though we suffer, we continue to love God. Our suffering may even provide us with the means with which to love God. In doing so, we offer ourselves, and our suffering, as a gift to the Almighty. This is not easy love. It is difficult, but it can lead to a more mature faith.

In the Book of Proverbs, we get a slightly different sense of chastisement through suffering. Here we understand that God loves us and brings us suffering as a result of that love, hoping that it will bring us to a deeper and more profound faith.

Targum

While the word *targum* may be used to refer generally to translation of any sort, it usually refers to the Aramaic translations of the Bible. For the sake of broad popular understanding of the Torah and Bible, the translation of sacred text into the vernacular has been necessary. However, the translation also serves as an interpretation and commentary and helps scholars to understand words, ideas, and concepts of the original Hebrew that might be unclear. The translation into Aramaic was among the first of translations into another language. (The Septuagint similarly is a translation into Greek.) The most important of these is the translation of the Torah by Onkelos the Proselyte (third century C.E.). Thus, when scholars speak of *the Targum,* they are usually making reference to *Targum Onkelos.* The *Jonathan Targum* is a freer translation of the Bible, erroneously attributed to Jonathan ben Uzziel, which dates no earlier than the seventh century C.E. An earlier fragmentary version is known as the *Jerusalem Targum.*

Prooftexts

Prooftexts are a system that the Rabbis employ as a basic principle for supporting the legal claims they make. It is a hermeneutic that combines the oral tradition with the written law. By basing their statements on a particular sacred text (generally from the Torah), the Rabbis are able to claim authenticity and gain authority. This is particularly important because in most cases, the Rabbis are not permitted to speak on their own behalf.

Primordial Waters

On the second day of Creation, according to the account of Genesis, God made a firmament by separating the waters from above and below, which the Holy One gathered into the seas and separated from the dry land (see Genesis 1:6–10). Apparently, these waters already existed before the creation of the world. These primordial waters also appear in ancient Babylonian creation myths.

GLEANINGS

Divine Commandments

Ask even knowledgeable Jews what the word *mitzvah* means and you will often be told, "good deed." But in reality, *mitzvah* means "commandment." The difference between "good deed" and "commandment," though subtle, is significant. "Good deed" implies a voluntary act, "commandment" an obligatory one. In contemporary Western society, most people believe voluntary acts to be on a higher plane than obligatory ones; after all, they reason, isn't a person who does an act voluntarily nobler than one who does it because he feels obligated? Yet the Talmud takes precisely the opposite point of view: "Greater is he who is commanded and carries out an act, than he who is not commanded, and carries it out" (*Kiddushin* 31a). Apparently, the rabbis of the Talmud believed that obligatory acts will be carried out with greater consistency and staying power than voluntary ones.

Joseph Telushkin, *Jewish Literacy: The Most Important Things to Know About the Jewish Religion, Its People, and Its History* (New York: William Morrow and Company, 1991), 495

Obligation without External Discipline—and Hope

The goal for the individual Jew and the Jewish community remains what it has always been, to create lives of such everyday sanctity and societies of such holiness that God's kingdom will become fact among us. Restoring personalism to Judaism makes personal piety again possible, even mandatory. Ethics can no longer displace God's presence in our lives. Our recent tradition had so little confidence in human power that it waited with virtual resignation for God to bring the Messiah. The liberals had such unbounded confidence in human power that they as good as dispensed with God in trusting to themselves and in humankind's progressive enlightenment to bring the Messianic Age. A sense of Covenant makes messianism a partnership between God and the people of Israel. It requires patience on our part as well as continued religious action; yet it gives us courage despite our failures and hope despite an infinite task which laughs at our successes, for God too is bringing the Messiah.

Eugene B. Borowitz, Cnoices in Modern Jewish Thought: A Partisan Guide
(New York: Behrman House, 1983), 288–89

Response

Holiness demands a response, an answer. We cannot simply say, "That's nice. Now on to something else." (Indeed if we can, it was not holiness we knew.) An encounter with the Sacred Unity of All Creation places a demand on our behavior. Sometimes the obligation is nothing more than a promise to remain silent in its Presence or to return to this place again. Other times we are driven to make more sustained changes in our actions and to persuade others to join us. We have "heard" something; something has been "laid upon us." We feel personally obligated, commanded. To ignore this summons would violate the wonder of the moment and the covenant it whispers.

Lawrence Kushner, The Book of Words: Talking Spiritual Life, Living Spiritual Talk
(Woodstock, Vt.: Jewish Lights Publishing, 1993), 91

God Gives Us Hope

God gives us hope in a way that no human agent can. Among humans, Murphy's Law operates: Anything that can go wrong will. But at the divine level, there is another, opposite law: Anything that should set right sooner or later will. God is the answer to the question, What is the point of trying to make the world better if problems of war, hunger, injustice, and hatred are so vast and stubborn that I can't even make a dent in them in my lifetime? God assures us, in a way that no mortal can, that what we do not achieve in our lifetime will be completed beyond our lifetime and in part because of what we did in our lifetime. Human beings may be mortal, appearing on earth for just a few years, but God's will is eternal. Ecclesiastes worried, What is the point of all the good I do if I die and all my good deeds are forgotten? The answer is that good deeds are never wasted and not forgotten. What cannot be achieved in one lifetime will happen when one lifetime is joined to another. People who never knew each other in life become partners in making good things happen, because the Eternal God gives their deeds a measure of eternity.

Harold S. Kushner, *When All You've Ever Wanted Isn't Enough*
(New York: Summit Books, 1986), 184

CHAPTER FOUR

ד:א שִׁמְעוּ בָנִים מוּסַר אָב וְהַקְשִׁיבוּ לָדַעַת בִּינָה:

**4:1 CHILDREN, LISTEN TO A PARENT'S TEACHING; PAY
ATTENTION TO GAIN UNDERSTANDING.**

When a parent speaks to a child and asks, "Do you hear me?" that parent is not
asking about the child's hearing ability. Rather, the parent is asking whether the child
is prepared to obey the parent's instructions. Similarly, *sh'ma* is used here to express
the same thing. The writer wants the reader to pay attention, as a child should to a
parent. Although *musar* is translated elsewhere as "discipline" to imply physical
chastisement, the sense here is much broader. Thus, it is translated as "teaching." The
last two words of the verse, *l'daat binah* (literally, "to know understanding"), are
translated idiomatically into English as "to gain understanding." Such understanding
must be achieved. It is not something that is easily gained.

ד:ב כִּי לֶקַח טוֹב נָתַתִּי לָכֶם תּוֹרָתִי אַל־תַּעֲזֹבוּ:

**4:2 LOOK, A GOOD DOCTRINE HAS BEEN GIVEN TO YOU;
[IT IS] MY TORAH, DO NOT FORSAKE IT.**

Like other verses from Proverbs (such as 3:17–18), this verse has made its way into
the liturgy, following the reading of the Torah, before it is returned to the ark. It is
sound advice, emerging from the practical experience of the writer. It also reflects the
"torah" of Proverbs.

ד:ג כִּי־בֵן הָיִיתִי לְאָבִי רַךְ וְיָחִיד לִפְנֵי* אִמִּי : ‏*סבירין ומטעין "לבני"

**4:3 WHEN I WAS MY FATHER'S LITTLE CHILD, A BELOVED
BABY TO MY MOTHER**

Although *ben* may be translated as son, the context suggests a tender feeling of father
to child that transcends the relationship established merely by fathering a child. The
translation of *yachid* (only) as *nivchar v'chaviv* (beloved) follows the suggestion of
Rashi. The writer wants to paint a sentimental picture of a young child receiving
ethical instruction from parents for the first time.

ד:ד וַיֹּרֵנִי וַיֹּאמֶר לִי יִתְמָךְ־דְּבָרַי לִבֶּךָ שְׁמֹר מִצְוֹתַי וֶחְיֵה:

4:4 YOU TAUGHT ME AND SAID, "LET YOUR MIND HOLD
ONTO MY WORDS. KEEP MY MITZVOT AND LIVE."

In order to be gender sensitive, we have taken a verse written with the third-person pronoun and made it more personal as a way of bringing the individual into covenantal relationship with God while expressing the deference intended by the writer. We have translated *libecha* (your heart) as "your mind." The verse contains an implicit promise that if the children adhere to the moral guidance offered by parents, they will lead productive lives. The biblical injunction resonates with the contemporary "Have a life."

ד:ה קְנֵה חָכְמָה קְנֵה בִינָה אַל־תִּשְׁכַּח וְאַל־תֵּט מֵאִמְרֵי־פִי:

4:5 GET WISDOM. GET UNDERSTANDING. DON'T FORGET.
DON'T TURN AWAY FROM MY WORDS.

By using *kneih* (usually translated as "buy," which we have translated as "get"), the writer suggests that the acquisition of wisdom comes at a price. It is not automatic. This realization is the beginning of understanding.

ד:ו אַל־תַּעַזְבֶהָ וְתִשְׁמְרֶךָ אֱהָבֶהָ וְתִצְּרֶךָ:

4:6 DON'T LET HER GO, FOR SHE WILL GUARD YOU; LOVE
HER AND SHE WILL WATCH OVER YOU.

Wisdom is again given a voice. The writer admonishes the reader to hold onto wisdom as one would hold tightly to the one he loves.

ד:ז רֵאשִׁית חָכְמָה קְנֵה חָכְמָה וּבְכָל־קִנְיָנְךָ קְנֵה בִינָה:

4:7 WISDOM BEGINS WITH GETTING MORE WISDOM; GET
UNDERSTANDING WITH ALL THAT YOU POSSESS.

The familiar way to translate the first half of this verse is as "the beginning of wisdom is to get wisdom." The second half is understood by Abraham ibn Ezra as using a portion of one's wealth to acquire wisdom. He understands that sometimes we have to use our resources to acquire wisdom, especially when it does not come through experience. If a portion is not enough, then use it all.

ד:ח סַלְסְלֶהָ וּתְרוֹמְמֶךָּ תְּכַבֵּדְךָ כִּי תְחַבְּקֶנָּה:

4:8 CHERISH HER AND SHE WILL EXALT YOU; EMBRACE HER
AND SHE WILL HONOR YOU.

The personification of wisdom continues in this verse. In later rabbinic Hebrew, *salsal* (cherish) comes to mean "curl the hair." If it had that meaning in biblical Hebrew, it would be difficult to understand the intent of the writer.

ד:ט תִּתֵּן לְרֹאשְׁךָ לִוְיַת־חֵן עֲטֶרֶת תִּפְאֶרֶת תְּמַגְּנֶךָּ:

4:9 SHE WILL GIVE YOU A GRACEFUL GARLAND FOR YOUR
HEAD; SHE WILL PRESENT YOU WITH A CROWN OF
GLORY.

In this verse we hear an echo of 1:9; an individual's wisdom will be obvious to all.

ד:י שְׁמַע בְּנִי וְקַח אֲמָרָי וְיִרְבּוּ לְךָ שְׁנוֹת חַיִּים:

4:10 LISTEN, MY YOUNG FRIEND. SEIZE MY WORDS SO THAT
YEARS MAY BE ADDED TO YOUR LIFE.

Again, the author promises that a long life will be the tangible result of wisdom.

ד:יא בְּדֶרֶךְ חָכְמָה הֹרֵתִיךָ הִדְרַכְתִּיךָ בְּמַעְגְּלֵי־יֹשֶׁר:

4:11 I HAVE SHOWN YOU THE WAY OF WISDOM; I HAVE LED
YOU ON THE RIGHT PATHS.

The best moral teaching is done more by example than by precept. A spin on the well-known saying yields: "Don't just do as I say; do as I do." Consistent with much of biblical literature, the image of a path suggests that one must begin by taking the first step—and then you are on your way. The ideal teacher of values shows the student how to choose the right way and where to take the correct first step. The writer continues the instruction with the next verse.

ד:יב בְּלֶכְתְּךָ לֹא־יֵצַר צַעֲדֶךָ וְאִם־תָּרוּץ לֹא תִכָּשֵׁל:

4:12 WHEN YOU GO, YOUR STRIDE NEED NOT BE SHORT;
IF YOU RUN, YOU WON'T STUMBLE.

Once you recognize the path to wisdom, you will be able to proceed more quickly toward the goal of acquiring it. Therefore:

ד:יג הַחֲזֵק בַּמּוּסָר אַל־תֶּרֶף נִצְּרֶהָ כִּי־הִיא חַיֶּיךָ:

4:13 Grab hold of instruction, don't let go; watch her, for she is your life.

Instruction is a means to acquiring wisdom. Once acquired, it will guide and enhance your life. It follows that those who refuse to follow the course of wisdom invite disaster. So the writer threatens the reader in the next verses by warning what could happen.

ד:יד בְּאֹרַח רְשָׁעִים אַל־תָּבֹא וְאַל־תְּאַשֵּׁר בְּדֶרֶךְ רָעִים:

4:14 Don't enter the course of the wicked; don't take strides in the way of those who are evil.

If you do, you will pay for it.

ד:טו פְּרָעֵהוּ אַל־תַּעֲבָר־בּוֹ שְׂטֵה מֵעָלָיו וַעֲבוֹר:

4:15 Reject it. Don't go near it. Turn from it and pass it by.

The teacher-writer warns against taking the first step on the path of evil.

ד:טז כִּי לֹא יִשְׁנוּ אִם־לֹא יָרֵעוּ וְנִגְזְלָה שְׁנָתָם אִם־לֹא יכשולו יַכְשִׁילוּ:

4:16 They can't sleep until they have done something wrong. They are robbed of sleep until they cause someone to stumble.

The writer portrays the wicked as so wrapped up in doing wrong that they are unable to rest until they have done their nefarious deeds. Even then, they cannot rest, because they continue to plot evil.

ד:יז כִּי לָחֲמוּ לֶחֶם רֶשַׁע וְיֵין חֲמָסִים יִשְׁתּוּ:

4:17 They feed on the bread of wickedness, and they drink the wine of violence.

As the innocent eat bread and wine, the stuff of life, the wicked consume wickedness and violence.

ד:יח וְאֹרַח צַדִּיקִים כְּאוֹר נֹגַהּ הוֹלֵךְ וָאוֹר עַד־נְכוֹן הַיּוֹם:

4:18 WHILE THE COURSE OF THE RIGHTEOUS IS LIKE THE
DAWN, WHICH GETS BRIGHTER AS THE DAY PROCEEDS

As virtue, like light, manifests itself gradually, so those who are virtuous will be gradually recognized as they pass through life day-by-day. The virtuous who walk in the light are contrasted with the wicked in the next verse.

ד:יט דֶּרֶךְ רְשָׁעִים כָּאֲפֵלָה לֹא יָדְעוּ בַּמֶּה יִכָּשֵׁלוּ:

4:19 THE WAY OF THE WICKED IS MURKY; THEY WILL
STUMBLE, YET NOT KNOW WHY.

The wicked, blinded by vice, will stumble. They won't even know which evil deed caused their downfall.

ד:כ בְּנִי לִדְבָרַי הַקְשִׁיבָה לַאֲמָרַי הַט־אָזְנֶךָ:

4:20 MY YOUNG FRIEND, PAY ATTENTION TO MY WORDS.
GIVE EAR TO WHAT I AM SAYING.

The writer again calls the student to attention because ethical instruction, perhaps more than any other kind, requires the student's constant focus. Virtue is not easy to learn or to teach.

ד:כא אַל־יַלִּיזוּ מֵעֵינֶיךָ שָׁמְרֵם בְּתוֹךְ לְבָבֶךָ:

4:21 DON'T LET THEM SLIP OUT OF YOUR SIGHT; HOLD
THEM DEEP IN YOUR MIND.

For ethical maxims to be placed into action in daily life, they must always be present in your mind and constantly reviewed.

ד:כב כִּי־חַיִּים הֵם לְמֹצְאֵיהֶם וּלְכָל־בְּשָׂרוֹ מַרְפֵּא:

4:22 THEY ARE LIFE TO THOSE WHO FIND THEM, HEALING
TO ALL FLESH.

As previously promised, ethical living will enhance the quality of life.

ד:כג מִכָּל־מִשְׁמָר נְצֹר לִבֶּךָ כִּי־מִמֶּנּוּ תּוֹצְאוֹת חַיִּים:

4:23 MORE THAN ANYTHING ELSE YOU WATCH OVER, PROTECT YOUR MIND, FOR ALL OF LIFE COMES FROM IT.

Evil affects the mind and the ability of the individual to deal with the challenges of everyday living.

ד:כד הָסֵר מִמְּךָ עִקְּשׁוּת פֶּה וּלְזוּת שְׂפָתַיִם הַרְחֵק מִמֶּךָּ:

4:24 TAKE THE FALSE FROM YOUR MOUTH, AND KEEP THE PERVERSE FAR FROM YOUR LIPS.

Honesty in speech is a basic element of ethical living.

ד:כה עֵינֶיךָ לְנֹכַח יַבִּיטוּ וְעַפְעַפֶּיךָ יַיְשִׁרוּ נֶגְדֶּךָ:

4:25 KEEP YOUR EYES LOOKING STRAIGHT AHEAD, AND DIRECT YOUR EYELIDS FORWARD.

The ethical person must keep his or her goals ever present in the mind. Like someone on a journey, you have to keep your eyes focused ahead of you, so that you can keep the end in sight and be careful not to bump into anything that would cause you to stumble.

ד:כו פַּלֵּס מַעְגַּל רַגְלֶךָ וְכָל־דְּרָכֶיךָ יִכֹּנוּ:

4:26 EXAMINE THE PATH UPON WHICH YOUR FEET STAND, AND LET YOUR WAYS BE STRAIGHT.

Your path in life should take you to the place that you have chosen. Proceed through life focused on that goal.

ד:כז אַל־תֵּט־יָמִין וּשְׂמֹאול הָסֵר רַגְלְךָ מֵרָע:

4:27 DON'T TURN RIGHT OR LEFT; REMOVE YOUR FOOT FROM EVIL.

The writer suggests that evil is the act of turning away from the proper goal—or the result of it. As Aristotle suggested with the notion of a golden mean—which Maimonides further interpreted—the middle path is the proper place on which to travel through life.

Covenantal Relationship

The covenantal relationship is an idea championed by the contemporary theologian Eugene B. Borowitz. Basing this idea primarily on the I-Thou relationship as articulated by the philosopher/theologian Martin Buber, Borowitz suggests that the paradigmatic relationship for the relationship between individuals can be seen in the covenantal relationship established between God and the Jewish people in the revelation of Torah at Sinai. Our behaviors and interactions should constantly be reflective of that relationship of mutual expectations and responsibilities. Moreover, it is this relationship that should guide and govern our lives.

The Golden Mean

Although the use of the term "golden mean" first occurred in 1587, the notion of moderation and the balancing of extremes as an ethical goal first occurs in Artistotle's *Ethics*. From *Ethics*, Maimonides takes the notion into his *Sh'monah P'rakim* (Eight Chapters), the introduction to his commentary to *Pirkei Avot*. Maimonides presents a kind of behavioral therapy: since the mean between the extremes is the ideal, a person who has moved from the mean—a miser, for example—is brought back to the mean by moving him or her in the opposite direction by being trained for a period to act as a spendthrift. Hopefully, after such therapy, the former miser will be moved to the mean and will be neither miser nor spendthrift.

Moses Maimonides

Moses Maimonides was born on March 30, 1135, in Cordoba, Spain. He is called Rambam in rabbinical literature, an acronym constructed from the name Rabbi Moses ben Maimon. In some places, he is also called HaNesher HaGadol, the Mighty Eagle. With his family, he fled his birthplace in 1148 when it fell to the Almohads and their religious persecution. During the ten years his family wandered through Spain—about which little is known—scholars speculate that he began his commentary to the Mishnah, wrote a short piece on the calendar and an essay on logic, and collected notes for his commentary to several tractates of the Talmud.

Maimonides moved to Fez, North Africa, in 1160. Troubled by the large number of Jews who converted to Islam there, he penned several pieces, including *Letter of Consolation, Letter on Forced Conversion,* and *Letter of the Sanctification of the Divine Name.* Following a short residence in the Land of Israel, Maimonides and his family settled in Egypt, first in Alexandria and then in Fostat (Old Cairo). After about a year in Egypt, he completed his commentary on the Mishnah (1168) and subsequently finished his *Sefer HaMitzvot* (1170), *Mishneh Torah* (1180), and *Guide for the Perplexed* (1190). In 1177, Maimonides was named head of the Jewish community. He died in 1204.

GLEANINGS

Sweet Words

Know that there is truth that can be conveyed in words. But there is a greater truth that words cannot contain. It is to capture and share this truth that symphonies are written, masterpieces sculpted, and sacred rituals passed from generation to generation. The disciple goes, not to hear words, but to watch and learn. For in the life of the master, every action, no matter how seemingly trivial, is filled with intention and meaning and truth.

> Edward Feinstein, in *Voice of the Spirit: Inspirations Based on the Music of Craig Taubman,*
> ed. Janet Bain Fattal (Los Angeles: Sweet Louise Music, 1998)

Wide Turns and the Narrow Path

Anyone who has ever driven an automobile over a winding mountain road knows the dangers of the narrow turn. We look for wide roads, even though they do not completely protect us from accidents. So it is with Judaism. We believe in the wide path, with enough choice and leeway on all sides (Nachmias). We concede the possibility of wrong choices, but we trust each individual to make the best, and not the worst of his opportunities.

> W. Gunther Plaut, *The Book of Proverbs: A Commentary* (New York: UAHC Press, 1961), 69

Faces of Children

If we are indeed created in God's image, then the value of a single human life—like God's—is immeasurable. With that premise from which to venture forth, I begin our journey by seeking out—why not—the Website for *Life* magazine. I find it at *www.pathfinder.com/Life/*. I click on a photo essay that seems likes a perfect springboard for this quest, an exposé of the first year in the life of Ella Rosalind Baker, born in London in August 1995. Her father, a photographer, has recorded every key moment of Ella's life in a journal that to this point has reached sixty thousand words, and in a series of photos, many of which appear at this site. Individually, they look like any of the hundreds of baby photos that a coworker is just dying to show you until you say to yourself, "Enough already" and excuse yourself to make an urgent phone call. But when seen together, this collage of sixteen shots taken over the course of fifty-two weeks has a stunning time-lapse effect. One after the other, I click on the individual photos to enlarge them to full-screen size, and this little flower of a baby unfolds before me. Here she is sleeping, here she yawns, here wide-eyed and pensive, here giggling, with hair ever-growing, here in a cradle, here in a dress.

Is it possible to bond with a total stranger? Is it possible to love this neighbor as thyself? Is it possible to see in her development the unfolding face of the divine image?

Joshua Hammerman, *thelordismyshepherd.com: Seeking God in Cyberspace* (Deerfield Beach, Fla.: Simcha Press, 2000), 215

Seeing What Needs to Be Done

I don't know of any other way to maintain or sustain a meaningful relationship of any kind except to take responsibility for it. I know that *thinking* about my responsibilities, engaging in quiet, honest reflection, may help me better hold up my end of the bargain. I know that what I feel often influences what *I* do. But since I have yet to master the art of telekinesis I have yet to see my feelings change a single thing or single soul outside of myself. Feelings seldom change the world, but actions *always* do. I don't want to live in a world in which I have to depend on my neighbor's *feelings* to predict her behavior. I do want to be part of a community in which everyone feels *obligated* to behave in a certain way. With obligation as the prevailing rule of conduct, I can count on others to do the right thing and they can count on me to do the same, regardless of how we feel, because safeguarding the sanctity of the community is *more important* than our individual emotional needs at any point in time. How can there be a community of common intention and integrity if everyone does what they think is right *only* when it "feels" right for them or *only* when it makes them feel good about themselves? How can we know what will make one person feel good about themselves and another awful? How can we measure human conduct by that standard? How can we depend upon each other if we are all hostages to mood and motivation? The simple answer is that we can't. Torah acknowledges that truth. We wouldn't need commandments if we all *felt* like doing them. It's precisely because we don't always feel like it that we *need* them. That's why we're *commanded* to do them. We are obliged, and that means "have to"—*not* "may—if I feel like it that particular day." Obligation is just another word for responsibility and responsibilities don't go away simply because we grow tired of them or find them too difficult to assume. Our ability to shoulder responsibility willingly, kindly and wisely is the litmus test of our continuing growth and development as human beings. Obedience as a manifestation of responsibility is a profound expression of our respect for other people and our reverence for God; a recognition that all our actions have consequences and that all our relationships have a holy dimension. The law of cause and effect is immutable whether in physics or in human behavior.

Lee Meyerhoff Hendler, *The Year Mom Got Religion: One Woman's Midlife Journey into Judaism* (Woodstock, Vt.: Jewish Lights Publishing, 1998), 157–58

CHAPTER FIVE

הֵ:א בְּנִי לְחָכְמָתִי הַקְשִׁיבָה לִתְבוּנָתִי הַט־אָזְנֶךָ:

5:1 MY YOUNG FRIEND, PAY ATTENTION TO MY WISDOM.
GIVE EAR TO MY UNDERSTANDING,

Again and again, the writer directs the student to pay attention.

הֵ:ב לִשְׁמֹר מְזִמּוֹת וְדַעַת שְׂפָתֶיךָ יִנְצֹרוּ:

5:2 IN ORDER TO MAINTAIN SCHEMES AND HAVE YOUR LIPS
PRESERVE KNOWLEDGE.

When *m'zimot* (schemes) was used in the singular in 1:4, we translated it as
"purpose." Here it is used to mean plans that should be kept secret, information that
should not be shared. Wisdom is knowing when to speak and when to keep silent,
when to disclose and when to conceal.

הֵ:ג כִּי נֹפֶת תִּטֹּפְנָה שִׂפְתֵי זָרָה וְחָלָק מִשֶּׁמֶן חִכָּהּ:

5:3 FOR THE LIPS OF A STRANGER DRIP WITH HONEY,
WHOSE MOUTH IS SMOOTHER THAN OIL.

It is difficult to render this verse as gender sensitive without changing the metaphor
completely. The author returns to the character of a "foreign woman" introduced in
2:16, whom we have characterized simply as a "stranger." This "stranger" is able to
seduce simply through speech and is thereby able to dredge out any secret. It should
be noted that the attraction of a "foreign woman" or "handsome stranger" exists in
many cultural contexts. Such a woman is able to do all the things that the men within
the group would forbid the women from the same group to do. This projected
attraction of the stranger tells us more about the secret desires of men than it does the
seductive character of woman, whether they are part of the reference group or
outside of it.

ה:ד וְאַחֲרִיתָהּ מָרָה כַלַּעֲנָה חַדָּה כְּחֶרֶב פִּיּוֹת:

5:4 AS BITTER AS WORMWOOD WILL BE HER OUTCOME, AS
SHARP AS A DOUBLE-EDGED SWORD.

We have translated *acharitah* as "her outcome." Others have chosen to render it as "her end," which may conceal an intentionally vulgar play on words. In any case, the writer warns the young student that as sweet as illicit behavior may seem, its result will be bitter. Moreover, sexual activity with a stranger is dangerous, as the writer points out in the following verse.

ה:ה רַגְלֶיהָ יֹרְדוֹת מָוֶת שְׁאוֹל צְעָדֶיהָ יִתְמֹכוּ:

5:5 HER FEET DESCEND DOWN TO DEATH; HER STEPS
PROCEED TO THE GRAVE.

Things have not changed. The same advice that the writer of Proverbs offers here is suggested by people today. Because sexual indiscretions are so enticing, dire punishments are threatened. Since the teaching of Proverbs is directed to this world, it is important to note the translation of *sheol* as "grave" both here and in 1:12, the place where the dead are brought for burial. Some have translated it as "netherworld" or "hell," which suggests an otherworldly orientation, a view that we believe was not that of the author of Proverbs.

ה:ו אֹרַח חַיִּים פֶּן־תְּפַלֵּס נָעוּ מַעְגְּלֹתֶיהָ לֹא תֵדָע:

5:6 SHOULD YOU EXAMINE THE COURSE OF LIFE, WOULD
YOU NOT KNOW THAT HER PATHS ARE PERVERSE?

The Hebrew text in this verse is difficult to translate. Following the commentary by Abraham ibn Ezra, we have taken both imperfect verbs as referents to the second person. Furthermore, we read the second half of the verse as a question. The teacher asks the student to reflect on the situation of the world. In doing so, the student will see that illicit sexual behavior will end in disaster.

ה:ז וְעַתָּה בָנִים שִׁמְעוּ־לִי וְאַל־תָּסוּרוּ מֵאִמְרֵי־פִי:

5:7 NOW BOYS, LISTEN TO ME. DON'T TURN AWAY FROM
ANYTHING I HAVE SAID.

Mei-imrei fi (literally, "the words of my mouth") has been translated as "anything I have said." One has the impression that this added call to attention is required after the warning against illicit sexual behavior. Perhaps this is because sexual sins are the most attractive, particularly to the young.

הֹח הַרְחֵק מֵעָלֶיהָ דַרְכֶּךָ וְאַל־תִּקְרַב אֶל־פֶּתַח בֵּיתָהּ:

5:8 KEEP AWAY FROM HER; DON'T COME CLOSE TO HER DOOR.

The house is in the city. The city provides both temptation and anonymity. If you get close to the house, you will be tempted to enter. And if you enter, you may sin. So don't tempt fate; keep away!

הֹט פֶּן־תִּתֵּן לַאֲחֵרִים הוֹדֶךָ וּשְׁנֹתֶיךָ לְאַכְזָרִי:

5:9 LEST YOU GIVE HONOR TO OTHERS AND YOUR YEARS TO THE CRUEL.

This is a difficult verse. *Hod* can mean "glory," "majesty," or "vigor." We have translated it as "honor." Thus, the first half of the verse means that to engage in illicit sexual behavior is to be bereft of honor. The second half of the verse raises the question as to who are the "cruel." The commentator Rashi thought that the word referred to the Prince of *Geihinom*. Perhaps, following Gersonides, the "cruel" may be untrammeled desire that leads the sinner ever deeper into sin and despair by overriding all controls. Such sinners become willing to trade everything to meet their desires. Hence one should watch out, according to the following verse:

הֹי פֶּן־יִשְׂבְּעוּ זָרִים כֹּחֶךָ וַעֲצָבֶיךָ בְּבֵית נָכְרִי:

5:10 LEST STRANGERS BE SATISFIED BY YOUR EXERTION AND YOUR TOIL BE IN A FOREIGNER'S HOUSE.

If sexual desire can occupy one's consciousness so extensively that one is willing to pay for sexual favors, then, without a doubt, it can impoverish the individual. All that one owns will end up in someone else's hands.

הֹיא וְנָהַמְתָּ בְאַחֲרִיתֶךָ בִּכְלוֹת בְּשָׂרְךָ וּשְׁאֵרֶךָ:

5:11 YOU WILL LAMENT WHEN YOUR END COMES, WHEN YOUR FLESH AND BODY FAIL.

Then it will be too late. The inability to sin is not the same as repentance. Repent now! Change your ways now, for:

51

ה:יב וְאָמַרְתָּ אֵיךְ שָׂנֵאתִי מוּסָר וְתוֹכַחַת נָאַץ לִבִּי:

5:12 YOU WILL SAY, "I HATED DISCIPLINE. MY MIND
REJECTED REPROOF.

In the future, as you look back on the present, you will be sorry that you did not change, but you will be stuck with the life that you have created for yourself. Future tears will not dissolve away present sins. The person you will have become will not be affected by the words you will then say.

ה:יג וְלֹא־שָׁמַעְתִּי בְּקוֹל מוֹרָי וְלִמְלַמְּדַי לֹא־הִטִּיתִי אָזְנִי:

5:13 "I DID NOT OBEY THE VOICE OF THOSE WHO TAUGHT
ME. I DID NOT DIRECT MY EAR TO THOSE WHO
INSTRUCTED ME.

Again, using the literary device of parallelism that is common in the Bible, the teacher imagines what the young person will say when that person becomes old and is saddened by the direction his or her life has taken. That young person might say:

ה:יד כִּמְעַט הָיִיתִי בְכָל־רָע בְּתוֹךְ קָהָל וְעֵדָה:

5:14 "I HAD PARTICIPATED IN ALMOST EVERY EVIL IN THE
MIDST OF THE CONGREGATION AND ASSEMBLY."

Here again the writer imagines what the young person will say looking back at his or her life.

ה:טו שְׁתֵה־מַיִם מִבּוֹרֶךָ וְנֹזְלִים מִתּוֹךְ בְּאֵרֶךָ:

5:15 DRINK WATER OUT OF YOUR OWN CISTERN AND
RUNNING WATER OUT OF YOUR OWN WELL.

Rashi takes this verse to refer to the study of Torah, while Ibn Ezra and some modern commentators read this as a euphemism for sexual intercourse within marriage. If it means the latter, as we believe that it does, then the writer is advising the reader to satisfy sexual desires by marrying young and staying faithful.

ה:טז יָפוּצוּ מַעְיְנֹתֶיךָ חוּצָה בָּרְחֹבוֹת פַּלְגֵי־מָיִם:

5:16 Let your springs be spread out and let there be
streams in the streets.

Following Rashi's understanding of the previous verse, "springs" and "streams" refer
to students whom you will raise up. If we follow Ibn Ezra's understanding of the verse,
then "springs" and "streams" refer to children.

ה:יז יִהְיוּ־לְךָ לְבַדֶּךָ וְאֵין לְזָרִים אִתָּךְ:

5:17 They will be your very own and not yours and
some strangers'.

In keeping with Rashi's interpretation, you will gain honor through your teaching,
honor you need to share. Following in the line of Ibn Ezra's interpretation, restricting
your sexual intercourse to your spouse will make sure that your children are not of
questionable parentage.

ה:יח יְהִי־מְקוֹרְךָ בָרוּךְ וּשְׂמַח מֵאֵשֶׁת נְעוּרֶךָ:

5:18 May your spring be blessed and [may you] rejoice
in the spouse of your youth.

Terms like "cistern" and "well" and "spring" are often used as euphemisms for
women, as they are in this verse. Such usage speaks of an attitude that certainly needs
improvement, although it is rather interesting from a psychospiritual point of view.
Nevertheless, the reader is advised to marry and remain with one's spouse to avoid
sexual temptation and marital difficulty, something that did not begin with our own
time. As Kohelet wrote, "...It has already been for a long time" (Ecclesiastes 1:10).

ה:יט אַיֶּלֶת אֲהָבִים וְיַעֲלַת־חֵן דַּדֶּיהָ יְרַוֻּךָ בְכָל־עֵת בְּאַהֲבָתָהּ תִּשְׁגֶּה
תָמִיד:

5:19 A lovely doe, a charming goat, may her breasts
intoxicate you every moment. May her love make
you reel always.

It may be acceptable for a woman to be compared to a doe, but it does seem strange
for that same woman to be likened to a goat. Yet to the ancients both of these animals
were symbols of beauty and sexual prowess. In rather direct language, the reader is
advised to confine sexual activity to one's spouse.

ה:כ וְלָמָּה תִשְׁגֶּה בְנִי בְזָרָה וּתְחַבֵּק חֵק נָכְרִיָּה:

5:20 MY YOUNG FRIEND, WHY REEL AFTER A STRANGE
WOMAN? WHY EMBRACE THE BODY OF A FOREIGN
WOMAN?

Cheik is translated as "body," but it may also have the meaning of "lap." Again, the "foreign woman," also implying the "forbidden woman," is presented here as the great temptation. The same holds true for the "foreign man." Marriage is presented as the means for managing sexual desire and a protection against temptation.

ה:כא כִּי נֹכַח עֵינֵי יְהוָה דַּרְכֵי־אִישׁ וְכָל־מַעְגְּלֹתָיו מְפַלֵּס:

5:21 FOR THE WAYS OF THE HUMAN ARE PRESENT TO THE
EYES OF GOD. YOU WEIGH ALL OUR PATHS.

We have changed the direction of the second half of the verse from third person to the second in order to make it more gender inclusive. If the exhortations against illicit sexual activity presented in the last few verses have not already made the gravity of such sin clear, then a divine warning is added: Whatever the young, presumptive reader will do, God will know about it. Therefore, watch out. Be careful. Even sexual sins, which may be hidden from the view of other humans, are plainly seen by God.

ה:כב עֲוֹנוֹתָיו יִלְכְּדֻנוֹ אֶת־הָרָשָׁע וּבְחַבְלֵי חַטָּאתוֹ יִתָּמֵךְ:

5:22 THE WICKED PERSON IS TRAPPED BY ONE'S OWN
INIQUITIES AND HELD BY THE CORDS OF ONE'S
OWN SIN.

The writer presents a more prudential approach. Whether or not the sinner is aware of it, the consequences of sin remain with the sinner. Just as a trap catches and holds the unwary animal, so sin will catch and hold the sinner.

ה:כג הוּא יָמוּת בְּאֵין מוּסָר וּבְרֹב אִוַּלְתּוֹ יִשְׁגֶּה:

5:23 LACKING DISCIPLINE, THE SINNER WILL DIE; BECAUSE
OF OVERWHELMING FOOLISHNESS, THE SINNER WILL
BE UNSTEADY.

Desire might lead to a kind of intoxication, causing a person to be unsteady and reel as if drunk. Illicit activity will similarly cause a person to stagger.

Sheol

Sheol was another name for Geihinom, outside the western wall in Jerusalem. Geihinom is mentioned in the Bible in various places (including Joshua 15:8) as a valley that formed the boundary between the tribes of Benjamin and Judah. This valley served as a dump where the city's refuse was placed and the carcasses of animals and the criminals were thrown. Jeremiah prophesied that the area would become a "valley of slaughter" and a burial place (Jeremiah 7:32). Thus, in postbiblical literature, it took on the identity of hell, where the wicked are punished. However, no allusion to this really exists in the Bible. In Genesis, *Sheol* is simply the abode of the dead (Genesis 37:35). The Rabbis located *Geihinom* in the bowels of the earth (Babylonian Talmud, *Eiruvin* 19a) and in the heavens or beyond the mountain of darkness (Babylonian Talmud, *Tamid* 32b). For the Talmud, the form of punishment for the wicked is not clearly articulated, but it is associated with some form of fire.

Prince of Geihinom

Geihinom, "the Valley of [Ben Hinom]" (south of Jerusalem), was known in biblical times as a place of child sacrifice (see II Kings 23:10) and the worship of Molech (Jeremiah 2:23). In the rabbinic imagination, this became the place of enduring punishment for sinners after their death. According to the Talmud, there is a *sar shel Geihinom,* a "prince of *Geihinom*," who reproves sinners (Babylonian Talmud, *Sanhedrin* 52a) and to whom is given heretics and those of the ruling authority (Babylonian Talmud, *Avodah Zarah* 17a). It is thought that Jewish sinners—following the confession of their sins—fare better in *Geihinom* than others (Babylonian Talmud, *Eiruvin* 19a).

Parallelism

Parallelism is a literary technique that is best seen in the Book of Psalms. However, it is employed throughout the Bible in a variety of forms. The author states an idea in one verse that is then restated in a second verse. This is its parallel. The restatement (the parallel) is generally either synonymous to the first verse (adding no new information) or complementary to it (adding a slight nuance in its restatement).

GLEANINGS

On Life and Death

In biblical times, Judaism's main emphasis was on life not death. Judaism was born into a world that worshiped and glorified death. A primary sacred document of the ancient Egyptians was *The Book of the Dead,* chronicling and extolling the journey to eternity. Egyptian slaves spent entire lifetimes building elaborate burial tombs to shelter their kings and nobles in death, surrounded by the finest of life's material goods—gold, silver, precious jewels, delicate fabrics, fine foods, companion animals, and even clay figurines of entire armies.

To counter this preoccupation with death, the Hebrew Bible teaches nothing of an afterlife. According to the Bible, immortality was achieved by living a good, worthy, meaningful, productive life on this earth, and by leaving progeny—children who would carry on the good deeds and the good name of their parents.

Yet the Bible does not teach that death means complete oblivion. It implies an eternity of the soul—the unique God-given spark of life that makes the material body into a living, breathing human being—when God tells Abram, "As for you, you shall *go to your fathers* in peace; you shall be buried at a ripe old age" (Genesis 15:15). When Abraham (remember, his name was changed at the time of the covenant of circumcision) dies, the Bible describes his death by saying, "And Abraham breathed his last, dying at a good, ripe age, old and content, and *he was gathered to his people* . . ." (Genesis 25:8).

While it does not define it in any clear way, the Bible describes a place called *sheol,* a netherworld to which souls descend at the time of death.

The Bible thus implies that death means the end of physical existence, but does not mean a total cessation of being. Rather, there is an eternity to the soul, which will somehow "live on" and be reunited with the souls of ancestors who have previously died.

Wayne Dosick, Living Judaism: The Complete Guide to Jewish Belief, Tradition, and Practice
(San Francisco: HarperSanFrancisco, 1995), 313–14

Wisdom for the Future

Sexuality is a form of intimacy. Like other forms of intimacy, such as friendship, being part of a support group, mentoring, and parenting, there are risks associated with taking on too much too soon, as many a new step-parent finds out. In my experience, sexual relationships are most successful when we think through our desires and how best to satisfy them. Unsafe sex—which can spread life-threatening diseases—clearly violates the Jewish religious affirmations of the sanctity of life. The larger Jewish wisdom about human relations—not to lie, cheat, manipulate, harm, coerce, or behave abusively—applies to the sexual realm. Self-knowledge, good communication, respect for others—spiritual goals encouraged by Jewish ethical values—are the most important tools for a healthy, satisfying sexual life. Lesbianism, bisexuality, and various other minority sexual preferences are within the range of normal human desire. They are not pathologies or inherently immoral, and do not require massive apologetics or justifications.

For Judaism to play a significant role in the ethical, physical, and spiritual development of Jewish women, it must deal with contemporary reality. Silence and denial will not serve the needs of Jewish women of all ages for moral guidance about sexuality or any other challenging life theme. One goal of religion is to awaken people to the sacred and meaningful in daily life. To do this, it is important that Jewish religious leaders and institutions articulate theories and models of sexuality that speak to the Jewish women of today.

Jane Rachel Litman, "When the Siren Stops Singing," in *Lifecycles,* vol. 2, *Jewish Women on Biblical Themes in Contemporary Life,* ed. Debra Orenstein and Jane Rachel Litman (Woodstock, Vt.: Jewish Lights Publishing, 1997), 196

The Spiritual Life

The spiritual life is like a tree with its roots above, pointing to that which transcends us. The spiritual life aims at transcendence while it affirms a meaning beyond absurdity, the presence of the lasting behind the screen of the ephemeral. Consideration of the afterlife directs our attention toward that which is lasting, toward that and who can survive us. In this regard, Dostoyevsky wrote, "If you were to destroy in mankind the belief in immortality, not only love, but every living force maintaining the life of the world would at once be dried up."

Thoughts about self-perpetuation can lead to actions aimed at making life more meaningful, more beautiful, more saturated with significance. Yet, so doing does not necessarily satisfy our curiosity as to what might yet await us. Various religious traditions not only accept the belief in an afterlife as an article of faith, but also offer a variety of views of what the nature of that afterlife might be like.

So far, no incontestable scientific evidence for or against an afterlife exists. But this should not be surprising. If life after death is a completely different dimension of existence than the one we presently inhabit, and if scientific measurement only relates to our present dimension, then it is understandable why the dimension of afterlife existence cannot be detected through scientific investigation.

Byron L. Sherwin, *Crafting the Soul: Creating Your Life as a Work of Art* (Rochester, Vt.: Park Street Press, 1998), 183

Family Relations

The faithful man, enjoying full marital relations with his wife, will have many children. A large family was considered a blessing. Only for a relatively short time, in the first half of the twentieth century, did Jewish families shrink to one or two children. In the second half of the 1900's, larger families are making their appearances once again, at least in America, but the number of children in the average Jewish family still falls considerably behind the average non-Jewish family.

The frankness with which Jewish tradition treated sexual questions is one reason for the high standard of Jewish morality throughout the ages. Sex was nothing to be ashamed of; it was a normal, necessary, and enjoyable part of life. There was no need for furtiveness and therefore no room for lascivious stories and dubious jokes. The Talmud...give[s] some wholesome sexual advice: Proper marital relations in your youth will assure continued fertility in old age.

W. Gunther Plaut, *The Book of Proverbs: A Commentary* (New York: UAHC Press, 1961), 77

Sex in Cyberspace

Sexuality is not in itself evil. I can imagine loving, married couples making great use of adult Websites, much as they do with adult videos. I'm also not so certain that the accessibility of Internet sex sites will lead our children to lives of depravity. The impact of the site I visited was neither titillation nor disgust, but a yawn. When I looked at it, I felt sad, as I did in Amsterdam, that people have to sell their bodies to gain self-worth. But the hard fact is that, once the clothes are off, there is little left that is sexy. What's sexy is the anticipation, the unfolding and the emotional attachment—the love. Unwrapping a Torah scroll is sexy. Hindu temple art is sexy. When you click on a Website and everyone is already naked and having at it, one can hardly call it sexy, evil, tempting or anything else but just plain boring.

Joshua Hammerman, *thelordismyshepherd.com: Seeking God in Cyberspace*
(Deerfield Beach, Fla.: Simcha Press, 2000), 200

CHAPTER SIX

וּ:א בְּנִי אִם־עָרַבְתָּ לְרֵעֶךָ תָּקַעְתָּ לַזָּר כַּפֶּיךָ:

6:1 MY YOUNG FRIEND, WHETHER YOU HAVE BECOME
GUARANTOR FOR A NEIGHBOR OR MADE A DEAL WITH
A STRANGER

The teacher turns now to other foolish acts that might have been undertaken by the
young student, namely, mistakes in business dealings: to become a guarantor for
someone you know or to make a deal with someone you don't know. Either act may
cause you to lose. When you agree to be a guarantor, you are agreeing to repay a
person's loan if he or she forfeits on that loan. You, as guarantor, cannot control the
behavior of the person who took out the loan, and you cannot compel its repayment.
To make a deal (the Hebrew says, *takata . . . capecha*, "you struck hands") with
someone you don't know may be bad business, because you don't know how that
person conducts his or her business and you may lose money as a result. While this
may be strange advice in this context, it was not unusual, since Jews have historically
been involved with loaning money. It was one of the few businesses they were
allowed to maintain in societies that restricted them from trades and professions.

וּ:ב נוֹקַשְׁתָּ בְאִמְרֵי־פִיךָ נִלְכַּדְתָּ בְּאִמְרֵי־פִיךָ:

6:2 YOU WILL BE SNARED BY THE WORDS OF YOUR MOUTH,
TRAPPED BY THOSE VERY WORDS.

"Silence is golden." What you say may bring disaster upon you. You can't be held to
a commitment that you did not make. But if you made a commitment, then you have
to stand by it.

וּ:ג עֲשֵׂה זֹאת אֵפוֹא בְּנִי וְהִנָּצֵל כִּי בָאתָ בְכַף־רֵעֶךָ לֵךְ הִתְרַפֵּס
וּרְהַב רֵעֶיךָ:

6:3 MY YOUNG FRIEND, DO THIS AND BE SAVED [FROM
DISASTER], NOW THAT YOU ARE IN YOUR NEIGHBOR'S
HANDS: GO GROVEL OR BERATE YOUR NEIGHBOR.

Two opposite courses of action are proposed. Either become most abject or most
annoying. Either become unnaturally silent or begin to yell. However you do it,
convince your neighbor to let you out of your surety contract. This verse contains two

interesting Hebrew words. *Hitrapeis* (grovel) may be translated literally as "become like mire or muck." *R'hav* can mean "press" or "harry." Both are extreme forms of behavior. The author employs these dramatic words to emphasize the importance of getting free from a contract that one should not have entered into.

ו:ד אַל־תִּתֵּן שֵׁנָה לְעֵינֶיךָ וּתְנוּמָה לְעַפְעַפֶּיךָ:

6:4 DON'T LET YOUR EYES SLEEP NOR ALLOW SLUMBER TO TAKE OVER YOUR EYELIDS.

Don't sleep on it. Take action now. Don't let another day pass. You don't know what can happen in a day's time.

ו:ה הִנָּצֵל כִּצְבִי מִיָּד וּכְצִפּוֹר מִיַּד יָקוּשׁ:

6:5 ESCAPE LIKE A DEER FROM THE HAND [OF A HUNTER] OR LIKE A BIRD FROM THE HAND OF A BIRD CATCHER.

Just as a deer would try to get out of a trap and a bird would attempt to get loose from a snare, so the unwary surety should try to get out of the contract. Having dealt with the folly of unconsidered words, the author of Proverbs now deals with the folly of laziness.

ו:ו לֵךְ־אֶל־נְמָלָה עָצֵל רְאֵה דְרָכֶיהָ וַחֲכָם:

6:6 LAZYBONES, TAKE A LOOK AT THE ANT; SEE WHAT SHE DOES AND GET SMART.

Now the teacher turns to nature to provide lessons for living. While it is difficult to capture the idiom the writer is using in Hebrew, anyone who is familiar with the tendency of teenagers to sleep late in the morning recognizes the behavior that is implicit in the idiom quite well.

ו:ז אֲשֶׁר אֵין־לָהּ קָצִין שֹׁטֵר וּמֹשֵׁל:

6:7 SHE HAS NEITHER A RULER NOR AN OFFICER NOR AN OVERSEER.

The biblical Hebrew terms *katzin* (ruler), *shoteir* (officer), and *mosheil* (overseer) seem to have equivalent meanings. In modern Hebrew, these words have taken on different meanings, with *katzin* referring to an officer in the army *(Tzahal)* and *shoteir* referring to a police officer. The point that the writer is making is that ants seem self-directed, while the young student seems to lack all direction in life.

ו:ח תָּכִין בַּקַּיִץ לַחְמָהּ אָגְרָה בַקָּצִיר מַאֲכָלָהּ:

6:8 SHE PREPARES HER FOOD IN THE SUMMER AND
GATHERS HER FOOD AT HARVEST TIME.

The instinctual life of insects and their ability to prepare ahead of time for their needs continue to amaze the human observer.

ו:ט עַד־מָתַי עָצֵל תִּשְׁכָּב מָתַי תָּקוּם מִשְּׁנָתֶךָ:

6:9 LAZYBONES, HOW LONG ARE YOU GOING TO LIE
SLEEPING? WHEN ARE YOU GOING TO GET UP?

Staying in bed is no way to face the day.

ו:י מְעַט שֵׁנוֹת מְעַט תְּנוּמוֹת מְעַט חִבֻּק יָדַיִם לִשְׁכָּב:

6:10 JUST A LITTLE MORE SLEEP, JUST A LITTLE SNOOZE,
JUST A SHORT NAP.

This is what the lazy person says to him- or herself. Having presented a picture of the lazy person, indicating how that person thinks, the writer is now going to tell him or her the consequences of such action. We have translated the idiom "just a little folding of the hands to lie down," the posture one might assume to take a short nap, as "just a short nap."

ו:יא וּבָא־כִמְהַלֵּךְ רֵאשֶׁךָ וּמַחְסֹרְךָ כְּאִישׁ מָגֵן:

6:11 YOUR POVERTY WILL COME RUNNING, AND YOUR
PRIVATION WILL BE LIKE A PERSON WITH A SHIELD.

Poverty will come so quickly to people who are lazy that they will not be able to do anything about it. Like a person who would have to duel with an opponent who had a shield, so will the indolent individual be at a loss to defend oneself from impoverishment.

ו:יב אָדָם בְּלִיַּעַל אִישׁ אָוֶן הוֹלֵךְ עִקְּשׁוּת פֶּה:

6:12 A USELESS PERSON, A DECEITFUL INDIVIDUAL IS THE
ONE WHO WALKS WITH A FALSE MOUTH

Only a twisted personality twists the truth. The use of deceit has become so common in our time that it is nearly an acceptable behavior now. We even use the term "spin doctor" to refer to such behaviors. The author of Proverbs describes the techniques of the then contemporary spin doctor in the next verse.

וּ:יג קֶרֵץ בעינו בְּעֵינָיו מֹלֵל ברגלו בְּרַגְלָיו מֹרֶה בְּאֶצְבְּעֹתָיו:

6:13 THE ONE WHO GIVES A WINK WITH THE EYE, WHO MAKES A SIGN WITH THE FOOT, WHO POINTS WITH THE FINGER.

Not everything has to be put into words. Using parts of the body, the deceitful person can suggest notions that still can hurt or put forth ideas that change the original meaning.

וּ:יד תַּהְפֻּכוֹת בְּלִבּוֹ חֹרֵשׁ רָע בְּכָל־עֵת מדנים מִדְיָנִים יְשַׁלֵּחַ:

6:14 PERVERSITY IS IN THE MIND; YOU DEVISE EVIL AT EVERY MOMENT; YOU SET OFF SQUABBLES.

This verse has been rendered in the second person, rather than the third-person masculine (as it appears in the original Hebrew) to make the translation more inclusive. However, we risk changing the sentiment of the author, since the author of Proverbs is not calling the student reader evil or perverse. Words can wound and even kill. One must be careful of what one says lest harm befall others. In our day, there are those who enjoy saying what ought not be said and encourage others to do so as well, even inciting them to fight with one another as a result. We call them talk show hosts.

וּ:טו עַל־כֵּן פִּתְאֹם יָבוֹא אֵידוֹ פֶּתַע יִשָּׁבֵר וְאֵין מַרְפֵּא:

6:15 THEREFORE, SUDDENLY DISASTER WILL COME. ALL OF A SUDDEN, YOU WILL BE BROKEN BEYOND REPAIR.

Again, the writer directs our attention to the one who does evil. There is more pious hope than prudential wisdom. Evil has a life of its own. Its demise is rarely sudden. The evil of talebearing has a very long "half-life." Perhaps this is the reason why the writer invokes the view of God in the next verse.

וּ:טז שֶׁשׁ־הֵנָּה שָׂנֵא יְהֹוָה וְשֶׁבַע תֹּעֲבוֹת תּוֹעֲבַת נַפְשׁוֹ:

6:16 THERE ARE SIX THINGS THAT GOD HATES AND SEVEN THINGS THAT GOD CONSIDERS AS ABOMINATIONS:

The use of numbers as a rhetorical device is first found in the writings of the prophet Amos (1:3 and 1:6): "For three transgressions of Damascus, and for four... [and] ... for three transgressions of Gaza, and for four...." Here we have six and seven. One may count six things in the following verses but not seven. Hence the numbers six and seven suggest an indefinite number rather than a specific listing.

ו׃יז עֵינַיִם רָמוֹת לְשׁוֹן שָׁקֶר וְיָדַיִם שֹׁפְכוֹת דָּם־נָקִי׃

6:17 EYES THAT ARE HAUGHTY, A TONGUE THAT LIES, AND
HANDS THAT SHED INNOCENT BLOOD

This is the beginning of the kinds of things that God does not like.

ו׃יח לֵב חֹרֵשׁ מַחְשְׁבוֹת אָוֶן רַגְלַיִם מְמַהֲרוֹת לָרוּץ לָרָעָה׃

6:18 A MIND THAT DEVISES DECEITFUL THOUGHTS, FEET
THAT RUN RAPIDLY TO DO EVIL

The list continues.

ו׃יט יָפִיחַ כְּזָבִים עֵד שָׁקֶר וּמְשַׁלֵּחַ מְדָנִים בֵּין אַחִים׃

6:19 FALSE WITNESS WHO EXHALES LIES AND THE ONE
WHO SETS OFF SQUABBLES BETWEEN BROTHERS
[AND SISTERS].

Here again the writer repeats the theme that words can wound. However, now
the writer offers a divine foundation or emphasis for what was already taught.
The Hebrew word *yafiach* might be translated as "blow" or "breathe." The image
is presented of a person for whom lying is so natural that it comes as easily as
breathing does.

ו׃כ נְצֹר בְּנִי מִצְוַת אָבִיךָ וְאַל־תִּטֹּשׁ תּוֹרַת אִמֶּךָ׃

6:20 MY YOUNG FRIEND, KEEP THE COMMANDMENT OF
YOUR FATHER, AND DON'T LET YOUR MOTHER'S
TEACHING SLIP AWAY.

The second half of this verse is the same as the second half of 1:8. The author uses
the term *mitzvah* (commandment) to refer to the father's instructions. This suggests
that the terms mitzvah and torah had not yet been employed to specifically refer to
divine instruction. The one who would gain wisdom is told to reflect on the kind of
teaching that might be offered by one's parents. This suggests that the one seeking
wisdom is probably rather young. Wisdom is what those who are older are willing to
pass down to those who are younger.

ו:כא קָשְׁרֵם עַל־לִבְּךָ תָמִיד עָנְדֵם עַל־גַּרְגְּרֹתֶךָ:

6:21 TIE THEM TO YOUR MIND ALWAYS; FASTEN THEM TO
YOUR NECK.

Since the biblical author understood the heart to be the seat of thought, we have translated *libcha* (your heart) as "your mind." The verbal root *anad* occurs once more in the Bible in Job (31:36). There it is associated with a crown. Since the verb seems to be used in reference to an ornament or jewelry, we have chosen to translate it as "fasten them." In any case, the writer wants to tell the reader to hold tight and not let go of the instruction, particularly when faced with sexual temptation (Job 5:24ff.).

ו:כב בְּהִתְהַלֶּכְךָ תַּנְחֶה אֹתָךְ בְּשָׁכְבְּךָ תִּשְׁמֹר עָלֶיךָ וַהֲקִיצוֹתָ הִיא
תְשִׂיחֶךָ:

6:22 WHEN YOU WALK AROUND, IT WILL GUIDE YOU. WHEN
YOU LIE DOWN, IT WILL WATCH OVER YOU. AND WHEN
YOU WAKE UP, IT WILL TALK TO YOU.

The writer hopes that the ethical instruction being offered will guide the individual at every moment and in every activity.

ו:כג כִּי נֵר מִצְוָה וְתוֹרָה אוֹר וְדֶרֶךְ חַיִּים תּוֹכְחוֹת מוּסָר:

6:23 FOR A COMMANDMENT IS A LAMP AND INSTRUCTION
IS LIGHT, AND THE WAY OF LIFE IS THE REPROOF
OF DISCIPLINE

Since this verse is so often quoted through an interpretation, it may be difficult to accept a different translation. For example, since *torah* refers to what a Sage teaches rather than what was divinely revealed at Sinai (see Proverbs 13:14), we have translated it here as "instruction." Similarly, we translate *musar* as "discipline." Wisdom will provide illumination for us all along the path of life, particularly in the face of temptation.

ו:כד לִשְׁמָרְךָ מֵאֵשֶׁת רָע מֵחֶלְקַת לָשׁוֹן נָכְרִיָּה:

6:24 TO GUARD YOU FROM AN EVIL PERSON, FROM THE
BEGUILEMENT OF AN ALIEN LANGUAGE.

Once again, the author wants to warn the reader about a foreign person (literally, "woman") as the source of temptation. What the person says may be as alluring as how she or he looks.

ו:כה אַל־תַּחְמֹד יָפְיָהּ בִּלְבָבֶךָ וְאַל־תִּקָּחֲךָ בְּעַפְעַפֶּיהָ׃

6:25 DON'T COVET HER BEAUTY IN YOUR MIND, AND DON'T
LET [THE WINKING OF] HER EYELIDS CAPTURE YOU.

The woman whom the writer has in mind does not even have to speak. Just looking at her can threaten a person's chastity. She does not even have to expose much of her body. Just a wink can cause you to lose your mind! Such fear may ultimately reveal more about the mind-set of the writer-teacher than the reality of the temptation. In the most pragmatic terms, the writer warns the reader of Proverbs that succumbing to temptation will result in economic loss.

ו:כו כִּי בְעַד־אִשָּׁה זוֹנָה עַד־כִּכַּר לָחֶם וְאֵשֶׁת אִישׁ נֶפֶשׁ יְקָרָה תָצוּד׃

6:26 FOR THE SAKE OF A WHORE, A PERSON WILL BE REDUCED
TO A LOAF OF BREAD, WHILE AN ADULTERESS WILL
HUNT FOR ONE'S PRECIOUS LIFE.

As presented and as might be expected, the fault lies with the woman (as temptress), rather than the man. If she is unmarried, she is a whore. As a whore, she will bleed the young man of all of his money. Of course, it is worse if the woman is married. His participation in *her* adultery may cost him his life. The message is clear, even if it is cast in extremely sexist terms by the author of Proverbs. Illicit sex can cost you your money or your life. No one will escape a penalty for illicit sex.

ו:כז הֲיַחְתֶּה אִישׁ אֵשׁ בְּחֵיקוֹ וּבְגָדָיו לֹא תִשָּׂרַפְנָה׃

6:27 CAN A PERSON RAKE FIRE INTO HIS OR HER LAP AND
NOT BURN HIS OR HER CLOTHES?

This is the image that the writer is suggesting: someone brushes burning coals into a pocket of a garment and then is surprised when the garment catches fire. The underlying notion is familiar: play with fire and you will get burned!

ו:כח אִם־יְהַלֵּךְ אִישׁ עַל־הַגֶּחָלִים וְרַגְלָיו לֹא תִכָּוֶינָה׃

6:28 CAN ONE WALK ON BURNING COALS AND NOT GET
SCORCHED FEET?

This is another example. As the writer understands it, such a walk would have an unfortunate outcome.

ו:כט כֵּן הַבָּא אֶל־אֵשֶׁת רֵעֵהוּ לֹא יִנָּקֶה כָּל־הַנֹּגֵעַ בָּהּ:

6:29 SIMILARLY, THE ONE WHO HAS SEXUAL RELATIONS WITH
HIS NEIGHBOR'S WIFE, WHOEVER TOUCHES HER WILL
NOT ESCAPE BLAME.

This verse follows from the previous one. Adultery, however tempting, will be
punished in one way or another. The temptations decried in this passage are the result
of the same situation that made the writing of the Book of Proverbs possible in the
first place, namely, the emergence of the city as a social institution. In a city whose
inhabitants are involved with commerce, it is possible to meet a variety of people. The
writer implies that one can meet different women in the city and be deluded into
believing that one can also be protected by the city's anonymity. There are
possibilities, and there are temptations.

ו:ל לֹא־יָבוּזוּ לַגַּנָּב כִּי יִגְנוֹב לְמַלֵּא נַפְשׁוֹ כִּי יִרְעָב:

6:30 NO ONE DESPISES A HUNGRY THIEF WHO STEALS TO
SATISFY DESIRE.

The writer now contrasts the situation of the adulterer with the situation of the thief.
Unlike the thief who steals because he or she is hungry, the one who commits
adultery, satisfying desire, cannot claim that were he not to sin, he would die as a
result. Instead, it is the opposite. Sinning puts one's life at risk. On the other hand,
the thief can claim that were he or she not to sin through stealing, his or her life
would be at risk.

ו:לא וְנִמְצָא יְשַׁלֵּם שִׁבְעָתָיִם אֶת־כָּל־הוֹן בֵּיתוֹ יִתֵּן:

6:31 IF THE THIEF IS DISCOVERED, THE THIEF MUST PAY
BACK SEVENFOLD AND MAY HAVE TO GIVE BACK ALL
THE WEALTH OF ONE'S HOUSE.

Even if motivated to steal out of hunger, thievery is still punishable. The term *hon
beito* (wealth of one's house) may be used by the author ironically. After all, had the
thief a great deal of wealth, then why would he or she be compelled to steal?

ו:לב נֹאֵף אִשָּׁה חֲסַר־לֵב מַשְׁחִית נַפְשׁוֹ הוּא יַעֲשֶׂנָּה:

6:32 THE ADULTERER LACKS SENSE. ONLY ONE WHO WOULD
DESTROY EVERYTHING WOULD DO IT.

The many meanings of *nefesh* (soul, desire, life) provide added illumination to this
verse. It was because of desire that the sinner was motivated to commit adultery.

That sin will then affect the life of the one who commits sin in this world. It will later affect the soul of the sinner in the next world as well.

ו:לג נֶגַע־וְקָלוֹן יִמְצָא וְחֶרְפָּתוֹ לֹא תִמָּחֶה:

**6:33 THE SINNER WILL FIND AFFLICTION AND DISHONOR
AND REPROACH THAT CANNOT BE WIPED AWAY.**

Depending on the source of the *nega,* one may translate the word as "wound." Perhaps the "wound" comes at the hands of a jealous spouse or even lashes directed by the court. Alternatively, the term could be translated in accordance with both Rashi and Ibn Ezra as "affliction" resulting from divine punishment.

ו:לד כִּי־קִנְאָה חֲמַת־גָּבֶר וְלֹא־יַחְמוֹל בְּיוֹם נָקָם:

**6:34 FOR JEALOUSY IS THE RAGE OF A SPOUSE; ON THE DAY
OF VENGEANCE, HE WILL NOT FORGIVE.**

The young person who would anticipate the delights of an adulterous relationship with a complacent lover should similarly anticipate the anger of the betrayed spouse.

ו:לה לֹא־יִשָּׂא פְּנֵי כָל־כֹּפֶר וְלֹא־יֹאבֶה כִּי תַרְבֶּה־שֹׁחַד:

**6:35 NO RANSOM WILL HE TAKE, NOR WILL HE BE
COMPLIANT, NO MATTER HOW YOU INCREASE THE
BRIBES.**

The spouse who is cheated will exact revenge. The young adulterer will be unable to find the means to pay his way out of that man's wrath.

Jews as Moneylenders

The negative stereotype and ethnic slur of Jews as moneylenders emerged from the limited professional opportunities available to Jews. Since they were prohibited from learning crafts and joining guilds and professional associations, they looked toward viable occupations that could be easily transported from one country to another, in the case of dispersion. In particular, during the Middle Ages, the Catholic Church prohibited the charging of interest between Christians, reflective of a reading of three passages in the Bible (Exodus 22:24; Leviticus 25:36–37; and Deuteronomy 23:20–21). The Rabbis reinterpreted this prohibition by means of a legal fiction. They determined that loans were really partnerships. While the Rabbis considered this approach appropriate for commerce, they prohibited the charging of interest to individuals who were in need.

The Use of Numbers

While numbers have great religious symbolism, few are given any real significance in the Bible. There are, however, a few exceptions to this. The number seven, for instance, is most prominent. It is reflected in the seven days of creation, the Sabbath as the seventh day, the Sabbatical year, the Jubilee year of seven times seven, and the *Omer* cycle of seven times seven days. In Jericho seven priests blew seven shofars seven times on seven days in seven circuits (Joshua 6:1ff.). Other numbers of note include ten (the potentially righteous of Sodom, plagues in Egypt, commandments, tithes) and forty (days of the Flood, Moses on the mountain, years in the desert).

Adultery

While the term "adultery" is not often heard in contemporary society, with people preferring to invoke euphemisms like "relationship" or "affair" instead, the Bible is quite clear about what is meant (see Exodus 20:13; Deuteronomy 5:17). As a result, biblical authors use adultery as a metaphor to describe unfaithful relationships, particularly between God and the people of Israel. The Rabbis considered adultery to be so important that it is one of the three cardinal precepts that must not be transgressed even in the face of death. In classic Jewish law, the principle came with its own male bias. Even the test of the bitter waters of *sotah* (see Numbers 5:12–31) was directed against the woman and not the man, although adultery by a husband became grounds for a divorce. While sexual relationships between a married man and a married woman were considered to be capital offenses, a relationship between a married man and an unmarried woman was not punishable, since polygamy was permitted in the ancient world.

While rabbinic law specified other consequences of adultery, what the Book of Proverbs makes clear is that when the Bible forbids adultery, it is speaking about something beyond the context of marital relationships. It is a prohibition against breaking a sacred trust that is epitomized in marital union.

GLEANINGS

Defining Jewish Macho

And a ... way of defining Jewish macho was in its understanding of *male sexuality*. Secular culture said, "Go out and sow your wild oats. Boys will be boys, and men will be men." Judaism demanded sexual restraint outside of marriage. Joseph was praiseworthy because he rejected the advances of Potiphar's wife. "Who is heroic?" the sages asked in *Pirkei Avot,* the ethical maxims of the Mishnah. "The one who conquers his *yetzer,* the one who can control his inclinations, the one who has command over his libido."

Jeffrey K. Salkin, *Searching for My Brothers: Jewish Men in a Gentile World*
(New York: G. P. Putnam's Sons, 1999), 4–5

The Torah of Light

The Rabbis compare God's law to a burning candle: the Torah is the candle's light, while mitzvah is the body of the candle itself. Torah cannot exist without the concrete presence of the mitzvah. Religion cannot be effective if it is merely form without content or content without form. Judaism as well as Christianity has wrestled with the problem of balancing form and content, ritual and spirit, the priestly and the prophetic. It is in the nature of reform movements to rebel against the encroachments of antiquated forms by first abandoning rituals almost to the vanishing point and then again to recapture them in part.

W. Gunther Plaut, *The Book of Proverbs: A Commentary* (New York: UAHC Press, 1961), 92

CHAPTER SEVEN

זַ:א בְּנִי שְׁמֹר אֲמָרָי וּמִצְוֹתַי תִּצְפֹּן אִתָּךְ:

7:1 MY YOUNG FRIEND, LISTEN TO WHAT I AM SAYING AND
STORE UP MY INSTRUCTIONS WITH YOU.

In this verse, as well as in the next verse, the word *mitzvot* (usually translated as
"commandments") does not have the same meaning as it does in later rabbinic
literature. Here it simply means the instruction of a teacher, rather than the direction
of a Deity.

זַ:ב שְׁמֹר מִצְוֹתַי וֶחְיֵה וְתוֹרָתִי כְּאִישׁוֹן עֵינֶיךָ:

7:2 FOLLOW MY INSTRUCTIONS AND LIVE WITH MY
TEACHING AS YOU WOULD THE PUPIL OF YOUR EYE.

Sight depends on the pupil of the eye. Life depends on adherence to the ethical
instructions that are being taught by the teacher.

זַ:ג קָשְׁרֵם עַל־אֶצְבְּעֹתֶיךָ כָּתְבֵם עַל־לוּחַ לִבֶּךָ:

7:3 TIE THEM TO YOUR FINGERS; WRITE THEM ON THE
SLATE OF YOUR MIND.

Although some commentators have taken the first clause of this verse as a parallel to
the ritual of *t'fillin*, it seems more likely that it refers to the practice (ancient as it is
modern) of tying a string around the finger to serve as a reminder. It is important that
the ethical instructions be remembered, particularly when the student is apt to forget
them during moments of temptation.

זַ:ד אֱמֹר לַחָכְמָה אֲחֹתִי אָתְּ וּמֹדָע לַבִּינָה תִקְרָא:

7:4 CALL WISDOM YOUR SISTER AND UNDERSTANDING
YOUR FRIEND.

A sister and a friend may serve as defense from an attack by the woman who is
characterized in the next verse. The verse could easily be directed to a man as "call
wisdom your brother and understanding your friend," thus instructing the female
student to be careful of the *man* described in the next verse.

זּ:ה לִשְׁמָרְךָ מֵאִשָּׁה זָרָה מִנָּכְרִיָּה אֲמָרֶיהָ הֶחֱלִיקָה:

7:5 THIS KEEPS YOU FROM A STRANGER, FROM A FOREIGNER
WHO BEGUILES WITH WORDS.

While we have chosen to translate this text without reference to gender, the author
returns to the notion of sexual temptation. This idea emerges in various cultures. The
reader is warned that while foreigners or strangers can be physically attractive, even
exotic, their speech can also be attractive and thereby beguiling. The text literally says,
"She smoothes her words," that is, she makes her words easy to swallow and leads
the innocent to commit sexual sin.

זּ:ו כִּי בְּחַלּוֹן בֵּיתִי בְּעַד אֶשְׁנַבִּי נִשְׁקָפְתִּי:

7:6 WHEN AT THE WINDOW OF MY HOUSE, I LOOKED
DOWN THROUGH THE LATTICE

Indirectly we learn that the urban environment of the city is a source of temptation,
for only in the city were houses built in such a way. Additionally, the kind of
anonymity necessary for illicit sexual activity would be easier to find in a large urban
environment than in rural areas (or in the suburbs) because there would be less
chance to be seen by others.

זּ:ז וָאֵרֶא בַפְּתָאיִם* אָבִינָה בַבָּנִים נַעַר חֲסַר־לֵב: יתיר א׳

7:7 I LOOKED AMONG THE FOOLS, AND I SAW A BOY
LACKING SENSE.

In wisdom literature such as Proverbs, sin is folly. Those who sin are described as
foolish. Thus, one who courts temptation is a fool.

זּ:ח עֹבֵר בַּשּׁוּק אֵצֶל פִּנָּהּ וְדֶרֶךְ בֵּיתָהּ יִצְעָד:

7:8 HE PASSES THROUGH THE STREET NEAR HER CORNER
AND SAUNTERS ON THE WAY TO HER HOUSE.

Again, the writer of Proverbs directs the instruction to a male reader who may be led
to sin by a woman. The same can be said of a female reader who may sin with a
male: "*She* passes through the street near *his* corner and saunters on the way to *his*
house." This verse offers us some insight into the mind of the writer. It is clear that the
intended reader is up to no good. His (or her) naïveté is related to his (or her) youth.
Because the older writer better understands the sexual drive, he (or she) is not as
gullible as is the young reader.

71

זּ:ט בְּנֶשֶׁף־בְּעֶרֶב יוֹם בְּאִישׁוֹן לַיְלָה וַאֲפֵלָה:

7:9 IT IS TWILIGHT, THE EVENING OF THE DAY, THE DARKEST
OF THE NIGHT, THICK DARKNESS.

The young reader thinks that he or she can get away with sin because it is veiled by the darkness. But just as sin can be concealed in layers, there are also gradations of darkness. In the twilight, few people can see what he or she does. In the darkness of the evening, even fewer will be able to observe his or her actions, nor are there as many people in the street at night who might be in a position to observe. And in the darkest part of the night, none will be able to see his or her activities.

זּ:י וְהִנֵּה אִשָּׁה לִקְרָאתוֹ שִׁית זוֹנָה וּנְצֻרַת לֵב:

7:10 HERE THE WOMAN COMES TOWARD HIM, DRESSED
LIKE A WHORE WITH HER MIND MADE UP [WHAT SHE
IS PREPARED TO DO].

While the verse is written for male readers, the text is also meant for women. Thus, it can be rendered, "Here the man comes toward her, dressed like a gigolo with his mind made up [what he is prepared to do]." The fool's dreams seem realized. The woman (or man) seems to be more than willing. The way she (or he) is dressed suggests that even before she (or he) is approached, she (or he) is ready for sex. However, as the end of the chapter will indicate, the person under discussion is not a prostitute. She will not engage in sex for money. She is a homemaker whose spouse is away on a business trip. Thus, she wants to have sex with the young man for pleasure, her pleasure. While this may be a liberating thought for some feminists, this posture, according to the author of Proverbs, is even worse than prostitution.

זּ:יא הֹמִיָּה הִיא וְסֹרָרֶת בְּבֵיתָהּ לֹא־יִשְׁכְּנוּ רַגְלֶיהָ:

7:11 LOUD AND STUBBORN, HER FEET DO NOT STAY
AT HOME.

זּ:יב פַּעַם בַּחוּץ פַּעַם בָּרְחֹבוֹת וְאֵצֶל כָּל־פִּנָּה תֶאֱרֹב:

7:12 SOMETIMES IN THE STREET, SOMETIMES IN THE
SQUARE, LYING IN WAIT AT EVERY CORNER.

זּ:יג וְהֶחֱזִיקָה בּוֹ וְנָשְׁקָה־לּוֹ הֵעֵזָה פָנֶיהָ וַתֹּאמַר לוֹ:

7:13 SHE GRABS HIM AND KISSES HIM AND BRAZENLY SAYS
TO HIM:

Alternatively, we may choose to read the text as "he grabs her and kisses her and brazenly says to her. . . ." However, were we to simply change the subject and object of the verse and switch the societal gender roles, the implication would be markedly different. For the writer of Proverbs, this verse tries to articulate a young man's dream-come-true. A married woman (read: schooled in the art of sexuality) makes the first move. If she becomes pregnant as a result of their lovemaking, she can easily explain away the child as her spouse's progeny. According to the writer of Proverbs, the ideal woman should stay at home, be submissive and quiet, and wait for her spouse to initiate sexual activity. We can deduce that the behavior of the ideal man should mirror this activity. From a modern perspective, this is not a marital partnership.

זּ:יד זִבְחֵי שְׁלָמִים עָלָי הַיּוֹם שִׁלַּמְתִּי נְדָרָי:

7:14 I HAVE THE SACRIFICE OF THE PEACE OFFERINGS FOR
TODAY. I HAVE PAID MY VOWS.

This is what the wanton woman says. Sex is promised, as is a good meal consisting of pieces of meat that she has brought home from the Temple. Since meat was only eaten as part of a sacrificial meal, as the root *z-v-ch* and the noun *mizbe-ach* suggest, her statement announces a meat meal along with sex.

זּ:טו עַל־כֵּן יָצָאתִי לִקְרָאתֶךָ לְשַׁחֵר פָּנֶיךָ וָאֶמְצָאֶךָּ:

7:15 THIS IS WHY I CAME OUT TO MEET YOU, TO LOOK FOR
YOU, AND I FOUND YOU.

This is not coincidental or spontaneous sexuality. This is a planned encounter. She is out looking for sex.

זּ:טז מַרְבַדִּים רָבַדְתִּי עַרְשִׂי חֲטֻבוֹת אֵטוּן מִצְרָיִם:

7:16 I HAVE COVERED MY COUCH WITH CLOTH CONTAINING
EMBROIDERED EGYPTIAN YARN.

The picture is not seductive enough, so the writer graphically tempts the senses.

נַפְתִּי מִשְׁכָּבִי מֹר אֲהָלִים וְקִנָּמוֹן: **יז:ז**

7:17 I HAVE SCENTED MY BED WITH MYRRH, ALOE, AND
CINNAMON.

These are the delights of the senses of sight and smell.

לְכָה נִרְוֶה דֹדִים עַד־הַבֹּקֶר נִתְעַלְּסָה בָּאֲהָבִים: **יח:ז**

7:18 LET'S GORGE OURSELVES WITH SEX UNTIL MORNING.
LET'S TRY DIFFERENT WAYS OF MAKING LOVE.

The Hebrew roots *ravah* (translated as "gorge") and *alas* (translated as "try") relate to
eating and drinking. The first means to "drink one's fill." The second means "to taste
or sample."

כִּי אֵין הָאִישׁ בְּבֵיתוֹ הָלַךְ בְּדֶרֶךְ מֵרָחוֹק: **יט:ז**

7:19 MY HUSBAND IS NOT AT HOME; HE HAS GONE ON A
LONG TRIP.

This is why the woman invites the young man to her bed. Again, the subject of
the verse can be changed, as can be the intended target: "My wife is not at
home; she has gone on a long trip." While this may not have been the case in
ancient society where women did not travel on business, it certainly can be said of
the modern world.

צְרוֹר־הַכֶּסֶף לָקַח בְּיָדוֹ לְיוֹם הַכֵּסֶא יָבֹא בֵיתוֹ: **כ:ז**

7:20 HE HAS LOTS OF MONEY, AND HE WILL NOT COME
HOME UNTIL THE MIDDLE OF THE MONTH.

Literally, "he has a bag of money in his hand, and he will not come home until the full
moon." The invited guest has nothing to fear. Not only will his intended lover's
spouse be away all night, he will also be gone for a couple of weeks. More pleasure
awaits him.

הִטַּתּוּ בְּרֹב לִקְחָהּ בְּחֵלֶק שְׂפָתֶיהָ תַּדִּיחֶנּוּ: **כא:ז**

7:21 WITH SUCH GREAT DOCTRINE, SHE ENTICED HIM; WITH
SUCH SLIPPERY SPEECH, SHE PUSHED HIM OVER.

The writer uses the word *lekach* in an ironic sense. It took very little to convince the
young man to have sex with her.

ז:כב הוֹלֵךְ אַחֲרֶיהָ פִּתְאֹם כְּשׁוֹר אֶל־טֶבַח יָבוֹא וּכְעֶכֶס אֶל־מוּסַר
אֱוִיל:

7:22 ALL OF A SUDDEN, *HE* GOES AFTER *HER*, LIKE AN OX TO
SLAUGHTER, LIKE A SHACKLE ON A FETTERED FOOL.

While we may not relate to the image that the writer is painting, the intent is clear. Admittedly, the Hebrew of the last clause is a bit difficult to translate. The word *eches* occurs only twice in the entire Bible. Here it appears in the singular, but it appears in a plural form in Isaiah 3:18. In Isaiah, the sense seems to be of "anklets" that make a tinkling sound. The commentator Rashi explains that the word refers to the "venom" of a snake sent to bite and punish the one who sins.

If one takes *musar* as the construct form of *musahr* (discipline), then the meaning of the clause is "as a shackle is for the discipline of a fool," that is, a kind of necessary consequence. However, if one assumes that *musar* is a form of *mosar*, then it is translated as "fetters." This would suggest a more casual connection to sin and its punishment. The shackle is part of a chain that binds a convicted felon.

ז:כג עַד יְפַלַּח חֵץ כְּבֵדוֹ כְּמַהֵר צִפּוֹר אֶל־פָּח וְלֹא־יָדַע כִּי־בְנַפְשׁוֹ
הוּא:

7:23 UNTIL AN ARROW PIERCES HIS LIVER AS QUICKLY AS A
BIRD FALLS INTO THE SNARE, HE WILL NOT KNOW THAT
IT IS AT THE COST OF HIS LIFE.

The attraction of sin should be balanced by the certainty of punishment. If an arrow pierces a person's liver, the wound is mortal. If a bird falls into a snare, its fate is death. While the sexual partner that the author describes may be very tempting to the reader, the author wants to make sure that the reader realizes that the eventuality of such sexual activity is certain death.

ז:כד וְעַתָּה בָנִים שִׁמְעוּ־לִי וְהַקְשִׁיבוּ לְאִמְרֵי־פִי:

7:24 NOW, YOUNG FRIENDS, HEAR ME OUT. LISTEN TO THE
WORDS OF MY MOUTH.

The author entreats the reader to listen carefully.

זכה אַל־יֵשְׂטְ אֶל־דְּרָכֶיהָ לִבֶּךָ אַל־תֵּתַע בִּנְתִיבוֹתֶיהָ:

7:25 Don't let your mind go astray after her ways.
Don't wander in her paths.

Sin begins in the mind, as a fantasy in the imagination of the potential sinner (which we all are). Then it is carried out in practice. If your mind goes astray, your body will follow.

זכו כִּי־רַבִּים חֲלָלִים הִפִּילָה וַעֲצֻמִים כָּל־הֲרֻגֶיהָ:

7:26 She has cast down many, and she has killed
many more.

The reader is warned not to be egocentric and self-absorbed. He is neither the first nor the last whom she has seduced.

זכז דַּרְכֵי שְׁאוֹל בֵּיתָהּ יֹרְדוֹת אֶל־חַדְרֵי־מָוֶת:

7:27 Her house is the way to hell, going down to the
rooms of death.

The Hebrew text for "ways" is plural, requiring a plural verb for "going down." *Sheol*, which we have translated as "hell," may be translated as "the pit." It suggests the underworld, but it is unclear whether or not a fully developed notion of hell existed in the mind of the writer of Proverbs. It is clear that this is different from what is generally known as hell in the English language, a concept colored by Christian theology and then transported into general, secular Western culture.

City Dwelling

Much of the Bible, particularly in the Torah, is focused on the agricultural life of the Jewish people. Thus, the social structures of ancient Jewish history evolve around a nomadic, agrarian society. In the Book of Proverbs, we are introduced to the idea of city dwelling. While the urban environment changes the behavioral expectations of men, it impacts even more greatly on women. The urban environment offered women more freedom and therefore more exposure to others and to society. The author of Proverbs felt that such freedom would lead her to immodesty and inappropriate activity. For the male writer, this translates into illicit sexual activity.

Youth

In secular culture throughout the Western world, particularly in North America, youth is celebrated. Youth is considered to be the ideal age, and everything is done in order to preserve it. We color our hair, have plastic surgery done on our bodies, even "lie" about our age. In Judaism, the older adult, personified by gray hair, is celebrated for the wisdom that comes with learning from life's experience. However, it is possible to wonder if the past was romanticized. Perhaps the biblical commandment in Leviticus 19:32, "You shall rise up before the gray-haired and show deference to the old. Fear God. I am *Adonai*," bespeaks an age when honor was not properly paid to the aged.

Construct Form

This is a technical aspect of Hebrew grammar that does not have a direct parallel in the English language. When two words are brought into a relationship to one another, like a compound noun, the vowel structure changes somewhat because the accent of the first word is shifted to the second word. Such is the case in Proverbs 7:22.

GLEANINGS

Holiness and Sexuality

God, as best we understand God, is not neutral but holy. We human beings, knowing God, should try to bring that character of holiness into our lives. We are, when we are mature, free to do so, but we do not. This is the central problem of human history. By God's grace the Jews came as a people to know God and understand itself as bound to God and God's service in history. This extraordinary but continual community experience of relationship, now dramatic, as at the mountains—Sinai, Carmel, and Zion—now everyday, as in the long centuries of biblical struggle to integrate this consciousness, changed this people's character. The Jews pledged themselves as a people, its individuals and its community alike, to live by God's demands on them. Further, it took upon itself obligations that went beyond what all people are required to do so that it would reflect the highest standards of human behavior and endure as a particular people dedicated to God's service in history. It vowed to live that way until all humankind should come to know that God so well that they too would transform their lives in terms of God's reality. Generation after generation, the Jews renewed that promise, and now they and that service are inseparably intertwined. Though often, individually and as a community, they have failed to live up to that pact, God, they knew, never rejected them and their activity on God's behalf. Rather, in the mysterious way in which God managed to give continuing order to the universe, God sustained the people of Israel and would not let it, as a whole, disappear from history until its task had been completed. This relationship of mutual love and obligation between God and the people of Israel, Jews call the Covenant.

The Covenant is carried out by the Jews when it is made the basis of their existence and thus applied to every aspect of life. (Any religious-secular dichotomy has, therefore, little meaning in Judaism.) Yet, the Jewish community has found no more central and significant form for the individual Jew to live in that Covenant than the personal covenant marriage. In its exclusiveness and fidelity it has been the chief analogy to the oneness of the relationship with God as the source of personal worth and development. In marriage's intermixture of love and obligation the Jew has seen the model of faith permeating the heart and thence all one's actions. Through children, Jews have found the greatest personal joy while carrying out the ancient Jewish pledge to endure through history for God's sake. Though Judaism knows sex can be one of the easiest ways to degradation, through the marriage covenant, it has made sexuality a chief means of serving God and becoming righteous. So Judaism has always deplored sexual immorality as a sin against God and human dignity alike.

Eugene B. Borowitz, "When Is It Moral to Have Intercourse?" in *Exploring Jewish Ethics: Papers on Covenant Responsibility* (Detroit: Wayne State University Press, 1990), 255–56; originally published as "Speaking Personally," in *Choosing a Sex Ethic: A Jewish Inquiry* (New York: Schocken Books, 1969)

Sexuality and Morality

How did sex become so important to us in the late twentieth century that we created a culture of narcissism embracing sexuality as its definition of human essence? Our "sex" both defines us and separates us from one another as each sexualized self belongs to one of a rapidly expanding set of categories—not just heterosexual or homosexual, we are now sadomasochistic, or one of many brands of fetishists, or vanilla or butch lesbians or.... The privilege of our sexual identities extends to our utterances. Each of us speaks "the truth" about him- or herself, the sexual truth—and since nobody can speak for anybody else, we cannot cross the great divide to understand anybody else. As for sexual morality, it too has been fashioned by the self alone, tailored to the individual's desire for pleasure. The loneliness of the long-distance sexualist. Whatever happened to dreams of community?

Slowly more and more folks have realized that it isn't so simple after all. What about violent pornography? What about people's responsibilities to one another? What about the dubious fruits of unbridled sexual predation? Is a language available to discuss these questions or are we doomed to fall back into the usual "Thou shalt nots"? Pro-sex or anti-sex: two sides of the same coin. But most of us are neither "pro" nor "anti" as these terms are usually construed. Instead, we are troubled—troubled by the moral vacuousness of an earlier vision of sexual liberation, troubled by the moral censoriousness of current demands to return to ancient *diktats*....

We are moving toward a vision of sexuality that is both mysterious and powerful. For instance, feminists who are mothers are articulating what they previously *felt* in the interstices of their bodies and souls—that maternal sexuality coexists complicatedly with male/female sexuality. Sue Miller's *The Good Mother* unearths this conundrum with great sensitivity and power, highlighting, for example, the strangeness of the mother's breast simultaneously as an object of male desire and fantasy and a source of loving nourishment to an infant. Perhaps sexuality is the giving to another who can respond in an equal, intimate way. We cannot return to the good old days when men were men and women were women and homosexuals had the good taste to stay in closets. Nor do I and others, long skeptical of how sexual liberation got billed on the social marquee, want such a return. We have struggled too long to carve out more equitable relations between men and women. We have seen too much pain inflicted upon our homosexual brothers and sisters because they *are* who they are. A politics of limits, of which sexuality is one feature, respects a zone of privacy where what goes on between people is nobody's business but their own and those who love them.

Jean Bethke Elshtain, "Rethinking Sexuality: What's the Matter with Sex Today?" *Tikkun* 3, no. 2
(March/April 1988): 42

CHAPTER EIGHT

ח:א הֲלֹא־חָכְמָה תִקְרָא וּתְבוּנָה תִּתֵּן קוֹלָהּ:

8:1 LOOK, WISDOM CALLS OUT AND UNDERSTANDING
SENDS FORTH HER VOICE.

Wisdom and understanding were lacking in the person for whom the previous chapter was written. Yet, these are not things that we should regard as hidden or difficult to find. They are available to anyone who bothers to look for them. In contrast to the characterization of the "evil woman" who would lead young men astray, the writer personalizes wisdom and understanding as virtuous women. While the temptress concealed herself in order to entice young men, wisdom and understanding stand out in the open, revealed.

ח:ב בְּרֹאשׁ־מְרֹמִים עֲלֵי־דָרֶךְ בֵּית נְתִיבוֹת נִצָּבָה:

8:2 AT THE HIGHEST POINT NEAR THE ROAD, SHE PRESENTS
HERSELF AT THE CROSSROADS.

While it might be suspicious for others to take this posture (such as was the case with Tamar in Genesis 38:14), wisdom can unabashedly do so.

ח:ג לְיַד־שְׁעָרִים לְפִי־קָרֶת מְבוֹא פְתָחִים תָּרֹנָּה:

8:3 NEXT TO THE GATES, AT THE ENTRANCE TO THE CITY,
AT THE ENTRY TO THE DOORS, SHE SHOUTS.

While the previous chapter suggested that it is improper for a woman to shout, wisdom is permitted to do so. Wisdom may speak to a young person, and that young person should listen and be responsive.

ח:ד אֲלֵיכֶם אִישִׁים אֶקְרָא וְקוֹלִי אֶל־בְּנֵי אָדָם:

8:4 TO YOU, GENTLE ONES, I CALL; MY VOICE IS FOR ALL
HUMANKIND.

The commentator Ibn Ezra sees the social difference—as do many modern biblical scholars—between *ishim* ("gentle ones," usually translated as "gentlemen") and *b'nei adam* ("all humankind," usually translated as "children of man"). For Ibn Ezra, the former are the rich and the latter are the poor, but wisdom applies to both rich and poor.

ח:ה הָבִינוּ פְתָאיִם* עָרְמָה וּכְסִילִים הָבִינוּ לֵב׃   יתיר א׳

8:5 SIMPLE ONES, UNDERSTAND CUNNING. FOOLS, USE YOUR MIND.

As we have noted (see 1:4), *ormah* is something not possessed by those who are unintelligent. In both Hebrew clauses, the imperative *havinu* (understand) is used. For the commentator Gersonides, who reads Proverbs as philosophy, this verse directs those who are simple to learn logic.

ח:ו שִׁמְעוּ כִּי־נְגִידִים אֲדַבֵּר וּמִפְתַּח שְׂפָתַי מֵישָׁרִים׃

8:6 LISTEN! I AM ABOUT TO SAY MARVELOUS THINGS; FROM THE OPENING OF MY LIPS COMES FORTH FAIR THINGS.

N'gidim, which we have translated as "marvelous things," may also mean "princes." Hence, the commentators Rashi and Ibn Ezra translate the phrase as "important, praiseworthy" things. In 1:3, we translated *meisharim* as "correct behavior." Here we use "fair things" as a more appropriate translation for this context. From this kind of instruction, the student will know how to conduct his or her life in an equitable manner.

ח:ז כִּי־אֱמֶת יֶהְגֶּה חִכִּי וְתוֹעֲבַת שְׂפָתַי רֶשַׁע׃

8:7 FOR MY MOUTH SPEAKS TRUTH; WICKEDNESS IS AN ABOMINATION TO MY LIPS.

Unlike others who may speak falsehood, whether they be those who lived at the time of the writer of Proverbs or in our own time, the writer speaks only the truth.

ח:ח בְּצֶדֶק כָּל־אִמְרֵי־פִי אֵין בָּהֶם נִפְתָּל וְעִקֵּשׁ׃

8:8 ALL THE WORDS OF MY MOUTH ARE CORRECT. NOTHING AMONG THEM IS TWISTED OR PERVERSE.

The writer affirms the accuracy of his own doctrine. The teacher's words are available to all.

ח:ט כֻּלָּם נְכֹחִים לַמֵּבִין וִישָׁרִים לְמֹצְאֵי דָעַת:

8:9 THEY ARE PLAIN TO THE ONE WHO UNDERSTANDS AND
FAIR TO THOSE WHO FIND KNOWLEDGE.

No special knowledge is required for the kind of ethical instruction being offered. The teacher's words are self-evident to any person who can understand them. They will be obviously straightforward to any seeker of knowledge.

ח:י קְחוּ־מוּסָרִי וְאַל־כָּסֶף וְדַעַת מֵחָרוּץ נִבְחָר:

8:10 ACCEPT MY DISCIPLINE RATHER THAN SILVER; [TAKE]
KNOWLEDGE RATHER THAN GOLD.

Possessions in themselves cannot offer instruction for life. Rather, personal possessions may actually distract a person from his or her ethical task.

ח:יא כִּי־טוֹבָה חָכְמָה מִפְּנִינִים וְכָל־חֲפָצִים לֹא יִשְׁווּ־בָהּ:

8:11 FOR WISDOM IS BETTER THAN CORAL, AND ALL THINGS
DESIRED CANNOT COMPARE WITH IT.

Many translators of Proverbs translate *p'ninim* as "rubies" or "pearls." We have chosen to translate it as "coral" following the direction of certain scholars. Although jewelry of any kind may be precious, it is only a decoration for the body. Wisdom is the ultimate adornment of the soul.

ח:יב אֲנִי־חָכְמָה שָׁכַנְתִּי עָרְמָה וְדַעַת מְזִמּוֹת אֶמְצָא:

8:12 I, WISDOM, DWELL WITH CUNNING, AND I WILL FIND
OUT THE KNOWLEDGE OF SCHEMES.

As is clear from the contrasting Hebrew terms used, *ormah* (cunning) and *m'zimot* (schemes), wisdom is presented here as a means of defense against the nefarious plans of others. While cunning is amoral, wisdom is moral. Because wisdom is so closely related to being clever, it knows the results of cleverness and can so inform the individual. Because wisdom provides knowledge of how schemes operate, it can help the individual fend against them.

ח:יג יִרְאַת יְהֹוָה שְׂנֹאת רָע גֵּאָה וְגָאוֹן וְדֶרֶךְ רָע וּפִי תַהְפֻּכוֹת שָׂנֵאתִי:

8:13 THE FEAR OF *ADONAI* IS THE HATRED OF EVIL; I HATE PRIDE, ARROGANCE, AN EVIL WAY, AND A PERVERSE MOUTH.

An ethical notion that is particular to Judaism is being taught here: reverence for God includes the hatred of evil. And this hatred is necessarily of this world. In the general worldview of the writer of Proverbs, as specifically articulated in this chapter, evil begins with falsehood. If we are unwilling to maintain what is true, we will end up stuck with what is false and therefore evil. The prophet Isaiah put it best when he wrote, "Woe to those who call evil good and good evil, that put darkness for light and light for darkness" (Isaiah 5:20).

ח:יד לִי־עֵצָה וְתוּשִׁיָּה אֲנִי בִינָה לִי גְבוּרָה:

8:14 COUNSEL IS MINE, AS IS PRUDENCE. I AM UNDERSTANDING. I HAVE POWER.

According to Ibn Ezra, the writer of this verse uses language very precisely. The reason that the verse says "I *am* understanding" rather than "I *have* understanding" is that if there is no understanding, there can be no wisdom. The phrase, "I have power," says Ibn Ezra, is to be understood in the same sense as "wisdom provides more strength to a wise person than ten rulers can give to a city" (Ecclesiastes 7:19). Gersonides notes that "counsel" refers to those sciences that are involved with action, such as medicine and agriculture.

ח:טו בִּי מְלָכִים יִמְלֹכוּ וְרֹזְנִים יְחֹקְקוּ צֶדֶק:

8:15 SOVEREIGNS RULE BY ME AND DIGNITARIES RIGHTLY DECREE.

The reader may feel that this verse and the one that follows are pious hopes rather than the testimony of history. The familiar word *tzedek* is understood as an adverbial accusative, "rightly."

ח:טז בִּי שָׂרִים יָשֹׂרוּ וּנְדִיבִים כָּל־שֹׁפְטֵי צֶדֶק*:   *בנוסח אחר "שפטי ארץ"

8:16 OFFICIALS OFFICIATE BY ME, AS DO PRINCES, ALL JUDGES OF THE EARTH.

One may wonder whether the writer is presenting differing ranks of a particular society who use wisdom as their guide as they rule.

ח:יז אֲנִי אהביה אֹהֲבַי אֵהָב וּמְשַׁחֲרַי יִמְצָאֻנְנִי:

8:17 I LOVE THOSE WHO LOVE ME, AND THOSE WHO
DILIGENTLY SEEK ME WILL FIND ME.

One may note a different nuance in this verse. Suddenly, wisdom is no longer self-evident or easily accessible. Wisdom needs to be "diligently" sought out.

ח:יח עֹשֶׁר־וְכָבוֹד אִתִּי הוֹן עָתֵק וּצְדָקָה:

8:18 RICHES AND HONOR ARE WITH ME, AS IS SPLENDID
WEALTH AND RIGHTEOUSNESS.

The *Targum* translates *ateik,* a rather uncommon word, as a noun (*mazala,* "luck"). We have translated it as an adjective: "splendid." Having argued for the value of wisdom on its own, the author now moves toward pragmatism: wisdom will get you wealth. Kohelet differs: "Better is wisdom with an inheritance...for there is the double protection of wisdom and money" (Ecclesiastes 7:11, 12).

ח:יט טוֹב פִּרְיִי מֵחָרוּץ וּמִפָּז וּתְבוּאָתִי מִכֶּסֶף נִבְחָר:

8:19 MY FRUIT IS BETTER THAN GOLD, EVEN FINE GOLD,
AND MY PRODUCE IS BETTER THAN CHOICE SILVER.

The writer now uses agricultural metaphors to suggest that wisdom produces excellent results. However, just as fruit must grow before it can be properly harvested, so does wisdom take time to develop and be nurtured. At this point in the author's argument for wisdom, one may wonder whether worldly wealth is the ultimate goal for the acquisition of wisdom or whether it is merely an inducement for those who are just beginning on the path toward finding wisdom. The next verse helps us to resolve this issue.

ח:כ בְּאֹרַח־צְדָקָה אֲהַלֵּךְ בְּתוֹךְ נְתִיבוֹת מִשְׁפָּט:

8:20 I WILL WALK ON THE COURSE OF RIGHTEOUSNESS, ON
THE PATHWAYS OF JUDGMENT.

In an ideal situation, "judgment" is "justice." Perhaps this is why the Hebrew *mishpat* can be translated with either word. However, the promise of the next verse may cause the reader to wonder whether judgment and justice are, in fact, the same thing.

ח:כא לְהַנְחִיל אֹהֲבַי יֵשׁ וְאֹצְרֹתֵיהֶם אֲמַלֵּא:

8:21 THOSE WHO LOVE ME WILL INHERIT SUBSTANCE; I WILL
FILL THEIR TREASURIES.

Those who have inherited possessions tend to feel that they have gained wisdom, as
well. That's what is expressed in the popular saying, "If you are so smart, why aren't
you rich?"

ח:כב יְהוָֹה קָנָנִי רֵאשִׁית דַּרְכּוֹ קֶדֶם מִפְעָלָיו מֵאָז:

8:22 GOD ACQUIRED ME AS THE FIRST OF THE WAY, PRIOR TO
THE WORKS OF OLD.

The translation of this verse follows the understanding from *B'reishit Rabbah* 1:1 that
the Torah (read: wisdom, according to the Rabbis) was created prior to Creation and
then served as a blueprint for Creation. Just as a sovereign ruler engages an architect
to build and an architect uses plans, so the Holy One of Blessing used the Torah as the
divine plan for creating the world. Using a kind of rabbinic algebra, the Rabbis read
the first word of the Torah, *B'reishit,* as *b-reishit* (with *reishit*), that is, "with the first."
Here, "the first" means wisdom/Torah. Hence, with wisdom/Torah did God create the
world *(bara Elohim).*

ח:כג מֵעוֹלָם נִסַּכְתִּי מֵרֹאשׁ מִקַּדְמֵי־אָרֶץ:

8:23 I WAS SHAPED FROM OF OLD, FROM THE BEGINNING,
FROM THE PRIMEVAL TIMES OF THE EARTH.

Wisdom makes the claim that it is more ancient than the world itself.

ח:כד בְּאֵין־תְּהֹמוֹת חוֹלָלְתִּי בְּאֵין מַעְיָנוֹת נִכְבַּדֵּי־מָיִם:

8:24 I WAS BROUGHT FORTH BEFORE THERE WERE DEPTHS,
BEFORE THERE WERE FOUNTAINS HEAVILY LADEN WITH
WATER.

Continuing the theme of the previous verse, this verse offers us a glimpse into ancient
cosmology, as well.

ח:כה בְּטֶרֶם הָרִים הָטְבָּעוּ לִפְנֵי גְבָעוֹת חוֹלָלְתִּי:

8:25 I WAS BROUGHT FORTH BEFORE THE MOUNTAINS WERE
SET IN, BEFORE THE HILLS.

Wisdom was there before the creation of the world.

ח:כו עַד־לֹא עָשָׂה אֶרֶץ וְחוּצוֹת וְרֹאשׁ עַפְרוֹת תֵּבֵל:

8:26 BEFORE GOD MADE THE EARTH AND FIELDS, EVEN
BEFORE THE DUST OF THE EARTH.

First the writer looks down, and then the writer will look up.

ח:כז בַּהֲכִינוֹ שָׁמַיִם שָׁם אָנִי בְּחוּקוֹ חוּג עַל־פְּנֵי תְהוֹם:

8:27 I WAS THERE WHEN GOD ESTABLISHED THE HEAVENS,
WHEN GOD SET A CIRCLE UPON THE FACE OF THE DEEP

The circle is omnidirectional.

ח:כח בְּאַמְּצוֹ שְׁחָקִים מִמָּעַל בַּעֲזוֹז עִינוֹת תְּהוֹם:

8:28 WHEN GOD CONGEALED CLOUDS ON HIGH, WHEN
GOD STRENGTHENED THE FOUNTAINS OF THE DEEP

Wisdom preceded every aspect of the creative process.

ח:כט בְּשׂוּמוֹ לַיָּם חֻקּוֹ וּמַיִם לֹא יַעַבְרוּ־פִיו בְּחוּקוֹ מוֹסְדֵי אָרֶץ:

8:29 WHEN GOD SET THE DIVINE DECREE UPON THE SEA SO
THAT THE WATERS WOULD NOT MOVE BEYOND ITS
BORDERS, ACCORDING TO THE DIVINE DECREE, WHEN
GOD ESTABLISHED THE FOUNDATIONS OF THE EARTH.

More literally, "when . . . the waters would not transgress God's mouth." However, we
have translated *piv* (God's mouth) as "the divine decree." Some may translate it as
"God's command." The writer also uses the verb *chakak* (to decree) in a number of
senses. We have translated *b'chuko* (when God decreed) as "when God established."
In both cases, we have avoided the gender-specific third-person pronoun when
referring to God.

ח:ל וָאֶהְיֶה אֶצְלוֹ אָמוֹן וָאֶהְיֶה שַׁעֲשֻׁעִים יוֹם יוֹם מְשַׂחֶקֶת לְפָנָיו
בְּכָל־עֵת:

8:30 I WAS WITH THE ETERNAL THEN AS AN INFANT, AND
I WAS GOD'S DAILY DELIGHT, PLAYING BEFORE THE
ALMIGHTY AT ALL TIMES

The word *amon*, literally "one brought up," is translated by some as "nursling." It was
often used by the Rabbis as *oman* (artisan), which made possible their midrash on
Torah as the plan for the world. Thus, wisdom/Torah was the artisan/architect with
God prior to Creation.

ח:לא מְשַׂחֶקֶת בְּתֵבֵל אַרְצוֹ וְשַׁעֲשֻׁעַי אֶת־בְּנֵי אָדָם:

8:31 PLAYING WITH GOD'S ENCOMPASSING EARTH AND WITH
THE DELIGHTS OF HUMANKIND.

The phrase *teiveil artzo* is difficult to translate. *Teiveil* is often translated as "world,"
but "world of the earth" makes little sense. Some translate the phrase *b'nei adam* as
"humankind," rather than its lowest stratum, as some believe the phrase indicates.

ח:לב וְעַתָּה בָנִים שִׁמְעוּ־לִי וְאַשְׁרֵי דְּרָכַי יִשְׁמֹרוּ:

8:32 NOW MY YOUNG FRIENDS, LISTEN TO ME: THOSE WHO
WILL KEEP MY WAYS WILL BE HAPPY.

The teacher-writer, speaking on behalf of wisdom, appeals to the student readers,
promising them happiness if they follow in the ways of wisdom.

ח:לג שִׁמְעוּ מוּסָר וַחֲכָמוּ וְאַל־תִּפְרָעוּ:

8:33 LISTEN TO MY INSTRUCTION AND WISE UP. DON'T
DISRESPECT IT.

In this verse, we have used a colloquialism to translate the text's own idioms. Like
most idioms, the simple Hebrew text contains a number of ambiguities. *Sh'ma* (listen)
may also mean "obey." *Musar,* as we explained in 1:2, may mean "instruction" or
"discipline." Thus, the first clause may mean "listen to my instruction" or "obey and
be disciplined." The commentator Ibn Ezra explains the first clause through a
reference to a statement in the Mishnah, "For the one whose fear precedes one's
wisdom, that person's wisdom will endure" (*Pirkei Avot* 3:11). Ibn Ezra takes the first
two words (*shimu musar*) to mean "obey and be disciplined," since "fear of sin"
refers to behavior. Whatever the kind of instruction, *musar* is more than the simple
imparting of ideas. Similarly, Ibn Ezra takes *al tifra-u* to mean "don't change the
order." In other words, ordered behavior must precede wisdom. The commentator
Rashi offers "don't negate it," which we have translated as "don't *disrespect* it."

ח:לד אַשְׁרֵי אָדָם שֹׁמֵעַ לִי לִשְׁקֹד עַל־דַּלְתֹתַי יוֹם יוֹם לִשְׁמֹר מְזוּזֹת
פְּתָחָי:

8:34 HAPPY IS THE ONE WHO HEARS ME, WHO KEEPS WATCH
DAILY AT MY DOORS, WHO GUARDS THE DOORPOSTS OF
MY ENTRYWAYS.

The writer anticipates what will be asked of wisdom in the first verse of the next
chapter ("build her house"). Such a house will have doors and entryways. The advice
to the reader: learn wisdom; enter the house of wisdom.

חːלה כִּי מֹצְאִי מצאי מָצָא חַיִּים וַיָּפֶק רָצוֹן מֵיְהֹוָה׃

8:35 FOR THE ONE WHO FINDS ME FINDS LIFE AND WILL
ATTAIN THE FAVOR OF *ADONAI*.

After promising material benefits in 8:21, the writer again promises spiritual benefits.

חːלו וְחֹטְאִי חֹמֵס נַפְשׁוֹ כָּל־מְשַׂנְאַי אָהֲבוּ מָוֶת׃

8:36 THE ONE WHO MISSES ME DOES HARM TO THE SELF; ALL
THOSE WHO HATE ME LOVE DEATH.

As this final verse in the chapter suggests (as is the case in Judges 20:16), the root
meaning of *chata* (sin) is "missing the mark." If wisdom is the source of life, then
turning away from wisdom (sin) paves the path leading to death.

Sin

The term "sin" is not used very often in English by Jews. When the word *cheit* is
used to refer to sin, it is usually qualified by its literal meaning as "missing the
mark"—drawn from an analogy to an archer and his (or her) bow. There are other
terms that reflect the same sentiment in Hebrew, such as *avon* or *pesha*, although each
comes with its own specific context and meaning. *Aveirah*, however, clearly refers to a
transgression of Jewish law, whether it is articulated in the Bible or in rabbinic
literature. More specifically, an *aveirah* is the departure by humans from any right path
designated by God. The Rabbis attribute human sinning to spiritual lethargy rather
than to any inherent moral deficiency. While Judaism does not speak of the original sin
that is known to Christianity, no human is free from sin. However, no sin is
unpardonable by God.

GLEANINGS

Perfection

Expecting perfection is illusionary. Yet many people live their lives in anxiety and
frustration because they fear not being perfect—not being in perfect health, not being
perfect spouses, children, colleagues, friends, and so on.

For people who are obsessed with perfection, making a mistake is an irreparable
catastrophe that they expect will inevitably call down the wrath of others upon them.
Yet making a mistake can become an opportunity for learning something new, for
moral development, and for discovering the healing power of forgiveness and love.
No one would punish a child learning how to walk because the child stumbles and

falls. Yet some people berate themselves as they go through life. They fail to realize that their existence is not fixed, but ever changing and moving. Being perfect is not part of our nature, but being able to learn from and correct our mistakes is. That's why pencils still have two sides, lead and an eraser. The horror of not achieving perfection can inhibit our actions, paralyze our talents, and stifle our quest for virtuous living.

Byron Sherwin, Why Be Good? Seeking Our Best Selves in a Challenging World
(New York: Daybreak Books, 1998), 19

Our Ultimate Wisdom

Human wisdom has its limits. When we have stretched these limits as far as we can, our tradition teaches us to turn to wisdom's ultimate source—God. We take comfort in knowing that we are not alone when we face life's extraordinary challenges and opportunities. If we can even fleetingly appreciate the One who, as the daily prayer says, "graciously endows humankind with knowledge, and teaches us understanding..." we can rely upon a relationship with God that will help us when our own good sense falters. Thus our greatest wisdom is knowing that we can turn to God and, in that intimacy, sense what we should do. "For the Lord gives wisdom, and knowledge and understanding are God's decree" (Prov. 2:6). After Job describes how difficult it is to find wisdom, he finally admits: "God understands the way to it; God understands its source.... God says to humanity, 'See! Revering the Lord, that is wisdom, and shunning evil, that is understanding'" (Job 28:23, 28).

Eugene B. Borowitz and Francine Weinman Schwartz, The Jewish Moral Virtues
(Philadelphia: Jewish Publication Society, 1999), 22

The Source of Light

Jacques Lipschitz, the sculptor, spent his youth in Paris. One day a painter complained that he was dissatisfied with the light he painted and went off to Morocco, seeking a change. He found that the light in his Moroccan canvases was no different. Lipschitz then told him, "An artist's light comes from within, not from without."

Even as we are all artists in life, we must strive to kindle the light within. All that we touch and feel only serves as a stimulus. The true creative spark lies within our heart and soul.

We must learn to kindle our inner spiritual light. We can do this by developing the ability to trust ourselves and our own judgments. The nurturing of our inner spiritual fire is a lifetime enterprise. We must follow that light wherever it leads us.

Bernard S. Raskas, Jewish Spirituality and Faith (Hoboken: N.J.: Ktav Publishing House, 1989), 43

CHAPTER NINE

ט:א חָכְמוֹת בָּנְתָה בֵיתָהּ חָצְבָה עַמּוּדֶיהָ שִׁבְעָה:

9:1 WISDOM HAS BUILT HER HOUSE AND HEWN SEVEN
PILLARS FOR HER.

The text presents us with an interesting grammatical challenge to resolve. The subject *chochmot* is in the plural, while the verb *bantah* is in the singular. The commentator Rashi found no difficulty with the disparity. He simply understood "her house" to mean the world that God built using wisdom/Torah. Among the medieval philosophers, *chochmot* came to mean "sciences." Thus, Gersonides concludes that the acquisition of the sciences precedes the acquisition of *t'vunah,* knowledge.

ט:ב טָבְחָה טִבְחָהּ מָסְכָה יֵינָהּ אַף עָרְכָה שֻׁלְחָנָהּ:

9:2 WISDOM HAS PREPARED THE MEAT, MIXED THE WINE,
AND SET THE TABLE.

Wisdom has prepared a banquet. Like a proper host, wisdom has done what needs to be done in the appropriate order. First, an animal needs to be slaughtered for its meat *(tavchah tivchah).* Since wine was produced in the ancient world as a thick syrup, it has to be prepared for drinking by mixing it with water. Once the main course and the refreshments are prepared, it is then time to set the table.

ט:ג שָׁלְחָה נַעֲרֹתֶיהָ תִקְרָא עַל-גַּפֵּי מְרֹמֵי קָרֶת:

9:3 WISDOM SENT OUT THE SERVANT, CALLING OUT AT THE
HIGHEST PARTS OF THE CITY.

With the meal now prepared and the table set, wisdom sends out house servants as messengers with invitations to come to the banquet. To make sure that people will attend the banquet, wisdom ascends to the high points of the city to call out a further invitation: Let everyone come, even those who do not [yet] appreciate wisdom.

ט:ד מִי־פֶתִי יָסֻר הֵנָּה חֲסַר־לֵב אָמְרָה לּוֹ:

9:4 LET THE ONE WHO IS FOOLISH TURN HERE. TO ONE
LACKING SENSE, WISDOM SAYS

To the person who would not otherwise turn toward wisdom, this message is given:
Come as if you are coming to a banquet, to a fine meal. Come for whatever attracts
you to it.

ט:ה לְכוּ לַחֲמוּ בְלַחֲמִי וּשְׁתוּ בְּיַיִן מָסָכְתִּי:

9:5 COME EAT MY BREAD AND DRINK THE WINE THAT
I MIXED.

ט:ו עִזְבוּ פְתָאיִם* וִחְיוּ וְאִשְׁרוּ בְּדֶרֶךְ בִּינָה: יתיר א׳

9:6 LEAVE FOOLS AND LIVE; MAKE STRIDES ON THE PATH
OF UNDERSTANDING.

The one who would be wise must forsake the company of fools. To go on the path of
understanding requires proceeding in a measured manner. Hence, the word *ishru*
(stride) is used. The commentator Ibn Ezra takes the "path of understanding" to mean
a study of the sciences.

ט:ז יֹסֵר לֵץ לֹקֵחַ לוֹ קָלוֹן וּמוֹכִיחַ לְרָשָׁע מוּמוֹ:

9:7 THE ONE WHO DISCIPLINES A MOCKER WILL GAIN
SHAME, AND THE ONE WHO REPROVES A WICKED
PERSON WILL GET A BLEMISH.

As the commentator Ibn Ezra notes, such people have no hope of change. To be
involved with them will only damage the one who attempts to make the correction.
This idea is continued in the next verse.

ט:ח אַל־תּוֹכַח לֵץ פֶּן־יִשְׂנָאֶךָּ הוֹכַח לְחָכָם וְיֶאֱהָבֶךָּ:

9:8 DON'T REPROVE A MOCKER LEST THE MOCKER HATE
YOU; REPROVE A WISE PERSON AND THAT PERSON WILL
LOVE YOU.

It should be noted that the mocker presents a problem that is different from the
challenge we face with a wicked person. A person may sin even though he or she
accepts the basic assumptions of Jewish tradition, whether these have been learned
through the Torah or through wisdom. Such sinning may be considered a temporary

triumph of the *yetzer hara* (evil inclination) over *yetzer hatov* (good inclination). Until that person repents, he or she may be considered wicked. The mocker presents a different problem for us. The mocker is not prepared to accept the basic tenets of Jewish tradition. Hence, it is of no use to apply to that person the words of Leviticus 19:17, "Reprove your neighbor." Such reproof works with a wise person precisely because that person, familiar with the verse from Leviticus, is willing to abide by it and your instruction. When you attempt to reprove someone who does not accept the framework of rebuke, you incur his or her enmity. And this has no purpose.

ט:ט תֵּן לְחָכָם וְיֶחְכַּם־עוֹד הוֹדַע לְצַדִּיק וְיוֹסֶף לֶקַח:

9:9 GIVE TO A WISE PERSON, AND THAT PERSON WILL GET WISER; INFORM A RIGHTEOUS PERSON, AND THAT PERSON WILL GAIN INSIGHT.

Taking the word *tein* as "give" requires us to insert something that is "given," such as "instruction." As a result, some translate "give instruction to a wise person." The *Targum* (which assumes the Aramaic root *tnah*, "teach") translates the word as *aleif* (teach). Thus, it translates the first clause of the verse as "teach a wise person, and that person will get wiser." This translation seems to make more sense. It should be noted that we have translated *lekach* here (as it we did in 1:5) as "insight," something immediately acquired.

ט:י תְּחִלַּת חָכְמָה יִרְאַת יְהֹוָה וְדַעַת קְדֹשִׁים בִּינָה:

9:10 THE BEGINNING OF WISDOM IS THE FEAR OF *ADONAI*, AND UNDERSTANDING IS THE KNOWLEDGE OF THE HOLY.

K'doshim (holy) is understood as the plural of "majesty." The commentator Gersonides takes the word to refer to the angels, which he believes are the separate intelligences. For him, the knowledge of such beings is required for the ultimate knowledge of Deity.

ט:יא כִּי־בִי יִרְבּוּ יָמֶיךָ וְיוֹסִיפוּ לְךָ שְׁנוֹת חַיִּים:

9:11 FOR THROUGH ME YOUR DAYS WILL BE MANY AND THE YEARS OF YOUR LIFE WILL BE INCREASED.

Once again, wisdom makes a promise to the reader: Follow me and live longer!

אִם־חָכַמְתָּ חָכַמְתָּ לָּךְ וְלַצְתָּ לְבַדְּךָ תִשָּׂא: **ט:יב**

9:12 IF YOU ARE WISE, YOU ARE WISE FOR YOURSELF; IF YOU
MOCK, YOU ALONE WILL BEAR [THE CONSEQUENCES].

Mockery is the great threat to this system, since it belies the very framework of
assumptions upon which the system works. Examples of questions that might be
considered mockery include: Does wisdom indeed bring long life? Does it bring well-
being? Does it nurture happiness?

אֵשֶׁת כְּסִילוּת הֹמִיָּה פְּתַיּוּת וּבַל־יָדְעָה מָה: **ט:יג**

9:13 THE STUPID PERSON IS LOUD, FILLED WITH
FOOLISHNESS, AND DOES NOT KNOW ANYTHING.

If *eishet k'silut* is translated literally (a stupid woman), then reading this verse out of
context would yield quite a bit of sexism. However, the writer is attempting to
describe the characteristics of the antithesis of wisdom. Since the author originally
personified wisdom as a dignified, elegant woman, here he suggests her opposite.
Unlike wisdom, stupidity or folly speaks loudly, without thinking, and certainly
without knowledge. Even so, such an intellectual deficiency is attractive to some
people.

וְיָשְׁבָה לְפֶתַח בֵּיתָהּ עַל־כִּסֵּא מְרֹמֵי קָרֶת: **ט:יד**

9:14 THIS PERSON SITS AT THE OPENING OF THE HOUSE, ON
A CHAIR AT THE HIGH POINT OF THE CITY

This person sits at the entryway, in plain view to all, available to anyone who
passes by.

לִקְרֹא לְעֹבְרֵי־דָרֶךְ הַמְיַשְּׁרִים אֹרְחוֹתָם: **ט:טו**

9:15 TO CALL TO THEM WHO GO PAST ON THE ROAD, WHO
WALK STRAIGHT ON THEIR COURSES.

Stupidity is available to everyone.

מִי־פֶתִי יָסֻר הֵנָּה וַחֲסַר־לֵב וְאָמְרָה לּוֹ: **ט:טז**

9:16 WHOEVER IS FOOLISH, LET THAT PERSON TURN IN
HERE. TO THE ONE WHO LACKS SENSE, THE STUPID
ONE SAYS:

טזז מַיִם־גְּנוּבִים יִמְתָּקוּ וְלֶחֶם סְתָרִים יִנְעָם:

9:17 "STOLEN WATERS ARE SWEET, AND SECRET BREAD IS DELIGHTFUL."

The teacher hopes that unlike the fool and the one who lacks sense, the reader will realize that illicit sexual activity will bring dire punishment. We have seen in Proverbs 5:15ff. that "water" can be a metaphor for sexual activity. If we review Genesis 39:6 through 39:9, we can understand the Rabbis' view of "bread" as another sexual metaphor.

טזיח וְלֹא־יָדַע כִּי־רְפָאִים שָׁם בְּעִמְקֵי שְׁאוֹל קְרֻאֶיהָ:

9:18 THE FOOLISH ONE DOES NOT KNOW THAT THE DEAD ARE THERE AND THAT THERE ARE THOSE WHO HAVE BEEN INVITED INTO THE DEPTHS OF HELL.

This passage parallels the advice given in 2:18. In that verse, as well as in the current one, one may assume that the *r'faim* mentioned are the spirits of the dead. The wise know that adultery is dangerous. Only fools think that they can get away with it.

Sexual Metaphors

While they are not discussed extensively, and since the Rabbis preferred to use what they called "clean language," sexual metaphors are often overlooked in the Bible and in rabbinic literature. The Purim *M'gillah*, for example, is replete with sexual metaphors. In this chapter, the innocuous terms of "bread" and "water" as life's sustaining forces are also used as sexual metaphors.

GLEANINGS

Setting the Proper Priority for Pleasure

Our tradition took a positive attitude to money, sex, and drinking because it unequivocally subordinated them to higher values. In Judaism, pleasure is not life's goal and its pursuit is not a major Jewish activity. Perhaps our lawgivers and rabbis realized what philosophers have often commented upon, that nothing makes finding happiness more unlikely than pursuing it vigorously. More convincingly, they simply looked at existence in a less self-centered way. They understood people to be intimately linked to God and other human beings. The meaning of our lives derives from this ultimate interdependence. As we fulfill our responsibilities to others and ourselves we carry out our obligations to God. The greatest pleasures come as a by-product of sanctifying life, the everyday and the exceptional times alike.

Eugene B. Borowitz, *Liberal Judaism* (New York: UAHC Press, 1984), 371–72

CHAPTER TEN

י:א מִשְׁלֵי שְׁלֹמֹה בֵּן חָכָם יְשַׂמַּח־אָב וּבֵן כְּסִיל תּוּגַת אִמּוֹ:

10:1 THE PROVERBS OF SOLOMON: A WISE CHILD MAKES ONE'S FATHER HAPPY, WHILE A FOOLISH CHILD IS THE GRIEF OF ONE'S MOTHER.

According to Jewish tradition, Solomon is the author of Proverbs. Since this superscription appears at the beginning of the tenth chapter, multiple authors or a composite authorship seems probable. Regarding the message of this verse, both commentators Rashi and Ibn Ezra offer an explanation that may not resonate with our modern sensibilities but is consistent with the reality of an earlier time. They suggest that since a mother is home more often than is a father, she sees the deficiencies of her children more readily.

י:ב לֹא־יוֹעִילוּ אוֹצְרוֹת רֶשַׁע וּצְדָקָה תַּצִּיל מִמָּוֶת:

10:2 TREASURES OF WICKEDNESS DO NOT AVAIL, BUT RIGHTEOUSNESS DELIVERS ONE FROM DEATH.

Tzedakah, "righteousness," is often translated as "charity" (charitable giving or righteous giving). There is a connection between the two meanings of the term: In an ideal society, everyone would have enough to satisfy his or her needs and would not be dependent on the generosity of others. Since contemporary society is not ideal, those who are dependent on others make their appeal for help on the basis of righteousness. Since we have not as yet created an ideal society, we owe "charity" to those who need it. In the past, it was not uncommon to find the phrase "righteousness delivers from death" on collection boxes *(pushkes).*

י:ג לֹא־יַרְעִיב יְהוָֹה נֶפֶשׁ צַדִּיק וְהַוַּת רְשָׁעִים יֶהְדֹּף:

10:3 GOD WILL NOT STARVE THE DESIRES OF THE RIGHTEOUS BUT WILL REJECT THE URGES OF THE WICKED.

Tzaddik and *rasha* are often contrasted. Depending on the context, the words may mean "righteous" and "wicked" or, alternately, "innocent" and "guilty." Not only does *nefesh* have the meaning of "soul," but it also means "desire" (cf. Genesis 23:8). What is contrasted in this verse is the difference between good and evil persons.

The former desire only what they need. The latter have insatiable desires. *Havah* (as it also appears in 11:6) suggests a more capricious desire. Since one of the goals of the author of Proverbs is to teach readers about balance and control, by using this term the author suggests that the difference between those who are good and those who are evil rests with the control of desire.

י:ד רָאשׁ עֹשֶׂה כַף־רְמִיָּה וְיַד חָרוּצִים תַּעֲשִׁיר:

10:4 AN IDLE HAND MAKES ONE POOR, WHILE A DILIGENT
HAND MAKES ONE RICH.

The simplicity of this verse invites a variety of possible translations. *Kaf* may mean "palm of the hand," or the "pan of a balance scale." *R'miah* may mean "idle, slack" or "lying, deceitful." Both Rashi and Ibn Ezra take the first clause to mean "a false scale pan will bring poverty." Rashi understands the second clause to mean "the hand of those who are diligent to properly decide legal cases will bring wealth." Ibn Ezra translates the clause similarly: "the hand of those who are diligent and honest will become honest." Not only can *yad* mean "hand," but it can also mean "tenon" or "peg." Hence, what might be described here would be a part of a scale pan, perhaps its arm. *Charutzim* (pl., "diligent") could be an abstract term. Hence, the translation of the verse might be "A false scale pan will bring poverty, while a proper beam will bring wealth." In the *Targum,* the verse is translated as "Poverty will cast down a deceitful person, while the hand of an honest person will make people rich."

י:ה אֹגֵר בַּקַּיִץ בֵּן מַשְׂכִּיל נִרְדָּם בַּקָּצִיר בֵּן מֵבִישׁ:

10:5 THE ONE WHO GATHERS IN THE SUMMER IS AN
INTELLIGENT OFFSPRING, BUT THE ONE WHO
SLUMBERS THROUGH THE HARVEST IS AN OFFSPRING
WHO BRINGS SHAME.

In this verse, the writer uses an agricultural image to present the notion that proper action requires proper timing. The one who gathers in the harvest in the summer has anticipated the autumn rains. Such action requires reflecting on past experiences and anticipating future events. The writer describes such a person as *maskil* (intelligent), a term that later in Jewish history describes the individual who incorporates notions of modernity when thinking about Judaism. The person who sleeps when he or she should be working is the kind of person about whom people talk. This person is not the kind who brings pride to one's parents.

י:ו בְּרָכוֹת לְרֹאשׁ צַדִּיק וּפִי רְשָׁעִים יְכַסֶּה חָמָס:

10:6 Blessings are on the head of the righteous, while the mouth of the wicked conceals violence.

What good people say reflects their goodness. What bad people say—even if it sounds good—hides their evil intentions.

י:ז זֵכֶר צַדִּיק לִבְרָכָה וְשֵׁם רְשָׁעִים יִרְקָב:

10:7 The memory of the righteous is a blessing; the name of the wicked should rot.

This first clause has entered the liturgy as part of the burial service. Our translation reflects common usage. An alternate translation might read, "The mention of the righteous is a blessing; the name of the wicked shouts rot." *Zeicher* (mention) may be seen as a parallel to *shem* (name), as it is indicated in Exodus 3:15, where a righteous person serves as a model for behavior. Such behavior increases the measure of good in the world. Such an increase is a blessing. The wicked person also serves as a model, and there are those who might pattern their lives after such a person. As the popular adage suggests, "The evil that people do lives after them," since that evil is imitated by others.

י:ח חֲכַם־לֵב יִקַּח מִצְוֹת וֶאֱוִיל שְׂפָתַיִם יִלָּבֵט:

10:8 A wise mind receives commandments, but a foolish chatterer shall be ruined.

The wise person knows when to speak and when to be silent. Folly is often found among those who speak too much. Those who are too willing to give others "a piece of their mind" often find that they have less of their mind left for themselves, as they often speak without thinking.

י:ט הוֹלֵךְ בַּתֹּם יֵלֶךְ בֶּטַח וּמְעַקֵּשׁ דְּרָכָיו יִוָּדֵעַ:

10:9 The one who walks with integrity will walk with security, but the one who perverts one's ways shall be found out.

Virtue is its own reward. Vice contains its own punishment. Decent behavior encourages decent behavior in others. Deceitful behavior cannot be hidden long.

יי קֹרֵץ עַיִן יִתֵּן עַצָּבֶת וֶאֱוִיל שְׂפָתַיִם יִלָּבֵט:

10:10 THE ONE WHO WINKS CAUSES SORROW, AND A FOOLISH
CHATTERER SHALL BE RUINED.

One can hurt another with words or without words. ''Winking'' here (as it was in 6:13) is a means of conveying innuendo. It can cause sorrow just as foolish words can do so. Perhaps for the purpose of emphasis, the last clause is the same as the last clause in verse eight.

ייא מְקוֹר חַיִּים פִּי צַדִּיק וּפִי רְשָׁעִים יְכַסֶּה חָמָס:

10:11 THE MOUTH OF THE RIGHTEOUS IS THE SOURCE OF
LIFE, BUT THE MOUTH OF THE WICKED CONCEALS
VIOLENCE.

As part of a signature style, the author repeats verses for emphasis, although some scholars call into question the process of editing Proverbs or the competency of the editor. The last clause in this verse is the same as the last clause of verse six. The writer returns to the theme of speech—explicit and concealed—as a means of conveying wisdom. The wise person would be able to appreciate the words of the righteous, as well as protect oneself from whatever is concealed by the words of the wicked. To be truly wise, one must differentiate between what is being said and what is really meant.

ייב שִׂנְאָה תְּעוֹרֵר מְדָנִים וְעַל כָּל־פְּשָׁעִים תְּכַסֶּה אַהֲבָה:

10:12 HATRED STIRS UP CONTROVERSIES, BUT LOVE COVERS
ALL OFFENSES.

We tend to assume the worst about those we dislike. Conversely, we tend to assume the best about those we love.

ייג בְּשִׂפְתֵי נָבוֹן תִּמָּצֵא חָכְמָה וְשֵׁבֶט לְגֵו חֲסַר־לֵב:

10:13 WISDOM IS TO BE FOUND ON THE LIPS OF THE ONE
WHO UNDERSTANDS, BUT A ROD IS FITTING FOR THE
BACK OF THE ONE WHO LACKS SENSE.

Wisdom belongs to those who already understand. According to the author, a fool deserves to be whipped.

י':יד חֲכָמִים יִצְפְּנוּ־דָעַת וּפִי־אֱוִיל מְחִתָּה קְרֹבָה:

10:14 THE WISE STORE KNOWLEDGE; A FOOL'S MOUTH IS
DESTRUCTION ABOUT TO OCCUR.

The contrast is made between the wise who speak little and the fool who talks too much. Because the fool speaks before thinking, what the fool says can bring misfortune upon him- or herself and upon others. Everything said by the fool is fraught with anxiety.

י':טו הוֹן עָשִׁיר קִרְיַת עֻזּוֹ מְחִתַּת דַּלִּים רֵישָׁם:

10:15 THE WEALTH OF A RICH PERSON IS A FORTIFIED CITY;
THE POVERTY OF THE POOR IS THEIR DESTRUCTION.

In this verse, the author writes from observation. Wealth provides protection and refuge from many problems. Poverty in itself is a problem. One of the Sages said that were he given the choice between poverty and all the curses in the Book of Deuteronomy, he would have chosen the curses.

י':טז פְּעֻלַּת צַדִּיק לְחַיִּים תְּבוּאַת רָשָׁע לְחַטָּאת:

10:16 THE WAGE OF THE RIGHTEOUS IS LIFE; THE PRODUCE
OF THE WICKED IS SIN.

Two terms are used to describe payment for work done. One is from the city (*p'ulah,* "wage"). The other is from the farm (*t'vuah,* "yield" or "harvest"). These two terms are used by the author to describe the different consequences of the activity of the righteous and the wicked. One enhances; the other blemishes life.

י':יז אֹרַח לְחַיִּים שׁוֹמֵר מוּסָר וְעוֹזֵב תּוֹכַחַת מַתְעֶה:

10:17 THE ONE WHO MAINTAINS DISCIPLINE IS ON THE PATH
OF LIFE; BUT THE ONE WHO REJECTS REPROOF LEADS
OTHERS ASTRAY.

Proper living is achieved not only through correct ideas, but also through a patterned way of life. *Musar* (discipline, instruction, chastisement) is the path of life that the reader of Proverbs is instructed to follow. There is no moral growth without moral reflection and without being held to account for one's actions. This verse and the next seem to be a restatement of the verse "You shall not hate your kin in your heart" (Leviticus 19:17). From that verse, the Rabbis deduce that if we do not reprove a person, we must hate him or her, since the unreproved person will continue to sin and incur unavoidable punishment.

יֹ״ח מְכַסֶּה שִׂנְאָה שִׂפְתֵי־שָׁקֶר וּמוֹצִא דִבָּה הוּא כְסִיל:

10:18 LYING LIPS COVER HATRED, BUT A FOOL ENGAGES
IN SLANDER.

Therefore, one should tell the truth and reprove a sinner out of concern for that
person. Not to reprove is to lie and to hate. One should tell the truth and not slander.

יֹ״ט בְּרֹב דְּבָרִים לֹא יֶחְדַּל־פָּשַׁע וְחֹשֵׂךְ שְׂפָתָיו מַשְׂכִּיל:

10:19 WITH MUCH TALKING THERE IS NO REFRAIN FROM
SIN, BUT THE ONE WHO RESTRAINS ONE'S LIPS IS
INTELLIGENT.

In his comment on the first clause of this verse, the commentator Rashi quotes *Pirkei
Avot* 1:17, "Whoever talks too much brings about sin." Rashi quotes only the end of
this statement from the Mishnah, because he assumes that the reader will know the
beginning: "Shimon (the son of Rabban Gamliel) said, 'All my life I was raised among
the Sages, and I never found anything better than silence.'" For the Rabbis and for
the writer of Proverbs, silence is a positive quality. The wise person thinks before
speaking, and thinking requires silence.

יֹ״כ כֶּסֶף נִבְחָר לְשׁוֹן צַדִּיק לֵב רְשָׁעִים כִּמְעָט:

10:20 THE TONGUE OF THE RIGHTEOUS IS WORTH CHOICE
SILVER, BUT THE MIND OF THE WICKED IS WORTH
LITTLE.

The verse continues the thought of the previous verse: if you must speak, you should
speak little. The speech of the righteous (and we understand that the author uses the
term "righteous" to mean "intelligent") is as rare as the best silver, while the wicked
(and we understand the author to refer to "wicked" when he means "foolish" or
"stupid") are intellectually deficient. Whatever the wicked say is of little worth.

יֹ״כא שִׂפְתֵי צַדִּיק יִרְעוּ רַבִּים וֶאֱוִילִים בַּחֲסַר־לֵב יָמוּתוּ:

10:21 THE LIPS OF THE RIGHTEOUS WILL FEED MULTITUDES,
WHILE FOOLS, LACKING SENSE, WILL DIE.

The commentator Rashi takes the first clause to mean that many people will be
sustained by the merit and prayers of the righteous. Ibn Ezra assumes that the clause
refers to the instruction that the righteous can provide. Gersonides, reflecting the
medieval philosophical tradition that distinguished between the philosophically
learned elite and the philosophically unlearned masses, understands the first clause to
say that not only do the lips of the righteous (which he equates with those who are

philosophically astute) provide life for them, those same lips guide the masses and provide for them as a shepherd provides for the sheep. Fools cannot help the masses. Moreover, since they lack correct ideas, they cannot help themselves. For Gersonides, incorrect ideas in this life negate the possibility of providence in this life and eternal life in the next. For him, folly leads to error, and error leads to death.

י:כב בִּרְכַּת יְהֹוָה הִיא תַעֲשִׁיר וְלֹא־יוֹסִף עֶצֶב עִמָּהּ:

10:22 THE BLESSING OF *ADONAI* MAKES ONE RICH, WHILE TOIL WILL ADD NOTHING.

Our translation of the second clause follows the suggestion of the commentator Ibn Ezra. He alludes to Genesis 3:17 and explains that the one who is blessed with God's favor will attain wealth without difficulty.

י:כג כִּשְׂחוֹק לִכְסִיל עֲשׂוֹת זִמָּה וְחָכְמָה לְאִישׁ תְּבוּנָה:

10:23 JUST AS IT IS PLEASANT FOR A FOOL TO CARRY OUT A SCHEME, SO IT IS [PLEASANT TO CARRY OUT] WISDOM FOR A DISCERNING PERSON.

This is a difficult verse. Its parallels are unclear. The commentator Rashi suggests that *kischok* means ''it is pleasant,'' which he implies from the context of the second clause. Thus, the translation might be ''As it is pleasant for a fool to carry out a scheme, so it is pleasant for a discerning person to acquire wisdom.''

י:כד מְגוֹרַת רָשָׁע הִיא תְבוֹאֶנּוּ וְתַאֲוַת צַדִּיקִים יִתֵּן:

10:24 WHAT THE WICKED FEAR SHALL COME UPON THEM; WHAT THE RIGHTEOUS DESIRE, GOD WILL GIVE.

Fear and hope. As presented, these are the basic elements of religion. The writer proposes that what the wicked fear may happen to them and what the righteous hope may happen to them. This verse reflects more the hope of the author than his or her experience.

י:כה כַּעֲבוֹר סוּפָה וְאֵין רָשָׁע וְצַדִּיק יְסוֹד עוֹלָם:

10:25 WHEN THE WHIRLWIND PASSES, NO WICKED PERSON CAN REMAIN, BUT THE RIGHTEOUS PERSON IS THE FOUNDATION OF THE WORLD.

The author would like to believe that natural calamities only affect the wicked, but experience tells us otherwise. Similarly, the righteous foundation of the world is a religious hope. Optimism is an anticipated posture for Jewish religious attitude.

יːכו כַּחֹמֶץ לַשִּׁנַּיִם וְכֶעָשָׁן לָעֵינָיִם כֵּן הֶעָצֵל לְשֹׁלְחָיו:

10:26 AS VINEGAR IS TO TEETH, AND AS SMOKE IS TO THE
EYES, SO IS THE LAZY PERSON TO THOSE WHO SEND HIM
[OR HER].

Vinegar and smoke irritate specific organs. And a lazy person is an irritant to
employers. Since wisdom literature is a product of city culture, it is concerned with an
important aspect of that culture: business.

יːכז יִרְאַת יְהֹוָה תּוֹסִיף יָמִים וּשְׁנוֹת רְשָׁעִים תִּקְצֹרְנָה:

10:27 FEAR OF GOD ADDS DAYS, WHILE THE YEARS OF THE
WICKED SHALL BE SHORTENED.

This is another example of how the author of Proverbs believes life should be. It can
be argued that the one who lives in accord with Torah may be saved from certain ills.
Thus, we continue to look for a direct correlation between virtue and its reward and
vice and its punishment.

יːכח תּוֹחֶלֶת צַדִּיקִים שִׂמְחָה וְתִקְוַת רְשָׁעִים תֹּאבֵד:

10:28 THE EXPECTATION OF THE RIGHTEOUS IS JOY, BUT THE
HOPE OF THE WICKED WILL BE DESTROYED.

The writer again proposes what ought to be, a proposal that has a certain internal
logic. The righteous have the right to expect that sooner or later, in this life or in the
next, they will be rewarded for their virtue. The joy of fulfilling the divine
commandments, what is called *simchah shel mitzvah*, will be echoed in the joy of
divine recompense. What the wicked hope for follows the pattern of life that they
developed. The wicked hope for things that are wicked. From a religious perspective,
such hopes should not be realized.

יːכט מָעוֹז לַתֹּם דֶּרֶךְ יְהֹוָה וּמְחִתָּה לְפֹעֲלֵי אָוֶן:

10:29 TO A PERSON OF INTEGRITY, THE WAY OF *ADONAI* IS A
FORTRESS, BUT TO THOSE WHO WORK INIQUITY, IT
BRINGS RUIN.

According to the commentator Rashi, "ruin" is the punishment for "those who leave
the way of *Adonai*." The commentator Ibn Ezra agrees and quotes the prophet Hosea
to support his argument: "Straight are the ways of *Adonai*; the righteous walk on
them, while the sinners stumble on them" (Hosea 14:10).

צַדִּיק לְעוֹלָם בַּל־יִמּוֹט וּרְשָׁעִים לֹא יִשְׁכְּנוּ־אָרֶץ: **י:ל**

10:30 THE RIGHTEOUS SHALL NOT BE MOVED FOREVER,
WHILE THE WICKED SHALL NEVER RESIDE IN THE LAND.

Rashi suggests that should the righteous fall, they will rise up again. The decline of the righteous will not be permanent. Ibn Ezra agrees, arguing that even if trouble befalls the righteous, their descendants will remain. Ibn Ezra continues his comment by saying that neither the memory of the wicked nor *their* descendants will remain.

פִּי־צַדִּיק יָנוּב חָכְמָה וּלְשׁוֹן תַּהְפֻּכוֹת תִּכָּרֵת: **י:לא**

10:31 THE MOUTH OF THE RIGHTEOUS BRINGS FORTH
WISDOM, BUT A PERVERSE TONGUE SHALL BE CUT OFF.

Interpreting *tzaddik* (righteous) as *tzodek* (correct), the commentator Gersonides says that the person who has correct ideas speaks wisdom. In other words, wisdom is that which is permanent and self-explanatory. The person who has incorrect ideas (those that do not conform to reality) speaks errors that are evanescent and fleeting.

שִׂפְתֵי צַדִּיק יֵדְעוּן רָצוֹן וּפִי רְשָׁעִים תַּהְפֻּכוֹת: **י:לב**

10:32 THE LIPS OF THE RIGHTEOUS KNOW FAVOR, BUT THE
MOUTH OF THE WICKED [KNOWS] PERVERSITY.

For Rashi, the "favor" achieved by the righteous is from God and from the people. For Gersonides, the "favor" comes only from human beings, since the *tzaddik*, that is, the philosopher, knows what people find useful and pleasant.

Poverty and Wealth

Poverty and wealth have been viewed by the Jewish people differently throughout history. If the three divisions of the *Tanach* are taken as reflecting three sequential periods of Jewish biblical history—the wilderness, the land, and the city, in which people are depicted respectively as shepherds, farmers, and city dwellers—then one quickly notes a changing attitude toward wealth, even as poverty was always viewed negatively. The Torah presents the shepherd experience as exemplified by the Patriarchs in the Land and the freed slaves in the wilderness. Shepherds, living in family groups or in tribes, seemed to have held wealth in common, with no real distinctions between rich and poor. It is significant that in the Torah, the noun *osher* (wealth) is found only once (in Leah and Rachel's complaint "that all the wealth from our father" belongs to them [Genesis 31:16]). The noun *ashir* (wealthy person) is found only once (in the requirement that the half-shekel offering, which may reflect a later period entirely, is to be collected equally from the rich and the poor [Exodus 30:15]). The verbal root *ashar*

104

(to be wealthy) is found only once (in the story of Abram's refusal to take spoil after winning a battle, lest one say, "I have made Abram rich" [Genesis 14:23]).

N'vi-im (Prophets), beginning with the Book of Joshua, presents the picture of shepherds leaving the wilderness and entering the Land. With the land came the opportunity of farming, but farming brought wealth to some and poverty to others. The early prophets, heirs to the earlier shepherd tradition, gave their response: Amos spoke against those who "sold the righteous for silver and the poor for a pair of shoes" (Amos 2:6), and Isaiah condemned those who "...beat My people to pieces and grind the faces of the poor" (Isaiah 3:15) and cried out, "Woe to them who join house to house...till there be no room" (Isaiah 5:8).

Though ostensibly an earlier text, the Torah contains some material that comes from a later period and addresses some of the problems caused by wealth. The *yoveil* (Jubilee) legislation (Leviticus 25:8ff.) sought to prevent the concentration of land in the hands of a few by requiring that after fifty years all land acquisitions were to be returned to the original owner. The *sh'mitah* (remission legislation in Deuteronomy 15) was designed to prevent borrowing for disaster relief from permanently impoverishing the unfortunate borrower.

The economy of the city intensified the problems of wealth and poverty. Hence, Proverbs, the book rooted in the urban experience, admonishes its reader that "a good name is better than great riches" (Proverbs 22:1), and Kohelet, the writer of Ecclesiastes, who presents himself as one who has amassed more wealth than any before him, concludes that ultimately "everything is futile and the pursuit of wind" (Ecclesiastes 2:17).

Rabbinic Judaism is the Judaism of the city. The rabbinic laws of Shabbat, as the early Zionists discovered, did not relate to the life of the farmer, but rather to the life of the city dweller. Rabbinic Judaism frequently uses business idioms (cf. *Pirkei Avot* 3:17), as the Rabbis understood commerce (cf. the three "Gates" of the Mishnah, *Bava Kama, Bava M'tzia,* and *Bava Batra*). They knew that money needed to be raised and capital investments had to be protected. Hillel's development of the legal fiction of the *p'rozbol* as a means of nullifying the *sh'mitah* (Babylonian Talmud, *Gittin* 36b) is a good example. Still, Rabbinic Judaism never praised poverty, teaching that a poor person was in many ways equivalent to a dead person (Babylonian Talmud, *N'darim* 64b), from which it can be deduced that as the latter decayed in the grave, the former decayed in life.

Averting the Decree

According to Jewish tradition, Yom Kippur is the culmination of a month of introspection (during Elul) followed by an intensive period of repentance initiated by Rosh HaShanah. On Yom Kippur, God judges us and determines what the course of our next year should be and whether we deserve another year of life. While the theology implicit in this idea can be debated, the lesson contained in the metaphor is rather clear. Here is the spiritual logic: the decisions we make about how we live our lives ultimately impact on the life we end up leading. Perhaps we come to these conclusions on our own. However, we make these decisions in the presence of God. The three factors that lead us to change our lives, and thereby help determine our future, are *t'filah* (prayer), *tzedakah* (charitable giving), and *t'shuvah* (repentance). By making these practices part of our daily lives, we are able to pave a path to our own future.

Deceitful Speech

The Rabbis were so concerned with the potential harm inherent in speech that, employing a word game, they suggested that harmful speech is equivalent to what the Bible calls *m'tzora* (a kind of serious skin affliction like leprosy). They used the root of the word *(m-tz-r)* as an acronym for *motzei shem ra* (the emergence of an evil reputation) and argued that gossip and slander were equivalent to murder. They then classified gossip of any kind as deceitful speech. Even when the details of the conversation were truthful, they were not to be spoken. Because the Rabbis felt that mostly women engaged in such gossip, they were particularly strident in their restrictions. However, they did not understand what has been argued by modern social scientists, that women often communicate with one another and establish relationships by sharing intimate details about themselves and others without any intent for harm.

GLEANINGS

The Power of Words

There is no greater wonder, and no greater attainment on the part of man, than his power of speech, by which, alone of all living creatures, he has learned to communicate clearly with his fellow-man, and transmit to him all the thoughts and feelings, in all their delicate shadings and subtleties, which animate his own mind and heart. And yet when you observe the hurt to himself and to others that his words effect you would be justified in saying that ninety times out of one hundred that man speaks it would be better that he be silent. Why is that? Surely it is good to let another heart know that in your heart there is love for him; surely he needs the gladness that that knowledge will give him. He needs the security, the warmth, the joy in living that this knowledge will give him; and while there are many ways of showing love, words are the gossamer wings on which love is carried from one soul to another, words carry the assurance of love, which the soul craves from the other.

Tehilla Lichtenstein, *Applied Judaism: Selected Jewish Science Essays,* ed. Doris Friedman
(New York: Society of Jewish Science, 1989), 542–43

The Problem of Revelation

The real problem is not that there is too little divine revelation but too much. I believe the Torah is divine revelation; I believe the 613 commandments are divine revelation; I believe Judaism is divine revelation; I believe that what I see of God now is divinely revealed, and that so is what every man sees of every god.

My problem is not the primitive, the extravagant, or the unexpected in Judaism. I should not know what to do with a religion that came on like the Boy Scout manual or like the Ethical Society. My problem is not a silent God, but a God who creates so immense a world, produces so enormous a Torah, communicates so embracing and so resonant a word that I can find no moment and no country without Him.

Arnold Jacob Wolf, in *The Condition of Jewish Belief: A Symposium Compiled by the Editors of "Commentary" Magazine* (Northvale, N.J.: Jason Aronson, 1989), 267–68

CHAPTER ELEVEN

יא:א מֹאזְנֵי מִרְמָה תּוֹעֲבַת יְהֹוָה וְאֶבֶן שְׁלֵמָה רְצוֹנוֹ:

**11:1 DECEITFUL SCALES ARE AN ABOMINATION OF *ADONAI*,
BUT A PERFECT WEIGHT [FINDS] DIVINE FAVOR.**

Mirmah (cunning or deceit) is contrasted here with *sh'leimah* (perfect, complete). To make scales that cheat customers requires cunning and forethought. To make weights that are true (in balance) requires honesty and thoroughness. For Judaism, a minimal definition of religiosity is a concern for truth. A minimal definition of Deity is a concern for goodness. To engage in everyday life in a manner designed to cheat others is to belie any claim to belief in God. Note that a concern for correct balances is included in the Holiness Code (Leviticus 19:36). Holiness has just as much to do with everyday commerce and business as it does with ritual and the synagogue. Also note that the author of Proverbs uses the strong word "abomination" in much the same way that the Torah uses it to refer to a variety of perceived transgressions.

יא:ב בָּא־זָדוֹן וַיָּבֹא קָלוֹן וְאֶת־צְנוּעִים חָכְמָה:

**11:2 PRESUMPTION COMES AND THEN SHAME, BUT THERE IS
WISDOM WITH THE HUMBLE.**

It is important that the intended reader praise wisdom *and* control pride. Being "smart" may mean being intelligent or being "too clever." Those who are truly intelligent will know how to act with others. The commentator Gersonides explains the verse by suggesting that those of us who are not adequately prepared for or do not properly engage in philosophical thought will soon discover, as will others, that our ideas do not reflect the reality of the world around us.

יא:ג תֻּמַּת יְשָׁרִים תַּנְחֵם וְסֶלֶף בֹּגְדִים ושדם יְשָׁדֵּם:

**11:3 THE INTEGRITY OF THE UPRIGHT LEADS THEM, BUT
THE PERFIDY OF THE TREACHEROUS WILL DESTROY
THEM.**

The writer tells the reader that the treacherous begin to believe their own lies and act on them. Like so many in the modern world, they begin to believe their own PR.

יא:ד לֹא־יוֹעִיל הוֹן בְּיוֹם עֶבְרָה וּצְדָקָה תַּצִּיל מִמָּוֶת:

11:4 RICHES WILL NOT AVAIL IN A DAY OF WRATH, BUT RIGHTEOUSNESS WILL SAVE ONE FROM DEATH.

It is not clear whether the ''day of wrath'' will befall an individual or a nation. A parallel notion is expressed in Proverbs 6:34–35 (money will not assuage the wrath of a husband whose spouse has been cheating on him). The notion that wealth, ''neither silver nor gold,'' would not save a nation from divine wrath is also expressed in Zephaniah 1:18. The second clause of this verse is expressed by the author in Proverbs 10:2.

יא:ה צִדְקַת תָּמִים תְּיַשֵּׁר דַּרְכּוֹ וּבְרִשְׁעָתוֹ יִפֹּל רָשָׁע:

11:5 THE RIGHTEOUSNESS OF PEOPLE OF INTEGRITY STRAIGHTENS THEIR PATH, BUT THE WICKED WILL FALL BY THEIR WICKEDNESS.

For the sake of gender inclusiveness, we have changed the verse from singular to plural. The path of life is in front of us. People who have walked in a straight path, who have chosen the right way, have become the persons formed by their choices. So too is the case with devious people. They become the persons formed by their choices.

יא:ו צִדְקַת יְשָׁרִים תַּצִּילֵם וּבְהַוַּת בֹּגְדִים יִלָּכֵדוּ:

11:6 THE RIGHTEOUSNESS OF THE UPRIGHT WILL SAVE THEM, BUT THE TREACHEROUS WILL BE TRAPPED BY THEIR OWN SCHEME.

Acts have outcomes. If we live properly, we should be delivered from evil. If we plot evil against others, we should not be surprised to find that we will be caught up in our own wrongdoing. However, since we have not discovered a one-to-one correlation between virtue and its reward, on the one hand, and vice and its punishment, on the other, the writer suggests a selective outcome in the world-to-come.

יא:ז בְּמוֹת אָדָם רָשָׁע תֹּאבַד תִּקְוָה וְתוֹחֶלֶת אוֹנִים אָבָדָה:

11:7 WHEN A WICKED PERSON DIES, THAT PERSON'S HOPE WILL BE LOST AND FALSE EXPECTATION PERISHES.

The last clause presents a variety of difficulties in translating from Hebrew to English. *Tochelet* means ''expectation'' or ''hope.'' *Onim* may be derived from *aven* (disaster or deception) or from *on* (generative, physical, or economic power). If we take *onim* to mean ''powerful,'' then we can translate the clause *tochelet onim avadah* as ''the expectation of the powerful perishes." Such a translation of the last clause may be a better parallel to the first clause of the verse.

יא:ח צַדִּיק מִצָּרָה נֶחֱלָץ וַיָּבֹא רָשָׁע תַּחְתָּיו:

11:8 THE RIGHTEOUS IS RESCUED FROM TROUBLE; AND THE WICKED ARRIVES IN HIS [OR HER] PLACE.

Rashi links the first clause of this verse to the previous verse. When a wicked person dies, a righteous person is delivered. Ibn Ezra explains the second clause differently, suggesting that the death of the wicked person actually acts as atonement for his or her misdeeds.

יא:ט בְּפֶה חָנֵף יַשְׁחִת רֵעֵהוּ וּבְדַעַת צַדִּיקִים יֵחָלֵצוּ:

11:9 THE DISLOYAL PERSON WILL DESTROY A NEIGHBOR BY [HIS OR HER] MOUTH, BUT THE RIGHTEOUS WILL BE DELIVERED BY KNOWLEDGE.

Chaneif may be translated either as "a hypocrite" or as "a godless person." Hence, we have translated it as "disloyal." Since Proverbs is a work focused on prudential wisdom, it continually emphasizes the importance of the power of speech. As the Rabbis noted, *l'shon hara* (evil language or evil tongue) can mean the telling of lies or the telling of the truth inappropriately. In contemporary society, the business of "spin doctors" is to distort truth or even lie outright in order to achieve political or business goals.

יא:י בְּטוּב צַדִּיקִים תַּעֲלֹץ קִרְיָה וּבַאֲבֹד רְשָׁעִים רִנָּה:

11:10 THE CITY REJOICES WHEN THE RIGHTEOUS RECEIVE GOOD, AND THERE IS JOY WHEN THE WICKED PERISH.

Given the conditional nature of this statement, the writer recognizes that the reward of virtue and the punishment of evil did not occur with frequency. Yet the claim of a moral structure for reality entails the possibility for such events.

יא:יא בְּבִרְכַּת יְשָׁרִים תָּרוּם קָרֶת וּבְפִי רְשָׁעִים תֵּהָרֵס:

11:11 THE CITY IS EXALTED BY THE BLESSING OF THE UPRIGHT, BUT IT IS DESTROYED BY THE MOUTH OF THE WICKED.

Speech has an effect on both those to whom it is directed and those who listen, even on the city itself of those who speak. The kind of speech uttered is determined by the nature of those who speak.

יא:יב בָּז־לְרֵעֵהוּ חֲסַר־לֵב וְאִישׁ תְּבוּנוֹת יַחֲרִישׁ:

11:12 ONE WHO LACKS SENSE WOULD HAVE CONTEMPT FOR
ONE'S NEIGHBOR, WHILE A DISCERNING PERSON
WOULD BE SILENT.

Again the writer is concerned with the effect of speech and is suggesting a series of appropriate behaviors. A sensible person does not express contempt for one's neighbor, no matter how much one might think it. A wise person keeps silent, particularly if there is nothing appropriate to say.

יא:יג הוֹלֵךְ רָכִיל מְגַלֶּה־סּוֹד וְנֶאֱמַן־רוּחַ מְכַסֶּה דָבָר:

11:13 THE TALEBEARER REVEALS A SECRET, BUT THE
TRUSTWORTHY PERSON CONCEALS A MATTER.

Civilized life requires knowing when to speak and when to be silent, when to uncover the hidden and when to leave it unexposed. Ibn Ezra comments that the phrase *holeich rachil* (literally, "going as a talebearer") is used in this verse because such a person hears a secret from one person and then goes to another to tell the secret of the first.

יא:יד בְּאֵין תַּחְבֻּלוֹת יִפָּל־עָם וּתְשׁוּעָה בְּרֹב יוֹעֵץ:

11:14 WHERE THERE IS NO GUIDANCE, THE PEOPLE WILL
FALL; HOWEVER, THERE IS DELIVERANCE WITH MANY
ADVISORS.

In a text that teaches prudence, we expect to be advised that political life requires thought and planning. While it might be argued that wisdom literature was a composite of training manuals for would-be political advisors, it is clear that even in the postmodern era, the development and preservation of society require requisite thought and planning. The commentator Gersonides takes the verse literally as a reference to strategy for war.

יא:טו רַע־יֵרוֹעַ כִּי־עָרַב זָר וְשֹׂנֵא תוֹקְעִים בּוֹטֵחַ:

11:15 EVIL WILL BEFALL THE ONE WHO IS SURETY FOR A
STRANGER, BUT THE ONE WHO HATES MAKING DEALS
WILL BE SAFE.

Tokim is an idiom that literally means "striking" as in striking hands or "shaking on it." The writer of Proverbs warns the reader not to get involved in "shady" business deals. This is even more important for the reader who has an interest in politics and wants to get involved in the business of government.

יא:טז אֵשֶׁת־חֵן תִּתְמֹךְ כָּבוֹד וְעָרִיצִים יִתְמְכוּ־עֹשֶׁר:

11:16 A GRACIOUS PERSON HOLDS ON TO HONOR AS THE
RICH HOLD ON TO WEALTH.

The advice that the author of Proverbs offers may not be politically correct. Thus, we have shaped the translation somewhat to fit our sensibilities. However, he suggests that a proper marriage to the right kind of woman can help boost one's career. Grace, which is one of the attributes that makes such a person "the right kind," is as enduring as is power to the wealthy. While one can lose one's grace as one can lose one's wealth, the author speaks through the prism of personal experience, as we all do.

יא:יז גֹּמֵל נַפְשׁוֹ אִישׁ חָסֶד וְעֹכֵר שְׁאֵרוֹ אַכְזָרִי:

11:17 THE KIND PERSON DOES GOOD TO THE SELF, BUT THE
CRUEL CAUSE TROUBLE TO THEIR OWN FLESH.

The commentator Rashi suggests that the verse refers to the way a person treats members of one's own family. Gersonides maintains that the verse reflects the way an individual responds to one's own individual needs. For example, a kind person is one who accepts the physical needs of the body, but the cruel person does not.

יא:יח רָשָׁע עֹשֶׂה פְעֻלַּת־שָׁקֶר וְזֹרֵעַ צְדָקָה שֶׂכֶר אֱמֶת:

11:18 A WICKED PERSON ACQUIRES A DECEITFUL WAGE,
BUT THE ONE WHO SOWS RIGHTEOUSNESS RECEIVES
A TRUE REWARD.

This verse presents us with a challenge in translation, since the common words that the author uses can have a variety of meanings. *Oseh* can mean "make" or "gain." *P'ulah* can mean "work" or "wage, the payment for work." *Tzedakah* can mean "righteousness" or "correctly." We have translated the verse so that it best relates to the verse that follows.

יא:יט כֵּן־צְדָקָה לְחַיִּים וּמְרַדֵּף רָעָה לְמוֹתוֹ:

11:19 THUS, RIGHTEOUSNESS IS FOR LIFE, AND PURSUING
EVIL LEADS TO DEATH.

Kein (yes) is sometimes used as "indeed" or "thus." The ultimate "true reward" from the preceding verse is life itself. For the writer of Proverbs, good adds to life, and evil diminishes it.

יא:כ תּוֹעֲבַת יְהֹוָה עִקְּשֵׁי־לֵב וּרְצוֹנוֹ תְּמִימֵי דָרֶךְ:

11:20 THOSE TWISTED OF MIND ARE AN ABOMINATION TO
GOD, BUT THOSE WHO ARE PERFECT IN THE WAY GAIN
DIVINE FAVOR.

The contrast is presented between those who are twisted (or crooked) and those who
are straight (or perfect). The devious are wicked. Those who proceed on straight and
clear paths are righteous.

יא:כא יָד לְיָד לֹא־יִנָּקֶה רָע וְזֶרַע צַדִּיקִים נִמְלָט:

11:21 HAND TO HAND, EVIL WILL NOT BE REMITTED, WHILE
THE SEED OF THE RIGHTEOUS WILL ESCAPE.

Yad l'yad (hand to hand) is easy to translate. However, the intention of the writer in
using these words is not clear. The *Targum* understands the phrase as ''the one who
stretches one's hands against one's neighbor will not be held guiltless.'' The
commentator Rashi understands it differently. He renders it as ''from the hand of God
to the hand of the sinner will come the punishment incurred for the evil done.'' Ibn
Ezra concurs with Rashi and adds that the punishment will come directly from God
and will be directed to the head of the sinner. Gersonides understands the initial
phrase *yad l'yad* to mean ''immediately,'' that is, the sinner will not be able to avoid
the sudden evils that will occur to him or her. Other commentators suggest that the
phrase is an idiom (my hand on it), as if the individual is taking some sort of an oath.
The context suggests to us that *yad l'yad* has the sense of ''indeed,'' that is, it is as
patently obvious as is one's hand.

There is a problem with *ra* in the first clause. It could mean ''evil'' or ''an evil
person.'' One might think that ''evil person'' is needed for parallelism, the familiar
literary style of the author. However, it might be argued that the use of the verb *nakeh*
(hold guiltless or remit) and the mention of *zera* (seed) is an allusion to the statement
that God is One, ''...extending kindness to the thousandth generation, forgiving
iniquity, transgression, and sin; *v'nakeih lo y'nakeh,* yet God does not remit all
punishment...'' (Exodus 34:7). Therefore, the mention of ''iniquity, transgression,
and sin'' requires the notion and noun for ''evil.''

יא:כב נֶזֶם זָהָב בְּאַף חֲזִיר אִשָּׁה יָפָה וְסָרַת טָעַם:

11:22 LIKE A GOLD RING IN A PIG'S SNOUT, SO IS A BEAUTIFUL
WOMAN BEREFT OF DISCRETION.

Again, we have a manifestation of the writer's sense of women. Beyond the specific
issue of gender, the writer wants to suggest two kinds of incongruities. The precious
ring will be placed in garbage because of the nature of pigs. And similarly, the
beautiful woman is not careful with whom she may associate. Because the Book of
Proverbs is the product of the city, people, particularly women, had much more

social freedom than did their rural counterparts. The city is a place of commerce, and the freedom that it implied for women was troubling to many men. Women were supposed to have discretion, but men were permitted their indiscretion—and their indiscretions.

יא:כג תַּאֲוַת צַדִּיקִים אַךְ־טוֹב תִּקְוַת רְשָׁעִים עֶבְרָה:

11:23 THE DESIRE OF RIGHTEOUSNESS IS ONLY FOR GOOD;
THE HOPE OF THE WICKED IS WRATH.

The contrast between the righteous and the wicked seems problematic. Do the wicked actually hope for wrath? Since we probably believe that the wicked deserve wrath, Rashi suggests that they are all certain to end in hell. Gersonides, whose commentary is philosophical in outlook and approach, explains that the wicked seek the wrong kind of outcome and therefore bring evil on themselves.

יא:כד יֵשׁ מְפַזֵּר וְנוֹסָף עוֹד וְחוֹשֵׂךְ מִיּשֶׁר אַךְ־לְמַחְסוֹר:

11:24 SOME DISBURSE AND YET HAVE MORE, WHILE OTHERS
WITHHOLD WHAT IS RIGHT AND END UP WANTING.

One has the feeling that some kind of business advice is being suggested in this verse, something like "You have to spend money to make money." This verse is generally used as a reference to charitable giving. As Ibn Ezra suggests, the person who gives charity will be rewarded. The person who withholds charity will be punished. Such a miscreant may end up in the position of needing the charity of others to survive.

יא:כה נֶפֶשׁ־בְּרָכָה תְדֻשָּׁן וּמַרְוֶה גַּם־הוּא יוֹרֶא*:   *יא' במקום ה'

11:25 A GENEROUS PERSON WILL BECOME RICH; THE ONE
WHO IS PROFUSE IN GIVING WILL BE PROFUSE IN
GETTING.

The two words that stem from the roots *dishein* and *raveh* are used as *t'dushan* and *marveh* and *yoreh*. These translate literally as "you will be made fat," "watered," and "be watered." We have translated them as "will become rich," "profuse in giving," and "profuse in getting." This suggests an allusion to the verse in Psalm 23:5, *dishanta vashemen roshi, kosi r'vayah*, usually translated as "You have anointed my head with oil. My cup runs over." According to Rashi, the words *nefesh b'rachah* (literally, "the soul of blessing") refer to a person who is generous with money, and the word *marveh* refers to a person who satisfies the needs of the poor. The verse continues the argument being made by the author of Proverbs: Virtue has a pragmatic purpose. Doing good will result in getting good. The notion of disinterested virtue in the history of ethics evolved much later than the period of time in which the Book of Proverbs was written.

יא:כו מֹנֵעַ בָּר יִקְּבֻהוּ לְאוֹם וּבְרָכָה לְרֹאש מַשְׁבִּיר:

11:26 THE PEOPLE WILL CURSE THE ONE WHO HOLDS BACK
GRAIN, WHILE A BLESSING WILL REST ON THE HEAD OF
ONE WHO DISPENSES IT.

Profit can be made out of disaster. In a period of famine, holding back on foodstuffs
was a means of increasing their value and price. A person who did so would be
cursed and would deserve whatever curse received. The author of Proverbs does not
ask, "Does fairness apply to all business transactions?" Rashi understands the clause
to refer to one who withholds Torah from potential students.

יא:כז שֹׁחֵר טוֹב יְבַקֵּשׁ רָצוֹן וְדֹרֵשׁ רָעָה תְבוֹאֶנּוּ:

11:27 ONE WHO SEARCHES FOR GOOD SEEKS FAVOR; EVIL WILL
COME TO THE ONE WHO SEEKS IT.

We may wonder who is the source of this desired "favor." As might be expected,
Rashi understands the source of the favor to be God. Ibn Ezra, on the other hand,
suggests that it means the favor of other persons. On a stylistic note, the author uses
three words that stem from roots that are synonymous: *shachar, bikeish,* and *darash.*
Shachar means "seek diligently." *Bikeish* means "ask, request, seek." *Darash* means
"inquire, investigate, seek." Proper translation is dependent on context and idiomatic
usage in Hebrew and English.

יא:כח בּוֹטֵחַ בְּעָשְׁרוֹ הוּא יִפֹּל וְכֶעָלֶה צַדִּיקִים יִפְרָחוּ:

11:28 THE ONE WHO TRUSTS IN WEALTH WILL FALL, BUT THE
RIGHTEOUS WILL FLOURISH AS FOLIAGE.

Ibn Ezra suggests that the person who puts trust in money will not be able to escape
those out to kill him or her. But those who put their trust in God will be saved.
Reflecting on the time period in Jewish history in which he was writing, wealth did not
save many members of the Jewish community.

יא:כט עֹכֵר בֵּיתוֹ יִנְחַל־רוּחַ וְעֶבֶד אֱוִיל לַחֲכַם־לֵב:

11:29 ONE WHO TROUBLES ONE'S HOUSEHOLD WILL
INHERIT THE WIND; THE FOOL IS THE SLAVE OF THE
WISE-MINDED.

Gersonides takes the first clause to refer to the one who mistreats his or her body to
such a point that it affects the mind.

יא:ל פְּרִי־צַדִּיק עֵץ חַיִּים וְלֹקֵחַ נְפָשׁוֹת חָכָם:

11:30 THE TREE OF LIFE IS THE FRUIT OF THE RIGHTEOUS; THE WISE WIN PEOPLE.

Both commentators Rashi and Gersonides understand the "tree of life" as eternal life. However, because of their diverging points of view, Rashi understands it as the reward for good deeds; Gersonides sees it as the reward for the cognition of correct ideas. For Rashi, we gain eternal life by doing good deeds. For Gersonides, it is gained by intellectual attainment.

יא:לא הֵן צַדִּיק בָּאָרֶץ יְשֻׁלָּם אַף כִּי־רָשָׁע וְחוֹטֵא:

11:31 TAKE NOTE: THE RIGHTEOUS ARE REPAID ON EARTH. HOW MUCH THE MORE WITH THE WICKED AND THE SINNER.

Rashi and Ibn Ezra differ on the meaning of "repaid." For Rashi, the righteous are punished in this life so they can be bereft of sin in the next life. For Ibn Ezra, the righteous are rewarded in this life as well. For both commentators, the fact that the righteous will receive a reward for their actions should be a warning to the wicked, who will receive a *reward* for their actions as well.

Reward and Punishment

The notion of reward and punishment in the next world was one of the things that the Rabbis introduced into Jewish belief and practice. It was part of their overall goal of wrestling community authority away from the priesthood. This stands in contradistinction to the biblical notion that such reward and punishment are proffered in this world, as is noted in this chapter and in others. However, as can be seen in this volume, rabbinic commentators interpret the writing of the author of Proverbs through their rabbinic lens and often see "this world" as the next.

Marriage

In the two tellings of the creation of the human being in the Torah (Genesis 1:26, 27; 2:7), one can find a justification for marriage in Judaism. In the first, *adam,* the human being, was created *zachar un'keivah* (male and female). Thus, to be human is somehow to unite male and female. In the second, the female is made from the rib of the man (Genesis 2:22). In either case, male and female are linked. Since the word *tzeila* (rib) also means "side," the Rabbis harmonized both accounts by saying that the first human had two sides, male and female, which were split (*B'reishit Rabbah* 17). *Tzeila* suggested something else to the Rabbis. Since the word "build" was used in connection to the rib (Genesis 2:22), and since the word "building" was an ancient term for a hairstyle, the

116

Rabbis imagined that God prepared Eve's hair for her wedding to Adam (Babylonian Talmud, *Shabbat* 95a). The verse "And God blessed them" (Genesis 1:28) was taken by the Rabbis to mean that God participated in the wedding of the primal human pair, along with the angels Michael and Gabriel. Since marriage was taken to be divinely ordained, it was assumed that it was the proper status for all.

The Rabbis moved the acquisition of a wife from an act of purchase to a symbolic transaction. The "bride price" was set at the smallest possible monetary unit. Moreover, the use of a *ketubah* as a future promise to pay rather than a present conveyance of funds made marriage easier. Though the man was the initiator of the process of betrothal and marriage, no woman was betrothed without her consent. The Rabbis developed a liturgy for weddings: the seven blessings. The wedding was transformed from a transaction to an act of worship in line with the very term for marriage, *kiddushin,* "sanctity." The rabbinic mind further believed that God arranged marriages and that such arrangements were no easy matter, involving God more than even the splitting of the Red Sea (*B'reishit Rabbah* 68:3, 4).

GLEANINGS

Scales in the Modern Marketplace

The modern marketplace is full of opportunity to cheat and to steal, to "look the other way" at dishonesty and deceit, to profit from ill-gotten gain.

But when you do what is right *because it is right,* when you measure accurately and count exactly, when you are scrupulous in your commerce and meticulous in your dealings, then your colleagues will respect you, your customers and competitors will believe you, and everyone will trust you.

And ultimately you will suceed, for everyone likes to deal with an honest man, everyone wants to do business with an honest woman.

In the Old West, there was no greater compliment than "He's as honest as the day is long."

Even today—especially today—there is still no greater tribute: Your honesty speaks your praise.

Wayne Dosick, *The Business Bible: Ten Commandments for Creating an Ethical Workplace*
(New York: William Morrow and Company, 1993), 63

CHAPTER TWELVE

יב:א אֹהֵב מוּסָר אֹהֵב דָּעַת וְשֹׂנֵא תוֹכַחַת בָּעַר:

12:1 THE ONE WHO LOVES DISCIPLINE LOVES KNOWLEDGE;
THE BRUTE HATES REPROOF.

Learning takes time. It requires discipline and the ability to accept and then transcend mistakes—and not repeat them. To teach, one must be able to correct a student without demeaning the student. Reproving another person is not easy. That is why the Torah teaches, "Reprove your neighbor, but incur no guilt as a result" (Leviticus 19:17). The midrash even includes a statement that implies the difficulty of this behavior, wondering if there was one person in the generation of Rabbi Akiva who knew how to give or accept criticism and reproof (*Sifra, K'doshim* 2:4).

יב:ב טוֹב יָפִיק רָצוֹן מֵיהֹוָה וְאִישׁ מְזִמּוֹת יַרְשִׁיעַ:

12:2 A GOOD PERSON WILL OBTAIN GOD'S FAVOR, BUT GOD
WILL CONDEMN THE SCHEMING PERSON.

Rashi understands the verse to mean that one who is good will bring good into the world. That's what "God's favor" is. The wicked person brings evil into the world through his or her schemes. Thus, God is forced to condemn it. Good and evil persons affect themselves and others by their behavior.

יב:ג לֹא־יִכּוֹן אָדָם בְּרֶשַׁע וְשֹׁרֶשׁ צַדִּיקִים בַּל־יִמּוֹט:

12:3 NO ONE WILL BE ESTABLISHED BY WICKEDNESS, BUT
THE ROOT OF RIGHTEOUSNESS WILL NEVER SLIP.

Ibn Ezra suggests that the second clause of the verse might be interpreted to mean that a root does not move once it is established in the ground; similarly the righteous will endure.

יב:ד אֵשֶׁת־חַיִל עֲטֶרֶת בַּעְלָהּ וּכְרָקָב בְּעַצְמוֹתָיו מְבִישָׁה:

12:4 A VIRTUOUS SPOUSE IS A CROWN, BUT THE ONE WHO
BRINGS SHAME CAUSES THE SPOUSE'S BONES TO ROT.

This is a difficult verse to translate into gender-free language. Even in doing so, the notion of a "spouse as a crown" sounds too close to the contemporary colloquialism "a trophy wife." It is acceptable only if one considers the reference as an allusion to the crown of Torah and of learning. The author of Proverbs wrote the verse literally as "a virtuous wife is a crown for her husband," giving credence to the assumption of his identity as a man. Many people translate the phrase *eishet chayil* as a "woman of valor" due to the liturgical use of the phrase from Proverbs 31:10ff. However, *chayil* has the sense of "power" and "competence." Perhaps reflecting his own life of poverty and failed romance, Ibn Ezra translates the phrase as a "woman of means."

יב:ה מַחְשְׁבוֹת צַדִּיקִים מִשְׁפָּט תַּחְבֻּלוֹת רְשָׁעִים מִרְמָה:

12:5 THE THOUGHTS OF THE RIGHTEOUS LEAD TO JUSTICE;
THE DELIBERATIONS OF THE WICKED LEAD TO DECEIT.

The difference between a righteous person and a wicked person will lead to a different conclusion even if the action looks the same. Their intentions are probably different. Those who are good people want just outcomes. Those who are wicked do not care about justice. They just want results that are self-serving.

יב:ו דִּבְרֵי רְשָׁעִים אֱרָב־דָּם וּפִי יְשָׁרִים יַצִּילֵם:

12:6 THE WORDS OF THE WICKED LAY IN WAIT FOR BLOOD,
BUT THE MOUTH OF THE UPRIGHT WILL SAVE THEM.

Rashi explains the first clause as relating to false testimony in a court of law, something the author probably did not have in mind. Ibn Ezra connects this verse with the one that precedes it and explains that the deceit of the wicked may have deadly consequences.

יב:ז הָפוֹךְ רְשָׁעִים וְאֵינָם וּבֵית צַדִּיקִים יַעֲמֹד:

12:7 THE WICKED ARE OVERTHROWN AND ARE NO MORE,
BUT THE HOUSE OF THE RIGHTEOUS WILL ENDURE.

The author seems to be writing more from the perspective of his theology than as a reflection of the reality he experiences.

יב:ח לְפִי־שִׂכְלוֹ יְהֻלַּל־אִישׁ וְנַעֲוֵה־לֵב יִהְיֶה לָבוּז:

12:8 ACCORDING TO ONE'S INTELLIGENCE SHOULD ONE BE
PRAISED; A PERVERTED MIND SHOULD BE DESPISED.

The writer makes a distinction between the ability to think and what is thought. Mere intelligence that is lacking moral direction is dangerous for the individual and for society.

יב:ט טוֹב נִקְלֶה וְעֶבֶד לוֹ מִמִּתְכַּבֵּד וַחֲסַר־לָחֶם:

12:9 BETTER TO BE DEMEANED AND HAVE A SLAVE THAN TO
BE HONORED AND LACK FOR BREAD.

Possessions do matter. This is particularly true in urban life. The Book of Proverbs aims to teach the reader the virtue of balance. Honor is important, but so is sustenance.

יב:י יוֹדֵעַ צַדִּיק נֶפֶשׁ בְּהֶמְתּוֹ וְרַחֲמֵי רְשָׁעִים אַכְזָרִי:

12:10 A RIGHTEOUS PERSON KNOWS ABOUT THE NEEDS
OF ANIMALS, BUT THE COMPASSION OF THE WICKED
IS CRUEL.

The writer suggests that it is the personality of wicked people that makes them act in a cruel manner, even to their own animals, even when they are ostensibly trying to be kind.

יב:יא עֹבֵד אַדְמָתוֹ יִשְׂבַּע־לָחֶם וּמְרַדֵּף רֵיקִים חֲסַר־לֵב:

12:11 THE ONE WHO TILLS ONE'S OWN GROUND WILL HAVE
PLENTY OF FOOD, WHILE THE ONE WHO PURSUES VAIN
THINGS LACKS SENSE.

This verse closely parallels Proverbs 28:19. It differs only in the final two words of the verse. One may wonder why the author of Proverbs talks about agriculture in a book that is directed to urban dwellers. For Rashi, food (literally, "bread") is a metaphor for study. Ecclesiastes 5:8 mixes references to the city and rural areas as well: "The advantage of land is paramount. Even a king is subject to the soil."

יב:יב חָמַד רָשָׁע מְצוֹד רָעִים וְשֹׁרֶשׁ צַדִּיקִים יִתֵּן:

12:12 A WICKED PERSON COVETS THE PREY OF EVIL PEOPLE;
THE ROOT OF THE RIGHTEOUS YIELDS FRUIT.

This is a difficult verse. *M'tzod* can mean "snare" or "net" and, by extension, "prey." It can even mean "stronghold." In 12:3, the author uses the phrase *shoresh tzaddikim*. Thus, the "root of the righteous" shall never slip. The *Targum*, as a reference to the meaning, translates the verb *yitein*, "he will give," as *nitkayeim*, "shall be established." Both Rashi and Ibn Ezra translate *yitein* as "yield," as in "yielding fruit." To attempt to combine both clauses of the verse, we suggest that the author means that a wicked person wants to get what others have by stealing from them, but a righteous person will work for it and thereby be sustained by his or her righteousness. Another possible translation might be as follows: "The wicked covet the stronghold of evil, while God gives the root of the righteous." In this case, the wicked need strongholds for their protection. But God protects the righteous.

יב:יג בְּפֶשַׁע שְׂפָתַיִם מוֹקֵשׁ רָע וַיֵּצֵא מִצָּרָה צַדִּיק:

12:13 THE EVIL PERSON IS SNARED BY TRANSGRESSIONS OF THE LIPS. THE RIGHTEOUS PERSON WILL EMERGE FROM TROUBLE.

Rashi contends that this verse is an allusion to the generation of the Flood and to Noah. The message of the verse is quite simple: Be careful about what you say.

יב:יד מִפְּרִי פִי־אִישׁ יִשְׂבַּע־טוֹב וּגְמוּל יְדֵי־אָדָם ישוב יָשִׁיב לוֹ:

12:14 BY THE FRUIT OF ONE'S MOUTH, ONE WILL BE SATISFIED; BY THE WORK OF ONE'S HANDS, ONE WILL RECEIVE RECOMPENSE.

Although the Hebrew includes several challenges for translation, the writer's point remains clear: There is a result that comes with every word spoken and every act performed.

יב:טו דֶּרֶךְ אֱוִיל יָשָׁר בְּעֵינָיו וְשֹׁמֵעַ לְעֵצָה חָכָם:

12:15 THE WAY OF THE FOOL IS RIGHT IN ONE'S OWN EYES, BUT THE WISE PERSON LISTENS TO ADVICE.

It is not surprising to find such a statement in a book devoted to giving advice. But the point remains valid. Wise people do not depend on their own minds alone. They know to seek the advice of others as well.

יב:טז אֱוִיל בַּיּוֹם יִוָּדַע כַּעְסוֹ וְכֹסֶה קָלוֹן עָרוּם:

12:16 THE ANGER OF A FOOL IS IMMEDIATELY KNOWN, BUT THE CLEVER PERSON'S SHAME IS HIDDEN.

We have translated *bayom* (literally, "on that day") as "immediately." Rashi suggests this translation, referring to the midrash that suggests that Adam sinned on the same day that he was created, that is, immediately. God prudently postponed Adam's punishment. *Arum*, depending on context, can mean "prudent," "guileful," or "clever." The contrast with the "fool" suggests "clever" as the most appropriate translation. Such a translation raises an important question: Should a sinner (cleverly) hide his or her sin? Should a sinner hide the shame that results from sinning?

יב:יז יָפִיחַ אֱמוּנָה יַגִּיד צֶדֶק וְעֵד שְׁקָרִים מִרְמָה:

12:17 THE ONE WHO TESTIFIES HONESTLY SPEAKS RIGHTLY,
BUT A FALSE WITNESS IS DECEIT.

Just as we have seen in Proverbs 6:19, *yafiach* (breathes forth) can be used to mean "testify." *Emunah* ("steadfastness," "faithfully"—later, "faith") is contrasted with *sheker* (falsity). Thus, it takes the meaning of "truly" or "honestly." *Tzedek*, generally translated as "righteousness," takes on the meaning of "accurate" or "correct" (as in *moznei tzedek*, "correct scales," Leviticus 19:36) when paired with *emunah*, as it is in Psalm 119:138. Thus, the verse contains two words that both mean "truly," "honestly," or "correctly." Ibn Ezra understands this construction of words to refer to judicial situations. Thus, it is advice to would-be witnesses.

יב:יח יֵשׁ בּוֹטֶה כְּמַדְקְרוֹת חָרֶב וּלְשׁוֹן חֲכָמִים מַרְפֵּא:

12:18 GOSSIP IS LIKE THE PIERCING OF A SWORD, BUT THERE
IS HEALING IN THE LANGUAGE OF THE WISE.

We come again to a warning about wise and unwise speech. Words once uttered can have a doleful effect, even if unintended. The wrong word can ruin a life. As the Rabbis understood it, Abel's murder by Cain arose out of a conversation in a field (*B'reishit Rabbah* 22). The wise person knows how to use words to heal rather than hurt.

יב:יט שְׂפַת־אֱמֶת תִּכּוֹן לָעַד וְעַד־אַרְגִּיעָה לְשׁוֹן שָׁקֶר:

12:19 THE LIP OF TRUTH ENDURES FOREVER, BUT THE LYING
TONGUE LASTS ONLY FOR A MOMENT.

Truth lasts, and falsity fades.

יב:כ מִרְמָה בְּלֶב־חֹרְשֵׁי רָע וּלְיֹעֲצֵי שָׁלוֹם שִׂמְחָה:

12:20 THOSE WHO DEVISE EVIL HAVE DECEIT IN THEIR
HEARTS, BUT THOSE WHO COUNSEL PEACE HAVE JOY.

According to Rashi, "those who devise evil" are so filled with nefarious plans that they have no room for feeling anything else except deceit. Ibn Ezra suggests that they keep thinking of ways to perpetuate their deceit. Gersonides draws the subjects of both parts of the verse together and suggests that the target of "those who devise evil" are "those who counsel peace."

יב:כא לֹא־יְאֻנֶּה לַצַּדִּיק כָּל־אָוֶן וּרְשָׁעִים מָלְאוּ רָע:

12:21 NO DISASTER WILL BEFALL THE RIGHTEOUS, BUT THE
WICKED WILL BE FILLED WITH EVIL.

This is more a statement of religious hope than of empirical reality. Perhaps this may be seen as a directive to us, to make sure that we avert disaster for the righteous. Such activity will isolate the wicked; their own evil will destroy them.

יב:כב תּוֹעֲבַת יְהֹוָה שִׂפְתֵי־שָׁקֶר וְעֹשֵׂי אֱמוּנָה רְצוֹנוֹ:

12:22 LYING LIPS ARE AN ABOMINATION TO GOD, BUT THOSE
WHO DEAL FAITHFULLY ARE GOD'S DELIGHT.

This is another example of the style of the writer of this book, in which two pairs of terms are cited in direct contrast. One pair is related to God, and the other pair is related to humans. *To-eivah* (abomination) and *ratzon* (will or delight) are related to God. *Sheker* (lying) and *emunah* (truly, faithfully) are related to humans.

יב:כג אָדָם עָרוּם כֹּסֶה דָּעַת וְלֵב כְּסִילִים יִקְרָא אִוֶּלֶת:

12:23 A CLEVER PERSON CONCEALS KNOWLEDGE, BUT THE
MIND OF FOOLS PROCLAIMS FOLLY.

Once again, we learn the value of silence. As has been noted previously, Rabbi Shimon ben Gamliel said, "All my life I have been brought up among the Sages, and I have found nothing better for a person than silence" (*Pirkei Avot* 1:17). Rashi notes that a clever person is careful about revealing matters of wisdom. The fool is not so careful about what is revealed and makes his or her stupidity apparent.

יב:כד יַד־חָרוּצִים תִּמְשׁוֹל וּרְמִיָּה תִּהְיֶה לָמַס:

12:24 A DILIGENT HAND WILL RULE, BUT A LAZY HAND WILL
BE RULED.

Mas, "forced labor" or "conscription," is presented by the author of Proverbs as punishment for laziness.

יב:כה דְּאָגָה בְלֶב־אִישׁ יַשְׁחֶנָּה וְדָבָר טוֹב יְשַׂמְּחֶנָּה:

12:25 WORRY WEIGHS THE MIND DOWN, WHILE A NICE WORD
MAKES IT HAPPY.

The *Targum* suggests an alternative translation: "Worry will make the mind anxious. A kind word will make the mind happy." In either case, the writer reminds us about the importance of kindness in words.

יב:כו יָתֵר מֵרֵעֵהוּ צַדִּיק וְדֶרֶךְ רְשָׁעִים תַּתְעֵם:

12:26 THE RIGHTEOUS PERSON IS BETTER THAN HIS OR
HER NEIGHBOR, BUT THE WAY OF THE WICKED
MISLEADS THEM.

While the *Targum* and Ibn Ezra translate this verse similarly, they feel that the first clause is trite. Gersonides suggests that the writer intends to say that the righteous person learns the best virtues from others and then emulates them. However, the wicked person learns the worst vices from others and emulates them.

יב:כז לֹא־יַחֲרֹךְ רְמִיָּה צֵידוֹ וְהוֹן־אָדָם יָקָר חָרוּץ:

12:27 A LAZY PERSON WILL NOT ROAST WHAT HE OR SHE HAS
HUNTED, BUT WEALTH IS DEAR TO A DILIGENT PERSON.

The verbal root *charach* (to roast) is used only in the Bible. While the writer uses a metaphor from hunting for food (something foreign to Jewish dietary law), the sense is clear: Don't waste what you have. The lazy person, having expended time and energy to hunt, is too lazy to make use of what he or she has hunted. The diligent person does not waste what took time and energy to acquire.

יב:כח בְּאֹרַח־צְדָקָה חַיִּים וְדֶרֶךְ נְתִיבָה אַל־מָוֶת: *סבירין ומטעין "אֶל", כלומר שׁנוי תנועה

12:28 THERE IS LIFE IN THE WAY OF RIGHTEOUSNESS; THERE
IS NO DEATH IN THE WAY OF THIS PATH.

This is a problematic verse. The Masoretic text has *al mavet,* "no death," as the last words of the verse. There are other manuscripts that read *el mavet* (to death). The author of the *Targum* may have had those manuscripts in mind, since the *Targum* sees the second clause as the antithesis of the first: "In the way of righteousness there is life, and in the way of transgression there is death." It is possible that the editor of the *Targum* was reviewing an alternative manuscript that replaced the redundant *v'derech n'tivah* (way) with *v'derech to-eivah* (way of the abomination). Such a text would support the reading of the *Targum* but not of the other classical commentators.

Masoretic Text

Jewish scribes working from 500 to 1000 C.E. were known as the Masoretes. They meticulously copied the Scriptures and preserved them. The work of the Masoretes produced the Masoretic text of the Bible (i.e., the current Hebrew text). They also set the musical notes for reading known in Yiddish as *trope* and in Hebrew as *taamei hamikra*.

GLEANINGS

Born into a Difficult Life

Sometimes a special soul is born into a difficult life because of a decision that the soul made while in the spiritual world. The soul does not so much need to right previous wrongs but rather wants to demonstrate the kind of qualities that can only be seen in hardship. A light shines more brightly in the darkness than in the presence of light. On a deeper level, such a soul chooses to descend into the physical world and to suffer. In this way, although the soul might not be consciously aware of the reasons for its choice, it elevates its position in the next world by giving encouragement and faith to others. For example, a soul may want to demonstrate the quality of forgiveness, compassion or faith. Because of this choice at a soul level, the soul is placed in life situations where there will be much opportunity to practice these qualities. As such, a person's life serves as a model for others close to him and possibly to the world as to how a person can maintain goodness and forgiveness in the face of extreme adversity.

Melinda Ribner, *New Age Judaism: Ancient Wisdom for the Modern World*
(Deerfield Beach, Fla.: Simcha Press, 2000), 100

CHAPTER THIRTEEN

יג:א בֵּן חָכָם מוּסַר אָב וְלֵץ לֹא־שָׁמַע גְּעָרָה:

13:1 BECAUSE OF A PARENT'S DISCIPLINE, A CHILD IS WISE;
A SCORNER DOES NOT ACCEPT REBUKE.

Our translation follows Rashi's understanding of this terse verse. For Gersonides, the difference between ''wise'' and ''scorner'' lies in the ability of a parent to impart wisdom and virtue to a child who is wise. However, the parent is unable to do so if the child scorns everything.

יג:ב מִפְּרִי פִי־אִישׁ יֹאכַל טוֹב וְנֶפֶשׁ בֹּגְדִים חָמָס:

13:2 IT IS APPROPRIATE THAT ONE SHOULD EAT FROM THE
FRUIT OF ONE'S MOUTH; BUT VIOLENCE IS THE DESIRE
OF THE TREACHEROUS.

Words should be used to benefit, rather than harm. The writer uses the term *bogdim* (treacherous) to suggest that there are those who cannot be trusted no matter what they say, for they intend harm. Rashi understands the first clause to refer to teachers of Torah, who provide good in this life and in the next.

יג:ג נֹצֵר פִּיו שֹׁמֵר נַפְשׁוֹ פֹּשֵׂק שְׂפָתָיו מְחִתָּה־לוֹ:

13:3 THE ONE WHO WATCHES ONE'S MOUTH GUARDS ONE'S
LIFE, BUT THE ONE WHO SPREADS ONE'S LIPS WIDE WILL
BE RUINED.

The verbal root *pasak* (spreads wide) occurs both here and in Ezekiel 16:25 with sexual meaning. Again we learn from the author the value of silence. Ibn Ezra understands the verse to suggest that saying the wrong thing can be dangerous.

יג:ד מִתְאַוָּה וָאַיִן נַפְשׁוֹ עָצֵל וְנֶפֶשׁ חָרֻצִים תְּדֻשָּׁן:

13:4 WHATEVER IT IS THAT THE LAZY PERSON WANTS, THAT PERSON WILL GET NOTHING; WHATEVER THE DILIGENT PERSON WANTS, THAT PERSON WILL GET IT IN ABUNDANCE.

Again, the author makes a contrast between diligence and laziness. This book, a book of the city, praises the assertive and self-initiating.

יג:ה דְּבַר־שֶׁקֶר יִשְׂנָא צַדִּיק וְרָשָׁע יַבְאִישׁ וְיַחְפִּיר:

13:5 THE RIGHTEOUS PERSON HATES THE FALSE WORD; THE WICKED PERSON ACTS ODIOUSLY AND SHAMEFULLY.

For Rashi, the difference between the righteous and the wicked is in their acceptance of falsehood. The righteous reject it, and the wicked accept it. In so doing, the wicked act "odiously and shamefully." The author of Proverbs reminds us of the importance of telling the truth. This is particularly important for people who have become accustomed to accepting lies and "spinning the truth."

יג:ו צְדָקָה תִּצֹּר תָּם־דָּרֶךְ וְרִשְׁעָה תְּסַלֵּף חַטָּאת:

13:6 RIGHTEOUSNESS KEEPS US UPRIGHT ON THE WAY, WHILE WICKEDNESS RUINS THE SINNER.

The last word of the verse *(chatat)* literally means "sin" and is taken by Rashi and Ibn Ezra to refer to *ish chatat* (a person who sins, a sinner). The verbal root *saleif,* which we have translated as "ruins," can also mean to "twist" or "upset," as in the prohibition against the taking of bribes (Exodus 23:8), for bribes *visaleif divrei tzaddikim,* "upset the pleas of the just."

יג:ז יֵשׁ מִתְעַשֵּׁר וְאֵין כֹּל מִתְרוֹשֵׁשׁ וְהוֹן רָב:

13:7 ONE MAY PLAY THE RICH PERSON AND HAVE NOTHING, BUT ANOTHER MAY PLAY THE POOR PERSON AND HAVE GREAT WEALTH.

Therefore, the teacher of Proverbs suggests, appearances may not reflect reality. If you are going to do business with someone, look beyond the appearance of the customer. And if you enter into a relationship with an individual, do not be deceived by appearances.

יג:ח כֹּפֶר נֶפֶשׁ־אִישׁ עָשְׁרוֹ וְרָשׁ לֹא־שָׁמַע גְּעָרָה:

13:8 THE RANSOM FOR A PERSON'S LIFE IS THAT PERSON'S
WEALTH; THE POOR HEAR NO REBUKE.

The second clause in the verse seems counterintuitive. Our experience seems to
support the first but denies the second. Facing the difficulty of the verse, Rashi
interprets the second clause to mean that the wealthy who give charity should not
reproach the poor for receiving it. He also suggests that the terms "rich" and "poor"
refer to varying levels of Torah knowledge. Rashi's interpretations move the reader
away from the challenges posed by a literal reading of the verse.

יג:ט אוֹר־צַדִּיקִים יִשְׂמָח וְנֵר רְשָׁעִים יִדְעָךְ:

13:9 THE LIGHT OF THE RIGHTEOUS BURNS BRIGHTLY, BUT
THE LAMP OF THE WICKED WILL BE EXTINGUISHED.

The verb *yismach,* which ends the first clause, in another context might be translated
as "will rejoice," reflecting the usual meaning assigned to the verbal root *samach.*
However, the context of the verse and the contrast of the onomatopoeic root *daach*
(to extinguish, to quench) suggest another meaning: that *yismach* is based on the
Ugaritic word for "to burn brightly." Gersonides takes the verb *yismach* to mean
"rejoice" and explains that the light of the righteous rejoices as a result of
the acquisition of concepts and the development of the acquired intellect.
For Gersonides, the righteous are those who hold correct ideas.

יג:י רַק־בְּזָדוֹן יִתֵּן מַצָּה וְאֶת־נוֹעָצִים חָכְמָה:

13:10 ONLY PRIDE PRODUCES CONTENTION, BUT THERE IS
WISDOM WITH THOSE WHO ARE WELL ADVISED.

Wise people listen to advice. Foolish persons will not listen to advice and,
consequently, will create problems for themselves and others. There are parallels
between this verse and an earlier verse (11:2). The last clause of this verse has the
words *v'et noatzim chochmah,* "there is wisdom with those who are well advised."
The last clause of 11:2 contains the words *v'et tz'nuim chochmah,* "there is wisdom
with the humble." Some would suggest that the last verse of 13:10 be emended to
tz'nuim, since both words contain the same consonants in Hebrew.

יג:יא הוֹן מֵהֶבֶל יִמְעָט וְקֹבֵץ עַל־יָד יַרְבֶּה:

13:11 WEALTH GOTTEN BY VANITY SHOULD BE DIMINISHED,
BUT WHAT IS GATHERED BY HAND WILL BE INCREASED.

Hevel (breath, vanity) is contrasted with *al yad* (by hand). Perhaps on the basis of
"breath," Rashi understands the verse to refer to the study of Torah. Ibn Ezra suggests

that the first clause refers to unlawful means such as theft, but the second clause, "gathered by hand," refers to hard work.

יג:יב תּוֹחֶלֶת מְמֻשָּׁכָה מַחֲלָה־לֵב וְעֵץ חַיִּים תַּאֲוָה בָאָה:

13:12 HOPE DELAYED SICKENS THE HEART, BUT LONGING
ACHIEVED IS THE TREE OF LIFE.

Rashi explains the first clause to refer to a person who promised something to another person but does not perform it. Hope is a crucial element in life. It carries us forward, particularly amidst the daily challenges of living.

יג:יג בָּז לְדָבָר יֵחָבֶל לוֹ וִירֵא מִצְוָה הוּא יְשֻׁלָּם:

13:13 WHOEVER DESPISES THE WORD WILL BE INJURED,
BUT WHOEVER REVERES A COMMANDMENT WILL BE
REWARDED.

From the parallel in the second clause, Rashi takes "the word" to refer to the words of Torah. He takes *yeichavel,* from the verbal root *chaval,* to mean "becomes a debtor." Ibn Ezra takes another sense of the same word to mean "becomes injured."

יג:יד תּוֹרַת חָכָם מְקוֹר חַיִּים לָסוּר מִמֹּקְשֵׁי מָוֶת:

13:14 THE DOCTRINE OF THE WISE IS THE SOURCE OF LIFE
[THAT HELPS] TO TURN FROM THE SNARES OF DEATH.

Rashi understands the two clauses of this verse as related to one another. The wise teach how to avoid the snares of death, and this teaching is the source of life.

יג:טו שֵׂכֶל־טוֹב יִתֶּן־חֵן וְדֶרֶךְ בֹּגְדִים אֵיתָן:

13:15 GOOD INTELLIGENCE PRODUCES FAVOR. THE WAY OF
THE TREACHEROUS IS HARD.

The last word of this verse is problematic. *Eitan* usually means "continual" or "constant." Both Rashi and Ibn Ezra understand the word to mean "hard." The *Targum* translates *eitan* as *teivad,* "will perish." Some scholars have suggested that emending the word to *eidam* (their calamity) would make most sense in this context.

יג:טז כָּל־עָרוּם יַעֲשֶׂה בְדָעַת וּכְסִיל יִפְרֹשׂ אִוֶּלֶת:

13:16 A CUNNING PERSON ACTS WITH KNOWLEDGE, WHILE
A FOOL DISPLAYS FOLLY.

Again the author teaches us that the difference between the *arum* (the cunning person) and the *k'sil* (fool) rests in knowledge and its use. It is important to remember that the word *arum* has no specific moral context. It simply describes how a person uses knowledge to act.

יג:יז מַלְאָךְ רָשָׁע יִפֹּל בְּרָע וְצִיר אֱמוּנִים מַרְפֵּא:

13:17 A WICKED MESSENGER WILL FALL INTO EVIL, BUT A
FAITHFUL ENVOY BRINGS HEALING.

Rashi offers the case of Balaam, the wicked messenger. He seems to be suggesting that a person acting on behalf of another person should keep the concerns of that person in mind.

יג:יח רֵישׁ וְקָלוֹן פּוֹרֵעַ מוּסָר וְשׁוֹמֵר תּוֹכַחַת יְכֻבָּד:

13:18 THE ONE WHO REJECTS DISCIPLINE WILL GAIN POVERTY
AND SHAME, BUT THE ONE WHO ACCEPTS REPROOF
WILL BE HONORED.

To acquire wisdom, discipline is indispensable. A lack of discipline will diminish both esteem and wealth.

יג:יט תַּאֲוָה נִהְיָה תֶעֱרַב לְנָפֶשׁ וְתוֹעֲבַת כְּסִילִים סוּר מֵרָע:

13:19 LONGING ACHIEVED IS SWEET TO THE SOUL; TURNING
FROM EVIL IS AN ABOMINATION TO FOOLS.

How we face the future colors the way we live in the present. The person who yearns for something gains great satisfaction when he or she achieves or receives what was yearned for. Decent people yearn for the removal of evil from their midst. Only fools do not yearn for the elimination of evil.

יג:כ הלוך הֹלֵךְ אֶת־חֲכָמִים וחכם יֶחְכָּם וְרֹעֶה כְסִילִים יֵרוֹעַ:

13:20 THE ONE WHO WALKS WITH THE WISE BECOMES WISE,
BUT THE COMPANION OF FOOLS WILL BE HARMED.

The point is clear. We are affected by those with whom we come into contact, particularly by those with whom we have an extended relationship. Thus, it is predicable that the author of Proverbs would advise the young reader, the intended audience, to seek the company of the wise.

יג:כא חַטָּאִים תְּרַדֵּף רָעָה וְאֶת־צַדִּיקִים יְשַׁלֶּם־טוֹב:

13:21 EVIL PURSUES SINNERS, BUT GOOD IS REPAID TO THE RIGHTEOUS.

Rashi's understanding of this verse challenges our own experiences. He suggests that evil will pursue a wicked person until he or she is ultimately destroyed by it.

יג:כב טוֹב יַנְחִיל בְּנֵי־בָנִים וְצָפוּן לַצַּדִּיק חֵיל חוֹטֵא:

13:22 A GOOD PERSON WILL BEQUEATH AN INHERITANCE TO GRANDCHILDREN, BUT A SINNER'S WEALTH WILL BE KEPT FOR THE RIGHTEOUS.

Virtue has an effect on the present, but it also has an effect on the future. In Ecclesiastes (or *Kohelet*), another book of wisdom in the Bible, whose views were considered by many Rabbis to be heretical, a different view is presented regarding the bequeathing of wealth through the generations: "For sometimes a person whose fortune was made with wisdom, knowledge, and skill must hand it on to become the portion of someone who did not work for it. That too is futile and a great evil" (Ecclesiastes 2:21).

יג:כג רָב־אֹכֶל נִיר רָאשִׁים וְיֵשׁ נִסְפֶּה בְּלֹא מִשְׁפָּט:

13:23 THERE WILL BE PLENTY OF FOOD IN THE SOIL WORKED BY THE POOR, YET SOME ARE SWEPT AWAY WITHOUT JUSTICE.

This is a very difficult verse to translate. *Nir,* generally translated as "soil," also means "cultivated," as in virgin soil made cultivable for the first time. This word is joined as a construct form to the word *rashim* (poor). The relationship between the soil and the poor is unclear. The *Targum* omits any reference to the soil and paraphrases the verse: "The poor will have much food, and a person may die without justice." Rashi avoids the problem of translation by taking the verse as a parable of Torah study. Ibn Ezra explains that the poor may have much to eat if they properly work the soil. But the person who does not utilize the proper method of cultivation will be swept away. Gersonides explains the first clause by saying that the soil that the poor works should provide enough for everyone, but the landowners take most of the produce, and the poor are left poor as a result. He explains that the second clause means that often the innocent are unjustly condemned. Some scholars have suggested an emendation of the text to solve the problem by reading *y'sharim* (the upright) for *rashim* (the poor). Thus, the first clause of the verse would read: "There is plenty of food in the soil for the upright."

יג:כד חוֹשֵׂךְ שִׁבְטוֹ שׂוֹנֵא בְנוֹ וְאֹהֲבוֹ שִׁחֲרוֹ מוּסָר:

13:24 PARENTS WHO HATE THEIR CHILDREN SPARE THEM THE ROD OF DISCIPLINE, BUT PARENTS WHO LOVE THEIR CHILDREN SEARCH THEM OUT FOR DISCIPLINE.

This verse was written: "He who hates his son...." We have translated the verse to transcend its gender specificity. However, it is likely that, in the ancient world, any form of corporal discipline was meted out by a father and only to his son, not a daughter. Nonetheless, the Rabbis were uncomfortable with this verse (and with what Abraham did to his son Ishmael) and interpreted it to mean "The one who spares the rod will end up hating his son" and applied it to Abraham in order to explain how he could send his son Ishmael out into the wilderness. They claimed that Abraham never disciplined Ishmael even though Ishmael had developed evil ways. Although Abraham began by loving Ishmael, because he did not chastise his strident son, Abraham ended up hating him (*Sh'mot Rabbah* 1:1).

יג:כה צַדִּיק אֹכֵל לְשֹׂבַע נַפְשׁוֹ וּבֶטֶן רְשָׁעִים תֶּחְסָר:

13:25 THE RIGHTEOUS EAT UNTIL SATISFIED, BUT THE BELLY OF THE WICKED WILL NEVER BE SATISFIED.

Another way of translating this verse into a contemporary idiom might be: "The righteous eat to their heart's content, but the belly of the wicked will always be empty." This promise reminds us of the troubling verse in Psalms that is included at the end of *Birkat HaMazon:* "I have been young and now I am old. Yet I have never seen the righteous forsaken, nor his [or her] seed begging for bread" (Psalm 37:25). Some participants prefer to read this as: "Yet, I have never seen the righteous *so* forsaken that his or her seed begs for bread." The most persuasive reading of the text seems to be as a charge to those who are sitting and eating. We have an obligation to make sure that the righteous are not forsaken nor that their offspring go hungry. This text paints a picture for us of the ultimate vision: a time when no one goes hungry.

Ugaritic

This is an ancient Northwest-Semitic language that existed in northern Syria during the second millennium B.C.E. Archaeologists have found documents written in this language in Ras Shamra, site of the ancient Ugarit. These texts were written on clay tablets in a unique cuneiform alphabet script.

Kohelet

One of the books in the final section of the *Tanach,* the Writings or *K'tuvim, Kohelet* is also known by its English name, Ecclesiastes. As one of the Five Scrolls *(m'gillot)* in the Bible, it is read aloud as part of the celebration of Sukkot. *Kohelet* is a book of *chochmah,* "practical wisdom." It offers the reader guidance for daily living. The author placed a high priority on the Greek notion of rhetoric, a notable influence in his work. Following Egyptian tradition, the author placed his wisdom in the mouth of a king (Solomon) to give it authority. However, the Book of *Kohelet* is most likely not the work of Solomon, but rather of an intuitive, insightful individual who had a passion for life. He probably compiled the book in his old age, having lived a long and rich life, and reports on observations in his own voice, as well as the voice of a narrator, that is, the old man Kohelet.

Emendation of Texts

There is a delicate balance to be reached with regard to scholarly emendations (educated attempts at changing the text based on scholarly evidence). On the one hand, there probably were mistakes in the copying and transmission of texts from one generation to the next. But it is too easy to change the text to get it to make more sense when we can't make sense out of it on our own. Instead, we are urged to struggle with the texts and try to understand them as they were bequeathed to us. Often, scholars write off the editors and redactors of our sacred texts as primitive and seek to "correct" the "mistakes" they made. We would caution them: Not so fast!

GLEANINGS

Love Should Be the Motive

Life is a mirage and life is an effort—and the fullness of life for every individual depends on the strength and beauty of his vision and the strength and beauty of his effort.

And I would have my child know that one lives by truth—but that truth is only relative. That in this great world so full of positive impressions, sensations, and experiences, there is only one unchanging truth, and that is the spirituality of the world. This spirituality is evidenced in power—human and superhuman, in the creative powers of nature, and the creative powers of man.

I would tell my child and live for him an inner freedom—a freedom from fear, a freedom from the outlived traditions of the past, and from the futile allegiances of the present—a freedom which should enable him to think thru every experience, to act and to react freely, and to realize daily living with all the capacity of a free spirit.

I would tell him that life must be lived constructively, that love should be the motive power of action—I would have him know that hatred, envy, malice, evil in any form is a boomerang and consumes its begetter.

I would have him think that every human being has unrealized and almost unlimited possibilities which it is his joyous responsibility to fulfill. I would have him keep his sense of personal accomplishment balanced by realizing that any individual accomplishment is infinitely small, if one thinks in terms of the cosmos—of what is being done, what has been done and what remains to be done.

And in time I hope he shall come to know that a talent for living consists in a capacity for adjustment, that happiness and fulfillment consist in realizing life to the fullest at every moment and in losing one's self thru giving one's love and one's power to the sum of human welfare.

Can we teach those things—appreciation of truth and beauty—understanding of inner freedom—the joys of world love and service? Probably not! One can only sense them and perhaps impart them thru the quality of one's own being.

Rose Haas Altschuler, "Love Should be the Motive Power of Action," in This I Believe: Documents of American Jewish Life, ed. Jacob Rader Marcus (Northvale, N.J: Jason Aronson, 1990), 168

CHAPTER FOURTEEN

יד:א חַכְמוֹת נָשִׁים בָּנְתָה בֵיתָהּ וְאִוֶּלֶת בְּיָדֶיהָ תֶהֶרְסֶנּוּ:

14:1 A WISE WOMAN BUILDS HER HOUSE, BUT THE FOOLISH
WOMAN DESTROYS IT WITH HER OWN HANDS.

This verse contains an interesting grammatical construction. The author combines the plural term for "wisdom" with the plural term for "woman." Generally the plural form for "wisdom" is not used. The *Targum* translates the two words as *chakimta dinshaiya* (the wisest among women). What is interesting here is the contrast between the wise and foolish applied to women and their role in the home. As we shall see at the end of the Book of Proverbs, the writer indicates that women were more than homemakers. They also worked in the marketplace, for instance. This is why we decided to leave the verse in its original gender specificity. Rashi applies this verse to the events surrounding the rebellion of Korach (Numbers 16, 17): the wise woman was the wife of On ben Pelet; the foolish woman was the wife of Korach (see Babylonian Talmud, *Sanhedrin* 110a).

יד:ב הוֹלֵךְ בְּיָשְׁרוֹ יְרֵא יְהוָה וּנְלוֹז דְּרָכָיו בּוֹזֵהוּ:

14:2 THE ONE WHO FEARS GOD WALKS UPRIGHTLY, BUT THE
ONE WHO DESPISES GOD PERVERTS THE DIVINE WAY.

Fear of God entails proper behavior. Inappropriate behavior reveals a lack of commitment to God. For Judaism, behavior is an indication of belief. A *maamin*, "a believer," is one who is a *ne-eman*, "one who can be depended upon." And that is the person who fears God and walks uprightly. Both are from the root *aman*, meaning "certain," hence the word "amen."

יד:ג בְּפִי־אֱוִיל חֹטֶר גַּאֲוָה וְשִׂפְתֵי חֲכָמִים תִּשְׁמוּרֵם:

14:3 THE MOUTH OF THE FOOL IS THE BRANCH OF PRIDE;
THE LIPS OF THE WISE PRESERVE THEM.

Choter (literally, "shoot") occurs again only in Isaiah 11:1, where it has the meaning of "branch." The "branch of pride" may be interpreted in different ways. The *Targum* translates the word as *zakta d'tzaara* (the sting of pain). Rashi relates the words to Pharaoh's statement: "Who is God that I should heed God?" (Exodus 5:2). Ibn Ezra understands the words as referring to the ability of the proud to strike at others.

Gersonides understands the words as referring to the fool's pride that is self-destructive. Perhaps the first clause of the verse should be translated: "From the mouth of the fool comes the outgrowth [*choter*] of pride."

יד:ד בְּאֵין אֲלָפִים אֵבוּס בָּר וְרׇב־תְּבוּאוֹת בְּכֹחַ שׁוֹר:

14:4 WHERE THERE ARE NO OXEN, THE CRIB IS CLEAN,
YET THERE IS MUCH BENEFIT FROM THE STRENGTH
OF AN OX.

All things have a cost-benefit relationship. If one does not own oxen, then one need not clean their crib. However, owning oxen provides benefits to their owner. Not having an ox includes a benefit, and having an ox includes a different benefit. The astute person will know how to balance benefits against costs.

יד:ה עֵד אֱמוּנִים לֹא יְכַזֵּב וְיָפִיחַ כְּזָבִים עֵד שָׁקֶר:

14:5 A TRUSTWORTHY WITNESS DOES NOT LIE, WHILE A
FALSE WITNESS EXHALES LIES.

The second clause is repeated from 6:19. The meaning is the same: for the false witness, lying is as easy as breathing. Though truth-telling is required in all society, the commercial relationships of city life strain the ability of the individual to tell the truth. As a result, city life necessitates truth-telling.

יד:ו בִּקֶּשׁ־לֵץ חׇכְמָה וָאָיִן וְדַעַת לְנָבוֹן נָקָל:

14:6 WISDOM IS NOT FOR A SCORNER, BUT KNOWLEDGE IS
EASY FOR ONE WHO IS UNDERSTANDING.

The author contrasts two types of people and two kinds of information: one who pays no regard to anything and one who seeks to understand. The former will not be able to gain deeper insight into anything, while the latter will be able to gain and process new information. Here Proverbs parallels the view of the philosophy of science that holds that while provisional skepticism may be useful, absolute skepticism impedes the work of science.

יד:ז לֵךְ מִנֶּגֶד לְאִישׁ כְּסִיל וּבַל־יָדַעְתָּ שִׂפְתֵי־דָעַת:

14:7 GET FAR AWAY FROM A FOOL, FOR LIPS OF KNOWLEDGE
YOU ARE NOT GOING TO KNOW.

Although both Rashi and Ibn Ezra understand the first clause to prohibit being in the company of a fool, Ibn Ezra takes the *mem* of *mineged* to suggest "get far away."

He wants to make the point that a fool is not a fit companion for one who will become wise.

יד:ח חָכְמַת עָרוּם הָבִין דַּרְכּוֹ וְאִוֶּלֶת כְּסִילִים מִרְמָה:

14:8 THE WISDOM OF THE PRUDENT IS THE UNDERSTANDING
OF ONE'S WAY; THE FOLLY OF FOOLS IS GUILE.

Rashi and Ibn Ezra agree that "the wisdom of the prudent" enables that person to find his or her way. Rashi and Gersonides both think "the folly of fools" brings them further folly, while Ibn Ezra thinks that their folly misleads others. In an idiomatic translation, the first clause might read: "The wisdom of the clever one is to know where he [or she] is going." Having a goal is the first step. Fools, even if they want to do evil, fail because they lack a goal. Because it is purposeless, their deceit becomes folly.

יד:ט אֱוִלִים יָלִיץ אָשָׁם וּבֵין יְשָׁרִים רָצוֹן:

14:9 GUILT IS THE INTERMEDIARY FOR FOOLS; FAVOR IS FOR
THE UPRIGHT.

The meaning of the verb in the first clause, *yalitz,* is problematic. If it is derived from *meilitz* (interpreter, translator)—as in Genesis 42:23—it means "interpreter" or "intercedes, acts as intermediary." However, if the word is derived from *leitz* (mocker), it means "mocks." A second problem is the word *asham,* which means "guilt," "ransom for guilt," or even, as Rashi translates in Old French, "amends." A third problem, related to the first two, is whether *asham* is the subject or object in the first clause. The *Targum* translates the first clause as *k'silei matlin b'cheta,* "fools sneer at sin." Rashi takes the first clause to mean "amends are advised for fools." Ibn Ezra understands the first clause similarly to Rashi. As Gersonides puts it, the reason for the failure of some fools to achieve a desired goal, which they discovered after much arguing, was guilt for sin. That guilt was the one thing that they had in common. It was their intermediary! For the *Targum,* Rashi, Ibn Ezra, and Gersonides, the upright basked in each other's favor.

יד:י לֵב יוֹדֵעַ מָרַת נַפְשׁוֹ וּבְשִׂמְחָתוֹ לֹא־יִתְעָרַב זָר:

14:10 THE MIND KNOWS ITS OWN BITTERNESS, AND NO
OUTSIDER CAN MIX INTO ITS JOY.

Each human being is party to his or her own emotions. No one can truly know what another feels. The best we can do to gain a glimmer of what another feels is to imagine what we would feel in a similar situation. Rashi understands the verse to refer to the difficulties of Torah study.

יד:יא בֵּית רְשָׁעִים יִשָּׁמֵד וְאֹהֶל יְשָׁרִים יַפְרִיחַ:

14:11 THE HOUSE OF THE WICKED WILL BE DESTROYED, BUT
THE TENT OF THE UPRIGHT WILL FLOURISH.

For Ibn Ezra, the choice of terms for domicile ("house" and "tent") is purposeful. The upright reject the pleasures of the world and are content to dwell in tents. This is not the case with the wicked, who want to live in houses.

יד:יב יֵשׁ דֶּרֶךְ יָשָׁר לִפְנֵי־אִישׁ וְאַחֲרִיתָהּ דַּרְכֵי־מָוֶת:

14:12 THERE IS A STRAIGHT PATH IN FRONT OF A PERSON.
YET ITS ENDS ARE THE WAYS OF DEATH.

As the other writer of biblical wisdom literature observed, "Alas, the old person dies just like the fool," "[There is] a time for being born and a time for dying," and "There is no authority over the day of death" (Ecclesiastes 2:16; 3:2; 8:8). Wisdom cannot prevent death. Instead, wisdom can teach us how to accept death. The *Targum* translates the verse as *it orcha d'savrin b'nei nasha ditritza hi v'sofah orcha d'mota,* "There is a way when humans think is acceptable, but its end is the way of death." Rashi combines this verse with the previous one in a way that was typical of generations of the past. He says that the people of Israel in exile, although they may follow the right path, now suffer martyrdom "in all the ways of death." Hence, their minds know bitterness. In the future, they will rejoice. They will do so alone.

יד:יג גַּם־בִּשְׂחוֹק יִכְאַב־לֵב וְאַחֲרִיתָהּ שִׂמְחָה תוּגָה:

14:13 IN LAUGHTER, THE MIND IS PAINED, FOR THE END OF
JOY IS GRIEF.

This depressing statement seems like it belongs in the Book of *Kohelet:* "Of revelry I said, 'It is mad!' Of merriment, 'What good is that?'" (Ecclesiastes 2:2). The first person slips on a banana peel, and the second person laughs. There is a connection between laughter and pain, between joy and sorrow. It is not surprising that there is a disparagement of laughter and joy in a book devoted to the education of young persons (in its time, young men). According to the author, one must be serious—in all times and all places—if one wants to be successful.

יד:יד מִדְּרָכָיו יִשְׂבַּע סוּג לֵב וּמֵעָלָיו אִישׁ טוֹב:

14:14 FROM THE WAYWARD'S OWN WAYS WILL HE OR SHE BE
SATISFIED; THE GOOD PERSON, FROM GOD.

The difficulty of this verse is in the word *umei-alav* (literally, "from upon him") in the second clause. The *Targum* translates the word as *min d'chalteih,* "fear, fear of God."

The *Targum,* therefore, contrasts the wayward, who follow their own inclinations, and the good person, who follows God. The commentator Ibn Ezra translates *mei-alav* as "from God's branches," from the root *aleh* for "root." Hence, a good person will receive a divine reward. Rashi makes reference to Esau and Jacob as models of the "wayward" and the "good."

יד:טו פֶּתִי יַאֲמִין לְכָל־דָּבָר וְעָרוּם יָבִין לַאֲשֻׁרוֹ:

14:15 THE FOOL BELIEVES ANYTHING; THE CLEVER WHERE HE
OR SHE GOES.

We have paraphrased *ashuro,* the last word in the verse, as "where he or she goes." Literally, it means "his steps" and is so translated by Rashi. Although both Rashi and Ibn Ezra understand the fool as being willing to believe the wrong things, it seems probable that a book devoted to wisdom would stress the idea that the fault of the fool is in his or her willingness to believe without a basis for that belief.

יד:טז חָכָם יָרֵא וְסָר מֵרָע וּכְסִיל מִתְעַבֵּר וּבוֹטֵחַ:

14:16 THE WISE PERSON IS WARY AND AVOIDS EVIL; THE FOOL
IS INCENSED AND FALLS FLAT [ON HIS OR HER FACE].

The two verbs of the second clause of the verse present problems because they belong to homonymous roots. While it may appear that *mitabeir* comes from the root *avar,* "to cross over," it actually comes from the similar root *avar,* "to be angry." Likewise, *botei-ach* does not come from the root *batach,* "to trust." Rather, it comes from the similar root *batach,* "to fall prostrate." We take this verse as a lesson in prudence: The wise person knows what to be afraid of. The irate fool rushes in to his or her own hurt.

יד:יז קְצַר־אַפַּיִם יַעֲשֶׂה אִוֶּלֶת וְאִישׁ מְזִמּוֹת יִשָּׂנֵא:

14:17 ONE WHO IS EASILY PROVOKED WILL ACT FOOLISHLY,
AND ONE WHO SCHEMES WILL BE HATED.

This verse seems to be directed to those irascible, easily affronted persons who either act impulsively in an inappropriate manner or who devise plans to act in such a manner at a future time. The writer suggests that rational behavior requires reflection and that rage invites self-destruction.

יד:יח נָחֲלוּ פְתָאיִם* אוֶּלֶת וַעֲרוּמִים יַכְתִּרוּ דָעַת: יתיר א'

14:18 FOOLS INHERIT FOLLY, BUT THE CLEVER ARE CROWNED
WITH KNOWLEDGE.

Once again, the author contrasts the foolish with the clever. The former, without
reflection, take what is handed to them. The latter make the effort to know what can
be known and gain as a result. In his commentary, Gersonides points out that the
fools are easily beguiled, while the wise investigate the ideas that confront them with
great deliberation.

יד:יט שַׁחוּ רָעִים לִפְנֵי טוֹבִים וּרְשָׁעִים עַל־שַׁעֲרֵי צַדִּיק:

14:19 THE EVIL BOW BEFORE THE GOOD, AND THE WICKED AT
THE GATES OF THE RIGHTEOUS.

Rashi takes the verb *shachu* (to bow down) as what is called the "prophetic perfect":
The evil *will* bow in the future.

יד:כ גַּם־לְרֵעֵהוּ יִשָּׂנֵא רָשׁ וְאֹהֲבֵי עָשִׁיר רַבִּים:

14:20 THE POOR PERSON IS HATED BY ONE'S NEIGHBORS,
WHILE THE RICH PERSON HAS MANY FRIENDS.

Rashi softens the sting of this verse by suggesting that "poor" is a reference to Torah
learning. In whatever form, poverty is not an attractive state. One Rabbi said that it is
the worst manner of suffering (*Sh'mot Rabbah* 31), and another said that a poor
person could be considered as dead (Babylonian Talmud, *N'darim* 64b). Perhaps the
Sage made that comparison because the dead person decays in the grave and the
poor person is forced to decay while still alive.

יד:כא בָּז־לְרֵעֵהוּ חוֹטֵא וּמְחוֹנֵן עניים עֲנָוִים אַשְׁרָיו:

14:21 THE ONE WHO DESPISES A NEIGHBOR IS A SINNER,
BUT HAPPY IS THE ONE WHO DEALS GRACIOUSLY WITH
THE POOR.

This can be read as a response to the previous verse. This verse is reminiscent of
Rabbi Akiva's famous teaching that "Love your neighbor as yourself" (Leviticus 19:18)
is the most important principle in the Torah (*Sifra K'doshim, Parshata* 7:12).

יד:כב הֲלוֹא-יִתְעוּ חֹרְשֵׁי רָע וְחֶסֶד וֶאֱמֶת חֹרְשֵׁי טוֹב:

14:22 Those who devise evil will surely go astray, while those who devise good will have steadfast love and truth.

Wisdom literature is based on the assumption that proper behavior will bring about the desired results and improper behavior the opposite.

יד:כג בְּכָל-עֶצֶב יִהְיֶה מוֹתָר וּדְבַר-שְׂפָתַיִם אַךְ-לְמַחְסוֹר:

14:23 Whatever the toil, there is profit; from talk, there is only loss.

This is a surprising statement to be included in Proverbs. The commercial environment of the city is one of words. The author sees the city as a place where there is a lot of talking and rural areas as places of silence. He also sees speech as a vehicle that can take people to immoral behavior. Nevertheless, those who are engaged in physical labor are relegated to the bottom of the socioeconomic pyramid.

יד:כד עֲטֶרֶת חֲכָמִים עָשְׁרָם אִוֶּלֶת כְּסִילִים אִוֶּלֶת:

14:24 The crown of the wise is their wealth; the folly of fools is folly.

The tautology of the second clause is somewhat problematic. The *Targum* sought to set it up as a parallel to the first clause by translating it as ''the glory of the fools is their folly.'' Some scholars suggest that the text be emended (*ivelet* to *l'viat*) so that it can read ''the accompaniment of fools is folly.'' For Ibn Ezra, the verse teaches us that even if fools have wealth, they use it in a foolish way. Gersonides suggests that the folly of the foolish prevents them from learning what would deliver them from folly. Hence the folly of the fools remains folly.

יד:כה מַצִּיל נְפָשׁוֹת עֵד אֱמֶת וְיָפִחַ כְּזָבִים מִרְמָה:

14:25 A true witness saves lives; the one who exhales lies is deceit.

This is another problematic verse. The last clause here seems to need a word before ''deceit.'' The *Targum* translates the last clause as ''one who speaks falsehood is a deceitful person.'' Both Ibn Ezra and Gersonides add *ish* (man) before ''deceit'' and understand it as a ''person of deceit.''

יד:כו בְּיִרְאַת יְהֹוָה מִבְטַח־עֹז וּלְבָנָיו יִהְיֶה מַחְסֶה:

14:26 THERE IS CERTAIN STRENGTH IN THE FEAR OF GOD,
AND FOR ONE'S CHILDREN, IT IS A REFUGE.

Rashi applies this verse to Abraham the Patriarch, because the angel said to him,
"I know you fear God" (Genesis 22:12).

יד:כז יִרְאַת יְהֹוָה מְקוֹר חַיִּים לָסוּר מִמֹּקְשֵׁי מָוֶת:

14:27 THE FEAR OF GOD IS THE SOURCE OF LIFE, TO TURN
FROM THE SNARES OF DEATH.

For Gersonides, the philosopher, the fear of God is wisdom that, when attained, will
provide guidance. For Rabbinic Judaism, fear of God was translated into the laws and
rituals of Jewish observance.

יד:כח בְּרָב־עָם הַדְרַת־מֶלֶךְ וּבְאֶפֶס לְאֹם מְחִתַּת רָזוֹן:

14:28 A MULTITUDE OF PEOPLE IS THE GLORY OF THE
SOVEREIGN; THE RUIN OF A PRINCE IS THE LACK
OF PEOPLE.

What is suggested here is the relation of ruler to those who are ruled. If a ruler can
attract people, then he or she will be able to rule more easily. If that ruler is unable to
attract supporters, then he or she will be found in a precarious situation. Note the
difference between the sovereign and the prince. The prince who cannot attract
people will never become a sovereign ruler.

יד:כט אֶרֶךְ אַפַּיִם רַב־תְּבוּנָה וּקְצַר־רוּחַ מֵרִים אִוֶּלֶת:

14:29 ONE WHO IS SLOW TO ANGER HAS GREAT
UNDERSTANDING, BUT ONE WHO IS QUICK TO REACT
EXALTS FOLLY.

Throughout the Book of Proverbs, the importance of calm reflection is highlighted.
"Think before you act" is the implicit motto of the author. Gersonides takes the verse
to refer to the importance of prolonged investigation as the means of attaining
philosophical truth.

יד:ל חַיֵּי בְשָׂרִים לֵב מַרְפֵּא וּרְקַב עֲצָמוֹת קִנְאָה:

14:30 A HEALING HEART IS THE LIFE OF THE FLESH, BUT ENVY
IS THE ROTTENNESS OF THE BONES.

The *Targum* translates the verse as: "One who dissipates the anger of his heart is a
physician to his flesh, for as crumbling wood is envy in the bone." Ibn Ezra
understands the first clause to refer to a person who, by being calm, provides healing
for the body and the second clause to refer to the person who is zealous to do evil
and thus becomes "rottenness" to one's own bones.

יד:לא עֹשֵׁק־דָּל חֵרֵף עֹשֵׂהוּ וּמְכַבְּדוֹ חֹנֵן אֶבְיוֹן:

14:31 THE ONE WHO OPPRESSES THE POOR BLASPHEMES
ONE'S MAKER; THE ONE WHO IS GRACIOUS TO THE
NEEDY HONORS GOD.

The social concern manifest in this verse reflects the sentiment of the prophets who
decried those who ". . . sell the righteous for silver and the needy for a pair of shoes,
that pant after the dust of the earth and the head of the poor" (Amos 2:6–7). It may
be said that if the religious life is lived between God and one's fellow human being,
then that life is truly demonstrated in one's relation to those who can't do anything for
us, but who need us to do something for them. The author has already said it
previously, "The poor person is hated by one's neighbors, while the rich person has
many friends" (14:20). It is the weak who need justice. The strong can usually take
care of their own needs. It is the poor who are often oppressed, precisely because
they are already weak. The rich are rarely found in slums, except perhaps to collect
the rent.

יד:לב בְּרָעָתוֹ יִדָּחֶה רָשָׁע וְחֹסֶה בְמוֹתוֹ צַדִּיק:

14:32 IN EVIL, THE WICKED WILL BE CAST DOWN; EVEN AT
DEATH, THE RIGHTEOUS MAY TRUST.

If we understand the verse as it seems to be written, it reflects a belief in immortality
that is uncharacteristic of the period of time in which Proverbs was written. Thus,
some scholars suggest that by emending *v'moto* (literally, "in [at] his death") to *v'tumo*
(literally, "in his innocence"), it is possible to see an interesting contrast in the verse:
"In his evil, the wicked will be cast down; in his innocence, the righteous may trust."
Rashi follows rabbinic tradition, as would be expected, and takes the second clause to
mean that righteous people may be certain to enter paradise when they die.

יד:לג בְּלֵב נָבוֹן תָּנוּחַ חָכְמָה וּבְקֶרֶב כְּסִילִים תִּוָּדֵעַ:

14:33 WISDOM WILL REST IN THE MIND OF THE
UNDERSTANDING PERSON; IN THE INWARD PARTS
OF THE FOOL, IT MAY BE KNOWN.

It is not clear what the last word *tivadei-a* (may be known) means in the context of this verse. It may mean that wisdom is ultimately so pervasive that its effects can be discerned even among fools. In explaining the clause, Rashi quotes the talmudic proverb (*Bava M'tzia* 85b) "as a coin in a bottle makes a clinking sound, so an ignoramus boasts of the little knowledge that he [or she] has."

יד:לד צְדָקָה תְרוֹמֵם־גּוֹי וְחֶסֶד לְאֻמִּים חַטָּאת:

14:34 RIGHTEOUSNESS EXALTS A PEOPLE, BUT SIN IS A
SHAMEFUL THING FOR ANY PEOPLE.

This often quoted verse, albeit in a different form, contains a problem in translation. *Chesed* is a homonym with two totally different meanings. The most common meaning, found many times in the Bible, is "steadfast love." The other meaning, which seems to be in use here and in Leviticus 20:17, is "a shameful thing." The second form is found as a verb in Proverbs 25:10. Ibn Ezra takes the word to mean "steadfast love" and interprets the word *chatat* (sin) to mean (as it can) "sin offering." Thus, he explains that the acts of steadfast love that the nations perform are considered by God as a "sin offering."

יד:לה רְצוֹן־מֶלֶךְ לְעֶבֶד מַשְׂכִּיל וְעֶבְרָתוֹ תִּהְיֶה מֵבִישׁ:

14:35 A RULER'S FAVOR IS FOR THE INTELLIGENT SERVANT;
THE SOVEREIGN'S WRATH IS FOR THE ONE WHO
BRINGS SHAME.

The verse seems to express a truism. Still, the burden of the book is directed toward compelling individuals to act intelligently. Acting in such a manner that will cause shame to others is condemned.

The Social Conscience of the Prophets

The Hebrew prophets generally prophesied against Israel, challenging them to do right so that they would not be punished (or even destroyed) by God. Thus, they became the conscience of the Jewish people. The Reform Movement took its direction (in the form of ethical monotheism) from the teachings of the Hebrew prophets and developed a program of social activism as its hallmark.

Immortality in the Bible

Though there is no clear doctrine of immortality in the Bible, there are hints of a belief that somehow, at least for some, life transcends physical death. An example of such a belief is the story of Saul, Samuel, and the witch of En-dor (I Samuel 28:17). As modern readers, we see another example of immortality in the connection of one generation to another. For example, Abraham and Sarah lived on through Isaac, who with Rebekah lived on through Jacob. However, it was the rabbinic tradition that introduced the ideas of immortality of the soul to Jewish religion. As a result, the rabbinic read of the Bible includes the notion of immortality of the soul.

GLEANINGS

Saving the World One Soul at a Time

It's always so much easier to save the world. It's easier to sign a petition for a nuclear freeze than it is to quit smoking cigarettes, though both are matters of survival. It's easier to demand justice for all than it is to deal justly with those who stand near. It's easier to vote for a resolution on Ethiopia than it is to give succor to a neighbor who is out of work and out of hope and who despairs that there is anyone who gives a damn for him.

Thus does the *Mishnah* remind us: Save the single soul, and you will save the universe.

Alexander M. Schindler, "Report to the UAHC Board of Trustees, Bal Harbor, Florida,
November 30, 1984," as reprinted in *The Jewish Condition: Essays on Contemporary Judaism
for Rabbi Alexander M. Schindler,* ed. Aron Hirt-Manheimer (New York: UAHC Press, 1995), 134

Successful Charity

Jewish law instructs us that a successful charity drive is not, as is so often the case today, simply determined by the amount raised or the percentage gained over previous efforts. Not only recipients, but potential donors as well may require our attention. The fund administrators must exercise their Jewish hearts and heads to protect manic types from giving away so much that they soon need charity themselves. When we know that someone of means has fallen upon hard times, we must, most gingerly, preserve their dignity. Giving *tzedakah* may be structured by Jewish law, but we must never forget that it operates as an instrument of Jewish compassion.

Eugene B. Borowitz and Francine Weinman Schwartz, *The Jewish Moral Virtues*
(Philadelphia: Jewish Publication Society, 1999), 132

CHAPTER FIFTEEN

טו:א מַעֲנֶה־רַּךְ יָשִׁיב חֵמָה וּדְבַר־עֶצֶב יַעֲלֶה־אָף:

15:1 A SOFT ANSWER REMOVES RAGE, WHILE A HURTFUL
WORD INCREASES IRE.

The writer seems to speak from personal experience while offering a prescription for behavior: Watch what you say, and be careful whom you offend.

טו:ב לְשׁוֹן חֲכָמִים תֵּיטִיב דָּעַת וּפִי כְסִילִים יַבִּיעַ אִוֶּלֶת:

15:2 THE MOUTH OF THE WISE IMPROVES KNOWLEDGE, BUT
THE MOUTH OF FOOLS EXPRESSES FOLLY.

According to Ibn Ezra, the tongue of the wise corrects the information received so that it truly becomes knowledge. According to Gersonides, the speech of the wise improves the knowledge of those who listen to them by correcting their ideas.

טו:ג בְּכָל־מָקוֹם עֵינֵי יְהוָה צֹפוֹת רָעִים וְטוֹבִים:

15:3 THE EYES OF GOD ARE EVERYWHERE, OBSERVING THE
EVIL AND THE GOOD.

Since God sees all and knows all, there will be an outcome of all human actions. Those who do well will be rewarded. Those who do ill will be punished. This statement of piety had to be added to a book that prescribes prudential morality so that its author could not be accused of ignoring morality whose source is divine.

טו:ד מַרְפֵּא לָשׁוֹן עֵץ חַיִּים וְסֶלֶף בָּהּ שֶׁבֶר בְּרוּחַ:

15:4 A HEALING TONGUE IS A TREE OF LIFE, BUT PERFIDY IS
A BREACH OF SPIRIT.

Speech has an effect on others and on the self. Kindness and truth extend life. Cruelty and lies mar life.

טו:ה אֱוִיל יִנְאַץ מוּסַר אָבִיו וְשֹׁמֵר תּוֹכַחַת יַעְרִם:

15:5 A FOOL SPURNS A PARENT'S DISCIPLINE, BUT THE ONE
WHO KEEPS REPROOF IN MIND WILL BECOME CLEVER.

The verse is directed to a young person who wants to take on the mantle of
leadership. That person is to gain direction from both parent and teacher. From the
former, one receives discipline. From the latter, one receives instruction. Both require
the young person to absorb what they are teaching. Self-control comes from the
direction of the parent. The acquisition of knowledge comes from the teacher. Such
acquisition requires effort. The person who cannot exert self-control will never be
able to take on the difficulties entailed by study. The person who refuses to accept
criticism will never be able to master the truth.

טו:ו בֵּית צַדִּיק חֹסֶן רָב וּבִתְבוּאַת רָשָׁע נֶעְכָּרֶת:

15:6 THERE IS MUCH TREASURE IN THE HOUSE OF THE
RIGHTEOUS, BUT THE PRODUCE OF THE WICKED IS
TROUBLED.

Rashi applies the first clause to the Temple that David wanted to build. Gersonides,
who understands *tzaddik* as "correct" as well as "righteous," reads this to mean that
"the house of the righteous is doubly strong because of its intrinsic strength and
because of God's providence on it."

טו:ז שִׂפְתֵי חֲכָמִים יְזָרוּ דָעַת וְלֵב כְּסִילִים לֹא־כֵן:

15:7 THE LIPS OF THE WISE DISPENSE KNOWLEDGE—NOT SO
THE MIND OF FOOLS.

The difficulty of understanding this verse is found in the last word *kein*. It may mean
upright and steadfast, as it does in Genesis 42:11, or it could simply mean "yes."
Hence, the last phrase may mean "not so the mind of fools" or "the mind of fools is
not upright/steadfast." Rashi's comment on this verse indicates that he took *kein* to
mean "upright." However, Ibn Ezra, who suggests that "the fools did not know how
to dispense knowledge," takes the word to mean "yes."

טו:ח זֶבַח רְשָׁעִים תּוֹעֲבַת יְהוָה וּתְפִלַּת יְשָׁרִים רְצוֹנוֹ:

15:8 THE SACRIFICE OF THE WICKED IS AN ABOMINATION TO
GOD, WHILE THE PRAYER OF THE UPRIGHT [FINDS]
GOD'S FAVOR.

Rashi applies the first clause to the offerings of Balaam and Balak and the second
clause to Moses. Implicit in this verse is the prophetic notion that ritual observance

does not offset ethical misconduct. As Isaiah put it, "'To what purpose is the multitude of your sacrifices to Me?' God says. 'I am full of the burnt offerings of rams.... Cease to do evil. Learn to do well. Seek judgment. Relieve the oppressed. Judge the orphan. Plead for the widow'" (Isaiah 1:11, 16–17). The mention of prayer rather than sacrifice in the second clause suggests a development in the spiritual history of Israel even within the context of the Book of Proverbs.

טו:ט תּוֹעֲבַת יְהוָה דֶּרֶךְ רָשָׁע וּמְרַדֵּף צְדָקָה יֶאֱהָב:

15:9 THE WAY OF THE WICKED IS AN ABOMINATION FOR GOD, BUT GOD LOVES THE ONE WHO PURSUES RIGHTEOUSNESS.

The fulfillment of the goal of righteousness continues to elude us. For Gersonides, the wicked combine erroneous views and vicious acts, while the righteous combine correct views and ethical acts.

טו:י מוּסָר רָע לְעֹזֵב אֹרַח שׂוֹנֵא תוֹכַחַת יָמוּת:

15:10 FOR THE ONE WHO LEAVES THE COURSE THERE WILL BE TERRIBLE PUNISHMENT; THE ONE WHO HATES REPROACH WILL DIE.

The word *musar* (discipline) comes from the root *yasar* (to punish, to cause pain). The *Targum*, therefore, translates the word as *marduta* (chastisement, punishment). Taking his cue from the *Targum*, Rashi understands the first clause to mean that terrible suffering will be prepared for the one who leaves the course of behavior directed by God. Gersonides takes the last clause to mean that the person who will not accept reproof will die in an evil state.

טו:יא שְׁאוֹל וַאֲבַדּוֹן נֶגֶד יְהוָה אַף כִּי־לִבּוֹת בְּנֵי־אָדָם:

15:11 HELL AND DESTRUCTION ARE BEFORE GOD; SURELY SO ARE THE MINDS OF HUMAN BEINGS.

For the biblical writer, *Sheol* (hell) was a real place, although it was hidden from sight. For us, "minds" are real, although they may not be visible. For the writer of Proverbs, God can see what we cannot. This notion is included in Proverbs, whose main emphasis is on prudential wisdom, for a practical reason: if a rational argument will not bring you to do the right thing, then the threat of punishment surely will.

טו:יב לֹא יֶאֱהַב־לֵץ הוֹכֵחַ לוֹ אֶל־חֲכָמִים לֹא יֵלֵךְ:

15:12 A SCOFFER DOES NOT LOVE THE ONE WHO REPROVES
HIM [OR HER]; HE [OR SHE] WILL NOT GO TO THE WISE.

Although reproof is a means of moral improvement, the one who mocks morality will
see reproof as interference. To accept reproof is to accept a universe of ethical
discourse in which certain things are right and other things are wrong. Someone who
does not accept such a worldview will simply see reproof as unwarranted
interference. Since "the wise" who are described in this book are involved with
ethical deliberations, they would not be the people to whom a scoffer would go.

טו:יג לֵב שָׂמֵחַ יֵיטִב פָּנִים וּבְעַצְּבַת־לֵב רוּחַ נְכֵאָה:

15:13 A HAPPY MIND MAKES A CHEERFUL FACE, WHILE THE
SPIRIT IS BROKEN BY A TROUBLED MIND.

Rashi understands the verse to relate to God in an anthropopathic manner: If you
follow God's ways, you will make God rejoice. God's cheerful countenance will do
you good and fulfill all your wants. If you cause God pain, then God will manifest an
angry spirit against you. For Gersonides, "a happy mind" will produce good results in
philosophical investigation. This verse may arise out of an understanding of how
people feel rather than encouraging them to do something. After all, one cannot be
directed to have a "happy mind" or a "troubled mind."

טו:יד לֵב נָבוֹן יְבַקֶּשׁ־דָּעַת ופני וּפִי כְסִילִים יִרְעֶה אִוֶּלֶת:

15:14 A DISCERNING MIND SEEKS KNOWLEDGE, BUT THE
MOUTH OF A FOOL FEEDS ON FOLLY.

The difference between the intelligent person and the fool rests in their attitude
toward knowledge. The intelligent person wants to gain more and more; the fool does
not care. Knowledge takes time to acquire. As Maimonides pointed out, if you were to
ask a person whether she or he wants to know the origins and configurations of the
universe and the nature of the human soul, she or he would want to know, but if you
told the person it would take a week to learn these things, "... the person would not
do it but would be satisfied with deceptive imaginings" (*Guide for the Perplexed* 1:34).

טו:טו כָּל־יְמֵי עָנִי רָעִים וְטוֹב־לֵב מִשְׁתֶּה תָמִיד:

15:15 ALL THE DAYS OF THE POOR ARE BAD, WHILE THOSE
WHO HAVE A CONSTANT FEAST HAVE A HAPPY MIND.

Rashi interprets this verse, which describes the situation of the poor and the rich,
as follows: The poor suffer on the Sabbath and the Festivals (hence, "all the days");
the rich are happy because of their wealth. Judaism has never romanticized poverty.

Mishlei: A Modern Commentary on Proverbs

Gersonides understands "the poor" to be those poor in philosophical ideas. For him, the person who has a good intellect rejoices every day as if that person were at a constant banquet.

טו:טז טוֹב־מְעַט בְּיִרְאַת יְהוָה מֵאוֹצָר רָב וּמְהוּמָה בוֹ:

15:16 BETTER A LITTLE WITH THE FEAR OF GOD THAN GREAT TREASURE WITH CONSTERNATION.

Gersonides explains that it is better to have less money acquired with "fear of God," that is, in a decent manner, than great wealth acquired through the oppression of others.

טו:יז טוֹב אֲרֻחַת יָרָק וְאַהֲבָה־שָׁם מִשּׁוֹר אָבוּס וְשִׂנְאָה־בוֹ:

15:17 BETTER A DINNER OF VEGETABLES WHERE THERE IS LOVE THAN A FATTENED OX WITH HATRED.

This verse does not speak to the merits of being a vegetarian. A meat meal is more expensive than a meal of vegetables. Gersonides applies this verse to a matter of domestic relations, arguing that it is better to have a meal of vegetables with a spouse where there is love than a meal of rich meat with a spouse where there is enmity.

טו:יח אִישׁ חֵמָה יְגָרֶה מָדוֹן וְאֶרֶךְ אַפַּיִם יַשְׁקִיט רִיב:

15:18 A HOTHEAD PICKS A FIGHT, BUT A PATIENT PERSON QUIETS A QUARREL.

Rashi explains *ish cheimah* (literally, "a master/person with heat") as one whose rage cannot be suppressed. Gersonides translates the term as *kaasan* (an angry person). Both see such a person as an explosion about to happen, requiring little detonation.

טו:יט דֶּרֶךְ עָצֵל כִּמְשֻׂכַת חָדֶק וְאֹרַח יְשָׁרִים סְלֻלָה:

15:19 THE LAZY PERSON'S PATH IS HEDGED WITH THORNS, BUT THE PROPER PERSON'S COURSE IS SMOOTHED DOWN.

If the "hothead" mentioned in the previous verse was ready to act without thinking, the slothful person is unable to act, no matter how much thinking takes place. Wherever such a person looks, problems are seen. This person can't move because he or she feels fenced in. The "proper person" (one of the *y'sharim*, "upright") is able to move in any direction. That's why that person's course is "smoothed down." This word (*salal*) is used with the same meaning in Isaiah 57:14 and Jeremiah 18:15 and is used to mean "pave" in contemporary Hebrew.

150

טו:כ בֵּן חָכָם יְשַׂמַּח־אָב וּכְסִיל אָדָם בּוֹזֶה אִמּוֹ:

15:20 A WISE CHILD MAKES A FATHER HAPPY, BUT A FOOLISH
PERSON DESPISES ONE'S MOTHER.

Rashi understands the last clause to mean that a fool will cause other people to despise the fool's own parents. This is probably an allusion to the rabbinic statement applied to Esau, that people looking at the fool would say, "Cursed be the breasts that suckled this wicked person" (*Tanchuma, Ki Teiztei* 4).

טו:כא אִוֶּלֶת שִׂמְחָה לַחֲסַר־לֵב וְאִישׁ תְּבוּנָה יְיַשֶּׁר־לָכֶת:

15:21 FOLLY IS FUN FOR ONE WHO LACKS SENSE; AN
UNDERSTANDING PERSON MOVES PROPERLY.

The author again makes the contrast between intelligent and foolish people and between appropriate and foolish behavior. Gersonides understands this verse in a philosophic manner: The person who lacks understanding foolishly rejoices in the pursuit of erroneous arguments. The person who has understanding and discernment pursues a goal using proper reasoning.

טו:כב הָפֵר מַחֲשָׁבוֹת בְּאֵין סוֹד וּבְרֹב יוֹעֲצִים תָּקוּם:

15:22 PLANS ARE RUINED WITHOUT COUNSEL, BUT THEY
ARE ESTABLISHED WITH MANY ADVISORS.

Sod, used here to mean "counsel," usually has the meaning of "secret." Although both Rashi and Ibn Ezra translate the word as "counsel," "secret" may also fit, since (military and civilian) plans will not be easily put into operation once they are broadcast. However, if we take the word to mean "counsel," then the author intends to remind us that there is a practical consequence to wisdom: to develop long-term goals, the input of many people is necessary. This is a particularly important lesson for those who strive to be advisors in control of society—the intended readership of this book.

טו:כג שִׂמְחָה לָאִישׁ בְּמַעֲנֵה־פִיו וְדָבָר בְּעִתּוֹ מַה־טּוֹב:

15:23 MAY A PERSON HAVE JOY BECAUSE OF WHAT THE
MOUTH SAYS; HOW GOOD IS A WORD AT THE RIGHT
MOMENT.

This verse may be understood in both a general and particular way. Speech and the ability to communicate make us human. What is important is how we use the gift of speech—to help or to cause hurt. Moreover, learning how and when to speak is extremely important for those who seek roles in government.

טו:כד אֹרַח חַיִּים לְמַעְלָה לְמַשְׂכִּיל לְמַעַן סוּר מִשְׁאוֹל מָטָּה:

15:24 THE COURSE OF LIFE GOES UPWARD FOR THE INTELLIGENT, SO THAT A PERSON MAY TURN FROM HELL BELOW.

Upon reading this verse, Rashi calls our attention to the seraphim who stood above Isaiah in his prophetic vision (Isaiah 6:2). Ibn Ezra suggests that the intelligent seek to do the will of the Creator. Gersonides relates the verse to apprehension: the more profound notion is achieved by the more profound thinker. We have translated *Sheol* (sometimes called "the pit" or "netherworld") as "hell"; in the biblical period the term did not designate what would later be attributed to the same word. However, it is clear that the Book of Proverbs includes some notion of torment after death. It could be argued that the idea of a "netherworld" is an incipient concept of hell, particularly when the context of this verse suggests *Sheol* as a place of torment and judgment.

טו:כה בֵּית גֵּאִים יִסַּח יְהֹוָה וְיַצֵּב גְּבוּל אַלְמָנָה:

15:25 GOD WILL DEMOLISH THE HOUSE OF THE HAUGHTY BUT WILL ESTABLISH A BOUNDARY FOR THE WIDOW.

Lacking the support of family, the widow was a target for land encroachment. Here, the writer promises her divine assistance. The depravation of the powerless by the powerful in the economic order was also the target of prophetic denunciation. The prophet Isaiah castigated those who "join house to house, that lay field to field till there be no place" (Isaiah 5:8). Micah complained of those who ". . . covet fields and take them away by violence; and houses and take them away" (Micah 2:2).

טו:כו תּוֹעֲבַת יְהֹוָה מַחְשְׁבוֹת רָע וּטְהֹרִים אִמְרֵי־נֹעַם:

15:26 EVIL THOUGHTS ARE AN ABOMINATION TO GOD, WHILE PLEASANT WORDS ARE PURE.

The Hebrew here is deceptively difficult to translate. One has to determine what is the subject of the second clause and its meaning and which words contrast with other words. Should the clause be translated as "pure [thoughts] are pleasant" or should it be translated as "pleasant words are a pure setting"? The *Targum*'s translation of this clause suggests the latter translation. Ibn Ezra understands "pure" as unadulterated, like "pure silver," which is free from dregs.

טו:כז עֹכֵר בֵּיתוֹ בּוֹצֵעַ בָּצַע וְשׂוֹנֵא מַתָּנֹת יִחְיֶה:

15:27 THE GETTER OF GAIN TROUBLES ONE'S OWN HOUSE,
BUT THE ONE WHO HATES GIFTS WILL LIVE.

The *Targum* translates the beginning of this phrase as *m'chaneish mammon dish'kar,* "brings in money acquired by falsehood," perhaps following the usage of the idiom *botzei-a batza* (getter of gain) in Jeremiah (6:13; 8:10). Ibn Ezra interprets the verse as "one who steals." The author of Proverbs used the phrase in a negative sense in 1:19. It may be argued that aspirants to the corridors of power—the target readership of this book—should not be known as being only interested in monetary gain.

טו:כח לֵב צַדִּיק יֶהְגֶּה לַעֲנוֹת וּפִי רְשָׁעִים יַבִּיעַ רָעוֹת:

15:28 THE MIND OF THE RIGHTEOUS REFLECTS BEFORE
ANSWERING, BUT THE MOUTH OF THE WICKED
GUSHES OUT EVIL.

The translation of the first clause reflects the views of Rashi and Ibn Ezra. Again the author emphasizes the contrast between silent reflection and mindless speech. Gersonides sees the difference between the righteous and the wicked in terms of their approach toward their goals. The righteous are always interested in what is beneficial. The wicked are solely interested in what is malicious.

טו:כט רָחוֹק יְהוָֹה מֵרְשָׁעִים וּתְפִלַּת צַדִּיקִים יִשְׁמָע:

15:29 GOD IS FAR FROM THE WICKED BUT HEARS THE PRAYER
OF THE RIGHTEOUS.

In the midst of guidance on practical wisdom, the author offers a statement of piety. Even Maimonides, in his *Guide for the Perplexed* (3:28), reminds us that God's hearing the prayer of the righteous is a "necessary belief." Nevertheless, Gersonides suggests that the statement refers to the divine aid that will be received by the righteous, and not the wicked.

טו:ל מְאוֹר־עֵינַיִם יְשַׂמַּח־לֵב שְׁמוּעָה טוֹבָה תְּדַשֶּׁן־עָצֶם:

15:30 THE LIGHT OF THE EYES MAKES THE MIND HAPPY;
A GOOD REPORT MAKES THE BONES FAT.

For Rashi, "the light of the eyes" is the light of Torah. The mind is happy because students of Torah know how to answer the questions put before them. Gersonides takes the phrase somewhat differently. He suggests that "the light of the eyes" refers to the mind, which makes the intellect happy when apprehending philosophical notions. The "bones" refers to the body, which is able to rejoice on its own more physical level. Gersonides' comment is reminiscent of Maimonides' presentation of two perfections: intellect and body. The intellect is perfected by intellectual notions (the truth as far as it can be apprehended). The body is perfected by being in the best possible physical shape. The contrast between the views of Rashi and Gersonides reflects the different lenses through which this book is read.

טו:לא אֹזֶן שֹׁמַעַת תּוֹכַחַת חַיִּים בְּקֶרֶב חֲכָמִים תָּלִין:

15:31 THE EAR THAT LISTENS TO THE REPROACH OF LIFE WILL ABIDE AMONG THE WISE.

More requirements for the wise, worded only slightly differently, repeated for emphasis. If you don't listen to criticism, you will be unable to learn and grow. Gersonides makes it clear that one acquires wisdom through life. However, as discussed previously, what he means by wisdom is far different than what is meant by Rashi.

טו:לב פּוֹרֵעַ מוּסָר מוֹאֵס נַפְשׁוֹ וְשׁוֹמֵעַ תּוֹכַחַת קוֹנֶה לֵּב:

15:32 THE ONE WHO DISREGARDS DISCIPLINE IS SELF-HATING, BUT THE ONE WHO LISTENS TO REPROACH GAINS SENSE.

On the basis of the *Targum*'s translation of *lev* (heart, mind) as *chochmah* (wisdom), we have translated the word as "sense" (*seichel*, in contemporary jargon). The author repeats what was said previously: for the one who seeks to become wise, self-control is important, as is the ability to accept and act on criticism.

טו:לג יִרְאַת יְהוָה מוּסַר חָכְמָה וְלִפְנֵי כָבוֹד עֲנָוָה:

15:33 FEAR OF GOD IS THE DISCIPLINE OF WISDOM; HUMILITY COMES BEFORE HONOR.

The writer presents a lesson in spiritual logic: to gain, one must give. To gain wisdom, one must voluntarily place oneself within a covenantal relationship with God. In doing so, one obligates oneself to perform mitzvot and live a Jewish life, what is referred to as "fear of God." To gain honor from others, one must diminish oneself.

Maimonides on Perfection of the Intellect and the Body

As a philosopher and physician, Maimonides urged the perfection of the mind and the care of the body. Both are indispensable for community leadership. In the *Guide for the Perplexed* (3:27), Maimonides speaks of these two kinds of perfections: body and soul. The perfection of the body is beyond physical appearance and age. However, without it, the perfection of the soul, which is ultimate, cannot be achieved. The perfection of the body, that is, being healthy and in the best physical shape, requires other people, for no individual alone can obtain food, shelter, and even the bathing that is necessary for bodily perfection. Quoting Aristotle (*Politics*, 1:2), "man is political by nature," Maimonides suggests that the perfection of the body requires the perfection of the body politic. Perfection of the body politic requires the ordering of the affairs of society so that individuals can aid one another and avoid hurting each other.

The ultimate perfection of the soul is achieved entirely by intellectual means, as Maimoides puts it:

> It is clear that to this ultimate perfection there do not belong either actions or moral qualities and that it consists only of opinions toward which speculation has led and that investigation has rendered compulsory. (*Guide for the Perplexed* 3:27)

Poverty and Wealth

Judaism neither celebrates poverty nor condemns wealth. However, Judaism does advocate the responsibility of the wealthy to the poor, to express gratitude to God for what we have by sharing it with others who do not. This is the essence of *tzedakah*.

GLEANINGS

Maimonides on the Intellect

Maimonides wants us to think about the commandments as laws we ourselves deeply want. He recognizes that at first a person may not feel this way. To a child just beginning to learn Jewish law, the commandments may seem like a set of needless restrictions, yet a child's immediate intuitions do not reflect the deepest longings of the human soul. Contrary to what popular culture would have us believe, it may require effort, study, patience to determine what the writing on our heart actually says. Maimonides' position is that if we make this effort, if we knew what the perfection of the human soul consisted of, we would see no real conflict between God's will and our own. We would obey the commandments freely, knowingly, and with conviction. Far from surrendering anything, we would be acting in full possession of our best faculties. We would accept the true opinions inculcated by the Torah, not on faith, but after a long and careful examination of the issues. Then and only then could we say that we really love God. To talk this way is to talk about an ideal of human behavior that few of us realize, because the rational appropriation of the commandments involves nothing less than a complete transformation of the soul. . . .

Kenneth Seeskin, *Maimonides: A Guide for Today's Perplexed*
(West Orange, N.J.: Behrman House, 1991), 95–96

Discovering the Commandments

The event at Sinai places me here today. I believe that the Torah is a record of the response to that event whose precise nature is not clear to me from the texts. It is clear that it had an irrevocable impact upon a people for several thousands of years. I, as a member of that people, am affected by, and thus ultimately am a participant in, the event. The acceptance of the commandments was the response of the people at that time. Insofar as I wish to participate in and personally recover the event, I find that I must participate in the commandments. Insofar as there is a lack of clarity about the events, there is also a lack of clarity about the commandments. The 613 commandments are a test number, an entrance requirement to the club of the "authentic." They are a way of asking whether one accepts normative Orthodoxy. I can only understand them as a theoretical dogma. As a theoretical system I can accept them. I can hold that the totality of the law is binding upon me as well as upon all other Jews, but I am not willing to claim clear divine authority for any given one of them. There is a serious disagreement even among the great codifiers like Maimonides and Nachmanides as to which the 613 commandments are. I can accept the idea of the Law and its general structure. I am not certain about the authority of its particulars. There is a revelation, but its full content is not always obvious. There are commandments, but I must struggle to discover them. . . .

Some, whether in the ethical or ritual realm, are rare opportunities to be passed by only at my own deep personal loss. Rabbi [Menachem] Mendel of Kotzk once said, "I don't want you to sin, not because it is wrong, but because there isn't enough time."

Richard J. Israel, *The Condition of Jewish Belief: A Symposium Compiled by the Editors of "Commentary" Magazine* (Northvale, N.J.: Jason Aronson, 1989), 98–99

CHAPTER SIXTEEN

טז:א לְאָדָם מַעַרְכֵי־לֵב וּמֵיְהֹוָה מַעֲנֵה לָשׁוֹן:

16:1 THE DISPOSITIONS OF THE MIND ARE FROM HUMANS,
BUT THE UTTERANCE OF THE TONGUE IS FROM GOD.

Rashi, Ibn Ezra, and Gersonides all take this verse to mean that an individual is able to think but requires divine assistance in properly expressing those thoughts. This verse can also be understood in terms of human planning and divine action in much the same way as the Yiddish folk saying *Mann tracht und Gott lacht* (humans plan and God laughs) or the English expression "Man proposes and God disposes." Regardless of the creative spin on the verse, the author's point is clear: Humans are not as much in control as they think they are. There are plans for the universe much greater than our own.

טז:ב כָּל־דַּרְכֵי־אִישׁ זַךְ בְּעֵינָיו וְתֹכֵן רוּחוֹת יְהֹוָה:

16:2 THE WAYS OF A PERSON ARE PURE IN ONE'S OWN SIGHT,
BUT GOD WEIGHS SPIRITS.

Self-deception is a given. Each person seeks to justify his or her actions. The very idea of the existence of God suggests that there is a value by which individuals can judge—and not merely justify—their actions.

טז:ג גֹּל אֶל־יְהֹוָה מַעֲשֶׂיךָ וְיִכֹּנוּ מַחְשְׁבֹתֶיךָ:

16:3 REVEAL YOUR ACTS TO GOD SO THAT YOUR THOUGHTS
CAN BE MADE REAL.

This advice is offered as a result of the implicit theology of the previous verse. The translation of the first word, *gol*, follows the *Targum*'s translation of the word as coming from *galah* (reveal) rather than from the root *galal* (roll). Ibn Ezra suggests that we should make our ways known to God. The message of the verse is: Before doing anything, think: How would this plan of action be weighed in the divine balance?

טז:ד כֹּל פָּעַל יְהֹוָה לַמַּעֲנֵהוּ וְגַם־רָשָׁע לְיוֹם רָעָה:

16:4 EVERYTHING THAT GOD MADE IS FOR A DIVINE
PURPOSE, EVEN THE WICKED FOR AN EVIL DAY.

Although Rashi understands *lamaaneihu* as "for God's sake," Gersonides follows
Maimonides' view of the verse (as disclosed in the *Guide for the Perplexed* 3:13),
taking it to mean "for its sake, that is, for a particular purpose or benefit." Such an
understanding better links the first part of the verse to the second to read, "Everything
that God made has its purpose: an evil day is made for the wicked."

טז:ה תּוֹעֲבַת יְהֹוָה כָּל־גְּבַהּ־לֵב יָד לְיָד־לֹא יִנָּקֶה:

16:5 AN ARROGANT PERSON IS AN ABOMINATION TO GOD;
HAND TO HAND, THAT PERSON WILL NOT BE BLAMELESS.

G'vah lev (literally, "lifted up of heart/mind") is translated as "an arrogant person."
The first clause reminds us of 11:20, and the second clause parallels the first clause of
11:21. Both here and in 11:21, *yad l'yad* (hand to hand) suggests some kind of
oath or, at the very least, serves as an emphatic (indeed!). Ibn Ezra understands the
phrase to mean that the hand of God will punish the hand of the person who
oppressed others.

טז:ו בְּחֶסֶד וֶאֱמֶת יְכֻפַּר עָוֹן וּבְיִרְאַת יְהֹוָה סוּר מֵרָע:

16:6 GUILT MAY BE ATONED BY STEADFAST LOVE AND
TRUTH; TURNING AWAY FROM EVIL IS BY THE FEAR
OF GOD.

Chesed ve-emet ("steadfast love and truth," or "true, abiding love") suggests the
performance of acts of the highest level of disinterested piety. The Sages taught that
bringing the dead to burial was such an act, since the kindness could not be repaid by
the deceased (*B'reishit Rabbah* 96:5). There seems to be a further lesson: restitution
for a wrong act and the removal of the attendant guilt are best accomplished by doing
something that is truly good.

טז:ז בִּרְצוֹת יְהֹוָה דַּרְכֵי־אִישׁ גַּם־אוֹיְבָיו יַשְׁלִם אִתּוֹ:

16:7 WHEN A PERSON'S WAYS PLEASE GOD, EVEN THE
PERSON'S ENEMIES WILL MAKE PEACE WITH HIM
[OR HER].

This verse reflects the same sentiment as the previous verse. Both Rashi and Ibn Ezra
take the subject of *yashlim* (will make peace) as God. Gersonides explains that God
will remove evil qualities from that person and in that manner will cause the person's

enemies to make peace with him or her. The use of a singular verb with a plural noun suggests that the subject of *yashlim* is "one's enemies."

טז:ח טוב־מְעַט בִּצְדָקָה מֵרֹב תְּבוּאוֹת בְּלֹא מִשְׁפָּט:

16:8 BETTER A LITTLE WITH RIGHTEOUSNESS THAN GREAT INCOME WITHOUT JUSTICE.

This verse reflects the same sentiments as 15:16. Gersonides specifies "without justice" as meaning "by theft and robbery." *Mishpat* suggests "law" as well as "justice." *B'lo mishpat* may mean "outside of the law" (illegally).

טז:ט לֵב אָדָם יְחַשֵּׁב דַּרְכּוֹ וַיהֹוָה יָכִין צַעֲדוֹ:

16:9 A PERSON'S MIND CALCULATES ONE'S PATH, AND GOD PREPARES ONE'S STEPS.

This translation follows the view of Gersonides, who explains that while a person must plan on the best means to achieve a goal, moving the plan from an idea to action requires divine assistance. As it stands, the verse suggests that prior planning is the way to gain divine assistance.

טז:י קֶסֶם עַל־שִׂפְתֵי־מֶלֶךְ בְּמִשְׁפָּט לֹא יִמְעַל־פִּיו:

16:10 DIVINATION RESTS ON THE SOVEREIGN'S LIPS; THE RULER'S MOUTH DOES NOT ACT IN JUDGMENT.

The context of this verse makes it a difficult one. In the Torah, Balaam says, "Lo, there is no augury in Jacob, no divining [*kesem*] in Israel" (Numbers 23:23). Since the writer uses the word *kesem* in this verse, it would appear that there is *kesem* in Israel. In order to resolve a possible contradiction, Rashi applies the first clause to a scholar (and not a king!) sitting in judgment. Ibn Ezra makes the connection of *kesem* to astrology.

טז:יא פֶּלֶס וּמֹאזְנֵי מִשְׁפָּט לַיהֹוָה מַעֲשֵׂהוּ כָּל־אַבְנֵי־כִיס:

16:11 BALANCE AND SCALES OF JUSTICE BELONG TO GOD; ALL THE WEIGHTS IN THE BAG ARE GOD'S WORK.

Some would emend this verse by omitting *mishpat* (justice) and adding its *mem* to the previous word, forming *moznayim* (scales), so that the first clause would read: "Balance and scales belong to God." This would make the verse an exhortation to have just balances, as commanded in Leviticus, "You shall not falsify measures of length, weight, or capacity. You shall have an honest balance, honest weights..." (Leviticus 19:35–36). Taking the verse as it stands, Rashi refers the first clause to divine justice (he uses the Old French word *justicia*), which requites a person according to his or her deeds. It is not clear why this verse was placed between the previous verse and the one that follows.

טז:יב תּוֹעֲבַת מְלָכִים עֲשׂוֹת רֶשַׁע כִּי בִצְדָקָה יִכּוֹן כִּסֵּא:

16:12 ACTING WICKEDLY IS AN ABOMINATION FOR SOVEREIGNS; BY RIGHTEOUSNESS SHOULD THE THRONE BE ESTABLISHED.

The notion of a "righteous sovereign" rests in the realm of theory. In reality, sovereign rulers act as they want. That is by definition what makes them sovereign. "Acting wickedly" may be a matter of perspective. Perhaps a more honest statement would be: "Acting wickedly is the custom of sovereigns, would that any throne (any throne!) be established by righteousness!" Gersonides takes the aforementioned "sovereigns" to refer to the human intellect. For him, it is reprehensible that the intellect should act incorrectly or badly in relation to ideas or actions.

טז:יג רְצוֹן מְלָכִים שִׂפְתֵי־צֶדֶק וְדֹבֵר יְשָׁרִים יֶאֱהָב:

16:13 LIPS SPEAKING HONESTLY FIND THE FAVOR OF SOVEREIGNS; THEY LOVE THOSE WHO SPEAK UPRIGHTLY.

Continuing in his view of "sovereigns" as the human intellect, Gersonides explains that "lips" refers to the various sciences required to discover philosophical truth. Taken in its plain meaning, this verse presents an idealistic view of royalty. The next verse appears to be much more realistic.

טז:יד חֲמַת־מֶלֶךְ מַלְאֲכֵי־מָוֶת וְאִישׁ חָכָם יְכַפְּרֶנָּה:

16:14 A SOVEREIGN'S RAGE IS A MESSENGER OF DEATH, BUT A WISE PERSON WILL KNOW HOW TO ASSUAGE IT.

While "sovereign's rage" is in the singular, "messenger of death" is in the plural. Thus, we have translated it in the singular. *Y'chaprenah* (assuage) comes from the basic root *kafar* (to cover with pitch, to hide). *Kofer* is a derived term that means "ransom," that is, the covering over of an action deemed bad by a payment of money. It then comes to mean "remove" or "assuage." Only later does it gain the meaning of "atone for." As is attested by the story of King David's final days (I Kings 2:8) when David told Solomon that he should kill Shimei, to whom he had promised safety, the suppressed rage of a king can send a deferred messenger of death. The simple meaning of the verse presents a realistic view of royal displeasure.

טז:טו בְּאוֹר־פְּנֵי־מֶלֶךְ חַיִּים וּרְצוֹנוֹ כְּעָב מַלְקוֹשׁ:

16:15 LIFE IS IN THE LIGHT OF THE SOVEREIGN'S FACE, AND
ROYAL FAVOR IS AS A CLOUD OF SPRING RAIN.

The spring rain that is mentioned here is the promise "I will grant the rain for your land in season, the early rain and the late" (Deuteronomy 11:14). It should be noted that royal favor and disfavor are linked to specific acts. In a world of arbitrary power, one does not have to *do* anything to gain favor or suffer disfavor. Whatever happens depends on the whim of a royal ruler. A neutral reading of much of the Books of Samuel and Kings reveals that the rulers of Judah and Israel did indeed operate as kings, that is, as persons vested with arbitrary power not controlled by ethical reflection. As might be expected, Rashi understands the "sovereign" as God, the Sovereign of sovereigns. Gersonides understands the "light of the Sovereign's face" as the apprehensions of those ideas that provide eternal life and the "cloud of spring rain" as a metaphor for those mental abilities that aid in the attainment of those notions.

טז:טז קְנֹה־חָכְמָה מַה־טּוֹב מֵחָרוּץ וּקְנוֹת בִּינָה נִבְחָר מִכָּסֶף:

16:16 BETTER THAN GOLD IS THE ACQUISITION OF WISDOM,
AND BETTER THAN SILVER IS THE ACQUISITION OF
UNDERSTANDING!

While most translations include a word (such as "indeed" or "yeah") for the emphatic way this verse begins, we have chosen to express it by a simple exclamation point at the end of the verse. In this verse we turn from the power of human rulers to the power of wisdom. By noting what they are compared against, Gersonides remarks that "wisdom" is presented as having a greater value than understanding. He explains that the latter may refer to matters of ethics and political philosophy. His explanation reflects the medieval view that ethical perfection, while important, is only a preparatory step to the acquisition of wisdom.

טז:יז מְסִלַּת יְשָׁרִים סוּר מֵרָע שֹׁמֵר נַפְשׁוֹ נֹצֵר דַּרְכּוֹ:

16:17 THE TRACK OF THE UPRIGHT IS TO TURN AWAY FROM
EVIL; THE ONE WHO WATCHES ONE'S WAY WILL PRESERVE
ONE'S LIFE.

M'silat y'sharim, "the track of the upright," the first two words of the verse, became the title of the popular theological tract written by Rabbi Moses Chayim Luzzatto. As is indicated by its usage in Numbers, "We will keep to the beaten track" (Numbers 20:19), the word *m'silah* suggests a road less developed than a highway, yet nonetheless clearly marked. Thus, the author wants to suggest that by turning from

161

evil the upright proceed through life. Those who want to join the ranks of the upright need only turn from evil.

טז:יח לִפְנֵי־שֶׁבֶר גָּאוֹן וְלִפְנֵי כִשָּׁלוֹן גֹּבַהּ רוּחַ:

16:18 Presumption precedes destruction; a haughty spirit goes before a fall.

This is a difficult verse to translate because its common translation into English is well-known. *Gaon,* from the root *gaah* (to be high), is often translated as ''pride.'' In many contexts (see Ezekiel 16:56 and Hosea 5:5; 7:10), the word has the meaning of ''presumption,'' as we have chosen to translate it here. *Shever* (destruction) comes from the root *shavar* (to break). Thus, it refers to something already broken, hence ''destruction.'' *Govah ruach* (literally, ''big of wind/spirit'') is translated as ''a haughty spirit.'' *Chishalon* (fall), from the root *kashal* (stumble, trip), seems to have the sense of being tripped by something. *Gaon,* something high, is what is brought low and smashed. Something puffed up, a ''high wind,'' is what trips you up.

טז:יט טוֹב שְׁפַל־רוּחַ אֶת־עניים עֲנָוִים מֵחַלֵּק שָׁלָל אֶת־גֵּאִים:

16:19 Better humility with the poor than dividing up spoil with the proud.

Aniyim (the poor) is the word that appears in the text, what is called the *k'tiv.* However, according to tradition, one reads the text (thus it is called the *k'rei*) as *anavim* (the oppressed). Whether the text is read as ''poor'' or ''oppressed,'' this verse continues the instruction of the previous verse: Pride is dangerous; humility is helpful.

טז:כ מַשְׂכִּיל עַל־דָּבָר יִמְצָא־טוֹב וּבוֹטֵחַ בַּיהוָה אַשְׁרָיו:

16:20 The one who reflects on the matter will find good; happy is the one who trusts in God.

The Hebrew text is deceptively simple. The difficulty of the translation is in the word *davar,* which can mean either ''matter'' or ''word.'' Rashi takes it to mean both in this instance. Thus, he understands the first clause as advice to be careful in speech and to weigh one's actions. The second clause he understands as instruction to trust in God when, after reflecting on one's words and one's actions, one decides to act to fulfill a commandment. Ibn Ezra takes *davar* to mean ''matter'' and connects this verse to the previous one: The person who accepts humility as his or her personal status will find good. That person should trust that God will sustain him or her rather than be one of those who ''divides up spoil.''

טז:כא לַחֲכַם־לֵב יִקָּרֵא נָבוֹן וּמֶתֶק שְׂפָתַיִם יֹסִיף לֶקַח:

16:21 THE WISE-MINDED WILL BE CALLED A PERSON OF
UNDERSTANDING; SWEETNESS OF LIPS AIDS
INSTRUCTION.

For Rashi, the wise-minded person will be called "understanding" upon reflecting on what has been learned from his or her teacher. That person will be able to explain what was learned to his or her own students. For Ibn Ezra, the wise-minded person is able to understand something even before studying it. That person would still gain from a proper exposition of the matter. Ibn Ezra adds that "sweetness" may be an allusion to wisdom. Gersonides understands both clauses as referring to the person whose philosophical attainments have led him or her to political understanding and whose manner of speech has motivated the members of society to live together in harmony.

טז:כב מְקוֹר חַיִּים שֵׂכֶל בְּעָלָיו וּמוּסַר אֱוִילִים אִוֶּלֶת:

16:22 INTELLIGENCE IS THE SOURCE OF LIFE TO THOSE WHO
HAVE IT, BUT FOLLY IS THE INSTRUCTION OF FOOLS.

Musar is usually translated as "discipline," because it indicates the kind of instruction that is linked to physical chastisement. By using the term here, the writer mocks fools, suggesting that even hitting them would neither instruct nor improve them because they are oblivious to their folly.

טז:כג לֵב חָכָם יַשְׂכִּיל פִּיהוּ וְעַל־שְׂפָתָיו יֹסִיף לֶקַח:

16:23 A WISE MIND MAKES ONE'S MOUTH SPEAK
INTELLIGENTLY AND ADDS LEARNING TO ONE'S LIPS.

Once again we are told that the quality of one's speech effectively indicates the quality of one's mind. Gersonides sees in intelligent speech the difference between the wise person and the fool.

טז:כד צוּף־דְּבַשׁ אִמְרֵי־נֹעַם מָתוֹק לַנֶּפֶשׁ וּמַרְפֵּא לָעָצֶם:

16:24 PLEASANT WORDS ARE LIKE HONEYCOMB, SWEET TO
THE SOUL AND HEALING FOR THE BONES.

Pleasing speech has a positive effect on those who hear it. This is particularly good advice for those who aspire to counsel those in power. Gersonides provides a full philosophical explanation for the verse: wise words from a scholar are like sweetness to the sensitive aspect of the soul, sweetness that nourishes a person, and like medicine for bruised bones.

טז:כה יֵשׁ דֶּרֶךְ יָשָׁר לִפְנֵי־אִישׁ וְאַחֲרִיתָהּ דַּרְכֵי־מָוֶת:

16:25 THERE IS A PATH THAT SEEMS STRAIGHT TO A PERSON,
BUT WAYS OF DEATH ARE AT ITS END.

The translation follows the *Targum: d'mitchazya b'ainei b'nei nasha ditritza hi,* "that seem in people's eyes as straight." In commenting on this verse, Ibn Ezra—who was more popular as a poet than as a biblical critic—seems to speak from his own experience. He relates it to the previous verse and says that a person once involved with "pleasing words" may find "the ways of death" when he or she forsakes them.

טז:כו נֶפֶשׁ עָמֵל עָמְלָה לּוֹ כִּי־אָכַף עָלָיו פִּיהוּ:

16:26 A WORKER'S LIFE IS SUSTAINED BY LABOR, FOR ONE IS
COMPELLED BY ONE'S MOUTH.

The difficulty in this verse lies in the word *nefesh,* which can mean "life," "person," "desire," or "soul." It is a feminine noun governing the verb *amlah* (labors, works). The first clause could be translated, "the soul of the worker works for the worker" or "the desire of the worker works for the worker." Our translation follows the *Targum:* the soul of the worker is supported by the worker's labor. Rashi explains the verse as meaning that one works to meet one's needs and is driven by one's own hunger. The writer offers the reader sound advice: We must work in order to live. Watch what you are doing or you will end up digging ditches!

טז:כז אִישׁ בְּלִיַּעַל כֹּרֶה רָעָה וְעַל־שְׂפָתָיו כְּאֵשׁ צָרָבֶת:

16:27 A VILE PERSON DIGS UP EVIL, AND THERE IS A BURNING
FIRE ON HIS [OR HER] LIPS.

People search the past of others as fodder for character assassination or even blackmail. The author uses the word *tzaravet* (scorching, burning)—which also appears in Leviticus 13:23 to describe skin inflammations—to suggest that a person's words burn in the present and leave scars in the future. Rashi takes the verb *koreh* (dig up) to mean "plan" and understands the verse to mean that a vile person who plans evil is eager to put the plan into operation. It is as if the vile person's lips burn to do evil.

טז:כח אִישׁ תַּהְפֻּכוֹת יְשַׁלַּח מָדוֹן וְנִרְגָּן* מַפְרִיד אַלּוּף: *יֵ' זעירא

16:28 A PERVERSE PERSON PROJECTS CONTENTION, AND THE
BAD-TEMPERED PERSON DIVIDES CLOSE FRIENDS.

The word *nirgan* comes from the root *ragan,* which can mean either "to whisper" or "to grumble." Thus, some translate it as "whisperer." Others understand the word as "one who murmurs or slanders." Ibn Ezra takes *nirgan* to mean "talebearer." The *Targum* translates it as "an argumentative person." The context suggests that kind of person who can say nothing good about anyone, the one who "bad-mouths" everyone else. We have chosen to translate the word as "bad-tempered." Rashi understands *aluf* (close friend) as God. Thus, the person who can't say anything good separates oneself from God. But Gersonides understands *aluf* as "chief" (from Genesis 36:15–43; Exodus 15:15). He sees the verse referring to the kind of person who constantly stirs up discord until it causes a rebellion and separates the ruler from those who are ruled.

טז:כט אִישׁ חָמָס יְפַתֶּה רֵעֵהוּ וְהוֹלִיכוֹ בְּדֶרֶךְ לֹא־טוֹב:

16:29 THE VIOLENT PERSON ENTICES ONE'S NEIGHBOR TO
LEAD HIM [OR HER] ON A PATH THAT IS NOT GOOD.

In a clever turn of phrase, the author connects *ish chamas* (violent person) with the verb *y'fateh* (seduces, beguiles). Guile and seduction seem to be something of which a violent person could not make use. The author makes the point that violent people are able to employ other tactics, not solely threats of violence, to persuade others to join them. Sometimes, they simply talk them into it.

טז:ל עֹצֶה עֵינָיו לַחְשֹׁב תַּהְפֻּכוֹת קֹרֵץ שְׂפָתָיו כִּלָּה רָעָה:

16:30 BY CLOSING ONE'S EYES, ONE CAN DEVISE PERVERSITY;
ONE CAN COMPRESS ONE'S LIPS TO BRING ON EVIL.

Evil can be accomplished with a wink and a sneer. It does not require words. The *Targum* translates the first two words as *ramaz b'aynohi* (hint with the eyes, wink). Ibn Ezra understands the second clause as fulfillment of the first: a perverse plan must be carried out for it to really be perverse.

טז:לא עֲטֶרֶת תִּפְאֶרֶת שֵׂיבָה בְּדֶרֶךְ צְדָקָה תִּמָּצֵא:

16:31 THE GRAY-HAIRED HEAD IS THE CROWN OF GLORY. IT
WILL BE FOUND THROUGH THE WAY OF RIGHTEOUSNESS.

Having delineated the power of spoken and unspoken evil, the author hopes that one may survive its depredations. The doing of righteousness is a guarantee of long life. Rashi understands *tzedakah* as "charity," which, for him, is a means of prolonging life. Since Gersonides takes *tzedakah* to mean both "righteousness" and "correctness," he understands the verse to mean that old age is a crown of glory when it is the result of the acquisition of ideas and the performance of virtues (both wisdom and political science).

טז:לב טוֹב אֶרֶךְ אַפַּיִם מִגִּבּוֹר וּמֹשֵׁל בְּרוּחוֹ מִלֹּכֵד עִיר:

16:32 BETTER IS THE ONE WHO IS SLOW TO ANGER THAN
THE ONE WHO IS MIGHTY; BETTER IS THE ONE
WHO CONTROLS THE SELF THAN ONE WHO CONQUERS
A CITY.

The last clause is quoted by Ben Zoma as a prooftext for the statement "Who is
strong? The one who subdues the impulse to do evil" (*Pirkei Avot* 4:1). The *Targum*
and Ibn Ezra point out that *tov* (good, better) applies to both clauses of the verse.
Once we see that this book is devoted to those who strive to be counselors to those in
power, it is clear that maintaining self-control is extremely important. Anger gets in the
way of personal achievement and success.

טז:לג בַּחֵיק יוּטַל אֶת־הַגּוֹרָל וּמֵיְהֹוָה כָּל־מִשְׁפָּטוֹ:

16:33 THE LOT IS CAST INTO THE LAP, BUTS ITS JUDGMENT
COMES FROM GOD.

The first clause seems to be a proverb whose exact meaning is unclear. Following
Rashi's understanding of the verse, one may say that while chance is a part of
everyday life, God ultimately determines all things.

Moses Chayim Luzzatto (1707–1747)

A kabbalist and poet, Moses Chayim Luzzatto was also known as Ramchal. He was
head of the center of Jewish learning in Padua, Italy. Luzzatto had strong messianic
aspirations and was exiled to Amsterdam. Many of his books were burned by his
opponents. His most famous work was an ethical treatise called *M'sillat Y'sharim* (1740).

M'kor Chayim

Literally, "source of life," the term *m'kor chayim* was used as a title for a Neoplatonic
treatise written by the medieval liturgical poet and philosopher Solomon ibn Gabirol
(1021–1058/70). The original, written in Arabic, was lost. Considered to be the work of
a Christian philosopher, the text was translated into Latin under the direction of the
Archbishop of Toledo in the middle of the twelfth century and given the title *Fons Vitae*.
A Hebrew epitome was made by Shem Tov Falaquera (1225–1290) with the Hebrew
title *M'kor Chayim*. The French Jewish scholar Solomon Munk proved in 1845 that *Fons
Vitae* and the treatise *M'kor Chayim* were written by the same person.

Aspects of the Soul

The Greek philosopher Plato (427–347 B.C.E.) taught that the human soul has three parts: reason or mind, spirit, and desire. Since spirit and desire were linked to the body, they could not transcend death as could the mind, which was not so linked. Aristotle (384–322 B.C.E.), on the other hand, contended that the three parts of the human soul related to different functions of the body. Galen (129–199 C.E.), physician and philosopher, carried on Plato's threefold division of the soul. Thinkers in the Middle Ages understood him to believe that there were either three souls or one soul that operated on three levels. While Maimonides argued that the soul is what distinguishes between what is alive and what is not, he believed that each soul may be divided into three sections loosely based on the major functions of each division that he named vegetative, animal, and rational.

GLEANINGS

Ethical Perfection

This blurred distinction between "permitted and forbidden," between right and wrong, between good and bad, keeps chipping away at the bedrock of our society—and at the bedrock of our Jewish existence. The "blurred distinction" cannot hide from the ethical commandments of the Torah, the ethical (and passionate) pronouncements of the prophets, the ethical laws and precepts of the Talmud, the ethical principles of modern Zionism, and the centrality of ethical values in Reform Judaism. It cannot hide from the long-standing and proud Jewish claim that we were the ones who taught the world about the one ethical God, that we delivered the ethical message of that God to all of humankind: "It has been told you, O man [not 'O Jew'], what is good and what *Adonai* requires of you—to do justly, to love mercy, and to walk humbly with your God."

Jack Stern, "Jewish Ethics in the Daily Life of the Jew," in *The Jewish Condition: Essays on Contemporary Judaism for Rabbi Alexander M. Schindler*, ed. Aron Hirt-Manheimer (New York: UAHC Press, 1995), 119–20

Knowing the Heart

Even those who do not know the law or the prescribed ritual know the heart. They can teach their children to be outraged at injustice and to feel the anguish of the humiliated. They must be urged to study Torah for the purpose of strengthening and refining Jewish conscience. They can be taught the power of conscience afforded those who are part of the court below, members of the holy congregation who can nullify the evil decrees. The Heavenly Tribunal awaits the bestirring of the court

167

below. As the *Zohar* stated, "Whenever the thing below bestirs itself, there is a simultaneous stimulation of the counterpart above as the two realms form one connected whole." (*Zohar* II 156b)

Harold Schulweis, "*Does God Have a Conscience?*" in *The Jewish Condition: Essays on Contemporary Judaism for Rabbi Alexander M. Schindler*, ed. Aron Hirt-Manheimer (New York: UAHC Press, 1995), 116

Becoming Possibly Holy

In my morning prayers, I recite a list *mitzvot she-ein lahem shi'ur*—mitzvot without measure, boundless mitzvot. They can be done as often as we like. They are beautiful practices I try to integrate into my life, guidelines for being a decent person, and for the possibility of holy relations with others. *Gemilut chasadim*: deeds of loving-kindness. *Ha-pe'ah*—literally, leaving a corner of the harvest for the poor, but now, direct acts of charity. *Talmud Torah*: study. A second list of mitzvot has rewards both temporal and eternal: among them, honoring mother and father, welcoming guests, visiting the sick, honoring the dead, rejoicing with bride and bridegroom, enabling friendships. Many we do naturally, Jew or non-Jew alike, but to think of them as mitzvot adds to their power for me. Then the doing becomes more than doing, it becomes possibly holy.

Rodger Kamenetz, *Stalking Elijah: Adventures with Today's Jewish Mystical Masters* (San Francisco: HarperSanFrancisco, 1997), 273

CHAPTER SEVENTEEN

טוֹב פַּת חֲרֵבָה וְשַׁלְוָה־בָהּ מִבַּיִת מָלֵא זִבְחֵי־רִיב: **יז:א**

17:1 BETTER A DRY CRUST WITH CONTENTMENT THAN A
HOUSE FILLED WITH MEAT MEALS AND STRIFE.

The phrase *zivchei riv* (literally, "sacrifices of strife") points to the fact that in ancient
times, meat was eaten as part of a religious rite. Thus, *zevach* (to sacrifice) also meant
"to slaughter for a communal meal." The eating of meat marked a special occasion.
It was a luxury that was rarely enjoyed. The author contrasts eating little in peace
against eating a lot with strife. Rashi refers this verse to the destruction of the Temple:
better to have no sacrifices than to have the sins of Israel.

עֶבֶד מַשְׂכִּיל יִמְשֹׁל בְּבֵן מֵבִישׁ וּבְתוֹךְ אַחִים יַחֲלֹק נַחֲלָה: **יז:ב**

17:2 AN INTELLIGENT SERVANT WILL RULE OVER AN
OFFSPRING WHO CAUSES SHAME AND WILL DIVIDE THE
INHERITANCE WITH THE [OTHER] SIBLINGS.

Centuries ago, a slave or servant could inherit, as is suggested by Abraham's
comment, "One of my household will inherit me" (Genesis 15:3). The previous verse
(Genesis 15:2) identifies the servant as Eliezer. Here the author warns that even a
wealthy son or daughter who behaves badly could lose his or her inheritance to a
servant who acts appropriately. To those who are not wealthy, this verse also suggests
that they might achieve a socioeconomic level through their intelligence that is higher
than the one inherited from their families of origin.

מַצְרֵף לַכֶּסֶף וְכוּר לַזָּהָב וּבֹחֵן לִבּוֹת יְהֹוָה: **יז:ג**

17:3 AS THE SMELTING POT IS FOR SILVER AND THE FURNACE
IS FOR GOLD, SO GOD TESTS HEARTS.

The "smelting pot" and the "furnace" are the means by which silver and gold are
purified. Similarly, God tests and purifies the human heart.

יז:ד מֵרַע מַקְשִׁיב עַל־שְׂפַת־אָוֶן שֶׁקֶר מֵזִין עַל־לְשׁוֹן הַוֺּת׃

17:4 AN EVIL PERSON LISTENS TO LIPS OF DISASTER, HEEDING FALSEHOOD AS WELL AS A DESTRUCTIVE TONGUE.

The second clause is somewhat unclear. Following Gersonides, we might emend *sheker* to *m'shakeir* (one who speaks falsehood, a liar). "Heeding" (literally, "giving ear") might be translated as "upon" so that the clause reads "upon a destructive tongue." The message of the verse seems clear, nonetheless: Speech can bring tragedy. Wicked is the person who pays attention to words that cause calamity to others.

יז:ה לֹעֵג לָרָשׁ חֵרֵף עֹשֵׂהוּ שָׂמֵחַ לְאֵיד לֹא יִנָּקֶה׃

17:5 THE ONE WHO MOCKS THE POOR TAUNTS ONE'S MAKER; THE ONE WHO REJOICES AT CALAMITY SHALL NEVER REMAIN BLAMELESS.

The *Targum* clarifies the second clause of this verse by adding the word *d'chavrei* (of one's neighbor) after "calamity." Those who have forgotten the poverty of their own origins continue to mock the poor. Blaming those who have little for their predicament is easy to do for those who have lost their sense of responsibility to members of society. It is not coincidental that the word *tzedakah* means both "righteousness" and "charity." In an ideal world, governed by righteousness, none would need charity. The giving of charity is an act of retributive righteousness for the giver.

יז:ו עֲטֶרֶת זְקֵנִים בְּנֵי בָנִים וְתִפְאֶרֶת בָּנִים אֲבוֹתָם׃

17:6 GRANDCHILDREN ARE THE CROWN OF GRANDPARENTS, AND THE GLORY OF CHILDREN ARE THEIR PARENTS.

Any grandparent will attest that grandchildren are the ultimate delight. Just as a crown is not worn by a king or queen at all times, so grandchildren are not with grandparents at all times—as they are with their own parents. In raising their children, parents should strive to act so that they will be the glory of their children. Rashi states that "grandchildren are the crown" when they follow the proper path in their own lives and "parents are the glory" when they are righteous.

יז:ז לֹא־נָאוָה לְנָבָל שְׂפַת־יֶתֶר אַף כִּי־לְנָדִיב שְׂפַת־שָׁקֶר:

17:7 EXTRAVAGANT SPEECH DOES NOT BEFIT A FOOL, MUCH
LESS LYING LIPS A PRINCE [OR PRINCESS].

Speech should reflect the speaker. Thus, a fool should be careful about the extent of what he or she says. How much more so the person who is in a position of authority. Rashi understands *s'fat yeter* as speech that reflects pride. Ibn Ezra understands the words to mean that the fool will not go to the wise for advice. For Gersonides, *s'fat yeter* refers to those words that convey status that are of no benefit to the fool, since he or she lacks the requisite education to appreciate them.

יז:ח אֶבֶן־חֵן הַשֹּׁחַד בְּעֵינֵי בְעָלָיו אֶל־כָּל־אֲשֶׁר יִפְנֶה יַשְׂכִּיל:

17:8 A BRIBE IS A GEM IN THE EYES OF ONE WHO RECEIVES IT;
WHEREVER THEY TURN, THEY BECOME INTELLIGENT.

This is a sarcastic verse. The word *baalav* may refer to the one who offers the bribe or to the one who receives it. If we accept the former view, then the meaning of the second clause is that once the bribe is offered and accepted, those offering the bribe find their way to be smooth. Their views are accepted, and they are treated as if they are intelligent. However, if we accept the latter translation, once a bribe is offered and accepted, either the giver of the bribe is seen as intelligent in the way he or she does business or the taker of the bribe is seen as being smart for negotiating such a deal. In many cultures, the giving of bribes is the price of doing business. Like the contributors of "soft money" to political campaigns in contemporary society, those who give bribes expect something in return, something that they may not have received otherwise.

יז:ט מְכַסֶּה־פֶּשַׁע מְבַקֵּשׁ אַהֲבָה וְשֹׁנֶה בְדָבָר מַפְרִיד אַלּוּף:

17:9 ONE WHO SEEKS LOVE WILL COVER OVER A
TRANSGRESSION, BUT THE ONE WHO REPEATS THE
MATTER DISTANCES A FRIEND.

The difficulty of this verse is in the interpretation of *shoneh* (repeats) in the second clause. Rashi and Ibn Ezra differ as to what they regard as being repeated. For Rashi, it is the telling of the transgression that is repeated. The one harping on what the other has done will cause a loss of friendship and a separation from God, as is suggested in the verse "You should not take vengeance or bear a grudge" (Leviticus 19:18). For Ibn Ezra, what is repeated is the transgression itself. That is what will separate the transgressor from even the friends who are prepared to forgive. Here is the ethical challenge presented by the author: How far does friendship or loyalty go in covering up evil acts? Consider the "blue wall of silence" of police, for example. Perhaps there is a relationship between the depth of loyalty and the seriousness of a transgression.

יז:י תֵּחַת גְּעָרָה בְמֵבִין מֵהַכּוֹת כְּסִיל מֵאָה:

17:10 A REBUKE PENETRATES A PERSON OF UNDERSTANDING
BETTER THAN ONE HUNDRED LASHES AFFECTS A FOOL.

This simple verse can be taken three ways because of the various meanings of the word *teichat* (penetrates). The *Targum* translates it as "enters." Ibn Ezra applies a homonym and translates it as "descend." Rashi thinks that the word is a noun from *chatat* (to be shattered or filled with terror). Thus, he rewrites the verse as: "More terrifying is a rebuke to the one who understands than one hundred lashes for a fool." Some scholars want to emend the verse so that *teichat* becomes *achat* (one) and read it as: "Better one rebuke...." However it is specifically translated, the author again presents a contrast between the wise and the not-so-wise. The author suggests that it is easy to correct the shortcomings of the wise and difficult to correct the failings of the foolish.

יז:יא אַךְ־מְרִי יְבַקֶּשׁ־רָע וּמַלְאָךְ אַכְזָרִי יְשֻׁלַּח־בּוֹ:

17:11 A REBELLIOUS PERSON SEEKS ONLY EVIL, AND A CRUEL
ANGEL WILL BE SENT TO THAT PERSON.

M'ri (rebellion) presents us with a problem in the first clause. We can't know for sure whether it is an abstract notion or a reference to a person. Most commentators and translations suggest that it is a person. The remainder of the clause presents us with the same challenge. Is *ra* "evil" or "an evil person"? Perhaps we should translate it as: "An evil person seeks only rebellion." Such a translation seems to be supported by the second clause.

יז:יב פָּגוֹשׁ דֹּב שַׁכּוּל בְּאִישׁ וְאַל־כְּסִיל בְּאִוַּלְתּוֹ:

17:12 [BETTER TO] LET A BEREFT BEAR MEET A HUMAN THAN
A FOOL IN HIS [OR HER] FOLLY.

The word *shakul* (bereft) describes a parent who has lost a child (or an animal who has lost its young). The image is clear: one would rather deal with a wild animal crazed by grief than with a fool doing what a fool does.

יז:יג מֵשִׁיב רָעָה תַּחַת טוֹבָה לֹא־תָמִישׁ רָעָה מִבֵּיתוֹ:

17:13 EVIL WILL NEVER DEPART FROM THE HOUSE OF THE
ONE WHO REWARDS EVIL FOR GOOD.

In response to this statement, Gersonides offers two reasons. First, people will stop attempting to do good. Second, there will be divine punishment because people will be kept from achieving those perfections that generally protect one from evil.

172

Too often throughout the history of the Jewish people, evil has been rewarded in place of good.

יז:יד פּוֹטֵר מַיִם רֵאשִׁית מָדוֹן וְלִפְנֵי הִתְגַּלַּע הָרִיב נְטוֹשׁ:

17:14 LIKE SOMEONE RELEASING WATER, SO IS THE BEGINNING OF CONTENTION. THEREFORE, LEAVE BEFORE THE QUARREL BREAKS OUT!

Rashi explains that as one drills a hole in a water pipe, it lets out more water and the flow itself enlarges the hole. Similarly, contention starts with very little and ends with very much. Since quarrels develop a life of their own beyond their initial reasons, the wise person will either avoid them or turn away as quickly as possible from them. The imagery of water is especially relevant, as it continues to represent a major area of contention in certain parts of the world. Consider the role of water supply in the ongoing Middle East crisis.

יז:טו מַצְדִּיק רָשָׁע וּמַרְשִׁיעַ צַדִּיק תּוֹעֲבַת יְהֹוָה גַּם־שְׁנֵיהֶם:

17:15 ONE WHO ACQUITS THE GUILTY AND ONE WHO CONVICTS THE INNOCENT ARE BOTH ABOMINATIONS TO GOD.

The verse suggests a legal context. Thus, we have translated *rasha* as "guilty" and *tzaddik* as "innocent." Judicial corruption is certainly nothing new. The first of the literary prophets, Amos, condemned those who "...sold the innocent for silver and the poor for a pair of shoes" (Amos 2:6). In Proverbs 17:8, the author pointed out the power of bribes, the motivation for such corruption.

יז:טז לָמָּה־זֶּה מְחִיר בְּיַד־כְּסִיל לִקְנוֹת חָכְמָה וְלֶב־אָיִן:

17:16 WHAT POINT IS THERE FOR THE FOOL TO HAVE THE FEE IN HAND WHILE LACKING THE INTELLIGENCE TO ACQUIRE WISDOM?

Playing on the word *liknot* (buy, acquire), the author points out that wisdom can't be bought as one might buy other things. Rather, it has to be acquired by study and reflection. Only a fool would think otherwise. However, there is a connection between the paying of fees and the acquiring of wisdom. Prior to free, public education, education was limited to an elite group. The notion of widespread education, available to all who can master it, is a revolutionary idea.

יז:יז בְּכָל־עֵת אֹהֵב הָרֵעַ וְאָח לְצָרָה יִוָּלֵד:

17:17 A companion loves for all time, but a sibling is born to share trouble.

While most of the classic commentators take *harei-a* as "friend," the word is usually translated as "neighbor" (see Exodus 11:2 and Leviticus 19:18). This verse represents a psychospiritual reality. It argues that one's connection to a friend or neighbor is dependent on feelings. The notion of unconditional love "for all time" is seldom found among neighbors and friends. However, relatives, particularly siblings, are bound by blood. It is when trouble arises that you really need—and depend on—family.

יז:יח אָדָם חֲסַר־לֵב תּוֹקֵעַ כָּף עֹרֵב עֲרֻבָּה לִפְנֵי רֵעֵהוּ:

17:18 A person bereft of sense makes a deal, to act as surety for a neighbor.

As a comment on the previous verse, the author suggests that it is foolish to guarantee the debt of a neighbor. In 11:15, we were told that it is foolish to guarantee the debt of a stranger. And the neighbor is someone who is known! We may want to debate the author's conclusion: when it counts, even the love of a neighbor does not last forever.

יז:יט אֹהֵב פֶּשַׁע אֹהֵב מַצָּה מַגְבִּיהַּ פִּתְחוֹ מְבַקֶּשׁ־שָׁבֶר:

17:19 The one who loves transgression loves discord; the one who raises high one's door seeks disaster.

Rashi understands transgression to refer to actions against people, not God. The idiom *magbiah pitcho* (raises high the door) is no longer clear to us. The *Targum* translates it as "who lifts the gate." In trying to understand the verse, Rashi and Ibn Ezra refer to "watch the opening of your mouth" (Micah 7:5) and understand the phrase to mean "to speak proudly." While the specific details may not be clear, the author's sentiments are: Watch what you say. Don't offend people with your words.

יז:כ עִקֶּשׁ־לֵב לֹא יִמְצָא־טוֹב וְנֶהְפָּךְ בִּלְשׁוֹנוֹ יִפּוֹל בְּרָעָה:

17:20 A depraved mind will find no good, and the one with a perverse tongue will fall into evil.

The writer points out that we tend to find what we are looking for. The person who looks for evil will find it. The person who sees good in others will find it. The person who bad-mouths everything and everyone will drive people away.

יז:כא יֹלֵד כְּסִיל לְתוּגָה לוֹ וְלֹא־יִשְׂמַח אֲבִי נָבָל:

17:21 ONE BEGETS A FOOL TO ONE'S OWN SORROW, AND NO
PARENT REJOICES WHOSE CHILD IS A SIMPLETON.

Gersonides sees the parent's sorrow as continuing as long as the child displays that he
or she is not able to think deeply while, at the same time, he or she exhibits bad
behavior. While most parents think that their children are "geniuses," the writer
exhibits a common insensitivity to those children who are not quite so bright.
Throughout history there have been those who unfortunately believe that mentally
challenged children are divine punishment for the sins of their parents.

יז:כב לֵב שָׂמֵחַ יֵיטִב גֵּהָה וְרוּחַ נְכֵאָה תְּיַבֶּשׁ־גָּרֶם:

17:22 A HAPPY HEART IS BENEFICIAL FOR HEALING, BUT A
BROKEN SPIRIT DRIES UP THE BONES.

The word *geihah,* to mean "healing," is only used here. The *Targum* translates *yeitiv
geihah* (beneficial for healing) as *mashpir gufa* (improves the body). One wonders
whether Rashi read *nogah* (shining, brightness) instead of *geihah* to explain his
comment that when people rejoice in their lot in life, their faces shine. Gersonides
offers an explanation out of the natural world for the statement. He suggests that
when a person is happy, that person's blood flow increases and aids in healing.
When a person is unhappy, blood flow is decreased, which has a negative effect on
the bones.

יז:כג שֹׁחַד מֵחֵיק רָשָׁע יִקָּח לְהַטּוֹת אָרְחוֹת מִשְׁפָּט:

17:23 THE WICKED WILL TAKE A BRIBE FROM SOMEONE'S
BOSOM TO PERVERT THE CAUSE OF JUSTICE.

The one who takes a bribe does not care how it is done. So unconcerned about being
caught, he or she will come right up to the bribe giver and take the bribe. Rashi takes
the verse to refer to the mercy that God has for the repentant sinner. Ibn Ezra suggests
that "bosom" is mentioned to indicate that the bribe is given and taken in secret.

יז:כד אֶת־פְּנֵי מֵבִין חָכְמָה וְעֵינֵי כְּסִיל בִּקְצֵה־אָרֶץ:

17:24 WISDOM IS IN FRONT OF THE PERSON OF
UNDERSTANDING BUT [BEFORE] THE EYES OF THE
FOOL AT THE ENDS OF THE EARTH.

The difference between the wise and the foolish is in their ability to focus. Wise
people see clearly what is right in front of them. Foolish people look everywhere
except where it matters. Rashi applies the second clause of the verse to the foolish

person who is put off from studying various tractates of the Talmud because of their length. Were that student wise, he or she would study one and then another, and then master them all. Gersonides offers us a philosophical insight. He suggests that, were people to pay attention to everything, then they would gain great wisdom from investigating their causal connections.

יז:כה כַּעַס לְאָבִיו בֵּן כְּסִיל וּמֶמֶר לְיוֹלַדְתּוֹ:

17:25 A FOOLISH CHILD CAUSES A FATHER TO BE ANGRY AND
A MOTHER TO BE BITTER.

We already met the foolish child and the unfortunate parents in 10:1 and 15:20. This verse continues the thought initiated in 17:21. Like the other verses, this is both observation and warning. One can see what pain and anguish foolish children cause their parents. Therefore, one should try not to be a foolish child. For Rashi, Jeroboam ben Nebat is the foolish child. The father is God, and the mother is the congregation of Israel.

יז:כו גַּם עֲנוֹשׁ לַצַּדִּיק לֹא־טוֹב לְהַכּוֹת נְדִיבִים עַל־יֹשֶׁר:

17:26 IT IS NOT GOOD TO PUNISH THE INNOCENT NOR TO
SMITE THE NOBLE FOR THEIR RIGHTEOUSNESS.

The writer presents us with two aspects of the same idea. Innocence should be rewarded, not punished. However, this is as Kohelet noted, "In the place of justice, there is wickedness, and in the place of the innocent, the guilty" (reading *tzaddik* instead of *tzedek* and *rasha* instead of *resha*) (Ecclesiastes 3:16). Rashi relates this verse to God's forbearance in dealing with Israel.

יז:כז חוֹשֵׂךְ אֲמָרָיו יוֹדֵעַ דָּעַת וקר יְקַר־רוּחַ אִישׁ תְּבוּנָה:

17:27 THE ONE WHO CONTROLS ONE'S WORDS KNOWS
SOMETHING, AND THE ONE WHO IS DISPASSIONATE IS
A PERSON OF UNDERSTANDING.

Rashi notes that the person who is learned is not too wordy. Ibn Ezra sees this verse as a praise of silence. Like so many other verses, this verse praises control over thought and speech. The second clause of this verse contains a case of *k'tiv/k'rei* (the way the text is written and the way it is read). "Dispassionate" (literally, "cold of spirit") is the text as written, and "dignified" (*y'kar ruach*; literally, "precious of spirit") is the text as read. However, we have taken the *k'tiv* as the better reading, making more sense here than the *k'rei*.

יז:כח גַּם אֱוִיל מַחֲרִישׁ חָכָם יֵחָשֵׁב אֹטֵם שְׂפָתָיו נָבוֹן:

17:28 EVEN A FOOL IS CONSIDERED WISE WHEN SILENT, AND
THOSE WHO KEEP THEIR MOUTH SHUT ARE CONSIDERED
TO HAVE UNDERSTANDING.

A praise of thoughtful silence in contrast to ill-considered speech, this is a suggestion
to those readers who speak too often. It may also be a bit of guidance to those who
don't quite make the grade. If you want others to think highly of you, keep quiet.

Literary Prophets

The term "literary prophets" refers to those prophets whose oracles were preserved
in writings either by themselves, their disciples, or their scribes. It is synonymous with
the term "classical prophets." The primary literary remains of the preclassical or popular
prophets, on the other hand, as the other prophets are called, are the stories and
accounts of their lives that were transmitted orally by their followers. This is also a
chronological distinction made to classify the two groups of prophets.

Jeroboam ben Nebat

First king of post-Solomonic Israel, Jeroboam ben Nebat came from the town of
Zeredah in the land of Ephraim and reigned for about twenty-two years (ca. 928–907
B.C.E.). He had the reputation as a "mighty man of valor" (I Kings 11:28) because
(before he came to power) he had been placed in charge of the troops from Ephraim
and Manasseh to fortify Jerusalem. He rebelled against the king, supported by Ahijah
the Shilonite, but the rebellion failed and he fled to Egypt. Following Solomon's death,
Jeroboam returned and was appointed king when the leaders of the people—excluding
Benjamin and Judah—proclaimed their independence from the House of David. On
taking the throne, he countered the king of Judah's attempts to reconquer Israel and
widened the breach between the two territories. His reign was weakened by attacks
from Shishak, the king of Egypt, and he eventually lost to Abijam.

GLEANINGS

Dedicated to the Truth

One must fanatically detect falsehoods. One must search his soul every time he writes
a sentence. The fact scrubbed clean is more eternal than perfumed or rouged words.
The historian's desk is an altar on which he must sacrifice his most cherished
prejudices. One must be dedicated to the truth.

Jacob Rader Marcus, quoted in *CCAR Yearbook* 105–106 (1995–1996): 360

Worldly Goods

Worldly goods are of small material value. I am in possession of a far richer store. It is a way of life transmitted to me, through thousands of years, by prophet, sage and martyr of my people. It embodies a counsel for life which if taken diligently to heart and practiced by all men, would lead to larger understanding, less bloodshed, and more brotherhood. It is a counsel which thinks of man as "little lower than angels" rather than as kin to beasts. That counsel I gladly bequeath to all mankind, without regard to family ties or color or creed. It is a rich heritage which, without distinction, I will to friend and foe alike.

Samuel Wolk, "Man: A Little Lower Than Angels," in Jacob Rader Marcus, *This I Believe: Documents of American Jewish Life* (Northvale, N.J.: Jason Aronson, 1990), 220

CHAPTER EIGHTEEN

יח:א לְתַאֲוָה יְבַקֵּשׁ נִפְרָד בְּכָל־תּוּשִׁיָּה יִתְגַּלָּע:

18:1 THE ONE WHO HAS BECOME ISOLATED SEEKING ONE'S OWN DESIRE HAS BROKEN AWAY FROM ALL SOUND ADVICE.

It is unclear to what "seeking desire" and becoming "isolated" refer. The *Targum* drops the word for "seeking" and takes "isolated" *(nifrad)* to refer to a vagrant or restless person. Rashi takes "desire" to refer to one's evil inclination *(yetzer hara)*, which moves a person to isolate oneself, to separate oneself from God's guidance. Speaking from the experience of writing his commentaries in Mantua, Rome, and London, Ibn Ezra understands *l'taavah* as one's desire to pursue wisdom and *nifrad* as one's leaving home in order to do so. Gersonides takes the word *nifrad* as isolated in the philosophical sense of an abstract, nonmaterial idea and notes that the pursuit of such an entity is precisely the desire of the philosopher. All of these commentators have the same challenge in interpreting *yitgala* in the second clause, which may mean "break out" or "quarrel." For Rashi, the reproach of the solitary sinner will be revealed in the presence of *tushiyah* (sound advice, prudence, wisdom; that is, the presence of Torah scholars). Ibn Ezra takes *yitgala* to mean "mix together with." Upon arriving at a "place of wisdom," the wandering scholar will mingle with the scholars who reside there. Gersonides also takes the word to mean "associate with" or "become involved with." The one who is philosophically adept will use every law of thought in the investigation of the boundaries of the abstract and the immaterial.

As the phrase *m'vakesh toanah* (to seek an excuse, an occasion) is attested (see Judges 14:4), some scholars suggest emending *l'taavah* (to/for desire) to *l'toanah* (for an occasion). Following such an emendation, the verse would read: "The one who becomes isolated is looking for trouble. That person has broken away from all sound advice." Such a translation would stress the importance of community for the individual. After all, humans are political by nature.

יח:ב לֹא־יַחְפֹּץ כְּסִיל בִּתְבוּנָה כִּי אִם־בְּהִתְגַּלּוֹת לִבּוֹ:

18:2 A FOOL DOES NOT WANT UNDERSTANDING BUT RATHER SELF-REVELATION.

Gersonides understands the second clause to mean that fools will seek understanding when their heart/mind *(libo)* reveals to them what they are missing. According to the verse, fools are unwilling to learn from anything or anyone. What they know is already in their own mind.

יח:ג בְּבוֹא־רָשָׁע בָּא גַם־בּוּז וְעִם־קָלוֹן חֶרְפָּה:

18:3 WHEN THE WICKED COME, CONTEMPT, SHAME, AND DISGRACE [ALSO] COME.

Kalon (shame) and *cherpah* (disgrace) seem to be synonyms. The Yiddish phrase *a shanda und a charpah* indicates the worse kind of disgrace. Yet both Rashi and Ibn Ezra understand the two words as expressing a causal relation. For Rashi, the first word refers to some kind of sexual shame, perhaps adultery, which brings in its course the condemnation of the second. While not as specific, Ibn Ezra explains the two words as referring to what the sinner does and how people respond. He quotes the text from *Pirkei Avot* "one transgression leads to another" (4:1).

יח:ד מַיִם עֲמֻקִּים דִּבְרֵי פִי־אִישׁ נַחַל נֹבֵעַ מְקוֹר חָכְמָה:

18:4 A PERSON'S WORDS ARE DEEP WATER, A SPRING OF WISDOM, A BABBLING BROOK.

Novei-a (babbling, flowing) may be onomatopoeic. The writer makes two sets of contrasts to stress the importance of thoughtful speech: words that are spoken as against wisdom, which is not spoken but thought, and the silence of deep water as against the gurgling of a brook. Deep water makes no noise, while a person's words are heard. It is as if to say that most people's words convey no real meaning. Wisdom, which makes no noise, speaks to those prepared to listen. Its cues, like the soft gurgling sounds of the brook, proclaim that like water, it is refreshing and life-giving.

יח:ה שְׂאֵת פְּנֵי־רָשָׁע לֹא־טוֹב לְהַטּוֹת צַדִּיק בַּמִּשְׁפָּט:

18:5 IT IS NOT GOOD TO FAVOR THE GUILTY OR TO SUBVERT THE INNOCENT'S CASE.

We have already been told that there are corrupt rulers and judges (16:15) who accept bribes (17:23, 26). It is horrendous that the guilty should be favored for a fee and the innocent condemned because they lack that fee. Rashi offers us some solace. He says that it is not good in the long run for the guilty to be favored in this life, for they will pay for it in the next.

יח:ו שִׂפְתֵי כְסִיל יָבֹאוּ בְרִיב וּפִיו לְמַהֲלֻמוֹת יִקְרָא:

18:6 THE LIPS OF A FOOL ENTER A QUARREL, AND THE FOOL'S
        MOUTH CALLS FOR A BEATING.

The word *mahalumot* (blows, beatings) occurs twice in the Bible—in this verse and,
later, in 19:29. Rashi takes the word to be suffering brought on by folly. Ibn Ezra takes
the word to refer to the physical violence that the fool will cause.

יח:ז פִּי־כְסִיל מְחִתָּה־לוֹ וּשְׂפָתָיו מוֹקֵשׁ נַפְשׁוֹ:

18:7 THE FOOL'S MOUTH IS THE FOOL'S RUIN. THE FOOL'S
        LIPS ARE A SNARE FOR THE FOOL'S SOUL.

Mokeish (snare) is a device used to catch birds. The fowler has to tempt the bird to
come to earth and enter the trap. Thus, a snare suggests something that you must
approach in order to be caught. If you don't approach it, you are safe. The fool's lips,
however, are an ever-present danger. The fool's thoughtless speech may put his or her
life at risk at anytime. In modern Hebrew, *mokeish* is a landmine.

יח:ח דִּבְרֵי נִרְגָּן כְּמִתְלַהֲמִים וְהֵם יָרְדוּ חַדְרֵי־בָטֶן:

18:8 THE WORDS OF AN IRRITABLE PERSON ARE LIKE
        TEMPTATIONS. THEY GO DOWN TO ONE'S INSIDES.

The *nirgan,* "an irritating or bad-tempered person," was introduced in 16:28. This is
the kind of person who bad-mouths everyone and everything. Even so, there are
people who like to hear what this person has to say. Like "junk food," they are taken
deep inside.

יח:ט גַּם מִתְרַפֶּה בִמְלַאכְתּוֹ אָח הוּא לְבַעַל מַשְׁחִית:

18:9 THE ONE WHO IS LAX IN ONE'S WORK IS A PARTNER TO
        A DESTRUCTIVE OWNER.

The point seems clear. As the owner of property should not destroy it, so the worker,
hired to do a specific task, should carry out that task. Rashi understands the first
clause to refer to a scholar who has turned away from Torah studies. For him, such a
person is like Satan. Ibn Ezra connects this verse with the previous one: those who
listen to malicious gossip become so involved that they cease to do their own work
properly and thus destroy it. Gersonides understands the verse to refer to any person
doing any kind of work in a lazy manner. Since people expect work to be done
properly, such a person is likened to one who would lay destructive traps.

181

יח:י מִגְדַּל־עֹז שֵׁם יְהֹוָה בּוֹ־יָרוּץ צַדִּיק וְנִשְׂגָּב:

18:10 THE NAME OF GOD IS A STRONG TOWER TO WHICH
THE INNOCENT MAY RUN AND BE SECURE.

V'nisgav, "be made secure" (literally, "be lifted up"), conveys the notion that as the
one who enters a high tower gains safety, so the one who gives oneself over to God's
protection will be made secure. As is his wont, Gersonides understands the verse
philosophically. He interprets *tzaddik* (righteous) as *tzodek* (correct) and explains that
for every person who correctly understands the intellectual structure of the universe,
God will be "a strong tower" for that person to depend upon.

יח:יא הוֹן עָשִׁיר קִרְיַת עֻזּוֹ וּכְחוֹמָה נִשְׂגָּבָה בְּמַשְׂכִּתוֹ:

18:11 A RICH PERSON'S WEALTH IS THAT PERSON'S
STRONGHOLD AND A HIGH WALL IN THE IMAGINATION.

While the sense of this verse seems clear, its translation is not so obvious. The
Targum and others derive *b'maskito* (in the imagination) from *sachach* (cover) and
translate it as "in the camp." Although Rashi seems to relate his commentary to the
Targum, he suggests the word is related to *even maskit* (ornamental stone [Leviticus
26:1]). Thus, he refers to houses with inlaid floors and translates "a wall in a house
with inlaid floors." The second clause, however, is striking. It undermines the
superficial read of the first clause and reveals the author's true sentiment: A wealthy
person who relies on wealth for strength is self-deceiving. Only God can be relied on
for strength and support.

יח:יב לִפְנֵי־שֶׁבֶר יִגְבַּה לֵב־אִישׁ וְלִפְנֵי כָבוֹד עֲנָוָה:

18:12 BEFORE DESTRUCTION A PERSON'S HEART MAY BE
PROUD; THEREFORE, HUMILITY SHOULD PRECEDE
HONOR.

In this verse is an echo of 16:18: "Presumption precedes destruction; a haughty spirit
goes before a fall."

יח:יג מֵשִׁיב דָּבָר בְּטֶרֶם יִשְׁמָע אִוֶּלֶת הִיא־לוֹ וּכְלִמָּה:

18:13 ANSWERING BEFORE HEARING IS FOOLISH AND
SHAMEFUL.

Just as the author recommends an appropriate approach to speech, so does the
author suggest a particular way to listen. People must learn how to listen and to
respond only after reflection. To do otherwise is foolish, and the individual who does
not listen will only garner shame as a result.

יח:יד רֽוּחַ־אִישׁ יְכַלְכֵּל מַחֲלֵהוּ וְרֽוּחַ נְכֵאָה מִי יִשָּׂאֶֽנָּה:

18:14 A PERSON'S SPIRIT MAY BOLSTER SICKNESS, BUT WHO
CAN BEAR A BROKEN SPIRIT?

Gersonides points out that the human spirit can sustain the body and do much to
heal. The spirit, however, is unable to heal itself.

יח:טו לֵב נָבוֹן יִקְנֶה־דָּעַת וְאֹזֶן חֲכָמִים תְּבַקֶּשׁ־דָּעַת:

18:15 AN UNDERSTANDING MIND MAY ACQUIRE KNOWLEDGE,
BUT THE EAR OF THE WISE WILL SEEK IT.

Our translation follows Gersonides' understanding of the verse. While the understanding mind may acquire knowledge on its own, the wise person is aided in the
search for knowledge by listening to others. Thus, the pursuit of knowledge is a
cooperative venture.

יח:טז מַתָּן אָדָם יַרְחִיב לוֹ וְלִפְנֵי גְדֹלִים יַנְחֶֽנּוּ:

18:16 A PERSON'S GIFT GUARANTEES A PLACE FOR HIM
[OR HER] AND GIVES ACCESS TO THE GREAT.

The author returns with a cynical look at the world: money talks! Ibn Ezra is most
clear: the *g'dolim* (great) in this verse are those who take bribes. In order to soften the
author's comment, Rashi applies the word "gift" to the giving of *tzedakah*.

יח:יז צַדִּיק הָרִאשׁוֹן בְּרִיבוֹ יבא וּבָא־רֵעֵהוּ וַחֲקָרֽוֹ:

18:17 THE FIRST TO PLEAD MAY SEEM INNOCENT UNTIL
THE NEXT COMES AND INVESTIGATES.

Ibn Ezra connects this verse with the previous one. The one who gave the gift was the
one who was first to plead and seemed to be the one in the right—even though the
opponent's arrival and investigation proved that the first individual was wrong. The
bribe worked. The first person won the case. Gersonides takes the verse as a warning
to judges and suggests that they not give in to the tendency to believe the story of the
first person telling it. Rather, they should be careful and listen to both sides of a case
before making the judgment.

יח:יח מִדְיָנִים יַשְׁבִּית הַגּוֹרָל וּבֵין עֲצוּמִים יַפְרִיד:

18:18 CASTING A LOT BRINGS AN END TO DISPUTES AND
SEPARATES THE CONTENDERS.

This seems to be further advice for judges. If a matter seems too difficult to decide either because of the intricacies of the case or the influence of those in contention, it may be better to have the parties agree to cast lots (or, as we would say, "flip a coin"). If both parties agree, then there can be no recrimination after the case has been decided nor can the influence of one party or the other be directed against the judge. The *Targum* translates *goral* (lot) as *pitzta,* which can mean either "lot" or "arbitration."

יח:יט אָח נִפְשָׁע מִקִּרְיַת־עֹז ומדונים וּמִדְיָנִים כִּבְרִיחַ אַרְמוֹן:

18:19 A SIBLING SINNED AGAINST IS HARDER TO BE WON
OVER THAN A FORTIFIED CITY, AND SUCH QUARRELS
LIKE THE BARS OF A CASTLE.

In order to try to prevent such an occurrence from happening, the author reminds us that family quarrels are often very bitter. Rashi explains that such quarrels may separate relatives as surely as locked and barred gates prevent entrance to a castle.

יח:כ מִפְּרִי פִי־אִישׁ תִּשְׂבַּע בִּטְנוֹ תְּבוּאַת שְׂפָתָיו יִשְׂבָּע:

18:20 ONE'S BELLY WILL BE SATISFIED ONLY BY THE FRUIT OF
ONE'S MOUTH; BY THE PRODUCE OF ONE'S LIPS WILL
ONE BE SATED.

The author used the phrase "by the fruit of one's mouth" in 12:14 and 13:2. The author continues to remind us about the benefits of proper advice to the recipient and the giver.

יח:כא מָוֶת וְחַיִּים בְּיַד־לָשׁוֹן וְאֹהֲבֶיהָ יֹאכַל פִּרְיָה:

18:21 LIFE AND DEATH ARE IN THE POWER OF THE TONGUE;
THOSE WHO LOVE IT WILL EAT ITS FRUIT.

Proper advice has a wide effect on the society and on the individual who offers it. The development of such advice takes discipline and devotion. One has to love it in order to do it. If one does it well, then one can do well and be successful.

184

יח:כב מָצָא אִשָּׁה מָצָא טוֹב וַיָּפֶק רָצוֹן מֵיְהֹוָה:

18:22 ONE WHO FINDS A SPOUSE HAS FOUND GOOD AND
WILL OBTAIN FAVOR FROM GOD.

Some may argue that the text is insensitive to those who seek the love of a partner
and have yet to find it. Nevertheless, while this text originally referred to a man
finding a wife, it is an affirmation of finding a loving and sustaining partnership
through marriage.

יח:כג תַּחֲנוּנִים יְדַבֶּר־רָשׁ וְעָשִׁיר יַעֲנֶה עַזּוֹת:

18:23 THE POOR SPEAK PLEADINGLY; THE RICH ANSWER
WITH DISRESPECT.

Money is power. The poor are forced to ask for charity. In telling the reader that the
rich may not always respond respectfully, the author reminds those who are rich to
do so.

יח:כד אִישׁ* רֵעִים לְהִתְרוֹעֵעַ וְיֵשׁ אֹהֵב דָּבֵק מֵאָח: ·סבירין ומטעין "יש"

18:24 TO FRIENDS, A PERSON MUST SHOW ONESELF TO BE
FRIENDLY, AND A FRIEND MAY BE CLOSER THAN A
SIBLING.

Due to the various ways that the words in this verse may be understood, the verse
might be translated as "there are friends who cause hurt"—if *ish* (man, person) is
taken as *yeish* (there is) and if *l'hitro-ei-a* (is derived from "to harm, hurt" rather than
"friends"). Rashi adds that the reason that one should be friendly to others is that
when friends are needed, they will be available. At such a time, friends may be even
closer than family.

Satan

In the Bible, Satan is not used as a proper name nor is it a reference to a demonic
antagonist to God (except for its usage in I Chronicles 21:1). Instead, Satan is an
adversary—sometimes even human—who opposes and obstructs. The term is used in
another form in the court of law referring to the prosecutor and the role of the
antagonist in general. In Job, Satan is clearly subordinate to God and a member of the
celestial court.

Satan is given a much more prominent role in the Talmud and midrash. He is even
identified as the *yetzer hara* (the evil inclination) and the Angel of Death (Babylonian
Talmud, *Bava Batra* 16a). He appears as the tempter, but his role is more clearly defined
by the Rabbis as the accuser. References to Satan in the liturgy are sparse, although
Satan is mentioned in the *Hashkiveinu* of the evening service and the morning blessings
that precede *P'sukei D'zimra*.

The Name of God

"The name of God" is a familiar expression in biblical literature, but it occurs only here in Proverbs and stands for God's protective power. The commandment that we must not use God's name in vain grew into the tradition that the Hebrew letters YHVH (which form the so-called personal name of God) were to be pronounced only by the High Priest on Yom Kippur, in the Holy of Holies. After the destruction of the Temple, all public use of God's name ceased, and wherever it occurred in the Bible, the word *Adonai* (my God) was substituted. Even this substitute in time assumed sacred character, and many Jews use it only in prayer, and otherwise (for instructional purposes) use the composite *Adoshem* (the name of God) or simply *HaShem* (the name). The abuse of God's name in common speech, which many Jews have, unfortunately, learned from their environment, is in direct contrast to the best of Jewish tradition. In medieval times, the presumed power inherent in God's name gave rise to much mystical speculation. It was believed that if one knew God's real, secret name, one would thereby wield semidivine powers, like giving life to a clay golem (the Jewish antecedent of Frankenstein). But even the golem was to perform religious and communal service (adapted from W. Gunther Plaut, *The Book of Proverbs: A Commentary* [New York: UAHC Press, 1961], 196).

GLEANINGS

Time Is Finite

Time is finite and insight elusive. Sometimes the search seems futile, lonely, and unsure. But if there is meaning in life—real, deep, eternal meaning—it is hiding in that force which drives us to be with each other. A child's smile, the warmth of human love, surviving pain, God's beautiful earth and its creatures, knowing that the music of our lives must someday cease—therefore how precious is the melody while it lasts—all of this is meaning, all of this is sacred, all of this can be ours.

Steven Z. Leder, *The Extraordinary Nature of Ordinary Things*
(West Orange, N.J.: Behrman House, 1999), 5

CHAPTER NINETEEN

יט:א טוֹב־רָשׁ הוֹלֵךְ בְּתֻמּוֹ מֵעִקֵּשׁ שְׂפָתָיו וְהוּא כְסִיל:

19:1 BETTER A POOR PERSON WALKING IN INTEGRITY THAN
ONE WHO IS PERVERSE IN SPEAKING AND A FOOL.

This is a statement of the ideal that we should strive toward in our repair of the world.
Since "a fool" does not seem to be the right term to contrast with "a poor person,"
some suggest emending *k'sil* (fool) to *ashir* (rich person).

יט:ב גַּם בְּלֹא־דַעַת נֶפֶשׁ לֹא־טוֹב וְאָץ בְּרַגְלַיִם חוֹטֵא:

19:2 ALSO A SOUL WITHOUT KNOWLEDGE IS NOT GOOD,
AND BEING IN HASTE WITH ONE'S FEET LEADS ONE
TO SIN.

While the message of the author seems obvious, the reader may wonder what kind of
knowledge is being referenced. The *Targum* provides the answer: *man d'la yadi-a
nafshei* (the one who does not know the self). By adding the word *l'vishta* (to evil), the
Targum explains why those quick on their feet are sinners: they are running toward
evil. For Rashi, it is Torah knowledge that is lacking. Such a person is quick to sin.
Rashi suggests that this verse refers to a person who would force his spouse to engage
in sexual activity several times against her will. Ibn Ezra, on the other hand, contends
that this verse continues the message of the previous verse: The fool's lack of
understanding stymies the correction of one's perverse mouth. Such a fool becomes a
sinner by being quick to steal. Gersonides explains that the fool's quick surrender to
one's libidinal drives (he uses the word "passions") prevents the acquisition of correct
ideas. Perhaps the verse is a simple reminder of the importance of knowledge and the
importance of caution in using it.

יט:ג אִוֶּלֶת אָדָם תְּסַלֵּף דַּרְכּוֹ וְעַל־יְהֹוָה יִזְעַף לִבּוֹ:

19:3 A PERSON'S FOLLY WILL LEAD ONE ASTRAY, AND ONE'S
MIND WILL RAGE AGAINST GOD.

Rashi thinks that this verse describes a series of events in which one causes the next. A
fool sins. As a consequence, the fool receives divine punishment. Then the fool rails
against the punishment. As it stands, the verse continues the attack against folly, which
ultimately will lead to blasphemy.

יט:ד הוֹן יֹסִיף רֵעִים רַבִּים וְדָל מֵרֵעֵהוּ יִפָּרֵד:

19:4 WEALTH BRINGS MANY FRIENDS, BUT EVEN A FRIEND
PARTS COMPANY WITH THE POOR.

Echoing what was taught in 14:20, this verse reminds us about the reality that wealth attracts people and poverty does not. Rashi softens the lesson by suggesting that Torah learning, which attracts students, is the "wealth" referred to by the writer.

יט:ה עֵד שְׁקָרִים לֹא יִנָּקֶה וְיָפִיחַ כְּזָבִים לֹא יִמָּלֵט:

19:5 A FALSE WITNESS WILL NOT BE GUILTLESS, AND THE
ONE WHO EXHALES LIES WILL NOT ESCAPE.

The phrase, "one who exhales lies," was used by the author in 6:19, 14:5, and 14:25. By placing the advice between two verses that describe how power and wealth are used to gain friends, the author provides readers with an ethical goal: repair that world so that it will be as it is described in this verse.

יט:ו רַבִּים יְחַלּוּ פְנֵי־נָדִיב וְכָל־הָרֵעַ לְאִישׁ מַתָּן:

19:6 MANY SEEK THE FAVOR OF A GENEROUS PERSON, AND
EVERYONE IS A FRIEND TO THE ONE WHO GIVES GIFTS.

The *Targum* takes the word *nadiv* to mean "prince," but we have followed Ibn Ezra and translated it as "a generous person," an alternative meaning of the term. Rashi takes the last clause of the verse to refer to either those who give charity or who endow the teaching of Torah.

יט:ז כָּל אֲחֵי־רָשׁ שְׂנֵאֻהוּ אַף כִּי מְרֵעֵהוּ רָחֲקוּ מִמֶּנּוּ מְרַדֵּף אֲמָרִים
לֹא לוֹ־הֵמָּה:

19:7 THE BRETHREN OF A POOR PERSON HATES THAT
PERSON. EVEN FRIENDS KEEP THEIR DISTANCE. THE
POOR ONE PURSUES THEM WITH WORDS. THEY
ARE NOT.

This last clause is difficult to translate. Its relationship to the other clauses is unclear. Perhaps the poor person "pursues with words" instead of attempting to establish a relationship with brethren. Maybe that is what makes such a person poor. Since the phrase seems to be used in a pejorative manner, perhaps what is meant is that that same person pursues friendships by employing words rather than feelings. Many scholars suggest that the phrase includes a *k'rei/k'tiv*. The written word *lo* meaning "no" or "not" is read as *lo* meaning "him" or "his." The last word in the clause is *heimah* (they, them). Some scholars contend that the last phrase is a fragment of a proverb. As a result, we cannot ascertain its full meaning. Rashi takes the clause to refer to a person who uses words to curry favor by claiming that certain people are relatives or friends, even though such claims are unfounded. Ibn Ezra understands the phrase to refer to those who use language "to pursue," that is, to persecute cruel relatives and false friends.

יט:ח קֹנֶה־לֵּב אֹהֵב נַפְשׁוֹ שֹׁמֵר תְּבוּנָה לִמְצֹא־טוֹב:

19:8 THE ONE WHO DEVELOPS THE MIND LOVES LIFE; THE ONE WHO PRESERVES UNDERSTANDING WILL FIND GOOD.

Again, the author emphasizes the relationship between knowledge and goodness.

יט:ט עֵד שְׁקָרִים לֹא יִנָּקֶה וְיָפִיחַ כְּזָבִים יֹאבֵד:

19:9 A FALSE WITNESS WILL NOT BE GUILTLESS, AND THE ONE WHO EXHALES LIES WILL PERISH.

Except for the last word in the verse (*yoveid*, "he will perish"), this verse is the same as 19:5. Such repetitions may be a reflection of the editing of the Book of Proverbs. Perhaps texts that are preserved by memory—and then written down—are bound to contain duplications. Or maybe the writer is preserving popular proverbs that take slightly different forms and therefore convey slightly different lessons.

יט:י לֹא־נָאוֶה לִכְסִיל תַּעֲנוּג אַף כִּי־לְעֶבֶד מְשֹׁל בְּשָׂרִים:

19:10 DELIGHT IS NOT SEEMLY FOR A FOOL, EVEN LESS SHOULD A SLAVE RULE OVER ROYALTY.

In this verse, we sense bitter disappointment in the writer. Fools do achieve delight, and unworthy persons do rule. Gersonides suggests that perhaps folly should cause pain, but in reality, folly is sometimes followed by delight. Social inversion may depend solely on the character of the slave or of the royalty. Kohelet complained of the same thing: "I have seen slaves on horseback and nobles walking on the ground like slaves" (Ecclesiastes 10:7). Our challenge is not to be satisfied with the stratification of society only if we benefit from it. Rather, we must work to make changes in it.

יט:יא שֵׂכֶל אָדָם הֶאֱרִיךְ אַפּוֹ וְתִפְאַרְתּוֹ עֲבֹר עַל־פָּשַׁע:

19:11 ONE'S INTELLIGENCE IS MANIFEST IN ONE'S PATIENCE,
ONE'S GLORY IN ONE'S FORGIVENESS OF OFFENSE.

The writer provides the general reader with a model for behavior, even as the author has given the intended reader advice on the control of one's passions and the awareness of when it is better to forgive than to hold a grudge.

יט:יב נַהַם כַּכְּפִיר זַעַף מֶלֶךְ וּכְטַל עַל־עֵשֶׂב רְצוֹנוֹ:

19:12 A RULER'S WRATH ROARS LIKE A LION, AND THE RULER'S
FAVOR IS LIKE DEW ON THE GRASS.

Like a lion, a sovereign ruler can roar and rip. The wary are warned to keep clear. Like the dew, for those who obtain it, the sovereign's favor can sustain and enhance life. These striking images remind us that the book was written for a particular group of people who wanted to be counselors to kings and advisors to those in power. The author felt that they need to be reminded that life and death are in the hands of the ruler.

יט:יג הַוֹּת לְאָבִיו בֵּן כְּסִיל וְדֶלֶף טֹרֵד מִדְיְנֵי אִשָּׁה:

19:13 A FOOLISH SON IS THE RUIN OF ONE'S PARENT;
A CONTENTIOUS SPOUSE IS LIKE A LEAKING ROOF.

The same misogynous idea of the second clause (which we have transcended with a gender-free translation) is also expressed in 27:15. The sense is clear and can be translated for either spouse. Just as a leaking roof constantly allows rain to intrude, a contentious spouse allows one's partner no peace. Some suggest that this verse emerged from the freedom granted to women in a city environment that was seen as threatening for men.

יט:יד בַּיִת וָהוֹן נַחֲלַת אָבוֹת וּמֵיהֹוָה אִשָּׁה מַשְׂכָּלֶת:

19:14 A HOUSE AND RICHES ARE ANCESTRAL INHERITANCES,
BUT AN INTELLIGENT SPOUSE COMES FROM GOD.

This verse seems to suggest that possessions may pass down through the generations automatically, but finding a proper spouse takes an act of God.

יט:טו עַצְלָה תַּפִּיל תַּרְדֵּמָה וְנֶפֶשׁ רְמִיָּה תִרְעָב:

19:15 LAZINESS PUTS ONE IN A DEEP SLEEP, AND AN IDLE
PERSON WILL STARVE.

Rashi applied this verse to a lazy Torah scholar who will answer a question having not
prepared for it, as if asleep. Ibn Ezra takes the word for "deceit" *(r'miyah)* to mean
"deceitful," suggesting that a deceitful person will starve. Gersonides joins both
clauses together and suggests that a person who is too lazy to study the sciences will
be unable to attain correct ideas. As a consequence, that person will not be able to
perfect the soul or meet the needs of the body. A more idiomatic translation of the
first part of the verse might read: "Laziness makes you unconscious."

יט:טז שֹׁמֵר מִצְוָה שֹׁמֵר נַפְשׁוֹ בּוֹזֵה דְרָכָיו יומת יָמוּת:

19:16 ONE WHO KEEPS THE COMMANDMENT PRESERVES
ONE'S LIFE, BUT ONE WHO DESPISES THE DIVINE WAYS
SHALL BE PUT TO DEATH.

Taking *d'rachav* to refer to the "ways of God," Ibn Ezra explains that the sinner will
die an untimely death by divine fiat. Following Maimonides (*Guide for the Perplexed*
3:27), Gersonides explains that keeping "the commandment" means perfecting the
body and soul. Not achieving such perfection will bring a person to an early death.

יט:יז מַלְוֵה יְהֹוָה חוֹנֵן דָּל וּגְמֻלוֹ יְשַׁלֶּם־לוֹ:

19:17 GOD LENDS TO THE ONE WHO GRACIOUSLY GIVES
TO THE POOR; GOD SHALL REPAY THAT PERSON IN
RETURN.

Our translation follows Ibn Ezra, who explains that wealth is a trust to be used to assist
the poor. Those who do so graciously will receive their just reward. Rashi suggests that
charity that a person has given will plead for one's life when that person becomes ill.
However one understands the specifics of the verse, the author emphasizes the
importance of charity as one means of helping the poor.

יט:יח יַסֵּר בִּנְךָ כִּי־יֵשׁ תִּקְוָה וְאֶל־הֲמִיתוֹ אַל־תִּשָּׂא נַפְשֶׁךָ:

19:18 DISCIPLINE YOUR CHILD WHEN THERE IS STILL HOPE,
BUT DON'T SET YOUR MIND ON DESTROYING HIM
[OR HER].

While this is a strong statement, it reflects the notion of "spare the rod and spoil the
child." Discipline was once carried out by beatings. However, the author warns that
such discipline should be applied only when there is hope of a good outcome.

As Rashi points out, one should not strike a child with a mortal blow. (We would argue that one should not strike a child at all.) Ibn Ezra suggests that the second clause of the verse refers to the parent who should not consider supporting the family through crime, an avenue that would place one's children in mortal danger as a result.

יט:יט גרל גְּדָל־חֵמָה נֹשֵׂא עֹנֶשׁ כִּי אִם־תַּצִּיל וְעוֹד תּוֹסִף׃

19:19 THE IRASCIBLE PERSON WILL BEAR A PUNISHMENT;
WERE YOU TO SAVE SUCH A PERSON YOU WOULD HAVE
TO DO IT AGAIN.

The relationship between the two clauses in this verse is unclear. We have followed the *Targum*'s translation of the first clause. The *Targum* translates the second clause rather broadly: "the more that one is relieved, the more that one adds to one's burden." Rashi places the anger elsewhere in interpreting the verse thus: "If you forego your anger and save your enemy when you see evil befall that person, you will increase your days of happiness." Ibn Ezra relates the verse to the previous one that deals with the errant child who needs discipline and interprets: "Don't turn your attention away from that child and withhold discipline. However, if that child is exceptionally angry, leave that child alone when receiving an appropriate punishment. If you try to save the child, you will have to keep doing it." Gersonides sees irascibility as a terrible fault, causing the person to quarrel with other people. The attempt to save that person from the resulting problems only worsens the fault. This verse offers the reader caution: Don't lose your temper. Control your anger.

יט:כ שְׁמַע עֵצָה וְקַבֵּל מוּסָר לְמַעַן תֶּחְכַּם בְּאַחֲרִיתֶךָ׃

19:20 LISTEN TO ADVICE AND RECEIVE DISCIPLINE SO THAT
YOU WILL BE WISE FOR THE REST OF YOUR LIFE.

Ibn Ezra connects this verse with the next one and suggests what kind of advice to follow. The verse may suggest that there is a progression to advice. If one listens, then one can become wise.

יט:כא רַבּוֹת מַחֲשָׁבוֹת בְּלֶב־אִישׁ וַעֲצַת יְהֹוָה הִיא תָקוּם׃

19:21 MANY ARE THE THOUGHTS IN A PERSON'S MIND, BUT
IT IS THE COUNSEL OF GOD THAT STANDS.

One may think of many things, but what counts is what God wants of the person.

יט:כב תַּאֲוַת אָדָם חַסְדּוֹ וְטוֹב־רָשׁ מֵאִישׁ כָּזָב:

19:22 A PERSON'S LUST IS SHAMEFUL; A POOR PERSON IS
BETTER THAN A LIAR.

The difficulty in translating this verse lies in the word *chesed* (from the word in the verse *chasdo*). Generally, this word means "continuous love or mercy." But its homonym, which we find in Leviticus 20:17 and Proverbs 14:34, means "shame." Gersonides argues that "shame" makes more sense in the verse than does "love." However, Rashi and Ibn Ezra take the word to mean "kindness." Rashi understands the clause to mean that people like someone who performs acts of kindness, while Ibn Ezra understands it to mean that people want to extend kindnesses to those who deserve it.

יט:כג יִרְאַת יְהוָֹה לְחַיִּים וְשָׂבֵעַ יָלִין בַּל־יִפָּקֶד רָע:

19:23 FEAR OF GOD BRINGS LIFE; FOR [THE GOD-FEARING]
SHALL BE SATISFIED AND MAY REST WITHOUT BEING
VISITED BY EVIL.

Ibn Ezra suggests that God-fearing people do not remember even the trouble that has already befallen them.

יט:כד טָמַן עָצֵל יָדוֹ בַּצַּלָּחַת גַּם־אֶל־פִּיהוּ לֹא יְשִׁיבֶנָּה:

19:24 LAZY PEOPLE HIDE THEIR HANDS IN THE DISH AND DO
NOT EVEN PUT IT BACK IN THEIR MOUTHS.

This verse describes people who are so lazy that when they eat they do not even bother to feed themselves. Rather, they put their hands in the communal dish and leave them there. Ridiculous as this sounds, it presents another opportunity for the author to admonish the reader not to be lazy.

יט:כה לֵץ תַּכֶּה וּפֶתִי יַעְרִם וְהוֹכִיחַ לְנָבוֹן יָבִין דָּעַת:

19:25 HIT A MOCKER AND A FOOL WILL GET SMART; CORRECT
THE INTELLIGENT AND THAT PERSON WILL GAIN
UNDERSTANDING.

Rashi applies the first clause of this verse to Jethro, who converts to Judaism after seeing the punishment meted out to Pharaoh. Ibn Ezra understands *yarim* (will get smart) as "he or she will study [the art of being] cunning."

יט:כו מְשַׁדֶּד־אָב יַבְרִיחַ אֵם בֵּן מֵבִישׁ וּמַחְפִּיר:

19:26 THE ONE WHO DISHONORS ONE'S FATHER AND MAKES
ONE'S MOTHER RUN AWAY IS A SHAMEFUL AND
REPREHENSIBLE CHILD.

Gersonides reverses the verse: "A shameful and reprehensible child [one given over to one's lusts] will send thieves to dishonor one's father by seeking to share in the loot, and this will cause the child's mother to run away." To prevent such a horrendous occurrence, Gersonides warns that parents should discipline their children when they are young.

יט:כז חֲדַל־בְּנִי לִשְׁמֹעַ מוּסָר לִשְׁגוֹת מֵאִמְרֵי־דָעַת:

19:27 STOP, MY YOUNG FRIEND, OBEY DISCIPLINE AND DO
NOT STRAY FROM THE WORDS OF KNOWLEDGE.

Since it is difficult to relate the two clauses of the verse in the Hebrew, we have followed the general translation of the *Targum:* "Turn away, my young friend, and obey discipline and don't stray from the words of my mouth." Rashi adds a few words to the verse and reverses its order to read: "My young friend, don't go astray [or 'turn away'] from words of knowledge in order to obey discipline." Ibn Ezra interprets it somewhat differently: "My young friend, don't turn away from words of knowledge, but hearken, obey, discipline." Gersonides offers one of the most interesting interpretations of the text, as he applies the medieval philosophical distinction between the perfection of the body and the perfection of the soul: "My young friend, stop listening continually to the science of ethics at the cost of turning away from the words of knowledge." Gersonides adds that it is not fitting that a person should waste time in the further investigation of ethics, since ethics only prepare us for the important goal of attaining (philosophical) wisdom.

יט:כח עֵד בְּלִיַּעַל יָלִיץ מִשְׁפָּט וּפִי רְשָׁעִים יְבַלַּע־אָוֶן:

19:28 A GOOD-FOR-NOTHING WITNESS MOCKS JUSTICE, AND
THE MOUTH OF THE WICKED ANNOUNCES INIQUITY.

Two homonyms *(yalitz* and *y'vala)* that are contained in the verse make its translation and interpretation difficult. While the *Targum* understands *yalitz* as "mocks," Rashi, Ibn Ezra, and Gersonides assume that it is derived from *meilitz* ("interpreter," as in Genesis 42:23) and understand it as "testifies." Therefore, the verse would suggest that even an unworthy witness can attest to the truth. *Y'vala* can come from the root *bala* meaning "swallow" or *bala* meaning "announce." In either case, it serves as a wordplay on *b'liyaal* (good for nothing, wicked, useless). Ibn Ezra suggests the alternative meaning of *yalitz* (mocks) and joins it with another interpretation of *y'vala* (from "taking apart the sanctuary" in Numbers 4:20). Thus, he suggests that while the base witness mocks justice, iniquity will split the mouth of the wicked. Gersonides takes *y'vala* as "swallow" and argues that the mouth of the wicked swallows up and conceals iniquity.

:יט:כט נָכוֹנוּ לַלֵּצִים שְׁפָטִים וּמַהֲלֻמוֹת לְגֵו כְּסִילִים

19:29 JUDGMENTS ARE MADE AGAINST MOCKERS AND LASHES
FOR THE BACKS OF FOOLS.

Both Rashi and Ibn Ezra conclude that God is the source of the judgments made against mockers. Rashi specifies the punishment as *tzaraat* (a skin disease usually incorrectly identified as leprosy). Gersonides connects this verse with the previous one to suggest that a judgment against those who provide erroneous information to philosophers is a fit punishment, as are the accompanying lashes.

False Witness

"False witness" is a term that we encounter in the Ten Commandments, as well as throughout rabbinic literature and law. It refers specifically to an individual who testifies that he (only men are legal witnesses in traditional Judaism) saw someone do something when, in fact, he did not. In the Judaism that existed up to modern times, a false witness might cause an innocent person to be punished, even executed. Such a witness was worthy of the greatest condemnation. The condemnation of the false witness reminds the modern Jew of the importance of truth telling in every sphere of life.

GLEANINGS

Doing It in a Group

Judaism is a team sport.

You can play tennis up against the backboard but it isn't the same. Golf works just fine with one person and a bag—but it gets awfully lonely. You can hit the ball in the holes and blast out of the sand traps, but playing against yourself gets old fast—you can miss the conversation. We've all played pick-up games of football with four or five people, and done the backyard stickball thing with one friend and the little sister who gets to be the designated fielder. One-on-one can be a great game, a good way to spend an afternoon with a friend, but it isn't basketball. . . .

The bottom line is this: To keep at it Jewishly in the hard moments, you need the support of a peer group—and so does your child. Otherwise, the storms afford many other warmer ports.

Joel Lurie Grishaver, *40 Things You Can Do to Save the Jewish People*
(Los Angeles: Alef Design Group, 1993), 217, 219

CHAPTER TWENTY

כ:א לֵץ הַיַּיִן הֹמֶה שֵׁכָר וְכָל־שֹׁגֶה בּוֹ לֹא יֶחְכָּם:

20:1 WINE IS A MOCKER, STRONG DRINK A BRAWLER; ALL
WHO GO ASTRAY THEREBY WILL NOT BECOME WISE.

Ibn Ezra takes *homeh*, "brawler" (literally, "one who shouts"), as one who shouts for
more *sheichar* (strong drink). Although wine (and other forms of alcohol) are used in
Judaism for sacramental purposes, such as in *Kiddush* for Shabbat and the Festivals,
Jewish tradition condemns alcohol abuse.

כ:ב נַהַם כַּכְּפִיר אֵימַת מֶלֶךְ מִתְעַבְּרוֹ חוֹטֵא נַפְשׁוֹ:

20:2 THE FEAR OF THE RULER IS LIKE THE ROARING OF A
LION; THE ONE WHO PROVOKES THE RULER SINS
AGAINST ONE'S OWN LIFE.

The lion's roar warns the wary. The cautious keep in mind the power of the ruler and
warn those who are close to the seat of power. Gersonides takes the verse as a
parable of the human intellect. Its rule of the individual is as natural as the lion's roar.
Misusing the intellect is as fatal as is disregarding the roar of the lion.

כ:ג כָּבוֹד לָאִישׁ שֶׁבֶת מֵרִיב וְכָל־אֱוִיל יִתְגַּלָּע:

20:3 KEEPING FROM A FIGHT IS HONORABLE FOR A PERSON;
ANY FOOL CAN QUARREL.

This is another way of saying "Pick your battles." Everyone needs to know what
battles are worth fighting.

כ:ד מֵחֹרֶף עָצֵל לֹא־יַחֲרֹשׁ ישאל וְשָׁאַל בַּקָּצִיר וָאָיִן:

20:4 IN WINTER, THE LAZY PERSON WILL NOT PLOW;
AT HARVEST, THAT PERSON MAY ASK BUT WILL GET
NOTHING.

Rashi explains that the lazy person uses the cold as an excuse for sitting around and
doing nothing—including neglecting to study. Ibn Ezra adds that at harvest time, the
other farmers will not give the lazy farmer anything. Gersonides sees this as a parable

about intellectual activity. The person who is unwilling to seek the various kinds of perfection will be unable to attain them.

כ:ה מַיִם עֲמֻקִּים עֵצָה בְלֶב־אִישׁ וְאִישׁ תְּבוּנָה יִדְלֶנָּה:

20:5 IN THE MIND ADVICE IS LIKE DEEP WATER, WHICH AN UNDERSTANDING PERSON CAN DRAW UP.

A counselor to those in power must have the self-confidence to believe that he or she knows the proper advice to give—a lesson for all to learn. Moreover, that person should know that what counts is not superficial appearances but rather those things that are much more profound. Rashi refers the verse to the study of Torah. A *halachah* may be locked up in the mind of the teacher, but an able student can bring it forth. Ibn Ezra understands the verse as referring to the quality of wisdom in the mind of the pure, which, like deep water, is uncontaminated. For Gersonides, this verse is a parable concerning the nature of knowledge. Like something that is submerged, nature requires the effort of investigation to make it available.

כ:ו רָב־אָדָם יִקְרָא אִישׁ חַסְדּוֹ וְאִישׁ אֱמוּנִים מִי יִמְצָא:

20:6 ONE CAN CALL MANY PEOPLE FRIENDS, BUT WHO CAN FIND A TRUSTWORTHY PERSON?

The challenge of translating this verse is to discern the subject of the verb *yikra* (will call). We have followed the *Targum*, which translates *yikra* as *mitkaryan* (are called). Rashi understands the verse to mean that while many trust that others who promise them *chesed* (continuous love) will deliver, there are few who do so. Ibn Ezra understands the verse to mean that many proclaim that they will do *chesed*, but not many are willing to say that they have found a person whom they can trust. For Gersonides, finding a person who actually does *chesed* is as difficult as finding one who is trustworthy.

כ:ז מִתְהַלֵּךְ בְּתֻמּוֹ צַדִּיק אַשְׁרֵי בָנָיו אַחֲרָיו:

20:7 THE ONE WHO WALKS IN INTEGRITY IS RIGHTEOUS, AND HAPPY ARE THE CHILDREN WHO COME AFTER.

For Gersonides, walking in integrity suggests perfection in both ethics and ideas.

כ:ח מֶלֶךְ יוֹשֵׁב עַל־כִּסֵּא־דִין מְזָרֶה בְעֵינָיו כָּל־רָע:

20:8 A SOVEREIGN SITS ON THE THRONE OF JUDGMENT,
WINNOWING EVIL WITH HIS [OR HER] EYES.

A competent ruler can easily discern goodness and evil. Gersonides resorts to understanding the verse as a parable once again. For him, the sovereign ruler is the intellect, and "with his [or her] eyes" refers to the investigation (of wisdom). What is evil is improper ethical conduct and incorrect ideas.

כ:ט מִי־יֹאמַר זִכִּיתִי לִבִּי טָהַרְתִּי מֵחַטָּאתִי:

20:9 WHO CAN SAY, "I HAVE MADE MY MIND CLEAN; I AM
PURE FROM SIN"?

Ibn Ezra reminds us of what we already know, that no one is able to say that he or she has never sinned.

כ:י אֶבֶן וָאֶבֶן אֵיפָה וְאֵיפָה תּוֹעֲבַת יְהֹוָה גַּם־שְׁנֵיהֶם:

20:10 FALSE WEIGHTS AND FALSE MEASURES, BOTH ARE AN
ABOMINATION TO GOD.

Business requires common standards. Cheating in business is considered an affront to God. The writer reminds us that religious life should be manifest in our everyday activities.

כ:יא גַּם בְּמַעֲלָלָיו יִתְנַכֶּר־נָעַר אִם־זַךְ וְאִם־יָשָׁר פָּעֳלוֹ:

20:11 EVEN A CHILD IS KNOWN BY DEEDS WHETHER THE
ACTION IS PURE OR RIGHT.

Ibn Ezra reminds us that *yitnaker* (is known) may also mean "hidden" or "disguised," as in Genesis 42:7. He interprets the verse to mean that if you are free of sin and act correctly, your deeds will hide your youth, since people expect young people to act foolishly. Gersonides translates the words the same way and suggests further that a person might hide evil intentions by good acts. However, such a person would be a *naar* (a pun on both "fool" and "youth"), since that person does not allow his or her intellect to rule. Instead, that person allows the intellect to serve. One might translate the verse as trumpeting the power of disguise: even young people can disguise themselves by their deeds, whether (or not) their acts are pure or right.

כ:יב אֹזֶן שֹׁמַעַת וְעַיִן רֹאָה יְהֹוָה עָשָׂה גַם־שְׁנֵיהֶם:

20:12 THE EAR THAT HEARS, THE EYE THAT SEES; GOD HAS
MADE THEM BOTH.

Rashi takes the "ear that hears" as the one who listens to moral instruction and "the
eye that sees" as the one who foresees the future.

כ:יג אַל־תֶּאֱהַב שֵׁנָה פֶּן־תִּוָּרֵשׁ פְּקַח עֵינֶיךָ שְׂבַע־לָחֶם:

20:13 DON'T LOVE SLEEP OR YOU WILL BECOME POOR;
KEEP YOUR EYES OPEN AND HAVE PLENTY OF BREAD.

This is another warning against laziness. If you want to succeed, be aware (stay
awake). Watch what is going on around you.

כ:יד רַע רַע יֹאמַר הַקּוֹנֶה וְאֹזֵל לוֹ אָז יִתְהַלָּל:

20:14 "BAD, BAD." THAT IS WHAT THE BUYER SAYS AND THEN
BOASTS [ABOUT THE BARGAIN] UPON LEAVING.

To diminish the asking price of a product, the buyer denigrates it. Then after the
purchase, the buyer brags to friends about the deal he or she made and the bargain
he or she got. Rashi understands the verse differently. He suggests that the verse refers
to a person who engages in Torah study while impoverished and suffering hunger
pangs. Once that student has amassed great learning, then that student will praise
him- or herself for having achieved it even through suffering. Gersonides suggests that
the verse could not refer to the acquisition of knowledge, for such acquisition could
never be bad.

כ:טו יֵשׁ זָהָב וְרָב־פְּנִינִים וּכְלִי יְקָר שִׂפְתֵי־דָעַת:

20:15 THERE IS GOLD AND THERE ARE ALL KINDS OF
CORAL, BUT THE MOST PRECIOUS THING IS LIPS
OF KNOWLEDGE.

This verse expresses what the writer wants the reader to reflect on. Knowledge is
important, and so is the ability to articulate what the student has learned.

כ:טז לְקַח־בִּגְדוֹ כִּי־עָרַב זָר וּבְעַד נׇכְרִיָּה חַבְלֵהוּ:

20:16 TAKE THE GARMENT FROM THE ONE WHO IS SURETY
FOR A STRANGER, AND HOLD IN PLEDGE THE ONE WHO
IS SURETY FOR A FOREIGN WOMAN.

This verse is repeated with a slight alteration in 27:13. In 6:1–2, the author advises against being surety for a neighbor. How much more foolish is it for a stranger. In this verse we see what can happen.

כ:יז עָרֵב לָאִישׁ לֶחֶם שָׁקֶר וְאַחַר יִמָּלֵא־פִיהוּ חָצָץ:

20:17 THE BREAD OF FALSEHOOD IS SWEET TO A PERSON, BUT
AFTERWARDS ONE'S MOUTH IS FILLED WITH GRAVEL.

There is a wordplay in this verse from the preceding verse. There we read *arav* (surety). Here we read *areiv* (sweet). Rashi applies the verse to an act of adultery. Perhaps such an act is delightful at the beginning, but it causes pain and remorse at the end. Ibn Ezra takes it to apply to false testimony given in court. Gersonides takes it to refer to erroneous conclusions drawn from mistaken premises.

כ:יח מַחֲשָׁבוֹת בְּעֵצָה תִכּוֹן וּבְתַחְבֻּלוֹת עֲשֵׂה מִלְחָמָה:

20:18 THOUGHTS ARE MADE FIRM BY ADVICE; MAKE WAR
WITH PLANS.

This verse has the role of the reader directly in mind. The ruler may make plans, and the advisor may have the responsibility of "finalizing the plan." While plans are made at higher levels, they are usually carried out on lower levels, such as is the case with wars. Rashi understands the verse in a religious sense: to fight the forces of Satan in one's life, one should fast, make penitence, and pray. Gersonides takes the verse as a parable of philosophical activity, of separating the correct notion from the incorrect one.

כ:יט גּוֹלֶה־סּוֹד הוֹלֵךְ רָכִיל וּלְפֹתֶה שְׂפָתָיו לֹא תִתְעָרָב:

20:19 THE ONE WHO GOES AROUND TELLING TALES WILL
REVEAL SECRETS, SO DON'T GET INVOLVED WITH A
BLABBERMOUTH.

Watch what you say and be careful with whom you associate. Gersonides also reminds us that talebearers have a deleterious effect on society.

200

כ:כ מְקַלֵּל אָבִיו וְאִמּוֹ יִדְעַךְ נֵרוֹ באישון בֶּאֱשׁוּן חֹשֶׁךְ:

20:20 REGARDING THE ONE WHO CURSES ONE'S FATHER AND
MOTHER, MAY THAT PERSON'S LAMP BE SMOTHERED IN
THE THICKEST OF DARKNESS.

Rashi understands the extinguishing of the lamp as suggestive of the evil that will befall
such a person. Ibn Ezra considers the lamp to be the soul of the person who behaves
in such an inappropriate way toward parents.

כ:כא נַחֲלָה מבחלת מְבֹהֶלֶת בָּרִאשֹׁנָה וְאַחֲרִיתָהּ לֹא תְבֹרָךְ:

20:21 IN THE BEGINNING, AN INHERITANCE MAY BE QUICKLY
GAINED, BUT IN THE END, IT WILL NOT BE BLESSED.

Rashi applies this verse to the efforts of the tribe of Gad and the tribe of Reuben to
take their inheritance to the other side of the Jordan (Numbers 32). Ibn Ezra explains
why a quickly acquired inheritance will receive no blessing: it was stolen.

כ:כב אַל־תֹּאמַר אֲשַׁלְּמָה־רָע קַוֵּה לַיהֹוָה וְיֹשַׁע לָךְ:

20:22 DON'T SAY: "I WILL PAY BACK EVIL." HOPE FOR GOD,
AND GOD WILL SAVE YOU.

Vendettas initiate vicious cycles. Don't fight evil with evil. Instead, trust God, and you
will be redeemed from evil.

כ:כג תּוֹעֲבַת יְהֹוָה אֶבֶן וָאָבֶן וּמֹאזְנֵי מִרְמָה לֹא־טוֹב:

20:23 IT IS AN ABOMINATION TO GOD TO HAVE DIFFERENT
WEIGHTS, AND IT IS NOT GOOD TO HAVE A DECEPTIVE
BALANCE SCALE.

This verse reminds us of 20:10 and 11:1.

כ:כד מֵיְהֹוָה מִצְעֲדֵי־גָבֶר וְאָדָם מַה־יָּבִין דַּרְכּוֹ:

20:24 A PERSON'S STEPS ARE DETERMINED BY GOD;
HOW DOES ONE DISCERN ONE'S WAY?

This verse may be in conflict with the doctrine of free will. If our path is determined
by God, then how are we responsible for what we do on life's way? Were it argued
that the human task is to determine what God wants and then to do it, then—in some
way—we would be figuring out our own way in life. If we cannot make sense out of

our own way and our steps are predetermined, there would be no room for a system of mitzvot and no foundation on which to build Judaism.

כ:כה מוֹקֵשׁ אָדָם יָלַע קֹדֶשׁ וְאַחַר נְדָרִים לְבַקֵּר:

20:25 IT IS A SNARE TO SPEAK CARELESSLY OF THE HOLY AND
TO MAKE INQUIRY AFTER UTTERING VOWS.

The meaning of the verb *yala* in the first clause is unclear. The *Targum* understands it as "to vow." Following others, we have translated it as "to speak carelessly." Rashi relates the verb to Obadiah 1:16, "to swallow down, to slurp." He thereby interprets the first clause as the consequence of sin. "It is a snare [after having sinned] to swallow down [destroy] one's sanctity." Ibn Ezra understands it similarly. For him, "the holy" is something related to the sanctuary. For most commentators, the verse presents us with a warning not to make vows carelessly, a notion from Kohelet: "Keep your mouth from being rash, and do not let your throat be quick to bring forth speech before God" (Ecclesiastes 5:1).

כ:כו מְזָרֶה רְשָׁעִים מֶלֶךְ חָכָם וַיָּשֶׁב עֲלֵיהֶם אוֹפָן:

20:26 THE WISE RULER WINNOWS THE WICKED AND MOVES
THE WHEEL OVER THEM.

Rashi identifies the "wise ruler" as God and "the wicked" as Pharaoh. "The wheel" is the link between the wicked (and his or her actions) and the punishment that person receives. Because Pharaoh hardened his heart, suggests Rashi, his chariot wheels ran hard, thus preventing his escape from the encroaching waters of the Red Sea (Exodus 14:25). Ibn Ezra refers the verse to a human ruler who first crushes enemies with the wheel and then grinds (winnows) them down. Gersonides explains that the "ruler" is the human intellect, which scatters incorrect ideas ("the wicked"). Like the wheel, the ruler moves people away from the negative effect of such ideas.

כ:כז נֵר יְהֹוָה נִשְׁמַת אָדָם חֹפֵשׂ כָּל־חַדְרֵי־בָטֶן:

20:27 THE SOUL OF THE HUMAN IS THE LAMP OF GOD,
WHICH SEARCHES ALL THE INNER PARTS.

Rashi suggests that the human soul will offer evidence (on the Day of Judgment). Ibn Ezra understands the verse as two possible parables. First, the human soul—which is a divine emanation—illumines the heart (mind), which contains ideas. Second, the "lamp of God" refers to the human intellect. If it is owned by the ruler, then that ruler will be able to rightly govern, rewarding the virtuous and punishing the wicked. Gersonides takes the "soul of the human" as the intellect, which investigates "all the inner parts" of existing things to understand their secrets. However the verse is understood, it stresses the relationship between God and each individual.

כ:כח חֶסֶד וֶאֱמֶת יִצְּרוּ־מֶלֶךְ וְסָעַד בַּחֶסֶד כִּסְאוֹ:

20:28 MAY CONTINUOUS LOVE AND TRUTH PRESERVE THE RULER, AND MAY THE THRONE BE SUSTAINED BY UNENDING LOVE.

Gersonides suggests that the continuous love and truth that a ruler may extend to the people may strengthen their support for that ruler. Such love will have a positive impact on any relationship.

כ:כט תִּפְאֶרֶת בַּחוּרִים כֹּחָם וַהֲדַר זְקֵנִים שֵׂיבָה:

20:29 THE GLORY OF THE YOUNG IS THEIR STRENGTH, AND THE BEAUTY OF THE OLD IS THEIR GRAY HAIR.

Gersonides observed that physical prowess is the goal of young people, while gray hair signals the accumulation of wisdom. His may be a reflection of the statement by Maimonides that "... in the measure in which the faculties of the body are weakened and the fire of the desires is quenched, the intellect is strengthened..." (*Guide for the Perplexed* 3:51).

כ:ל חַבֻּרוֹת פֶּצַע תמריק תַּמְרוּק בְּרָע וּמַכּוֹת חַדְרֵי־בָטֶן:

20:30 SLASHES SCOUR AWAY EVIL, AS DO LASHES ON THE INNER PART OF THE BODY.

The *Targum* translates the first words, *chaburot petza* (slashes of the wound), with two words, *shuchanei ufudata* (scabs and punishment). Rashi quotes a rabbinic statement (Babylonian Talmud, *Shabbat* 33a) in order to link the word *tamrik* (scours) to *tamrukeha* (her cosmetics [Esther 2:9]), which states that the person who adorns oneself to do evil will end up with wounds through lashes. Making the same connection, Ibn Ezra connects this verse to the previous one: as physical strength marks out the young and gray hair the old, so do sounds and the wounds resulting from lashes designate the wicked. Gersonides offers a psychospiritual explanation: there are certain sins that leave an irremovable trace in the body. Perhaps the spiritual lesson of the verse is that suffering purifies the sinner.

Free Will

If God is omniscient and knows everything, then does the human have... this conundrum has perplexed Jewish thinkers for centuries. For if God knows everything and humans do not have free will, how can they be held responsible (and thus to be punished) for their actions? Thus, classic philosophers have held that persons have free will and God knows what choices humans will make. As a result, they are held responsible for their actions. Some contemporary Jewish thinkers, like Mordecai Kaplan, Harold Schulweis, and Harold Kushner, argue that God's power is limited and that God cannot know everything and cannot intervene in human affairs or the workings of nature.

Day of Judgment

While there are a variety of interpretations regarding what will happen when the Messiah comes, at the end of days, most will agree that it will be an individual and collective Day of Judgment. Individuals will be judged for their deeds as a prerequisite for living in the world-to-come. This Day of Judgment is approximated on Yom Kippur, which is also known as Yom HaDin, "the Day of Judgment."

GLEANINGS

Evil

A man once stood before God, his heart breaking from the pain and injustice in the world. "Dear God," he cried out, "look at all the suffering, the anguish and distress in Your world. Why don't You send help?"

God responded, "I did send help. I sent you."

I believe we are sent by God to conquer evil, soothe suffering, and create joy. When we reach out to people in pain, we do God's work. Why there needs to be pain and suffering in the first place is an understandable question but ultimately a pointless one. There are those who believe suffering is inflicted by God as punishment for sin. Others simply accept on faith that what seems like evil to us actually has a purpose in God's great plan, but being human means we can never fully appreciate its role. Then there are those who refuse to blame God for evil; they blame humanity instead. I am one of those. For me, for most of us, I suspect, God is not an omnipotent, supernatural power but a power manifest in humanity at its best. If this is so, then the answer to cruelty lies not in heaven but on earth. Salvation will come to us not from God above but from each other.

Steven Z. Leder, *The Extraordinary Nature of Ordinary Things*
(West Orange, N.J.: Behrman House, 1999), 39–40

CHAPTER TWENTY-ONE

כא:א פַּלְגֵי־מַיִם לֶב־מֶלֶךְ בְּיַד־יְהוָה עַל־כָּל־אֲשֶׁר יַחְפֹּץ יַטֶּנּוּ:

21:1 LIKE WATER CHANNELS, THE RULER'S HEART IS IN
THE HAND OF GOD; THE RULER MAY DIRECT IT AS
GOD DESIRES.

As the direction of water in irrigation channels follows the plan of the engineer who
constructed it, so is the ruler's mind directed by a divine mandate. This seems to
suggest that there is a divine right to the human monarchy. Gersonides suggests that
the verse teaches us that *even* a sovereign ruler is under divine control. He also
suggests that the verse means that sin does not proceed from God or from the
intellect (which he understands as the meaning of "ruler") but rather from other
aspects of the soul.

כא:ב כָּל־דֶּרֶךְ אִישׁ יָשָׁר בְּעֵינָיו וְתֹכֵן לִבּוֹת יְהוָה:

21:2 IN ONE'S OWN EYES, ONE IS ALWAYS RIGHT, BUT GOD
EXAMINES ALL MINDS.

The admission of personal error is one of the most difficult things to do. We feel
diminished should we be in error. The notion of truth and equity that is not linked to
person, place, or time is part of what we understand to be God.

כא:ג עֲשֹׂה צְדָקָה וּמִשְׁפָּט נִבְחָר לַיהוָה מִזָּבַח:

21:3 THE DOING OF RIGHTEOUSNESS AND JUSTICE IS MORE
ACCEPTABLE TO GOD THAN SACRIFICE.

This is an echo of the teaching of the prophets: justice is more prized than sacrifice.
It is not that ritual (whether in the form of animal sacrifice or prayer) is bad or
unnecessary in our religious lives. We require the crystallization of our belief in
concrete form. However, we are tempted to let our ritual acts suffice in our religious
lives and forego our ethical responsibilities.

כא:ד רוּם־עֵינַיִם וּרְחַב־לֵב נִר רְשָׁעִים חַטָּאת:

21:4 A HAUGHTY LOOK, A PROUD HEART—THE CULTIVATED
LAND OF THE WICKED IS SIN.

The difficulty of the second clause lies in the word *nir* (cultivated land). Its meaning is unclear. Perhaps it means that sin lays the foundation to sin further just as "cultivated land" permits the farmer to plant crops. The *Targum* translates *nir* as *ushraga* ("and the lamp") and draws a connection between the first clause and the second: "A haughty look, a proud heart, and the lamp for the wicked to sin." Just as a lamp enables a person to proceed in darkness, so pride prepares a wicked person to sin.

כא:ה מַחְשְׁבוֹת חָרוּץ אַךְ־לְמוֹתָר וְכָל־אָץ אַךְ־לְמַחְסוֹר:

21:5 THE PLANS OF THE DILIGENT LEAD ONLY TO PROFIT;
HASTE LEADS ONLY TO LOSS.

An idiomatic translation of the last clause might read: "haste makes waste." The author is advocating calm reflection in place of precipitous haste. Gersonides understands the last clause to refer to the person who acts without reflection or investigation.

כא:ו פֹּעַל אוֹצָרוֹת בִּלְשׁוֹן שָׁקֶר הֶבֶל נִדָּף מְבַקְשֵׁי־מָוֶת:

21:6 ACQUIRING TREASURES BY THE LANGUAGE OF LIES
IS A QUICKLY FLEETING VAPOR, [THEY ARE] SEEKERS
OF DEATH.

In the last clause Rashi reads *mikshei mavet* (snares of death) instead of *m'vakshei mavet* ("seekers of death" or "seeking death"). As a philosopher, Gersonides saw the acquisition of wealth in place of knowledge as the ultimate death of the intellect. The message of the verse: do not use lies (or speak untruth) as a means to acquire wealth.

כא:ז שֹׁד־רְשָׁעִים יְגוֹרֵם כִּי מֵאֲנוּ לַעֲשׂוֹת מִשְׁפָּט:

21:7 THE VIOLENCE OF THE WICKED WILL SWEEP THEM AWAY,
FOR THEY REFUSE TO DO RIGHT.

Violence becomes a drug to the one who employs it. As a result, the violent person is prevented from acting in any other way. Eventually, the violence will be directed at the violent person. Gersonides understands the verse to refer to those who become habituated to deriving erroneous conclusions from improper premises. At a certain point, such people are unable to derive correct conclusions even if they are given the proper premises.

206

כא:ח הֲפַכְפַּךְ דֶּרֶךְ אִישׁ וָזָר וְזַךְ יָשָׁר פָּעֳלוֹ:

21:8 TWISTED AND STRANGE IS THE HUMAN WAY, THOUGH
THE PURE PERSON'S WORK IS RIGHT.

Rashi understands the first clause to refer to people who, strangely enough, turn away
from mitzvot only to find that their way in life is twisted and does not follow a straight
path. Gersonides connects this verse with the previous one and holds that people
who have correctly developed premises will find their way to correct conclusions,
while others who have not done so will find the path to their conclusions twisted.
Simply put, if you can clarify the problem, you have a better shot at reaching a
resolution to it.

כא:ט טוֹב לָשֶׁבֶת עַל־פִּנַּת־גָּג מֵאֵשֶׁת מִדְיָנִים וּבֵית חָבֶר:

21:9 IT IS BETTER TO LIVE ON A CORNER OF THE ROOF THAN
TO LIVE IN THE HOUSE WITH A QUARRELSOME SPOUSE.

In his comment on this verse, Rashi quotes an *aggadah* (Babylonian Talmud, *Rosh
HaShanah* 31a) that suggests that the Divine Presence may depart from Israel if the
people act like a contentious spouse.

כא:י נֶפֶשׁ רָשָׁע אִוְּתָה־רָע לֹא־יֻחַן בְּעֵינָיו רֵעֵהוּ:

21:10 THE SOUL OF THE WICKED CRAVES EVIL; THEIR
NEIGHBOR FINDS NO FAVOR IN THEIR EYES.

Wicked people are so bent on doing evil that they do not even recognize their
neighbor. The author is suggesting that it is evil to disregard another human being. For
an evil person, another person does not have to be a stranger to have his or her
humanity denied. One can even live next door and not be thought of as a person.

כא:יא בַּעֲנָשׁ־לֵץ יֶחְכַּם־פֶּתִי וּבְהַשְׂכִּיל לְחָכָם יִקַּח־דָּעַת:

21:11 WHEN A MOCKER IS PUNISHED, A FOOL WILL GET
WISE; WHEN THE WISE IS INSTRUCTED, THAT PERSON
GAINS KNOWLEDGE.

This verse echoes the sentiment of 19:25. Rashi understands that the example of the
mocker will motivate the fool to repent.

כא:יב מַשְׂכִּיל צַדִּיק לְבֵית רָשָׁע מְסַלֵּף רְשָׁעִים לָרָע:

21:12 THE RIGHTEOUS ONE UNDERSTANDS THE HOUSE OF
THE WICKED, PERVERTING THE WICKED TO EVIL.

While this verse seems simple, it is problematic. Who is *tzaddik* (righteous)? Rashi assumes that it is God and takes *maskil* (understands) as "pays attention to" and *m'saleif* as "perverting" or "cutting off, destroying." For Ibn Ezra, *maskil* is either "gives understanding to" or "understands." Thus, he reads the verse as "God gives understanding even to those in the house of the wicked" or "God understands that the condition of those in that house will ultimately destroy them." Sensing that the word *m'saleif* also refers to the twisting or misrepresenting of ideas or situations, Gersonides considers *tzaddik* as the person whose virtue may bring good fortune to the house of the wicked. The onlooker, not knowing that there is an innocent person in the house among the wicked, may conclude that being wicked does not matter and will thus be moved to do evil.

כא:יג אֹטֵם אָזְנוֹ מִזַּעֲקַת־דָּל גַּם־הוּא יִקְרָא וְלֹא יֵעָנֶה:

21:13 THE ONE WHO STOPS UP ONE'S EARS TO PREVENT
HEARING THE CRY OF THE POOR WILL CRY OUT AND
NOT BE ANSWERED.

The person who does not give *tzedakah* will end up in need of it. So give *tzedakah*, because if you do need it someday, you want to be in a position of being worthy to receive it.

כא:יד מַתָּן בַּסֵּתֶר יִכְפֶּה־אָף וְשֹׁחַד בַּחֵק חֵמָה עַזָּה:

21:14 A GIFT GIVEN IN SECRET AVERTS ANGER, JUST AS A BRIBE
IN THE BOSOM [PREVENTS] STRONG WRATH.

"In the bosom" is an idiom for something done secretly. For Rashi, both the gift and the bribe are acts of *tzedakah*.

כא:טו שִׂמְחָה לַצַּדִּיק עֲשׂוֹת מִשְׁפָּט וּמְחִתָּה לְפֹעֲלֵי אָוֶן:

21:15 THERE IS JOY FOR THE INNOCENT WHEN JUSTICE IS
DONE BUT TERROR FOR THOSE WHO WORK INIQUITY.

The translation of this verse is dependent on how one understands the word *tzaddik*: "legally innocent" or "generally righteous." Rashi assumes that it is the latter, making a reference both to God, the ultimate Righteous One, and to the righteous individual. God rejoices when judging the righteous and granting a portion to that person in the world-to-come. Similarly, the righteous people rejoice when they are judged. Gersonides thinks that the righteous rejoice when they are judged because if they are judged to be innocent, they will be protected from the wrath of earthly kings.

כא:טז אָדָם תּוֹעֶה מִדֶּרֶךְ הַשְׂכֵּל בִּקְהַל רְפָאִים יָנוּחַ:

21:16 THE ONE WHO WANDERS FROM THE WAY OF
UNDERSTANDING WILL REST IN THE COMPANY OF
THE DEAD.

For Rashi, such a person is the one who departs from the way of Torah. For Ibn Ezra, it is the one who departs from wisdom. Gersonides understands this to mean that the one who departs from the way of the intellect will develop erroneous ideas about the world. For each of these commentators, there are rewards given for Torah, wisdom, and the activation of the intellect. For Rashi, the person will end up in *Geihinom*. According to Ibn Ezra, the person will simply be dead. And for Gersonides, the nature of the person's death will be determined by what correct ideas were apprehended by the individual while alive.

כא:יז אִישׁ מַחְסוֹר אֹהֵב שִׂמְחָה אֹהֵב יַיִן־וָשֶׁמֶן לֹא יַעֲשִׁיר:

21:17 ONE WHO LOVES JOY WILL BE A PERSON WHO WANTS;
THE ONE WHO LOVES WINE AND OIL WILL NOT
GET RICH.

If you want to be rich, then hold on to your money. If you spend your money on personal pleasures, you won't be able to invest it. Gersonides sees a distinction between the joys of the body and the joys of the mind. If you spend your money on wine, you won't be in a position to achieve any measure of intellectual perfection.

כא:יח כֹּפֶר לַצַּדִּיק רָשָׁע וְתַחַת יְשָׁרִים בּוֹגֵד:

21:18 THE WICKED ARE ATONEMENT FOR THE RIGHTEOUS,
AND THE FAITHLESS ARE IN PLACE OF THE UPRIGHT.

Why would the righteous need atonement? In what way can the "faithless" take the place of the "upright"? The verse teaches that the innocent will be delivered and the wicked will be punished. As an example, Rashi reminds us of the story of Mordecai and Haman.

כא:יט טוֹב שֶׁבֶת בְּאֶרֶץ־מִדְבָּר מֵאֵשֶׁת מדונים מִדְיָנִים וָכָעַס:

21:19 It is better to dwell out in the wilderness than
with a quarrelsome and vexatious spouse.

Here is another domestic image. Rashi again uses this metaphor to reflect on the
predicament of the Jewish people. Gersonides suggests that neither the pursuit of
anger nor the pursuit of pleasure is a proper concern of the intellectual thinker.

כא:כ אוֹצָר נֶחְמָד וָשֶׁמֶן בִּנְוֵה חָכָם וּכְסִיל אָדָם יְבַלְּעֶנּוּ:

21:20 There is desirable treasure and oil in the
dwelling of the wise, but a fool will swallow
it up.

For Ibn Ezra, the treasure is gourmet food. The "oil" represents the best of that food,
for it is the richest in content. The fool will buy such food and immediately eat it up.

כא:כא רֹדֵף צְדָקָה וָחָסֶד יִמְצָא חַיִּים צְדָקָה וְכָבוֹד:

21:21 The one who pursues righteousness and
continuous love will find life, righteousness,
and honor.

Ibn Ezra explains "pursues" as a metaphor. You should do a righteous act as quickly
as if you were running after it. Taking *tzedakah* to mean both "righteous acts" and
"correct ideas," Gersonides suggests that the person who pursues it will achieve life in
this world and reward in the next.

כא:כב עִיר גִּבֹּרִים עָלָה חָכָם וַיֹּרֶד עֹז מִבְטֶחָה:

21:22 One who is wise can attack a city garrisoned by
the mighty and conquer its vaunted strength.

Since Psalm 103:20 has the angels called *giborei koach* (mighty heroes) and Psalm
29:11 says that *"Adonai* gives *oz* [strength] to the people," Rashi applies this verse to
Moses, who ascended to heaven (*ir giborim*, "city of heroes") to bring down the
Torah (*oz*, "strength") to the people of Israel. Ibn Ezra takes the verse to mean that
wisdom is greater than power. Gersonides agrees with Ibn Ezra and invites the reader
to look at Ecclesiastes 9:16: "Wisdom is better than power."

כא:כג שֹׁמֵר פִּיו וּלְשׁוֹנוֹ שֹׁמֵר מִצָּרוֹת נַפְשׁוֹ:

21:23 WATCH YOUR MOUTH AND YOUR TONGUE, AND YOU
WILL SAVE YOUR LIFE FROM TROUBLE.

Ibn Ezra interprets the verse as "watch what you eat and what you say, and you will
save yourself a lot of trouble." Gersonides takes the verse as praise of silence.

כא:כד זֵד יָהִיר לֵץ שְׁמוֹ עוֹשֶׂה בְּעֶבְרַת זָדוֹן:

21:24 PROUD AND HAUGHTY SCORNER IS THE NAME OF ONE
WHO ACTS WITH BOUNDLESS DISRESPECT.

In a comment on the morally corrosive quality of pride, Gersonides notes that such a
person treats other people as if they were nothing.

כא:כה תַּאֲוַת עָצֵל תְּמִיתֶנּוּ כִּי־מֵאֲנוּ יָדָיו לַעֲשׂוֹת:

21:25 WHAT THE LAZY PERSON DESIRES WILL BE FATAL, FOR IT
WILL PREVENT ANY ACTION [FROM TAKING PLACE].

Desire joined to sloth prevents any action. The lazy person fixated on a particular
thing, yet unwilling or unable to act, will not direct his or her energies elsewhere and
will be unable to function in day-to-day life.

כא:כו כָּל־הַיּוֹם הִתְאַוָּה תַאֲוָה וְצַדִּיק יִתֵּן וְלֹא יַחְשֹׂךְ:

21:26 ALL [THE LAZY] PERSON DOES ALL DAY IS DESIRE, BUT
THE PROPER PERSON GIVES AND DOESN'T HOLD BACK.

For Rashi, it is God who provides for the lazy. For Ibn Ezra, the proper person takes
care of it. Gersonides understands *v'tzaddik* (the proper person) as "the one who is
correct." Such a person gives what is proper as a result of a knowledge of the arts and
sciences and on the basis of an assessment of the situation.

כא:כז זֶבַח רְשָׁעִים תּוֹעֵבָה אַף כִּי־בְזִמָּה יְבִיאֶנּוּ:

21:27 THE SACRIFICE OF THE WICKED IS AN ABOMINATION;
HOW MUCH THE MORE SO WHEN IT IS BROUGHT WITH
A WICKED PURPOSE.

The first clause parallels a similar clause in 15:8. Rashi relates the verse to the offerings
of Balaam and Balak (Numbers 23). The statement as it stands reflects the influence of
the prophets upon the sacrificial service. It is clear that at first, the offering of sacrifices

was considered sufficient to remove the effect of sin (see Leviticus 16). Later, the prophets taught that sacrifice without inner change was no way to remove the effect of sin.

כא:כח עֵד־כְּזָבִים יֹאבֵד וְאִישׁ שׁוֹמֵעַ לָנֶצַח יְדַבֵּר:

21:28 A FALSE WITNESS WILL PERISH, WHILE THE PERSON WHO RESPONDS MAY ALWAYS SPEAK.

Two words in the second clause make translating this verse difficult. *Lanetzach* may mean "victory" or "eternally." The *Targum* translates it as "firmly." Rashi takes it to mean *tamid* (continually). *Shomei-a* means "hear" or "hearken." So Rashi understands it to be a hearkening to the commandment: "You shall not testify falsely against your neighbor" (Exodus 20:13). Ibn Ezra understands it to refer to the person who, having heard of the death of the false witness, constantly explains it as the punishment for false testimony. Thus, we have translated *shomei-a* as "responds."

כא:כט הֵעֵז אִישׁ רָשָׁע בְּפָנָיו וְיָשָׁר הוּא יכין דרכיו יָבִין דַּרְכּוֹ:

21:29 THE WICKED PERSON HARDENS ONE'S FACE, BUT THE UPSTANDING PERSON UNDERSTANDS THE WAY.

To "harden one's face" is to act daringly. To do so is also to "harden one's heart." While it is not clear, "the way" (literally, "his way") probably refers to the divine pattern of life, which an upstanding person would understand and follow.

כא:ל אֵין חָכְמָה וְאֵין תְּבוּנָה וְאֵין עֵצָה לְנֶגֶד יְהוָה:

21:30 THERE IS NO WISDOM, THERE IS NO UNDERSTANDING, THERE IS NO COUNSEL THAT CAN STAND AGAINST *ADONAI*.

Although wisdom, understanding, and counsel are the primary concern for the author of the Book of Proverbs, the author nevertheless admits to their limitations: human thought cannot prevail over divine purpose.

כא:לא סוּס מוּכָן לְיוֹם מִלְחָמָה וְלַיהוָה הַתְּשׁוּעָה:

21:31 A HORSE MAY BE PREPARED FOR THE DAY OF WAR, BUT VICTORY BELONGS TO *ADONAI*.

Gersonides proves the veracity of the verse by noting that at times the weak may gain victory in battle over the strong. Perhaps this verse is an attempt to obviate the basic element of this volume: life depends on human planning.

Tzedakah

The term *tzedakah* is usually translated as "charity" but actually means "righteousness." Therefore, we choose to translate the word as "righteous giving." While some have articulated systems for the giving of charity, most notably the Eight Degrees of *Tzedakah* of Moses Maimonides, *tzedakah* is essentially Judaism's vehicle for redistributing wealth in the world. We thank God for what we have by sharing it with others. Thus, rich or poor, the giving of *tzedakah* is incumbent upon everyone.

GLEANINGS

Mystery

We end in the proper place: mystery. There is much we do not understand. What we do understand is that God is a God who commands; God is a God who, as the Exodus story tells us, liberates slaves. God has called us *l'takken olam b'malchut Shaddai,* "to mend the world under the sovereignty of the Almighty." A belief in a self-sufficient humanity, moving inexorably to a perfect world, has proven to be not only shallow but, in the face of Auschwitz, offensive. To believe this, in my opinion, in the face of recent and current history would require a greater leap of faith than any traditional religious teaching. What will prevent us from retreating into quietism and waiting for God to make everything right, total passivity in the face of great evil, is the Jewish belief in our partnership with God.

The belief that humanity can eradicate the evil inclination from the human heart by itself and that God is unnecessary is *hubris* or *chutzpah*. In contrast, Judaism teaches that God commands and we are called to fulfill these mitzvot. The movement of history from the present age to the age of the Messiah is, indeed, mysterious, but Judaism teaches us the realism of this hope. *P'tach libi b'toratecha u'v'mitzvotecha tirdof nafshi,* "Open my heart to Your Torah that my spirit may pursue Your commandments."

Michael S. Stroh, "Mending the World and the Evil Inclination: The Human Role in Redemption,"
in *Duties of the Soul: The Role of Commandments in Liberal Judaism,* ed. Niles E. Goldstein and
Peter S. Knobel (New York: UAHC Press, 1999), 91–92

CHAPTER TWENTY-TWO

כב:א נִבְחָר שֵׁם מֵעֹשֶׁר רָב מִכֶּסֶף וּמִזָּהָב חֵן טוֹב:

22:1 RATHER A GOOD NAME THAN MUCH WEALTH, AND
FAVOR IS BETTER THAN SILVER AND GOLD.

Both a "good name" and "favor" refer to the regard others have for a person. Such regard is not a function of wealth. Rather, it is a function of character. The writer of Proverbs emphasizes the importance of character because of the obvious temptation of wealth, particularly for readers whose intellectual prowess would lead them to gaining wealth.

כב:ב עָשִׁיר וָרָשׁ נִפְגָּשׁוּ עֹשֵׂה כֻלָּם יְהוָֹה:

22:2 RICH AND POOR HAVE MET TOGETHER; *ADONAI* HAS
MADE THEM ALL.

It is the rich who have to be instructed about the common humanity of all persons, not the poor who require such guidance. As the line in the play *The Dybbuk* has it, "The mirror is glass and the window is glass, but when you add silver to glass, you only see yourself."

כב:ג עָרוּם רָאָה רָעָה ויסתר וְנִסְתָּר וּפְתָיִים עָבְרוּ וְנֶעֱנָשׁוּ:

22:3 A CUNNING PERSON SEES EVIL AND HIDES FROM IT,
BUT FOOLS PASS BY AND ARE PUNISHED.

Ibn Ezra understands *arum* (cunning) as "prudent" and explains that the prudent avoid evil, while fools don't. As a result, they suffer the consequences. Gersonides understands the verse to mean that the wise can anticipate evil and avoid it, while fools cannot and hence suffer. Once again, the author of Proverbs presents us with a contrast between the fortunes of the wise and the foolish.

כב:ד עֵקֶב עֲנָוָה יִרְאַת יְהֹוָה עֹשֶׁר וְכָבוֹד וְחַיִּים:

22:4 THE RESULT OF HUMILITY IS THE FEAR OF *ADONAI* AND
WEALTH, HONOR, AND LIFE.

Both Ibn Ezra and Gersonides see a causal connection between "humility" and "fear of *Adonai*" and between "fear of *Adonai*" and "wealth, honor, and life." For Ibn Ezra, divine favor gotten by "fear of *Adonai*" will bring material goods for the latter. For Gersonides, "humility" will move the thinker to philosophical reflection, which, in turn, will bring the thinker to the political virtues of "wealth" and "honor" and the intellectual virtues, which provide "life."

כב:ה צִנִּים פַּחִים בְּדֶרֶךְ עִקֵּשׁ שׁוֹמֵר נַפְשׁוֹ יִרְחַק מֵהֶם:

22:5 THORNS AND SNARES ARE THE WAY OF THE CORRUPT;
ONE SHOULD KEEP FAR FROM THEM TO PRESERVE
ONE'S SOUL.

Rashi notes that as "snares" are hidden from view, so is the punishment that will befall the corrupt—but it is waiting. Gersonides thinks that the indifference to the situation and the carelessness of the "corrupt" person will cause his or her own downfall. The wise person does not court danger needlessly.

כב:ו חֲנֹךְ לַנַּעַר עַל־פִּי דַרְכּוֹ גַּם כִּי־יַזְקִין לֹא־יָסוּר מִמֶּנָּה:

22:6 EDUCATE A CHILD IN THE PROPER WAY AND EVEN AS
AN ADULT HE [OR SHE] WILL NOT TURN FROM IT.

The root *chanach*, which was first used to refer to Abram's trained servants (*chanichav*, Genesis 14:14), comes to mean "to dedicate" (as in Numbers 7:11); both meanings combine here in "to educate." It is the basis of the modern Hebrew word *chinuch* (education). Jewish education should be both training—how to do something— and dedication—why do something. Although the text has *naar* (lad), we have translated it as "child," since we educate both boys and girls and value both men and women.

כב:ז עָשִׁיר בְּרָשִׁים יִמְשׁוֹל וְעֶבֶד לֹוֶה לְאִישׁ מַלְוֶה:

22:7 THE RICH RULE THE POOR, AND THE BORROWER IS
SERVANT TO THE LENDER.

The writer describes a truth that we have all come to understand: wealth is power. Rashi attempts to soften the statement by referring it to the possession of learning rather than the possession of money. Thus, the ignorant will always need the scholar.

כב:ח זוֹרֵעַ עַוְלָה יקצור יִקְצׇר־אָוֶן וְשֵׁבֶט עֶבְרָתוֹ יִכְלֶה׃

22:8 THE ONE WHO SOWS INIQUITY SHALL REAP DISASTER;
THE ROD OF ONE'S RAGE WILL PASS AWAY.

Rashi understands the second clause to mean that the wicked person will lose the power to impose his or her will on others. The root *kalah* (pass away) suggests a process that comes to an end.

כב:ט טוֹב־עַיִן הוּא יְבֹרָךְ כִּי־נָתַן מִלַּחְמוֹ לַדָּל׃

22:9 BLESSED IS THE ONE WHO IS GENEROUS, FOR SUCH
A PERSON GIVES FROM HIS [OR HER] OWN BREAD TO
THE POOR.

Tov ayin (literally, "a good eye") is an idiom for one who is generous. The measure of generosity of such people is that they are willing to give of their own food to the poor. *Milachmo* (of one's own bread) suggests giving more than bread, since *lechem* can mean more than just bread and often refers to food in general.

כב:י גָּרֵשׁ לֵץ וְיֵצֵא מָדוֹן וְיִשְׁבֹּת דִּין וְקָלוֹן׃

22:10 DRIVE OUT THE MOCKER AND CONTENTION WILL
LEAVE; QUARRELING AND SHAME WILL CEASE.

For Rashi, the "mocker" represents the *yetzer hara,* "the evil inclination." Gersonides thinks that the "mocker" hates people by nature and gets a perverted pleasure out of causing others to quarrel. For the writer of Proverbs, mockers are dangerous because such people threaten the basic assumptions of the community. It is difficult to determine who is the mocker in our times, since there are different kinds of communities that make up our individual worlds, such as place, profession, class, and religion.

כב:יא אֹהֵב טהור טְהָר־לֵב חֵן שְׂפָתָיו רֵעֵהוּ מֶלֶךְ׃

22:11 ONE WHO LOVES PURITY OF HEART HAS GRACE UPON
ONE'S LIPS AND SHALL HAVE A RULER FOR A FRIEND.

Rashi takes the ruler to be God. Ibn Ezra thinks that the ruler is mortal and offers the example of Hushai, who was the friend of David (II Samuel 15:37). In either case, the lesson is clear: a heart that is pure and words that are kind will win favor.

כב:יב עֵינֵי יְהֹוָה נָצְרוּ דָעַת וַיְסַלֵּף דִּבְרֵי בֹגֵד:

22:12 THE EYES OF *ADONAI* PRESERVE KNOWLEDGE BUT
PERVERT THE WORDS OF THE DISLOYAL.

Ibn Ezra quotes the rabbinic saying "The Torah speaks in the language of the children
of humankind" (Babylonian Talmud, *Y'vamot* 71a; *Bava M'tzia* 31b) and explains that
"the eyes" refer to divine favor. Moreover, God will prevent the possessors of
knowledge from being injured by the plans of the disloyal. In a similar manner,
Gersonides interprets "the eyes of *Adonai*" as a reference to divine providence, which
will protect those who possess knowledge and will upset the plans of the disloyal.

כב:יג אָמַר עָצֵל אֲרִי בַחוּץ בְּתוֹךְ רְחֹבוֹת אֵרָצֵחַ:

22:13 THE LAZY PERSON SAYS, "THERE IS A LION OUTSIDE.
I CAN GET KILLED IN THE STREETS."

Rashi understands "the lazy person" as one who is too lazy to study Torah. Ibn Ezra
takes the verse to refer to a wicked person. Gersonides sees the verse as the kind of
excuse that a lazy person uses to avoid leaving the house. This verse may actually
refer to a person who is so frightened by the outside world that he or she may be
unable to act in any manner.

כב:יד שׁוּחָה עֲמֻקָּה פִּי זָרוֹת זְעוּם יְהֹוָה יפול יִפָּל־שָׁם:

22:14 THE MOUTH OF STRANGE WOMEN IS A DEEP PIT; THE
ONE WHO FALLS THERE WILL INCUR *ADONAI'S* WRATH.

Once again, we encounter the exogamous sexual attraction of the strange (or foreign)
woman. Such a notion is found frequently in literature: women inside the group are
considered virtuous, but women outside the group are considered immoral. Whether
the statement is correct or not is irrelevant. The author uses the notion to separate
one group from another. Contact with a "strange woman" is a particular problem
that emerges from the anonymity of city life. Only in the city, filled with commerce
and attracting different kinds of people, can the temptation of contact with such
women be found. Rashi understands "strange women" as a parallel for idolatry.
Because he is a philosopher, Gersonides takes the term to refer to incorrect ideas
based on imagination.

כב:טו אִוֶּלֶת קְשׁוּרָה בְלֶב־נָעַר שֵׁבֶט מוּסָר יַרְחִיקֶנָּה מִמֶּנּוּ׃

22:15 FOLLY IS FOUND IN A CHILD'S MIND, BUT THE ROD OF
DISCIPLINE WILL DRIVE IT FAR AWAY.

Physical chastisement was considered a necessary part of the education of a child.

כב:טז עֹשֵׁק דָּל לְהַרְבּוֹת לוֹ נֹתֵן לְעָשִׁיר אַךְ־לְמַחְסוֹר׃

22:16 DEFRAUDING THE POOR WILL MAKE ONE RICH, WHILE
GIVING TO THE RICH WILL MAKE ONE POOR.

Some have seen this cynical verse as problematic. However, the writer points out the truth even if it is not moral. One may look at society and see that those who are most defenseless are the easiest targets of the greed of others. Rashi takes "giving to the rich" to mean giving to idolatry. Gersonides understands "the poor" to refer to the appetitive faculty, that aspect of the mind involved with desire. He thereby explains that controlling desire "makes one rich." That is, it increases the acuity of the would-be philosopher.

כב:יז הַט אָזְנְךָ וּשְׁמַע דִּבְרֵי חֲכָמִים וְלִבְּךָ תָּשִׁית לְדַעְתִּי׃

22:17 INCLINE YOUR EAR AND LISTEN TO THE WORDS OF THE
WISE; LET YOUR MIND BE APPLIED TO MY KNOWLEDGE.

Rashi takes the first clause to mandate the study of Torah with any teacher, even one who is unworthy. The second clause, according to Rashi, is a warning to the student that, should the teacher be unworthy, the student should avoid being influenced by the teacher's actions. Gersonides thinks that the verse teaches the importance of the addition of Torah to philosophy.

כב:יח כִּי־נָעִים כִּי־תִשְׁמְרֵם בְּבִטְנֶךָ יִכֹּנוּ יַחְדָּו עַל־שְׂפָתֶיךָ׃

22:18 IF YOU KEEP THEM WELL WITHIN YOU, IT WILL BE
PLEASANT; MAY THEY BE ESTABLISHED ON YOUR LIPS.

B'vitnecha literally means "in your belly." We have translated it as "well within you." Rashi explains that the words of Torah will be fixed within your mind when you are able to articulate them. For Gersonides, the mind derives pleasure from absorbing the words of the wise.

כב:יט לִהְיוֹת בַּיהוָה מִבְטַחֶךָ הוֹדַעְתִּיךָ הַיּוֹם אַף־אָתָּה:

22:19 THAT YOUR TRUST BE IN *ADONAI*, THIS DAY, HAVE
I MADE IT KNOWN TO YOU, YES TO YOU.

The force of the emphatic *af atah* ("yes," or "yea to you") is unclear. What is clear, however, is that the style of the previous three verses is markedly different from those that preceded them. Rashi takes the verse to mean that one should pursue one's studies without worrying how to pay for them.

כב:כ הֲלֹא כָתַבְתִּי לְךָ שלשום שָׁלִישִׁים בְּמוֹעֵצֹת וָדָעַת:

22:20 HAVE I NOT WRITTEN YOU FOR SOME TIME
CONCERNING COUNSELS AND KNOWLEDGE?

The problem in this verse is the word *shilshom*, for which there is a *k'tiv* (written form) and *k'rei* (form to be read). According to the *k'tiv*, it means "three days ago, the day before yesterday." According to the *k'rei* form *(shalishim)*, it means "officers" and, by extension, "excellent things." The *Targum* translates it as *t'lata zimnin* (three times). Rashi takes the word to be a form of *shalosh* (three) and interprets that God has written three things: the Torah, the Prophets, and the Writings. Arguing from the context of the previous verse's *hayom* (today, this day), Ibn Ezra accepts the *k'tiv* and interprets it as "the day before yesterday." Gersonides follows the *k'rei* and interprets that as a sovereign ruler would send officers, so would counselors use knowledge to deal with political and intellectual matters. In our translation, we follow Ibn Ezra, accepting the *k'tiv*. Thus, we interpret the word *shilshom* as "for some time."

כב:כא לְהוֹדִיעֲךָ קֹשְׁטְ אִמְרֵי אֱמֶת לְהָשִׁיב אֲמָרִים אֱמֶת לְשֹׁלְחֶיךָ:

22:21 TO MAKE YOU KNOW THE CERTAINTY OF THE WORDS
OF TRUTH, THAT YOU MIGHT RETURN THE WORDS OF
TRUTH TO THE ONE WHO SENT YOU.

This is the only instance of the word *kosht* (certainty) appearing in the Bible, although it is the common Aramaic word for "truth." Perhaps because of a perceived redundancy, the *Targum* translates "the words" by *u'milei* (and the words). Rashi interprets *l'sholchecha* (the one who sent you) as *l'shoelcha* (the one who asks you—for a legal decision).

כב:כב אַל־תִּגְזָל־דָּל כִּי דַל־הוּא וְאַל־תְּדַכֵּא עָנִי בַשָּׁעַר:

22:22 DON'T ROB THE POWERLESS BECAUSE THEY ARE
POWERLESS; DON'T CRUSH THE POOR IN COURT.

The words *dal* and *ani* are synonyms. Depending on the context, each can mean "poor," "powerless," or "wretched." *Shaar* literally means "gate" but seems to mean "court" in the context of this verse and from the perspective of the author of Proverbs. In ancient times, courts met at the entrance to the city, a place open to the eyes of onlookers. This is a warning against those with power who do take advantage of the "powerless" and those with power who use the law to crush the weak. If this admonition is insufficient, then further warning is given in the next verse.

כב:כג כִּי־יְהֹוָה יָרִיב רִיבָם וְקָבַע אֶת־קֹבְעֵיהֶם נָפֶשׁ:

22:23 FOR *ADONAI* WILL PLEAD THEIR CAUSE AND WILL RUIN
THE LIFE OF THOSE WHO RUIN THEM.

The notion that God is the ultimate guarantor of the rights of the poor and the defenseless is echoed throughout biblical and rabbinic literature.

כב:כד אַל־תִּתְרַע אֶת־בַּעַל אָף וְאֶת־אִישׁ חֵמוֹת לֹא תָבוֹא:

22:24 DON'T BE THE BUDDY OF AN ANGRY PERSON, AND
DON'T GO ALONG WITH A PERSON WHO IS FILLED
WITH WRATH

Once again, the reader is warned about the danger of anger and the danger of associating with those who lose their temper. As Maimonides points out, the ideal ruler does not "let loose the reins of anger" (*Guide for the Perplexed* 1:54).

כב:כה פֶּן־תֶּאֱלַף ארחתו אֹרְחֹתָיו וְלָקַחְתָּ מוֹקֵשׁ לְנַפְשֶׁךָ:

22:25 LEST YOU LEARN FROM THE WAYS [OF THE ANGRY
PERSON] AND SET A TRAP FOR YOUR SOUL.

Association with an angry person may lead you to act similarly.

כב:כו אַל־תְּהִי בְתֹקְעֵי־כָף בַּעֹרְבִים מַשָּׁאוֹת:

22:26 DON'T BE AMONG THOSE WHO SHAKE HANDS AND
BECOME GUARANTORS FOR DEBTS.

This verse repeats the warning of 6:1. It is a common aspect of commercial law that a person who enters into a business relationship may be forced to accept the debts of the business as well as its assets. Again we note that *tokei kaf* (literally "striking hands") is an idiom that parallels "shaking hands" in contemporary English.

כב:כז אִם־אֵין־לְךָ לְשַׁלֵּם לָמָּה יִקַּח מִשְׁכָּבְךָ מִתַּחְתֶּיךָ:

22:27 IF YOU WON'T BE ABLE TO PAY, WHY SHOULD YOUR BED
BE TAKEN FROM UNDER YOU?

The careless investor may become bankrupt and lose everything, including one's bed.

כב:כח אַל־תַּסֵּג גְּבוּל עוֹלָם אֲשֶׁר עָשׂוּ אֲבוֹתֶיךָ:

22:28 DON'T REMOVE THE ANCIENT LANDMARK THAT YOUR
ANCESTORS MADE.

This verse seems to move away from the culture of the city toward the culture of the countryside. Rashi interprets the verse to refer to a matter of religious custom. Gersonides takes the verse to warn against the manipulation of real property as a way of oppressing one's neighbor.

כב:כט חָזִיתָ אִישׁ מָהִיר בִּמְלַאכְתּוֹ לִפְנֵי־מְלָכִים יִתְיַצָּב בַּל־יִתְיַצֵּב
לִפְנֵי חֲשֻׁכִּים:

22:29 THE PERSON YOU SEE AS SKILLFUL IN WORK WILL
STAND BEFORE RULERS, NOT BEFORE THE LOWLY.

Chashukim (literally, "those who are dark"), by context, is translated here as "the lowly." Ibn Ezra translates the word as "poor." The writer tells the readers to devote themselves to work in order to derive benefit from it.

A Good Name

This is a common metaphor for wisdom literature in general and the Book of Proverbs in particular. It fuels a great deal of discussion in rabbinic literature, as well. A good name (read: reputation) is extremely important for the biblical and rabbinic mind-set, so much so that the founder of Chasidism took the Hebrew for this concept as his name: Baal Shem Tov. Of course, in his case, he refers to God's good name or reputation, something that he talked about with his disciples and something that he believed that humans should emulate in their interactions with one another.

Humility

The human is placed in an awkward position. First, the human must be humble. However, the human has been given a measure of control over the earth and all its creatures. Human beings are made in the image of God, a little lower than angels. Therefore, it is a delicate balance that we must maintain. It is what led one Chasidic teacher to suggest that each individual keep a slip of paper in each pocket. In one pocket, the paper should read that the human is nothing but dust and ashes. And on the other paper should be the reminder that the human is a little lower than the angels. When feeling arrogant, we should access the statement that reminds us of our lowly place among the worms: dust and ashes. And when we are feeling downtrodden, we should remind ourselves (through reading the slip of paper) that we have been created only a little lower than the angels.

GLEANINGS

The Content of My Religion

My process of spirituality leads me to the content of my religion; the content of my religion leads me to a recycling of the process of my spirituality. The recycling of the process invites me to reexamine my content; my reexamined content invites me to explore once again the process of my spirituality which, in turn, enables me to be creative in the content of my religious experience....

Edward Zerin, "A Tale of Two Dilemmas," *CCAR Journal: A Reform Jewish Quarterly* (summer 1998): 61

What Is Spirituality?

For what is spirituality? What is the spirit? It is, I would suggest, what God and humankind have in common. It is the non-material, the non-corporeal, which stands in counter distinction to the physical, the sensual, which links us with other living human creatures, even with the beasts. It is the living soul, *nishmat chayim,* which God blew into man's nostrils. And it was man in that case. It is like the *ruach,* the wind that blew over chaos and transformed it into the universe as we now know it. The extent to which we give expression to the morally good in our everyday lives is the extent of our spirituality.

Alice Shalvi, "The Spiritual Transformation of Israel," *CCAR Yearbook* 105–106 (1995–1996): 73

CHAPTER TWENTY-THREE

כג:א כִּי־תֵשֵׁב לִלְחוֹם אֶת־מוֹשֵׁל בִּין תָּבִין אֶת־אֲשֶׁר לְפָנֶיךָ:

23:1 IF YOU SIT DOWN TO EAT WITH A RULER, YOU HAD
BETTER KNOW WHO IS BEFORE YOU.

More is at stake than table manners. As Rabban Gamliel said, "Watch out for the
ruling authorities. They befriend a person only for their own purposes" (*Pirkei Avot*
2:3). A simple invitation to dinner may be replete with multiple intentions.

כג:ב וְשַׂמְתָּ שַׂכִּין בְּלֹעֶךָ אִם־בַּעַל נֶפֶשׁ אָתָּה:

23:2 YOU PUT A KNIFE TO YOUR THROAT IF YOU ARE A
GLUTTON.

Rashi's understanding of *baal nefesh* (literally, "possessor of the soul") as *raavtan*
(glutton) illuminates the verse: if the ruler is stingy and you eat too much at the ruler's
table, you will put your life at risk. Rashi also presents the rabbinic view, which took
the verse as a parable of students who adjust their questions to the responses of their
teacher. Since Gersonides takes the prior verse as a parable for acquiring wisdom, he
takes this verse to teach that students would be wise to control their passions.

כג:ג אַל־תִּתְאָו לְמַטְעַמּוֹתָיו וְהוּא לֶחֶם כְּזָבִים:

23:3 DON'T YEARN FOR HIS [OR HER] DELICIOUS MORSELS,
FOR THEY ARE THE BREAD OF LIES.

Rashi continues the parable by asking such students to seek a proper teacher who will
answer any question. For Gersonides, lack of control will not provide the
understanding that will enable the student to acquire true wisdom and ultimate
knowledge.

כג:ד אַל־תִּיגַע לְהַעֲשִׁיר מִבִּינָתְךָ חֲדָל:

23:4 DON'T TIRE YOURSELF OUT TO GET RICH, AND GIVE UP
DEPENDING ON YOUR OWN UNDERSTANDING.

The *Targum* translates the last clause as *bivyuntach p'rak minei*, "with your
understanding break away from it [wealth]." Rashi refers the verse to Torah study,

cautioning students not to accumulate various versions of what they have learned because they will soon forget them. Gersonides understands the verse as an admonition: Don't let the pursuit get in the way of the acquisition of wisdom. Too often, people weary themselves in order to acquire wealth, only to find that they are too tired to enjoy or use it.

כג:ה הֲתָעִיף עֵינֶיךָ בּוֹ וְאֵינֶנּוּ כִּי עָשֹׂה יַעֲשֶׂה־לּוֹ כְנָפַיִם כְּנֶשֶׁר וְעִיף הַשָּׁמָיִם:

23:5 CAN YOU MAKE YOUR EYES FLY TOWARD SOMETHING
WHEN IT IS NOT THERE? IT [WEALTH] MAKES ITS WINGS
AND FLIES UP TO HEAVEN LIKE AN EAGLE.

As the American proverb suggests, "You can't take it with you." Wealth comes and goes. The author compares wealth to a bird that can fly away when it wants and all that its possessor can do is watch it as it wings its way toward heaven.

כג:ו אַל־תִּלְחַם אֶת־לֶחֶם רַע עָיִן וְאַל־תִּתְאָו לְמַטְעַמֹּתָיו:

23:6 IF SOMEONE HAS AN EVIL EYE, DON'T COVET HIS
[OR HER] BREAD; DON'T YEARN FOR HIS [OR HER]
DELICIOUS MORSELS.

Here the "evil eye" refers to an ungenerous person who looks askance at anything anyone else wants. This last clause is repeated from the first clause of 23:3. This verse repeats the ideas reflected in 23:3–4.

כג:ז כִּי כְּמוֹ־שָׁעַר בְּנַפְשׁוֹ כֶּן־הוּא אֱכֹל וּשְׁתֵה יֹאמַר לָךְ וְלִבּוֹ בַּל־עִמָּךְ:

23:7 THOSE PEOPLE HAVE CALCULATED IN THEIR MIND;
"EAT AND DRINK," THEY WILL SAY TO YOU, BUT THEY
DO NOT MEAN IT.

The last three words *v'libo bal imach* (he does not mean it) literally means "his heart is not with you." We have translated the verse in the plural to make it more inclusive. Knowing how to "read" someone is an important skill to acquire, particularly when dealing with those who wield a great deal of power. The author warns the reader that just being invited to a party is no indication of the goodwill of the host. In fact, the invitation may only be a ploy.

כג:ח פִּתְּךָ־אָכַלְתָּ תְקִיאֶנָּה וְשִׁחַתָּ דְּבָרֶיךָ הַנְּעִימִים:

23:8 YOU WILL VOMIT THE MORSEL YOU EAT. YOU WILL SPOIL
YOUR SWEET WORDS.

Watch out! the author warns the reader. A simple mistake in table manners may ruin
the impression you are trying to make on your host. Rashi explains that the host's bad
treatment of guests that causes you shame may even cause you to vomit. Gersonides
gives a simple explanation for gastric distress: the stingy host may have provided
guests with food that is so rotten that it causes them to vomit.

כג:ט בְּאָזְנֵי כְסִיל אַל־תְּדַבֵּר כִּי־יָבוּז לְשֵׂכֶל מִלֶּיךָ:

23:9 DON'T SPEAK IN THE EARS OF A FOOL, FOR THAT
PERSON WILL DESPISE THE SENSE OF YOUR WORDS.

Ibn Ezra takes the fool to be the stingy host. He suggests that it is a waste of time to try
to correct the host.

כג:י אַל־תַּסֵּג גְּבוּל עוֹלָם וּבִשְׂדֵי יְתוֹמִים אַל־תָּבֹא:

23:10 DON'T REMOVE THE ANCIENT LANDMARK, AND DON'T
ENTER INTO THE FIELDS OF ORPHANS.

The first clause repeats the first clause of 22:28. The second clause warns against
taking advantage of those who are not able to defend their own rights. As Rashi points
out, all persons owning land are bound by the commandments laid down in Leviticus
19:9–10 to allow the poor to glean the corners of the field, to gather in the grapes
that have not been harvested in the vineyard, and to pick up what was forgotten in
the field or in the vineyard. Still, it would be better if the fields of the orphans were
spared altogether. Rashi presents us with the problem of the clash between needs: the
poor lack everything; the orphans, even as orphans, do own land. Ethical decisions
often involve the balancing of rights and the conflict of competing goods.

כג:יא כִּי־גֹאֲלָם חָזָק הוּא־יָרִיב אֶת־רִיבָם אִתָּךְ:

23:11 THEIR REDEEMER IS STRONG; HE [OR SHE] WILL ARGUE
THEIR CAUSE WITH YOU.

The *go-eil* (redeemer) as mandated by Leviticus 25:25–26 is the relative who is
entrusted with the responsibility to protect the rights of other members of the family.
At times, that relative may be required to buy back the ancestral holding that the
poor member of the family was forced to sell. The *go-eil*, as indicated by Numbers
35:12, is also charged with avenging the murder of a relative. Both roles of the *go-eil*

extend to the idea of God as *go-eil* of the people of Israel. It seems that God is the intended *go-eil* of this verse. Both Ibn Ezra and Gersonides understand *go-eil* from this perspective.

כג:יב הָבִיאָה לַמּוּסָר לִבֶּךָ וְאָזְנֶךָ לְאִמְרֵי־דָעַת׃

23:12 BRING YOUR HEART TO DISCIPLINE AND YOUR EARS TO
WORDS OF KNOWLEDGE.

Gersonides understands *musar* ("discipline" or "personal conduct") as political philosophy. Such philosophy necessarily precedes further metaphysical instruction. In his comment, Gersonides encapsulates the view of Maimonides that "the perfection of the body," which includes the body politic, necessarily precedes "the perfection of the soul," which is the acquisition of metaphysical truths (*Guide for the Perplexed* 3:27).

כג:יג אַל־תִּמְנַע מִנַּעַר מוּסָר כִּי־תַכֶּנּוּ בַשֵּׁבֶט לֹא יָמוּת׃

23:13 DON'T WITHHOLD DISCIPLINE FROM A YOUNG PERSON;
WERE YOU TO HIT THAT PERSON WITH A STAFF, THAT
PERSON WOULD NOT DIE.

This statement emphasizes the difference in the views of child-rearing between the ancient world and the contemporary period. Similarly, those in the medieval world and many in the modern world considered hitting children as a divine mandate and "spare the rod and spoil the child" as divine wisdom. Beating children teaches them that adults can do to them what they cannot do to adults. Hence, children who are physically abused will often do to their own children what was done to them—unless there is an intervention of some sort. The Greek term *pedagogue*, like the Hebrew term *m'lameid*, originally meant the teacher who motivated students with beatings. Even Gersonides, the philosopher, accepted the notion that beating children was useful. He thought that hitting the student would save the student from a premature death and preserve the student's soul, which can achieve eternity.

כג:יד אַתָּה בַּשֵּׁבֶט תַּכֶּנּוּ וְנַפְשׁוֹ מִשְּׁאוֹל תַּצִּיל׃

23:14 SMITE THE CHILD WITH A STAFF AND YOU SAVE THE
CHILD FROM THE NETHERWORLD.

Like many other explanations of an imbalance of power, the justification for beating a child is construed as helping the child, saving him or her from a punishment in another world. What is tragic about the statement is that the author obviously believed what he or she wrote, attempting to convince others to believe it as well.

226

כג:טו בְּנִי אִם־חָכַם לִבֶּךָ יִשְׂמַח לִבִּי גַם־אָנִי:

23:15 MY YOUNG FRIEND, IF YOUR MIND WILL BE SMART,
EVEN MY MIND WILL REJOICE.

This verse suggests another means of motivation for the teacher: simple encouragement. Teaching is about encouraging others to learn.

כג:טז וְתַעְלֹזְנָה כִלְיוֹתָי בְּדַבֵּר שְׂפָתֶיךָ מֵישָׁרִים:

23:16 MY ENTIRE BEING WILL REJOICE WHEN YOUR LIPS
SPEAK CORRECTLY.

Ancients considered *chilyotai* (literally, "my kidneys")—which we have translated as "my entire being"—as the seat of emotion. Gersonides translates the term as "my thoughts." Here again the teacher motivates the student in a more contemporary— and acceptable—manner.

כג:יז אַל־יְקַנֵּא לִבְּךָ בַּחַטָּאִים כִּי אִם־בְּיִרְאַת־יְהֹוָה כָּל־הַיּוֹם:

23:17 DO NOT LET YOUR MIND ENVY THE SINNERS, BUT LET
THE FEAR OF GOD BE WITH YOU EVERY DAY INSTEAD.

Ibn Ezra suggests that the use of the article "*the* sinners" indicates that the student is acquainted with a particular group of sinners. Thus, this is not an abstract warning.

כג:יח כִּי אִם־יֵשׁ אַחֲרִית וְתִקְוָתְךָ לֹא תִכָּרֵת:

23:18 FOR SURELY THERE WILL BE AN END AND YOUR HOPE
WILL NOT BE CUT OFF.

The *acharit* (end) is what will occur either at the end of the student's life or at the end of time. In any case, some time in the future is meant. Hence, the author warns the student about present activities so that those activities do not negatively affect the future. For Rabbinic Judaism, that "end" will be the judgment in the world-to-come. Gersonides understands this verse as a warning about destructive activities and erroneous ideas.

כג:יט שְׁמַע־אַתָּה בְנִי וַחֲכָם וְאַשֵּׁר בַּדֶּרֶךְ לִבֶּךָ:

23:19 MY YOUNG FRIEND, LISTEN AND GET SMART; DIRECT
YOUR MIND TO THE RIGHT WAY.

Rashi notes that the wise heart/mind will not direct a person to sin.

כג:כ אַל־תְּהִי בְסֹבְאֵי־יָיִן בְּזֹלֲלֵי בָשָׂר לָמוֹ:

23:20 DON'T BE ASSOCIATED WITH DRUNKS OR GLUTTONS.

Gersonides warns that association with drunks and gluttons will affect one's behavior and lead to certain bad habits, which the author warns about in the next verse.

כג:כא כִּי־סֹבֵא וְזוֹלֵל יִוָּרֵשׁ וּקְרָעִים תַּלְבִּישׁ נוּמָה:

23:21 FOR THE DRUNK AND THE GLUTTON WILL BECOME POOR, AND STUPOR WILL DRESS ONE UP WITH RAGS.

Overindulgence will prevent a person from making a living, and poverty will be the result. The author needs to warn the reader that self-control in all things is a prerequisite for those wishing to counsel those in power. Lose control and you lose your power and your job.

כג:כב שְׁמַע לְאָבִיךָ זֶה יְלָדֶךָ וְאַל־תָּבוּז כִּי־זָקְנָה אִמֶּךָ:

23:22 LISTEN TO YOUR FATHER WHO BEGOT YOU, AND DON'T DESPISE YOUR MOTHER NOW THAT SHE IS OLD.

Gersonides takes the entire verse as a parable. "Father" is wisdom, and "mother" is a sensitive soul. The last clause is problematic. What kind of person would have to be warned not to despise his or her mother?

כג:כג אֱמֶת קְנֵה וְאַל־תִּמְכֹּר חָכְמָה וּמוּסָר וּבִינָה:

23:23 ACQUIRE THE TRUTH AND DON'T SELL IT, [ALONG WITH] WISDOM, DISCIPLINE, AND UNDERSTANDING.

Rashi takes *k'neih* (acquire) in its literal meaning of "buy" and tells the readers that if they cannot study for free, then they should pay for it. Even so, one should instruct without charge. Gersonides takes *chochmah* (wisdom) to refer to philosophy in general, *musar* (discipline) to refer to political philosophy, and *binah* (understanding) to refer to metaphysics—the mastery of which will perfect the acquired intellect, which achieves eternal life.

כג:כד גול יגול גִּיל יָגִיל אֲבִי צַדִּיק יוֹלֵד וְיוֹלֵד חָכָם וִישְׂמַח־בּוֹ:

23:24 THE PARENT OF THE RIGHTEOUS WILL GREATLY REJOICE; THE ONE WHO BEGETS A WISE CHILD WILL BE HAPPY.

This verse suggests the old Yiddish expression *nachas fun kinder* (joy from children).

כג:כה יִשְׂמַח־אָבִיךָ וְאִמֶּךָ וְתָגֵל יוֹלַדְתֶּךָ:

23:25 LET YOUR FATHER AND MOTHER BE HAPPY, AND MAY
SHE WHO BORE YOU REJOICE.

This kind of advice assumes a close relationship between parents and children. Such a relationship would have a positive effect on the child's motivation to study.

כג:כו תְּנָה־בְנִי לִבְּךָ לִי וְעֵינֶיךָ דְּרָכַי תרצנה תִּצֹּרְנָה:

23:26 MY YOUNG FRIEND, PAY ATTENTION TO ME; LET YOUR
EYES WATCH MY WAYS.

The teacher must be a role model for the student. Teaching by example is one of the most effective forms of educations. Ibn Ezra connects this verse with the next one.

כג:כז כִּי־שׁוּחָה עֲמֻקָּה זוֹנָה וּבְאֵר צָרָה נָכְרִיָּה:

23:27 YES, A PROSTITUTE IS A DEEP DITCH; A STRANGE
WOMAN IS A NARROW PIT.

In this verse, the *nochriyah* (strange woman) is the temptress, a projection of desire on someone who is forbidden because she is an outsider. No matter how this verse is interpreted, it is an insult to women. While it may be important to warn a young person to remain chaste and the texts could be less gender-specific and refer to both men and women, our modern sensibility suggests that the language of warning should not demean those who are perceived to be chastity's temptation. Such a posture leads us to treat another human being as an object. Ironically, the point of chastity is undermined by the very warning that treats as objects those persons felt to be the temptation. Language that describes sexual activity as existing without feeling and love is tantamount to describing intimacy itself as an object as well.

כג:כח אַף־הִיא כְּחֶתֶף תֶּאֱרֹב וּבוֹגְדִים בְּאָדָם תּוֹסִף:

23:28 LIKE A ROBBER, SHE LIES IN WAIT AND INCREASES THE
NUMBER OF FAITHLESS MEN.

Once again, the woman is presented as a predator. It is her fault that men sin. We know that this is not the case and the same can be said of men. However, men controlled the community in the ancient world and therefore placed parameters on women in order to control their own passions, which men were apparently unable to do on their own.

כג:כט לְמִי אוֹי לְמִי אֲבוֹי לְמִי מדונים מִדְיָנִים לְמִי שִׂיחַ לְמִי פְּצָעִים
חִנָּם לְמִי חַכְלִלוּת עֵינָיִם:

23:29 WHO WAILS? WHO CRIES WOEFULLY? WHO HAS
ARGUMENTS? WHO MUMBLES? WHO HAS WOUNDS
WITHOUT REASON? WHO HAS BLOODSHOT EYES?

Drunkenness brings the unwanted results of pain, slurred speech, arguments, scars,
and bloodshot eyes. Life in the city allows for commerce, bars, and the opportunity
for overindulgence with alcohol. The midrash commenting on Noah, whom the text
claims as the first drunkard, suggests that before a person drinks, that person behaves
like a lamb. After drinking, that person becomes a lion. After drinking more, the
person becomes a pig and then an ape (*Tanchuma B'reishit, Noach* 13).

כג:ל לַמְאַחֲרִים עַל־הַיַּיִן לַבָּאִים לַחְקֹר מִמְסָךְ:

23:30 THOSE WHO SPEND THEIR TIME SITTING WITH THE
WINE COME TO TRY THE MIXED WINE.

Our translation follows Ibn Ezra's comment that "sitting" is assumed by the verb
lamacharim (who delay, who tarry). What is suggested is that those who are described
here are not casual drinkers. They are alcoholics who spend their time in bars, trying
all kinds of alcoholic beverages. The problem of drunkenness, of alcoholism, seems to
be a problem of the past as well as the present.

כג:לא אַל־תֵּרֶא יַיִן כִּי יִתְאַדָּם כִּי־יִתֵּן בכיס בַּכּוֹס עֵינוֹ יִתְהַלֵּךְ
בְּמֵישָׁרִים:

23:31 DON'T LOOK AT THE WINE WHEN IT IS RED, WHEN IT
GIVES COLOR TO THE CUP, GOING DOWN SMOOTHLY.

Like current advertisements that tout the different kinds of wine for their color,
ancient merchandising similarly dealt with its appearance rather than its effect.
Although wine merchants may praise the appearance and taste of the product, people
drink wine (and other alcoholic beverages) for the effect, for how they make the
drinker feel. Here the reader is reminded about the effect.

כג:לב אַחֲרִיתוֹ כְּנָחָשׁ יִשָּׁךְ וּכְצִפְעֹנִי יַפְרִשׁ:

23:32 THE END RESULT IS THAT IT BITES LIKE A SERPENT;
IT POISONS LIKE A VIPER.

Rashi and Gersonides translate the verb *yafrish* (literally, "to cause to spread") in the second clause as "stings." We follow Ibn Ezra's view and have translated the word as "poisons"; that is, like a viper's venom, wine spreads its effects throughout the body. The spread of the effect through the body leads to strange things.

כג:לג עֵינֶיךָ יִרְאוּ זָרוֹת וְלִבְּךָ יְדַבֵּר תַּהְפֻּכוֹת:

23:33 YOUR EYES WILL SEE STRANGE THINGS, AND YOUR MIND
WILL SAY TOPSY-TURVY THINGS.

This is a further description of the effect of drunkenness. Since the author uses *zarah* to describe "strange" (foreign) women (Proverbs 2:16; 5:3, 20; 7:5), the *Targum*, Rashi, and Ibn Ezra take the plural *zarot* to refer to "strange women" and think that lust will be the effect of drunkenness. Such a translation would affect their understanding of *yiru* (you will see). Therefore, the *Targum*, Rashi, and Ibn Ezra would translate this verse as follows: "You will be looking for strange women." By taking the word *zarot* to refer to the effect of wine on the brain, which causes a person to hallucinate, Gersonides retains the meaning of *yiru* as "you will see."

כג:לד וְהָיִיתָ כְּשֹׁכֵב בְּלֶב־יָם וּכְשֹׁכֵב בְּרֹאשׁ חִבֵּל:

23:34 YOU WILL BE LIKE SOMEONE LYING DOWN IN THE
MIDST OF THE SEA OR ONE LYING AT THE TOP OF A
SHIP'S MAST.

The imagery seems clear, at least to anyone who has ever been drunk. Everything seems to spin from side to side, as if one were buffeted by waves. Everything seems to go back and forth and side to side and up and down as if one were a lookout at the top of a ship in the midst of a stormy sea. The author hopes that the description of the effects of too much drinking would keep one from drinking. The word *chibeil*, which appears at no other point in the Bible, is translated by the *Targum* as *ilfa* (ship) and by Rashi as *toren* (mast). Ibn Ezra takes the word to mean "anchor rope."

כג:לה הִכּוּנִי בַל־חָלִיתִי הֲלָמוּנִי בַל־יָדָעְתִּי מָתַי אָקִיץ אוֹסִיף אֲבַקְשֶׁנּוּ
עוֹד:

23:35 THEY HIT ME, AND I DIDN'T FEEL IT. THEY BEAT ME, AND I DIDN'T KNOW IT. WHEN AM I GOING TO WAKE UP? EVEN SO, I WILL DO IT AGAIN.

For active alcoholics, the deleterious effects of drink are not sufficient to keep them sober. The Rabbis in the midrash tell the tale of a drunken father whose sons wanted to change their father's behavior. While he was drunk, they put him in a cave in a cemetery. They hoped that he would be so frightened when he awakened that he would stop drinking. By chance, some wine traffickers went by the cave and decided to store some bottles of wine in it. When the sons came by to see what happened to their father, they found him asleep with a bottle in his mouth (*Vayikra Rabbah* 12, *Sh'mini*).

The Poor, the Widowed, and the Orphan

"The poor, the widowed, and the orphan" is a metaphor that the Bible uses (and is repeated in other sacred literature) to refer to the most vulnerable groups within the context of the Jewish community. While these terms—and their grouping—may no longer be politically correct, the text uses them with the best intention. Society has the responsibility to look out for those who may be most vulnerable due to circumstances that are generally beyond their control because others in the community may want to take advantage of their situation.

GLEANINGS

Love, Sex, and Friendship

Even though Judaism honors sexuality and discourages celibacy, it also recognizes the dangers of unbridled sexual lust. At times, the rabbis of old described sexual urges as "the evil impulse," not because they believed that sex was inherently evil, but because they believed sex without restraint could lead a man to disaster. Judaism teaches us that sexual pleasure is a divine gift. It also teaches us that sex without love, commitment, or respect is meaningless and unworthy of human beings. Judaism seeks to elevate to a higher spiritual level what some consider a purely physical act.

Allan C. Tuffs, *And You Shall Teach Them to Your Sons: Biblical Tales for Fathers and Sons* (New York: UAHC Press, 1997), 65–66

Understanding Our Sexual Selves

Men love to tell tall tales of their sexual exploits, particularly those feats accomplished in their young, single, irresponsible days. And they love to tell dirty jokes. No matter how you look at it, such behavior violates Jewish ethics, because it comes at the expense of others, often women. Of course, a man who refuses to participate in such conversations is usually scorned and considered not much of a man. For in America, sexual prowess is widely regarded as the measure of a man's worth.

The ancient rabbis understood the compelling power of sexuality. They frankly discussed nearly every aspect of the sexual self. One sage is depicted hiding under Rav Huna's bed as Huna and his wife are making love. When Huna discovered his student hiding under the bed, the student's explanation is simple and straightforward: "I have come to learn Torah from the master."

If Jewish teachings are so unabashed about sex, then why has traditional Judaism created the *mechitza,* literally, a wall of separation between men and women? Such a physical barrier has barred women from the central action in the synagogue. (Liberal Judaism has long-since abandoned separation. Even in many Orthodox synagogues, the separation is more symbolic than real; a small divider separates two adjacent sections of the sanctuary.)

In order to understand the *psychological* role of the *mechitza,* we need to recognize that it was introduced to rein in men more than women. The rabbis understood that men must continually struggle to control their *yetzer hara,* their evil inclination. Women have more self-control, so traditional Judaism placed restrictions primarily on women, knowing they would be more able to comply.

The rabbis knew the human heart only too well. They too were men. They didn't need Freud to explain things to them. Indeed, contemporary research confirms what our tradition has already known: that sexual desire is part of our natural genetic engineering. It motivates our species to continue itself. But it is love that helps the bonds of continuity soar heavenward.

Kerry M. Olitzky, *From Your Father's House . . . : Reflections for Modern Jewish Men* (Philadelphia: Jewish Publication Society, 1999) 104–06

CHAPTER TWENTY-FOUR

כד:א אַל־תְּקַנֵּא בְּאַנְשֵׁי רָעָה וְאַל־תתאו תִּתְאָיו לִהְיוֹת אִתָּם:

24:1 DON'T ENVY EVIL PEOPLE; DON'T WISH TO BE LIKE
THEM.

Gersonides points to the reason that some might envy the wicked: their apparent
success. As usual, virtue cannot be sold on the basis of success, while vice derided on
the basis of its failures. Ultimately, virtue stands alone. It is our acting on the stage of
our own expectations, our sense of whom we would like to be as persons, that is the
essential motivation for virtue. If material success is our marker, then virtue will never
win. When being and becoming the person we could be is the measurement for
success, then virtue will win.

כד:ב כִּי־שֹׁד יֶהְגֶּה לִבָּם וְעָמָל שִׂפְתֵיהֶם תְּדַבֵּרְנָה:

24:2 THEIR MINDS PONDER DESTRUCTION, AND THEIR
LIPS SPEAK MISCHIEF.

Unlike the truth that the author of Proverbs wants us to ponder (17:7), or the Torah
that the Psalmist invites us to review day and night (Psalm 1:2), the wicked ponder the
destruction of others.

כד:ג בְּחָכְמָה יִבָּנֶה בָּיִת וּבִתְבוּנָה יִתְכּוֹנָן:

24:3 A HOUSE IS BUILT BY WISDOM AND ESTABLISHED
BY UNDERSTANDING.

This image is continued in the following verse.

כד:ד וּבְדַעַת חֲדָרִים יִמָּלְאוּ כָּל־הוֹן יָקָר וְנָעִים:

24:4 ITS CHAMBERS ARE FILLED WITH KNOWLEDGE, AND ALL
ITS RICHES ARE DEAR AND PLEASANT.

Since Gersonides took *chochmah* (wisdom) of the previous verse to refer to things
that bring eternity and *bayit* (house) to refer to the individual person, it follows that
the "chambers" refer to the intellect, whose responsibility is to amass the proper
("correct") ideas.

כד:ה גֶּבֶר־חָכָם בַּעוֹז וְאִישׁ־דַּעַת מְאַמֶּץ־כֹּחַ:

24:5 A WISE PERSON IS STRONG, AND A PERSON OF
UNDERSTANDING INCREASES POWER.

For Gersonides, the strength of the wise person is in the control of material
possessions and directing oneself to the study of "correct" ideas.

כד:ו כִּי בְתַחְבֻּלוֹת תַּעֲשֶׂה־לְךָ מִלְחָמָה וּתְשׁוּעָה בְּרֹב יוֹעֵץ:

24:6 FOR WITH PLANS YOU MAKE WAR AND WITH MANY
ADVISORS YOU HAVE VICTORY.

The first clause echoes 20:18. The second clause is an echo of 20:5. This use of
materials already presented raises a possible question about the editing of the Book of
Proverbs. Perhaps the author wanted to emphasize the particular lessons. Or perhaps
the author had a different literary sense, for the final redactor certainly knew that the
texts were repeated in various places. According to Gersonides, the war to be fought
is with the *yetzer hara* (evil inclination), which he identifies with the appetitive faculty
of the soul. For him, the "advisors" are those aspects of the rational faculties of soul
that help the individual control desire.

כד:ז רָאמוֹת לֶאֱוִיל חָכְמוֹת בַּשַּׁעַר לֹא יִפְתַּח־פִּיהוּ:

24:7 WISDOM IS AS CORALS TO A FOOL; IN THE GATE, ONE
DOES NOT OPEN ONE'S MOUTH.

Ramot is the problem word in this verse. Relating the word to its use in Job (28:18),
Rashi understands it as some kind of precious stone (e.g., corals). Ibn Ezra and
Gersonides take it as an irregular form of *ramot,* "high." For Rashi, fools are so
entranced by various kinds of sciences that they fail to study Torah. For Ibn Ezra and
Gersonides, wisdom is far above fools, so that they are unable to attain it.

כד:ח מְחַשֵּׁב לְהָרַע לוֹ בַּעַל־מְזִמּוֹת יִקְרָאוּ:

24:8 THE ONE WHO DEVISES EVIL SHALL BE CALLED MASTER
OF SCHEMES.

We might wonder what criticism could affect such a wicked person. Surely, the
wicked person who "devises evil" is beyond being affected by what others think.

כד:ט זְמַת אִוֶּלֶת חַטָּאת וְתוֹעֲבַת לְאָדָם לֵץ:

24:9 THE SCHEME OF THE FOOL IS SIN, AND A MOCKER IS
AN ABOMINATION TO ANY PERSON.

As noted previously, the "mocker" is worse than the "fool," for the mocker denies the ethical framework that the fool misunderstands. The mocker denies God. The fool neither accepts divine good nor learns from experience, either his or her own or of others. Our world lacks the conformity that would make the mocker a threat. It assumes that there is one ethical system that he or she is challenging. There are just so many different and competing ethical frameworks that to accept one is, in effect, to mock another—though we have unfortunately seen the effect that one can have on the masses, particular during World War II.

כד:י הִתְרַפִּיתָ בְּיוֹם צָרָה צַר כֹּחֶכָה*:   יתיר ה'

24:10 IF YOU ARE LAX ON A DAY OF TROUBLE, YOUR OWN
STRENGTH WILL BE SMALL.

Both Rashi and Ibn Ezra understand the verse to mean that if you don't help your friend when your friend is in trouble, you will suffer when you need help. Gersonides takes the first clause to suggest that if one does not actively pursue the acquisition of wisdom now, then it will be more difficult to acquire later on.

כד:יא הַצֵּל לְקֻחִים לַמָּוֶת וּמָטִים לַהֶרֶג אִם־תַּחְשׂוֹךְ:

24:11 SAVE THOSE WHO ARE CONDEMNED TO DEATH, WOULD
YOU HOLD BACK FROM THOSE ABOUT TO BE KILLED?

Both Rashi and Ibn Ezra connect this verse with the previous one: being lax on a day of trouble may get someone killed. When the verse stands alone, the reader is left to ponder for whom the verse was written and in what context.

כד:יב כִּי־תֹאמַר הֵן לֹא־יָדַעְנוּ זֶה הֲלֹא־תֹכֵן לִבּוֹת הוּא־יָבִין וְנֹצֵר נַפְשְׁךָ
הוּא יֵדָע וְהֵשִׁיב לְאָדָם כְּפָעֳלוֹ:

24:12 SHOULD YOU SAY, "WE REALLY DON'T KNOW THIS,"
DOES NOT THE ONE WHO EXAMINES ALL HEARTS
UNDERSTAND? THE ONE WHO WATCHES YOUR SOUL
WILL KNOW AND WILL RENDER TO EACH PERSON
ACCORDING TO WHAT HAS BEEN DONE.

The writer suggests what the Torah states elsewhere: "You shall not stand idly by your neighbor's blood" (Leviticus 19:16). Even so, the duty to help a neighbor in distress is more of a moral requirement than it is a legal requirement. Perhaps that is the reason that none of our commentators make extended comments on this verse. Rashi limits himself to explaining that the first word, *ki*, in this context means "perhaps." Ibn Ezra is silent, and the usually wordy Gersonides is content with stating that God will know whether one exerted oneself in the acquisition of knowledge.

כד:יג אֱכָל־בְּנִי דְבַשׁ כִּי־טוֹב וְנֹפֶת מָתוֹק עַל־חִכֶּךָ:

24:13 MY YOUNG FRIEND, EAT HONEY BECAUSE IT IS GOOD, AND THE HONEYCOMB WILL BE SWEET TO YOUR PALATE.

This verse is the obvious introduction to the next verse.

כד:יד כֵּן דְּעֶה חָכְמָה לְנַפְשֶׁךָ אִם־מָצָאתָ וְיֵשׁ אַחֲרִית וְתִקְוָתְךָ לֹא תִכָּרֵת:

24:14 SO TOO IS THE KNOWLEDGE OF WISDOM TO YOUR MIND; IF YOU FIND IT, THERE WILL BE A FUTURE AND YOUR HOPE WILL NOT BE CUT OFF.

The last clause is quoted from 23:18. The *Targum* translates *d'eh* (knowledge) with a verbal imperative *itchakam* (know!). Rashi connects the verse with the previous one and suggests that as one would pursue the taste of honey, so one should pursue wisdom. Ibn Ezra suggests that one's wisdom will be appreciated by one's children. Gersonides understands the verse, particularly the last clause, to teach that by acquiring wisdom one will achieve human success in this life and eternity in the next life.

כד:טו אַל־תֶּאֱרֹב רָשָׁע לִנְוֵה צַדִּיק אַל־תְּשַׁדֵּד רִבְצוֹ:

24:15 O WICKED ONE, DON'T LIE IN WAIT WHERE THE RIGHTEOUS DWELL, DON'T RUIN WHERE THEY REST.

One might wonder which wicked people would be reading the Book of Proverbs in order to take the advice of the author. This verse acts as an introduction to the next verse.

כד:טז כִּי שֶׁבַע יִפּוֹל צַדִּיק וָקָם וּרְשָׁעִים יִכָּשְׁלוּ בְרָעָה:

24:16 ALTHOUGH THE RIGHTEOUS FALL SEVEN TIMES, THEY GET UP, YET IT IS DISASTER WHEN THE WICKED JUST STUMBLE.

This verse, like the previous one, is a warning to the wicked. Thus, they must be advice to those who might have a tendency toward doing evil. It can be assumed that the truly wicked would not be reading Proverbs in the first place.

כד:יז בִּנְפֹל אוֹיִבְךָ אַל־תִּשְׂמָח וּבִכָּשְׁלוֹ אַל־יָגֵל לִבֶּךָ:

24:17 DON'T REJOICE WHEN YOUR ENEMIES FALL, AND DON'T
BE HAPPY WHEN THEY STUMBLE

Although it may seem so, this verse is not an injunction on an ethical level. Rather, as the next verse indicates, it emerges from the fear that God will see you enjoying the spectacle of your enemies' failure.

כד:יח פֶּן־יִרְאֶה יְהוָֹה וְרַע בְּעֵינָיו וְהֵשִׁיב מֵעָלָיו אַפּוֹ:

24:18 SO THAT IT DOES NOT DISPLEASE *ADONAI*, LOOKING
ON AND TURNING AWAY IN ANGER.

We have translated the anthropomorphic *ra b'einav* (evil in God's eyes) as "displease *Adonai*." Gersonides sees a deficiency in the character of the person who would rejoice in the punishment of another. However, Saadyah Gaon expressed the view that part of the reward of the righteous was precisely their observing the punishment and the suffering of the wicked (*Books of Beliefs and Opinions,* treatise 9, chapter 9).

כד:יט אַל־תִּתְחַר בַּמְּרֵעִים אַל־תְּקַנֵּא בָּרְשָׁעִים:

24:19 DON'T EXCUSE YOURSELF BECAUSE OF EVILDOERS NOR
ENVY THE WICKED.

This verse, like some others, raises questions about the editing process of the Book of Proverbs. With the exception of the last word, *r'shaim* (wicked), it is a quotation of Psalm 37:1, which ends with the words *b'osei avlah* (doers of iniquity). Perhaps the editor liked the text and wanted to include it or it was a theme the editor wanted to emphasize. As the verse stands, the two clauses seem to contradict each other. The first suggests that the reader should not be troubled by "evildoers," since they have no future—as the next verse indicates. The second suggests that the reader, rather than being troubled by the "wicked," really wants to join them. To avoid what seems to be a contradiction, Ibn Ezra and Gersonides take *titchar* (excite) to mean *titareiv* (to be involved with).

כד:כ כִּי לֹא־תִהְיֶה אַחֲרִית לָרָע נֵר רְשָׁעִים יִדְעָךְ:

24:20 FOR AN EVIL PERSON HAS NO FUTURE; THE LAMP OF
THE WICKED WILL BE PUT OUT.

Although it might seem that *ra* (evil person) in the first clause refers to evil itself, the *Targum,* Ibn Ezra, and Gersonides understand it to refer to a person who is evil.

כד:כא יְרָא־אֶת־יְהֹוָה בְּנִי וָמֶלֶךְ עִם־שׁוֹנִים אַל־תִּתְעָרָב:

24:21 MY YOUNG FRIEND, FEAR *ADONAI* AND THE
SOVEREIGN RULER, AND DON'T GET INVOLVED WITH
PEOPLE OF RANK.

The difficulty in this verse lies in the meaning of *shonim* in the second clause. Coming from the root *shanah* (to change), the word can also be related to *sh'nei* (two). What is changed or what is done twice becomes the problem. Although the *Targum* translates the word by *shatyei* (those who are insane), the Septuagint and the *P'shita* translate the word as "persons of exalted rank," *apaythesis* and *shaytia* respectively. Rashi relates the word to those who believe in two divine powers. Ibn Ezra suggests that the word refers to those who repeat evil acts. Gersonides understands it to mean those who keep the mitzvot. All of these interpretations reflect what appears to be the author's intent to warn the reader not to get involved with second-rank people who want to change the status quo. Both the Korach rebellion in Numbers 16, as an early literary example, and the revolution in *Animal Farm,* as a late example, are initiated by those of secondary rank, that is, those of the ruling class who are not ruling during the time the story takes place. They turn to those who are ruled and claim that things would be different were they to be installed in power: then all people would be equal! If one is loyal to God and the sovereign ruler, that is, the civil order as it presently exists, then one should keep far away from those who want to change it.

כד:כב כִּי־פִתְאֹם יָקוּם אֵידָם וּפִיד שְׁנֵיהֶם מִי יוֹדֵעַ:

24:22 FOR SUDDENLY THEIR DESTRUCTION WILL COME,
AND WHO KNOWS WHAT RUIN WILL COME FROM BOTH?

Rashi takes the last clause to refer to the double destruction due to idolatry. Ibn Ezra expects that punishment for revolution will come from both God and the sovereign ruler. In the previous verse and in this verse, the author stresses the importance of social stability in the world in which wisdom literature operates.

כד:כג גַּם־אֵלֶּה לַחֲכָמִים הַכֵּר־פָּנִים בְּמִשְׁפָּט בַּל־טוֹב:

24:23 THESE THINGS ALSO RELATE TO THE WISE: FAVORITISM
IN COURT IS NOT GOOD.

At first, the first clause seems to suggest another editing challenge to resolve. It is as if the editor came upon another collection of wise sayings and appends them to the book without any concern for questions or repetitions. This may reflect a literary style that is not as self-conscious as modern literary approaches might suggest. Nevertheless, the second clause is troublesome, since showing partiality in judgment was prohibited in the Torah (Leviticus 19:15; Deuteronomy 16:19).

Why is it presented here at all and in such a weak manner as "not good"? Perhaps it is an afterthought of the author that was not taken out by the editor, or an affirmation of what the Torah has taught, as if to say, "Just a reminder...." Since the Torah is traditionally ascribed to divine authorship and wisdom literature reflects human experience, it could also be an attempt by the author to suggest that human experience often affirms what God has taught, such as in the case of the court, where humans are forced to act like God.

כד:כד אֹמֵר לְרָשָׁע צַדִּיק אָתָּה יִקְּבֻהוּ עַמִּים יִזְעָמוּהוּ לְאֻמִּים:

24:24 The one who says to the guilty, "You are innocent," will be cursed by the peoples and execrated by the nations.

After reading the previous verse and this verse, one has the feeling that the standard of justice prescribed by the aforementioned Torah verses had not reached all courts.

כד:כה וְלַמּוֹכִיחִים יִנְעָם וַעֲלֵיהֶם תָּבוֹא בִרְכַּת־טוֹב:

24:25 It shall be pleasant for those who reprove; upon them shall come a good blessing.

Ibn Ezra connects this verse with the previous one. Directed to the judges, the verse promises a good outcome for those who condemn the guilty rather than declaring them innocent.

כד:כו שְׂפָתַיִם יִשָּׁק מֵשִׁיב דְּבָרִים נְכֹחִים:

24:26 He will kiss the lips of the one who returns a proper verdict.

D'varim n'chochim (literally, "proper words") is translated in context as "a proper verdict." It is not clear who will be doing the kissing. Rashi explains the first words of the verse to suggest that the judge who delivered a proper verdict would be worthy of being kissed. Gersonides understands the first words as metaphor: since lying is hated and truth is loved, the lips that speak truth would invite kisses from all. It seems that this verse, like the previous one, encourages the judge to deliver a proper verdict. Nevertheless, one wonders whether these exhortations were more successful than those placed directly in the Torah.

כד:כז הָכֵן בַּחוּץ מְלַאכְתֶּךָ וְעַתְּדָהּ בַּשָּׂדֶה לָךְ אַחַר וּבָנִיתָ בֵיתֶךָ׃

24:27 ON THE OUTSIDE PREPARE YOUR WORK, GET IT READY
IN THE FIELD, AND THEN BUILD YOUR HOUSE.

The specified work is not clear from the plain meaning of the verse. Rashi first explains that what is to be prepared on the outside is the study of Bible, what is to be readied in the field is the Mishnah, and what is to be built as a house is the Gemara. His second explanation is more compelling. At first, one should acquire fields and vineyards and then graze animals in the field. Having provided oneself with a livelihood, one should then find a spouse. Gersonides predictably interprets the verse in a philosophical manner. He suggests that the first clause refers to those things observed by way of the senses. The second refers to the investigation of knowledge received through the senses. And the final clause refers to the intellectual notions.

כד:כח אַל־תְּהִי עֵד־חִנָּם בְּרֵעֶךָ וַהֲפִתִּיתָ בִּשְׂפָתֶיךָ׃

24:28 DO NOT BE A WITNESS AGAINST YOUR NEIGHBOR
WITHOUT REASON; DON'T DECEIVE WITH YOUR LIPS.

We have followed the interpretation of Ibn Ezra in the translation of the last clause. He takes *vahafitita* (literally, "and would you deceive?") as a question with an assumed negative response. As readers, we are forced to wonder what kind of testimony is being questioned. Perhaps it relates directly to the next verse.

כד:כט אַל־תֹּאמַר כַּאֲשֶׁר עָשָׂה־לִי כֵּן אֶעֱשֶׂה־לּוֹ אָשִׁיב לָאִישׁ כְּפָעֳלוֹ׃

24:29 DON'T SAY: WHAT ONE DID TO ME, I WILL DO TO
THAT PERSON. I WILL PAY BACK A PERSON ACCORDING
TO THE ACTION.

Revenge is always tempting, particularly in matters before a court. It may be that this verse continues the various injunctions directed first to the judge and now to the witnesses.

כד:ל עַל־שְׂדֵה אִישׁ־עָצֵל עָבַרְתִּי וְעַל־כֶּרֶם אָדָם חֲסַר־לֵב׃

24:30 I PASSED BY THE FIELD OF THE LAZY AND BY THE
VINEYARD OF A PERSON WHO LACKS UNDERSTANDING.

Rashi refers to the "lazy" as those who have not reviewed their study of the Talmud.

כד:לא וְהִנֵּה עָלָה כֻלּוֹ קִמְּשֹׂנִים כָּסּוּ פָנָיו חֲרֻלִּים וְגֶדֶר אֲבָנָיו נֶהֱרָסָה:

24:31 SEE, IT WAS TOTALLY OVERGROWN WITH THISTLES; THE
SURFACE WAS COVERED WITH BROKEN NETTLES, AND
THE STONE FENCE HAD FALLEN DOWN.

The author provides us with an image of a field that has been allowed to ruin due to
laziness. As might be expected, Rashi refers the verse to lazy students who have not
reviewed what they learned.

כד:לב וָאֶחֱזֶה אָנֹכִי אָשִׁית לִבִּי רָאִיתִי לָקַחְתִּי מוּסָר:

24:32 I LOOKED, I CONSIDERED, I SAW, AND I DERIVED
DISCIPLINE.

The context for this verse suggests that the abandoned field provided insight to the
writer, which is now conveyed to the reader. The lazy person has a price to pay. What
such a person would say is shown in the next verse.

כד:לג מְעַט שֵׁנוֹת מְעַט תְּנוּמוֹת מְעַט חִבֻּק יָדַיִם לִשְׁכָּב:

24:33 A LITTLE SLEEP, A LITTLE SLUMBER, JUST A LITTLE
TUCKING IN ONE'S HANDS TO REST.

That lazy person will discover what the author teaches us in the next verse.

כד:לד וּבָא־מִתְהַלֵּךְ רֵישֶׁךָ וּמַחְסֹרֶיךָ כְּאִישׁ מָגֵן:

24:34 YOUR POVERTY COMES MARCHING IN AND YOUR
NEED LIKE A PERSON WITH A SHIELD.

The last clause suggests that just as one who is without a shield is at a disadvantage
against one with a shield, the lazy person will be unable to stave off the results of
doing nothing or even just a little.

Virtue

The Platonic notion of virtue is the right relationship between the parts of the soul, and the Aristotelian notion is the mean between two extremes. Ethics may be defined as the doctrine of virtues dealing with good and bad and with moral duty and obligation. Thus, to be ethical (virtuous) one must align the parts of the soul complex in the Platonic world. For Aristotle and for those who followed him, like Maimonides, it was a matter of finding the middle ground.

Appetitive Faculty of Soul

According to most philosophers, the soul is divided into parts or faculties. The appetitive faculty consists of the many drives and urges that persuade the individual to nurture the body.

Saadyah Gaon

Saadyah ben Joseph (882–942), from Fayyum in Egypt, is considered by most to be the father of medieval Jewish philosophy. He was the first to develop the notions of Islamic theology and philosophy in an independent manner. Similarly, he was the first to develop a philosophic justification for Judaism. He received his training in Egypt, where he lived the first thirty years of his life. He subsequently lived in the Land of Israel, Syria, and Babylonia. In 928, he became the *gaon* (head) of the well-known rabbinical academy in Sura, Babylonia.

Saadyah was also a pioneer in Hebrew philology. He translated the Bible into Arabic, and his commentaries on it laid the foundation for a scientific interpretation of the Bible. Much of his extensive literary output focused on polemics against Karaism. (The Karaites were a Jewish sect that accepted the biblical text, *kara* in Aramaic, alone and rejected all rabbinic interpretation of oral law.) Saadyah's entire system of philosophy can be found in his book *Beliefs and Opinions*. His doctrine concerning the relationship between reason and revelation—which was accepted by most subsequent Jewish philosophers—provided the methodological foundation for his religious philosophy. For him, religious truth, a distinct form of truth, is found in revelation. Reason provides the common foundation for all religions. For Saadyah, only Judaism is the work of God; all other religions were developed by humankind and therefore falsely claim divine origin.

P'shita

The *P'shita* is the Syriac (Christian Aramaic) translation of the Bible. It served as the Bible for the Christians of Syria. It dates from possibly the second to fourth century C.E.

GLEANINGS

Judaism's Mind-Set

In biblical times, Torah created a simple arithmetic to fulfill the Covenant: the good plus the holy, as well as the (merely) Jewish, since some of the Commandments were neither inherently good nor manifestly holy, but they were Jewish, such as *sha'atnez* and *kashrut*. Hence the mind-set's simple arithmetic held that the observance of all the Commandments *in toto* by the Jewish people *in toto* ensured the peace and prosperity of the entire community as surely as one plus one equals two. The Prophets then amplified this covenantal mind-set, offering clear warning of the consequences if Israel failed to act in accordance with God's expectations. When the people subtracted the Commandments from the Covenant, they suffered. The Writings, especially Job, Ecclesiastes, and many of the Psalms, then nuanced the simple arithmetic of the Covenant, acknowledging that the observance of the Commandments would not always assure material reward. The simple arithmetic then evolved into an ethical tautology of A equals A: the reward for doing what is good, holy, and Jewish is doing what is good, holy, and Jewish. When this nuanced equation no longer sufficed, the Pharisees and then the rabbis turned the ethical tautology into utopian eschatology: the ultimate reward for keeping the Commandments will be realized with the advent of the *Mashiach* and the *'Olam HaBa*.

Mark Joel Mahler, "What Ever Happened to *Judaism* in Reform?"
CCAR Journal: A Reform Jewish Quarterly (summer 1998): 17–18

CHAPTER TWENTY-FIVE

כה:א גַּם־אֵלֶּה מִשְׁלֵי שְׁלֹמֹה אֲשֶׁר הֶעְתִּיקוּ אַנְשֵׁי חִזְקִיָּה מֶלֶךְ־יְהוּדָה:

25:1 THESE TOO ARE THE PROVERBS OF SOLOMON, WHICH
THE MEN OF HEZEKIAH, KING OF JUDAH, COPIED.

This chapter starts another section of the book. From these different sections, it appears that the editorial process included materials that emerged from different times and reflected different themes. Ibn Ezra suggests that this section was selected to be a separate entity by Hezekiah out of a mass of other proverbs of Solomon. Gersonides spins it a little differently. He suggests that these proverbs were separated out from the rest because they were more the product of a later period (namely, the period of the "men of Hezekiah") rather than the product of Solomon.

כה:ב כְּבֹד אֱלֹהִים הַסְתֵּר דָּבָר וּכְבֹד מְלָכִים חֲקֹר דָּבָר:

25:2 IT IS THE GLORY OF GOD TO HIDE A MATTER AND THE
HONOR OF RULERS TO SEARCH OUT A MATTER.

Rashi explains that what is hidden is the "account of the beginning" and the "account of the chariot," which, according to the Talmud (*Chagigah* 11b, 13a), could not be discussed. Rashi continues the investigation of the acts of kings and of Sages, for it reveals their brilliance in their methods of deducing the halachah.

כה:ג שָׁמַיִם לָרוּם וָאָרֶץ לָעֹמֶק וְלֵב מְלָכִים אֵין חֵקֶר:

25:3 THE HEAVENS FOR HEIGHT AND THE EARTH FOR DEPTH,
BUT UNSEARCHABLE ARE THE MINDS OF RULERS.

One wonders how this verse can be related to the previous one. The writer seems to suggest that just as we cannot measure the extremes of height or depth, similarly the extent of power is beyond measure. Rashi agrees. He suggests that the manifold tasks that sovereign rulers must undertake to meet the needs of their people, to establish laws for them, and to fight their battles are incomprehensible no matter how some speak of them or write of them. As might be expected, Gersonides reads the verse as a philosophical metaphor: although "above" and "below" are not precisely defined in terms of a line, reality implies some kind of stable definitions, for the highest "heaven" and the center of the "earth" suggest the ultimate distances above and below. Since the kind of concerns that engage the mind of a ruler constantly change, it is difficult to understand them.

כה:ד הָגוֹ סִיגִים מִכָּסֶף וַיֵּצֵא לַצֹּרֵף כֶּלִי:

25:4 REMOVE THE DROSS FROM SILVER AND OUT COMES A
VESSEL FOR THE SILVERSMITH.

Dross in the silver prevents the making of a proper utensil. Its removal is necessary to fulfill the purpose of the silversmith. The application of this statement is seen in the next verse.

כה:ה הָגוֹ רָשָׁע לִפְנֵי־מֶלֶךְ וְיִכּוֹן בַּצֶּדֶק כִּסְאוֹ:

25:5 REMOVE THE WICKED FROM THE PRESENCE OF THE
RULER AND THE THRONE WILL BE ESTABLISHED IN
RIGHTEOUSNESS.

As dross affects silver, the presence of a wicked person will affect the court of a sovereign ruler. Remove that person and the ruler's court will be known for righteousness. This verse reflects a situation in which corruption is found in high places. It is a spin on the famous quote of the bank robber Willy Sutton, who was asked why he robbed banks. "That is where the money is" was his answer.

כה:ו אַל־תִּתְהַדַּר לִפְנֵי־מֶלֶךְ וּבִמְקוֹם גְּדֹלִים אַל־תַּעֲמֹד:

25:6 IN THE PRESENCE OF THE RULER, DON'T GLORIFY
YOURSELF, AND IN THE PLACE OF THE GREAT,
DON'T STAND.

As we have seen throughout the Book of Proverbs, the author writes to provide information to those who would stride along the corridors of power and to help them develop proper attitudes. Here the writer gives the student further information about court etiquette: watch yourself, don't look too good, and don't put on airs. Remember your real status, and remember that you depend on the goodwill of those who are your superiors.

כה:ז כִּי טוֹב אֲמָר־לְךָ עֲלֵה הֵנָּה מֵהַשְׁפִּילְךָ לִפְנֵי נָדִיב אֲשֶׁר רָאוּ
עֵינֶיךָ:

25:7 IT IS BETTER THAT SOMEONE SAY TO YOU, "COME UP,"
THAN HAVE SOMEONE BRING YOU DOWN IN THE
PRESENCE OF ROYALTY, AS YOUR EYES HAVE SEEN.

Details about who sits where and who stands where reflect relationships of power.
The writer warns the young people for whom this book was ostensibly written to
watch out where they stand and where they sit.

כה:ח אַל־תֵּצֵא לָרִב מַהֵר פֶּן מַה־תַּעֲשֶׂה בְּאַחֲרִיתָהּ בְּהַכְלִים אֹתְךָ
רֵעֶךָ:

25:8 DON'T SPEED TO A QUARREL LEST YOU KNOW WHAT
TO DO AT THE END WHEN YOUR NEIGHBOR PUTS
YOU TO SHAME.

Although the first clause may remind us of Polonius's advice to Laertes in
Shakespeare's *Hamlet,* "Beware of entrance to a quarrel...," it does match exactly
the continuation of that piece of advice, "...but being in, Bear't that the opposed
may be beware of thee" (act 1, scene 3). Here the reader is warned to stay out of a
situation, the outcome of which cannot be predicted.

כה:ט רִיבְךָ רִיב אֶת־רֵעֶךָ וְסוֹד אַחֵר אַל־תְּגָל:

25:9 QUARREL WITH YOUR NEIGHBOR, BUT DON'T REVEAL
ANOTHER'S SECRET—

The sense of the first clause, and Rashi's commentary on it, suggest an "If you must"
(that is, if the quarrel is unavoidable). Yet here there are boundaries: keep the quarrel
between you and your neighbor. Don't involve a third party.

כה:י פֶּן־יְחַסֶּדְךָ שֹׁמֵעַ וְדִבָּתְךָ לֹא תָשׁוּב:

25:10 LEST THE ONE WHO HEARS IT WILL BRING SHAME ON
YOU AND YOUR EVIL REPUTATION WILL NEVER GO AWAY.

Y'chased'cha (will bring shame on you) occurs only here as a verbal root and only as a
noun in Leviticus 20:17 and Proverbs 14:34. What is remarkable is that the noun
chesed (steady love) has a partner that sounds the same and means the opposite:
chesed as "shame."

כה:יא תַּפּוּחֵי זָהָב בְּמַשְׂכִּיּוֹת כָּסֶף דָּבָר דָּבֻר עַל־אָפְנָיו:

25:11 LIKE APPLES OF GOD IN FILIGREES OF SILVER SO IS A
WORD WELL SPOKEN.

The author presents a piece of jewelry, made up of a gold core covered with a silver
filigree overlay, as the analog of a parable. The "silver apple" is seen at a distance;
coming closer, the inner "golden apple" is visible. A parable also has an outer and
inner aspect. The outer aspect conveys one meaning, the inner aspect another. The
comparative values of the two meanings is like the value of silver to gold. In the *Guide
for the Perplexed*, Maimonides makes use of this verse to signal to his intended reader
that he wrote the *Guide* in such a way that its hidden secrets can be glimpsed through
the filigree of its words (*Guide*, introduction). Gersonides tells his reader that since
many of the verses of this book are parables, his interpretation will provide a great
benefit to the person possessing a subtle intellect.

כה:יב נֶזֶם זָהָב וַחֲלִי־כָתֶם מוֹכִיחַ חָכָם עַל־אֹזֶן שֹׁמָעַת:

25:12 LIKE AN EARRING OF GOLD, AND AN ORNAMENT OF
FINE GOLD, IS ONE WHO OFFERS WISE REPROOF TO AN
EAR THAT LISTENS.

The delicate relation between the one who offers reproof and the one who receives it
received the attention of the Rabbis. Rabbi Tarfon wondered if there was anyone in
his generation who knew how to offer reproof and Rabbi Eliezer ben Azariah
wondered if there was anyone in his generation who knew how to receive it (*Sifra,
K'doshim, Parshata Bet, Perek Dalet*).

כה:יג כְּצִנַּת־שֶׁלֶג בְּיוֹם קָצִיר צִיר נֶאֱמָן לְשֹׁלְחָיו וְנֶפֶשׁ אֲדֹנָיו יָשִׁיב:

25:13 AS THE COLDNESS OF SNOW AT HARVESTTIME, SO IS A
DEPENDABLE MESSENGER TO THE ONE WHO SENT HIM;
HE REFRESHES THE SOUL OF HIS MASTER.

The image is clear: at the hot time of harvest, the cold of winter would be a delight,
but, as Rashi points out, not the snow, which would impede the harvest. Ibn Ezra also
takes the first clause to refer to the cold air—rather than snow—that might refresh an
overheated harvester. An equal delight would be a messenger who could be
depended upon, so that the one who sent that messenger on the journey could be
assured that the message would be transmitted.

כה:יד נְשִׂיאִים וְרוּחַ וְגֶשֶׁם אָיִן אִישׁ מִתְהַלֵּל בְּמַתַּת־שָׁקֶר:

25:14 ONE WHO WOULD BOAST OF A GIFT NOT GIVEN IS LIKE
CLOUDS AND WIND WITHOUT RAIN.

Much is promised and little is delivered. Our translation of *matat shaker* (literally,
"a false gift") as "a gift not given" follows the interpretation of Gersonides.

כה:טו בְּאֹרֶךְ אַפַּיִם יְפֻתֶּה קָצִין וְלָשׁוֹן רַכָּה תִּשְׁבָּר־גָּרֶם:

25:15 PATIENCE WILL PERSUADE A RULER, AND A SOFT
TONGUE WILL BREAK A BONE.

As Rashi understands it, the "ruler" here is God. It is good advice for the one who
wants to move through the corridors of power: patience is a necessary virtue.
Similarly, great care in speech must be taken, and it too is a virtue.

כה:טז דְּבַשׁ מָצָאתָ אֱכֹל דַּיֶּךָ פֶּן־תִּשְׂבָּעֶנּוּ וַהֲקֵאתוֹ:

25:16 IF YOU HAVE FOUND HONEY, EAT AS MUCH AS IS
SUFFICIENT FOR YOU, LEST YOU BE STUFFED AND
VOMIT IT UP.

Maimonides uses this verse as a parable of intellectual apprehension: one should
proceed only after proper training (*Guide* 1:31).

כה:יז הֹקַר רַגְלְךָ מִבֵּית רֵעֶךָ פֶּן־יִשְׂבָּעֲךָ וּשְׂנֵאֶךָ:

25:17 RARELY GO TO YOUR NEIGHBOR'S HOUSE LEST HE
[OR SHE] GET TIRED OF YOU AND HATE YOU.

The opening words of *hokar ragl'cha* literally mean "let your foot be rare." We have
translated the words idiomatically as "rarely go," which Rashi joins to the following
clause, "get tired of you." Just as one should eat no more honey than one can digest
(as in the previous verse), one should visit a neighbor no more than the neighbor can
stand. Rashi also gives a midrashic interpretation: avoid inadvertent sins lest you end
up bringing in too many sin offerings.

כה:יח מֵפִיץ וְחֶרֶב וְחֵץ שָׁנוּן אִישׁ־עֹנֶה בְרֵעֵהוּ עֵד שָׁקֶר:

25:18 A MALLET, A SWORD, AND A SHARPENED ARROW IS
THE FALSE WITNESS WHO TESTIFIES AGAINST ONE'S
NEIGHBOR.

As deadly as the implements are in the first clause of the verse, so is the person in
the second.

249

כה:יט שֵׁן רֹעָה וְרֶגֶל מוּעָדֶת מִבְטָח בּוֹגֵד בְּיוֹם צָרָה:

25:19 As a broken tooth, as a foot out of joint, so
   is trusting an untrustworthy person in time
   of trouble.

Trust may be a great thing, but you must be sure of the person being trusted. Just as
you would have difficulty chewing with a broken tooth or walking with a foot out of
joint, you only become aware of the problem of trusting the wrong kind of person
when you try doing it.

כה:כ מַעֲדֶה־בֶּגֶד בְּיוֹם קָרָה חֹמֶץ עַל־נָתֶר וְשָׁר בַּשִּׁרִים עַל לֶב־רָע:

25:20 As a fashionable garment on a cold day, as
   vinegar on washing soda, so is one singing
   songs to a broken heart.

This is a difficult verse to translate because two words are homonyms that contribute
to idioms. The first word, *maadeh*, can be derived from two different roots containing
the same three letters. *Adah* can mean either "to take off" or "to decorate." *Maadeh*
can be read either as a verb, the *hifil* (causative) participle, or a noun. If *maadeh* is
read as a verb from *adah*, "to remove," then the meaning of the first clause,
"removing a garment on a cold day," suggests an act of stupidity. Taking *maadeh* as a
verb from *adah*, "to decorate," yields "decorating a garment on a cold day." This
seems to make little sense. We have elected to take *maadeh* as a noun derived from
the latter root and translate it as a "fashionable" (or "ornamental") garment. This
suggests that the wearer chooses to wear the garment because it is stylish rather than
warm. Thus, it is a useless garment, as far as the author is concerned. The second
challenge of translation involves the last word in the verse, *ra*, which can be derived
from two different roots that contain the same three letters. *Raah* can mean either "to
do or be evil" or "shattered, broken." We have followed Ibn Ezra in taking *ra* here to
be derived from the second meaning and have translated it as "broken." The verse
suggests useless acts. When one is cold, a warm garment is more important than one
that is stylish or accessorized. When one wants to use washing soda (laundry
detergent), the bubbles that are produced by adding vinegar have no purpose. So too
is singing "happy" songs to one who is deeply troubled.

כה:כא אִם־רָעֵב שֹׂנַאֲךָ הַאֲכִלֵהוּ לָחֶם וְאִם־צָמֵא הַשְׁקֵהוּ מָיִם:

25:21 If your enemy is hungry, feed him [or her] with
   bread; if he [or she] is thirsty, provide him
   [or her] with water.

Here, as throughout the text, the author recommends virtuous behavior. Rashi applies
this verse to treatment of the *yetzer hara* (evil inclination). One should take it to the

beit midrash (study house) and feed it with the bread and water of Torah. Gersonides sees this kind of action as a means of training and improving one's ethical virtues. In this advice is perhaps the mechanism to attack one's enemy, to "kill him with kindness," as the next verse suggests.

כה:כב כִּי גֶחָלִים אַתָּה חֹתֶה עַל־רֹאשׁוֹ וַיהוָה יְשַׁלֶּם־לָךְ:

25:22 FOR YOU WILL HEAP COALS UPON HIS [OR HER] HEAD
AND *ADONAI* WILL REWARD YOU.

According to Ibn Ezra, when your enemies remember what you have done for them, they will be struck with such remorse that they will burn with shame, and it will be as if "coals" had been heaped on the top of their heads.

כה:כג רוּחַ צָפוֹן תְּחוֹלֵל גָּשֶׁם וּפָנִים נִזְעָמִים לְשׁוֹן סָתֶר:

25:23 THE NORTH WIND BRINGS THE RAIN, AND AN ANGRY
FACE BRINGS ON GOSSIP.

The difficulty in this verse can be found in the word *t'choleil* (brings) in the first clause. The inflected form could either be *piel* (from the root *chul*) or *polel* (from the root *chalal*). If it is the first, the meaning would be "brings." If it is the second, then the meaning would be "stops." Rashi takes the first meaning, while Ibn Ezra takes the second. One should note that the meaning of the second clause is dependent on the meaning of the first, particularly since there is no verb in the second clause. Rashi and Ibn Ezra agree that *l'shon sater* (literally, "a secret tongue") has the meaning of "gossip." The meaning of the verse depends on the view of the action of the "north wind." If Rashi is correct, then as the north wind *brings* rain, one's "angry face" will elicit gossip on the part of others. On the other hand, if Ibn Ezra is correct, then as the north wind stops rain from falling, the person who gossips will stop when the potential listener shows, with an angry face, disinterest in hearing it.

כה:כד טוֹב שֶׁבֶת עַל־פִּנַּת־גָּג מֵאֵשֶׁת מִדוֹנִים מְדְיָנִים וּבֵית חָבֶר:

25:24 IT IS BETTER TO LIVE ON A CORNER OF THE ROOF
THAN TO LIVE IN THE HOUSE ALONG WITH A
QUARRELSOME SPOUSE.

The author has already shared this verse with readers in 21:9. Thus, Rashi makes the same comment here as he did there, relating the verse to the departure of the *Shechinah*.

כה:כה מַיִם קָרִים עַל־נֶפֶשׁ עֲיֵפָה וּשְׁמוּעָה טוֹבָה מֵאֶרֶץ מֶרְחָק:

25:25 AS COLD WATER TO A WEARY SOUL, SO IS GOOD NEWS
FROM A FAR COUNTRY.

As a philosopher, Gersonides cannot resist explaining the effect of cold water that
dissipates the body's natural heat in order to provide a benefit for the soul. He then
compares this action to hearing good news about relatives and friends, which has a
positive effect on the soul.

כה:כו מַעְיָן נִרְפָּשׂ וּמָקוֹר מָשְׁחָת צַדִּיק מָט לִפְנֵי־רָשָׁע:

25:26 A TRAMPLED FOUNTAIN AND A FOULED SPRING, SO IT IS
WHEN THE RIGHTEOUS PERSON SLIPS BEFORE THE
WICKED PERSON.

Seeing pure water that becomes polluted by what stupid or evil people do brings the
same revulsion as seeing good people corrupted by bad people.

כה:כז אָכֹל דְּבַשׁ הַרְבּוֹת לֹא־טוֹב וְחֵקֶר כְּבֹדָם כָּבוֹד:

25:27 EATING TOO MUCH HONEY IS NOT GOOD, BUT THE
INVESTIGATION OF THEIR GLORY IS GLORY.

This is a difficult verse. Some modern literary critics assume that there must be a
contrast between two clauses. Therefore, they think that the word "not" must be
added in the second clause. In keeping with such a view, they think that the *vav* of
v'cheiker should be translated as "and." Hence, the entire word should be translated
as "and the investigation." They understand *k'vodam* (their glory) to refer to men and
women in general. The translation of the second clause accordingly would be "and
the investigation of their glory is *not* glory." Rashi and Ibn Ezra, however, take the
verse as it stands. Rashi understands "honey" as the proscribed topics of *Maaseh
B'reishit* (Account of the Beginning) and *Maaseh Merkavah* (Account of the Chariot).
Such topics should not be pursued. However, it is a glorious thing to investigate the
decisions of the Sages, which brought them glory. Ibn Ezra takes the "eating of
honey" as the pursuit of imaginary things and "investigation" as the investigation of
the wisdom of the righteous.

כה:כח עִיר פְּרוּצָה אֵין חוֹמָה אִישׁ אֲשֶׁר אֵין מַעְצָר לְרוּחוֹ:

25:28 LIKE A RAVAGED CITY WITHOUT A WALL, SO IS THE
PERSON WHO CANNOT EXERT SELF-CONTROL.

Just as a wall would have protected the city, so self-control would have protected
the individual.

Maaseh B'reishit *and* Maaseh Merkavah:
The Account of the Creation and the Account of the Chariot

The Mishnah (*Chagigah* 2:1) proscribes the public expounding of these notions. The first is prohibited in front of two people and the second before even one person "unless that person is a Sage and understands of one's knowledge." The mishnah continues and suggests the reason for such a prohibition: "For the one who reflects on four things, it would be better for that person not to have come into this world: what is above, what is below, what was before, and what will come after. One who has no regard to honor one's Maker, it would be better for that person not to come into the world." Somehow, either or both of these ideas are taken to ask the wrong kind of questions, questions viewed as sullying the honor due God. It may be that the mishnah here contains an attack on some kind of Gnostic knowledge or perhaps theories about the origin or operation of the world. These might threaten traditional belief. The discussion of this mishnah in general leads to the story of the four who "entered the Garden" of speculation (Babylonian Talmud, *Chagigah* 14b). Only Rabbi Akiva emerged unscathed.

Maimonides takes the "account of the creation" and the "account of the chariot" as evidence that certain notions should not be publicly presented (*Guide for the Perplexed*, introduction to part 1). He also tells his reader that the first term refers to physics and the second term refers to metaphysics. Probably neither the Rabbis of the Mishnah nor of the Talmud would have agreed.

GLEANINGS

Taking Our Mandate Seriously

If we are to take the concept of *tikkun olam* seriously, if we are to assume responsibility for the world in which we live and work toward creating a better one, we need new images of Divinity, images that invite us to work *with* God rather than under God's authority. This does not mean abandoning all of our previous images of God nor, I think, does it necessarily mean abandoning belief in God's transcendence. I concur with Larry Hoffman's assessment that "transcendent" need not mean "great, mighty, and awesome," that is, God as a Being who rules over us. Transcendent, as Hoffman writes, may simply mean "a being that exists independently and enters into relationship with us" as God's partners in the world's continual creation. Which images of divinity best convey this model of partnership is open for discussion. Undoubtedly, there will be disagreement among us as to which images are appropriate or worthy of inclusion in our prayers. But it is my fervent hope that...we—the Reform laity and clergy—not only affirm the reality of God...but also explore together our understanding of God's nature and the kinds of images through which this nature, as we perceive it, might best gain communal expression.

Ellen Umansky, "Charting Our Future—Liberal Judaism in the 21st Century IV,"
CCAR Yearbook 100 (1990): 66–67

CHAPTER TWENTY-SIX

כו:א כַּשֶּׁלֶג בַּקַּיִץ וְכַמָּטָר בַּקָּצִיר כֵּן לֹא־נָאוֶה לִכְסִיל כָּבוֹד:

26:1 LIKE SNOW IN SUMMERTIME AND RAIN AT HARVESTTIME,
SO IS HONOR UNSEEMLY FOR A FOOL.

Just as the first clause presents things that don't fit, so does the last clause. Rashi points out that snow would affect the drying of the kind of summer fruit that is described in II Samuel 16:2. For Gersonides, were the snow and the rain to fall as described by the author, not only would that go against the natural order, it would also be dangerous. So too does honoring a fool go against what is expected and is dangerous in the end.

כו:ב כַּצִּפּוֹר לָנוּד כַּדְּרוֹר לָעוּף כֵּן קִלְלַת חִנָּם לא לוֹ תָבֹא:

26:2 AS A SPARROW WANDERS AND AS A SWALLOW FLIES, SO A
CURSE UTTERED FOR NO REASON WILL COME HOME.

The difficulty in this verse is to be found in the last clause, in the word *lo,* which comes before the verb *tavo* (to come). As a *k'tiv* (the written form), it is *lo,* "not." As a *k'rei* (the form to be read), *lo* means "to him." The written and read forms provide two contradictory meanings to the verse. If the former, the author suggests that a curse uttered with no purpose in mind will, like some wandering bird, fly and have no effect. If the latter, the author would be suggesting that like a wandering bird that finally flies home, a curse uttered for no reason will return and have its baneful effect "to him" *(lo),* that is, against the one who uttered it. Hence, this would be understood as an idiom for "home." For Ibn Ezra, there is meaning in both the *k'tiv* and the *k'rei.* The two suggest that the mindless curse will harm only the one who delivered it and no one else, that is, "it won't come" and "it will come to him."

כו:ג שׁוֹט לַסּוּס מֶתֶג לַחֲמוֹר וְשֵׁבֶט לְגֵו כְּסִילִים:

26:3 A WHIP FOR A HORSE, A BRIDLE FOR A DONKEY, AND
A ROD FOR THE BACK OF FOOLS.

Having dealt with what is felt to be unnatural combinations, the writer now presents what is natural. The author suggests that just as one does not reason with animals and has to use physical force to direct them, so one should use such force to direct a fool. Implicit in this verse is the medieval notion that those who are not "learned" and who are not responsive to the direction of the intellectual elite are no better

254

than animals. (For example, see *Guide for the Perplexed* 1:8; 2:36; 3:51.) Rashi understands "fools" as those who are wicked.

כו:ד אַל־תַּעַן כְּסִיל כְּאִוַּלְתּוֹ פֶּן־תִּשְׁוֶה־לּוֹ גַם־אָתָּה:

26:4 DON'T ANSWER A FOOL ACCORDING TO THE FOOL'S FOLLY, LEST YOU BECOME A FOOL.

This verse is translated somewhat loosely to transcend the gender specificity of the author through the use of pronouns. There seems to be a contradiction with the verse that follows. Some commentators avoid this contradiction by interpreting them to refer to different topics. Thus, Gersonides tells the reader not to answer the fool when the fool discusses minor matters, but to answer the fool when the fool attempts to deal with science.

כו:ה עֲנֵה כְסִיל כְּאִוַּלְתּוֹ פֶּן־יִהְיֶה חָכָם בְּעֵינָיו:

26:5 ANSWER A FOOL ACCORDING TO HIS [OR HER] FOLLY, LEST THE FOOL BECOME WISE IN HIS [OR HER] OWN EYES.

Perhaps the author used a collection of folk sayings in composing the Book of Proverbs and it is only our contemporary literary sense that is uncomfortable with the contradiction of this verse and the previous one.

כו:ו מְקַצֶּה רַגְלַיִם חָמָס שֹׁתֶה שֹׁלֵחַ דְּבָרִים בְּיַד־כְּסִיל:

26:6 SENDING A MESSAGE BY A FOOL IS LIKE CUTTING OFF ONE'S FEET OR DRINKING VIOLENCE.

According to Rashi, "drinking violence" is a metaphor for the rage that your associates would feel upon learning that you have enlisted a fool as a messenger.

כו:ז דַּלְיוּ שֹׁקַיִם מִפִּסֵּחַ וּמָשָׁל בְּפִי כְסִילִים:

26:7 AS THE LEGS OF THE LAME DANGLE, SO IS A PARABLE IN THE MOUTH OF FOOLS.

While not a politically correct statement for modern sensibilities, ungainly motion is the image here. The halting gait of the physically challenged who has difficulty walking is compared to the fool who tries to be clever and make use of parables. Ibn Ezra applies a rhymed folk saying to explain the verse: *mashal b'li seichel k'guf b'li regel,* "a parable without sense is like a body without a foot."

כו:ח כִּצְרוֹר אֶבֶן בְּמַרְגֵּמָה כֵּן־נוֹתֵן לִכְסִיל כָּבוֹד:

26:8 LIKE FITTING A STONE IN A SLING, SO IS ONE WHO
GIVES HONOR TO A FOOL.

This is a difficult verse to translate, because the first and third words, *kitz'ror* and
margeimah, can have a number of meanings. *Tz'ror* can be a noun and mean "bag"
or "pebble," or it can be the infinitive of the root *tz-r-r* and mean "bind" or "fit."
Margeimah can mean "sling" or "heap of stones." Perhaps the modern Hebrew use
of the word *margeimah* for "mortar" or "mine thrower" is based on this verse. Taking
the first clause as translated above, one wonders what contrast would be presented in
the second clause. To use a sling, one has to fit a stone to it. The *Targum* may suggest
something different when it translates the first clause as *heich niktza d'tasa b'kila,* "like
fitting a sliver of foil in a sling." A sliver of foil is not a proper missile, because it is too
light. Hence, the two clauses would present instances of improper activity: a misused
sling and misplaced honor. If *tz'ror* even simply meant "pebbles" and *margeimah*
meant a "heap of stones," then the first clause would suggest the addition of
something useless to something already there and thus adding nothing of value. "Like
pebbles to a heap of stones" (similar to the expression "bringing coals to Newcastle"),
so is "one who gives honor to a fool." Rashi quotes the rabbinic application of this
verse: "The one who teaches Torah to an unworthy student is like one who casts
stones at a statue of Mercury [as an act of idolatry]."

כו:ט חוֹחַ עָלָה בְיַד־שִׁכּוֹר וּמָשָׁל בְּפִי כְסִילִים:

26:9 LIKE A THORN STUCK IN THE HAND OF A DRUNK, SO IS
A PARABLE IN THE MOUTH OF FOOLS.

The shriek of pain uttered by the unwary drunk when his hand is punctured by a
thorn makes as much sense as the words of a fool explicating a parable. The fool can
recite the words but is unable to understand what the parable means. Rashi suggests
that just as the thorn that is stuck in the hand of the drunk causes pain, so the parable
causes pain to the one who is unable to comprehend it.

כו:י רַב מְחוֹלֵל־כֹּל וְשֹׂכֵר כְּסִיל וְשֹׂכֵר עֹבְרִים:

26:10 A MASTER BEGINS ALL AND HIRES THE FOOL AND HIRES
THOSE WHO PASS.

This is a difficult verse to translate and understand. As we have seen in 25:23, the
verb *t'choleil* (in 25:23) and *m'choleil* (in 26:10) is problematic. Its translation is
dependent on the root from which it is derived. It could be from the *piel* form of *chul*
or the *polel* form of *chalal.* If it is from the first, then it could mean "to cause to turn,
to whirl." However, if it is from the second, then there are further problems to be

resolved, since there are three different possible roots, which are homonyms ("to profane," "to begin," "to pierce"). Rashi takes *rav* (master) to refer to God and *m'choleil* as "create." He interprets "hires" as *dan* (judges). Unlike a human master, God, says Rashi, involves the Divine Self with those who are "fools" and those who "pass" (passersby who are idlers). Ibn Ezra takes *rav* as a human ruler who controls everything, who by hiring fools compels the fool to work and also hires those who would otherwise "pass" (reject his rule). Gersonides takes *rav* to be a quarrelsome human ruler who "injures" *(m'choleil)* and kills but (oddly enough) does good to the foolish and the *ovrim* (passers, transgressors, and sinners).

כו:יא כְּכֶלֶב שָׁב עַל־קֵאוֹ כְּסִיל שׁוֹנֶה בְאִוַּלְתּוֹ:

26:11 LIKE A DOG RETURNING TO ITS VOMIT, SO A FOOL REPEATS HIS [OR HER] FOLLY.

Ibn Ezra notes that as the dog is not embarrassed to return to its vomit, the fool is not embarrassed to return to his or her folly. Gersonides explains that just as the dog does not realize that its body has already rejected what it is attempting to eat, so the fool does not recognize that his or her foolish acts are indeed folly.

כו:יב רָאִיתָ אִישׁ חָכָם בְּעֵינָיו תִּקְוָה לִכְסִיל מִמֶּנּוּ:

26:12 HAVE YOU SEEN A PERSON WHO IS WISE IN HIS [OR HER] OWN EYES? A FOOL HAS MORE HOPE THAN THAT PERSON.

In a book directed to potential intellectuals, it is always important to stress humility. Being wise does not mean being a "wise guy." Ibn Ezra explains why that person is "wise in his [or her] own eyes": the person is lazy. Laziness as a brake on action is presented in the next verse.

כו:יג אָמַר עָצֵל שַׁחַל בַּדָּרֶךְ אֲרִי בֵּין הָרְחֹבוֹת:

26:13 A LAZY PERSON SAYS, "THERE IS A LION IN THE WAY, A LION IN THE STREETS."

The lazy person is willing to make any excuse to avoid work. The lazy person can't go out in the field ("the way") nor go to work in the city ("in the streets"). Gersonides notes that such a person is not only unwilling to go out to work but is unwilling to remain inside and study philosophy.

כו:יד הַדֶּלֶת תִּסּוֹב עַל־צִירָהּ וְעָצֵל עַל־מִטָּתוֹ:

26:14 THE DOOR TURNS ON ITS HINGES AND THE LAZY
PERSON IN HIS [OR HER] BED.

Just as the door turns but does not move off its hinges, so the lazy person tosses and turns in his or her bed but does not get off of it.

כו:טו טָמַן עָצֵל יָדוֹ בַּצַּלָּחַת נִלְאָה לַהֲשִׁיבָהּ אֶל־פִּיו:

26:15 THE LAZY PERSON STICKS A HAND INTO THE DISH AND
IS TOO TIRED TO PUT IT IN HIS [OR HER] MOUTH.

Taman (literally, "hides") is here translated as "sticks." Lazy people are depicted as putting their hands deep into the communal dish but are unwilling or unable to take them out of the dish and put them and their contents into their mouths. Rashi explains the behavior as a means of keeping their hands warm in the hot food, since the room is so cold.

כו:טז חָכָם עָצֵל בְּעֵינָיו מִשִּׁבְעָה מְשִׁיבֵי טָעַם:

26:16 THE LAZY PERSON IS WISER IN HIS [OR HER] OWN EYES
THAN SEVEN WHO CAN GIVE A REASON.

Since the lazy person is lazy, he or she never gets involved with having to come up with a real answer to a question. Ibn Ezra suggests that the "seven" may refer to advisors to a sovereign ruler. Gersonides simply takes the word to mean "many."

כו:יז מַחֲזִיק בְּאָזְנֵי־כָלֶב עֹבֵר מִתְעַבֵּר עַל־רִיב לֹא־לוֹ:

26:17 LIKE ONE GRABBING THE EARS OF A DOG, SO IS THE
ONE WHO PASSING BY GETS EXCITED ABOUT A QUARREL
THAT IS NOT ONE'S OWN.

There is a play on words in this verse that is only heard in the Hebrew: *oveir* (from *avar*, "pass by" or "cross over") and *mitabeir* ("get angry" or "get excited"). In biblical times, dogs were not domesticated as pets but ran wild in the streets. Anyone who would touch a dog, let alone inflict pain on a dog by grasping its ears, would needlessly risk being bitten. So too there is needless risk in getting involved in another person's quarrel, to say nothing of becoming enraged by it. This is splendid advice for the person who seeks power: avoid needless arguments; such confrontations may come back to "bite" you.

כו:יח כְּמִתְלַהְלֵהַּ הַיֹּרֶה זִקִּים חִצִּים וָמָוֶת:

26:18 LIKE A CRAZED PERSON HURLING TORCHES OR ARROWS
OR DEATH

This verse is connected to the next one. Ibn Ezra understands *vamavet* (and/or death)
as lethal weapons.

כו:יט כֵּן־אִישׁ רִמָּה אֶת־רֵעֵהוּ וְאָמַר הֲלֹא־מְשַׂחֵק אָנִי:

26:19 SO IS THE ONE WHO DECEIVES ONE'S NEIGHBOR AND
THEN SAYS, "I AM ONLY KIDDING."

Intentions do not always count; actions always do. You may be angry or pretend to be
so and not intend to do any damage, yet the damage is done. A torch can start a fire,
an arrow can pierce the skin, and either can cause death. If you deceive your fellow
and cause injury, it does no good to say that the damage was unintended because the
act of deception was all in "fun." A practical joke can kill.

כו:כ בְּאֶפֶס עֵצִים תִּכְבֶּה־אֵשׁ וּבְאֵין נִרְגָּן יִשְׁתֹּק מָדוֹן:

26:20 IN THE ABSENCE OF WOOD, THE FIRE GOES OUT; WHERE
THERE IS NO TALEBEARER, THE QUARREL IS STILLED.

A fire that lacks fuel becomes extinguished. A quarrel that lacks provocation soon
ends. Both need to be fed if they are to keep going. The next verse continues
this proverb.

כו:כא פֶּחָם לְגֶחָלִים וְעֵצִים לְאֵשׁ וְאִישׁ מדונים מִדְיָנִים לְחַרְחַר־רִיב:

26:21 AS CHARCOAL IS TO EMBERS AND WOOD IS TO FIRE, SO
IS A CONTENTIOUS PERSON FOR IGNITING A QUARREL.

Again, the author presents a comparison of fuel to fire and words to quarrels.

כו:כב דִּבְרֵי נִרְגָּן כְּמִתְלַהֲמִים וְהֵם יָרְדוּ חַדְרֵי־בָטֶן:

26:22 THE WORDS OF A TALEBEARER, LIKE DELICACIES, GO
DOWN DEEP IN THE BODY.

The writer continues a warning as to what should not be said and what should
not be listened to. Gossip is attractive: it is tempting to listen to it and tempting to
spread it.

כו:כג כֶּסֶף סִיגִים מְצֻפֶּה עַל־חָרֶשׂ שְׂפָתַיִם דֹּלְקִים וְלֶב־רָע:

26:23 LIKE STONEWARE COVERED WITH SILVER DROSS, SO ARE
FERVENT LIPS AND A WICKED MIND.

This verse deals with the difference between appearance and reality. It uses pots as a metaphor for things that are not as they appear. At first glance, the stoneware looks like silver. It turns out that the silver is the worst kind; dross is what is left after the refining process. On final reflection, it becomes clear that the pots are really stoneware, essentially of little value. It is the same with people who say one thing with passion and coldly think of something else. Rashi explains *s'fatayim dolkim* (burning or fervent lips) as those that belong to people who pretend to be friends in order to gain the trust of others.

כו:כד בשפתו בִּשְׂפָתָיו יִנָּכֵר שׂוֹנֵא וּבְקִרְבּוֹ יָשִׁית מִרְמָה:

26:24 AN ENEMY DISGUISES WITH LIPS, BUT THERE IS STRONG
GUILE WITHIN.

The writer offers another example of appearance versus reality: Words may not mean what they seem. Those who speak them may have hidden agendas.

כו:כה כִּי־יְחַנֵּן קוֹלוֹ אַל־תַּאֲמֶן־בּוֹ כִּי שֶׁבַע תּוֹעֵבוֹת בְּלִבּוֹ:

26:25 WHEN ONE MAKES ONE'S VOICE SOUND GRACIOUS,
DON'T BELIEVE IT; THAT PERSON HAS SEVEN
ABOMINATIONS ON THE MIND.

Again, what one says may not be what one means. The nicest of words may conceal the vilest of intentions.

כו:כו תִּכַּסֶּה שִׂנְאָה בְּמַשָּׁאוֹן תִּגָּלֶה רָעָתוֹ בְקָהָל:

26:26 HATRED MAY BE COVERED BY DECEIT, BUT ONE'S EVIL
WILL BE REVEALED BEFORE A COMMUNITY.

The verse suggests that the more people know a person, the less possible it is for that person's villainy to be hidden. Ibn Ezra connects this verse with the one that follows.

כו:כז כֹּרֶה־שַּׁחַת בָּהּ יִפֹּל וְגֹלֵל אֶבֶן אֵלָיו תָּשׁוּב:

26:27 WHOEVER DIGS A PIT WILL FALL INTO IT, AND THE
ONE WHO ROLLS A STONE WILL HAVE IT ROLL BACK
ON ONESELF.

Rashi applies this verse to Abimelech in the Book of Judges (chapter 9), who attempted to establish himself as king, slew seventy people, and in turn was killed. Evil ultimately destroys itself.

כו:כח לְשׁוֹן־שֶׁקֶר יִשְׂנָא דַכָּיו וּפֶה חָלָק יַעֲשֶׂה מִדְחֶה:

26:28 A LYING TONGUE HATES THOSE WHOM IT CRUSHES,
AND A FLATTERING TONGUE WORKS RUIN.

Those who defame others rationalize their misdeeds by hate. Somehow, they say, their victims deserve it. Flattery—which is another form of lying—does not aid those to whom it is directed. By giving them a wrong view of themselves, it may bring them to ruin. Since *midcheh* (ruin) comes from the word *dachah* (to thrust), Rashi notes that flattery may thrust a person away from God.

Abimelech

Abimelech is the son of Gideon, the son of Joash (Judges 8:30–32). In addition to this Abimelech, there is another one, identified as the king of Gerar. He is mentioned in Genesis 20 and 21 in relation to Abraham and in Genesis 26 in relation to Isaac. He is reported as taking Sarah and Rebekah, respectively, into his palace after their husbands identify them as their sisters in order to save their own lives. In both cases, the plot is discovered before Abimelech engages in a sexual relationship with them. Since he is innocent, he becomes indignant and escapes punishment. There are those who suggest that these two stories are variants of the same tradition. Both Abraham and Isaac are engaged in a dispute with Abimelech over wells. But it is clear that Isaac must dig into the well where his father had dug before he can discover his true self.

GLEANINGS

To Be a Reform Jew

Why be Jewish?...[To be a Jew] is to be committed to certain values to which Jews have always been committed: to love of family, to education, to philanthropy, to individual righteousness, and to the idea of a unique Jewish destiny.

To be a Jew is to believe that if only our children would come to know and experience this tradition; if only they would know the drama of Jewish history, the richness of Jewish life, the grandeur of Jewish ethics, and the majesty of Jewish faith; if only they would know these things, they would not hesitate to choose Judaism as their own.

Eric H. Yoffie, "To Be a Reform Jew," *CCAR Journal: A Reform Jewish Quarterly* (summer 1998): 2

CHAPTER TWENTY-SEVEN

כז:א אַל־תִּתְהַלֵּל בְּיוֹם מָחָר כִּי לֹא־תֵדַע מַה־יֵּלֶד יוֹם:

27:1 DON'T BOAST ABOUT TOMORROW, FOR YOU DON'T
KNOW WHAT A DAY CAN BRING.

Gersonides understands the first clause to refer to what you would like to do and the second clause to refer to the impediments to your proposed actions. The old Yiddish saying *Man tracht und Gott lacht* (literally, "humans plan and God laughs"), translated as the idiom "Man proposes and God disposes," captures the sentiment of the author in this verse.

כז:ב יְהַלֶּלְךָ זָר וְלֹא־פִיךָ נָכְרִי וְאַל־שְׂפָתֶיךָ:

27:2 LET SOMEONE ELSE PRAISE YOU AND NOT YOUR
OWN MOUTH; LET IT BE A STRANGER AND NOT YOUR
OWN LIPS.

Ibn Ezra suggests that "your own mouth" and "your own lips" refer to what one might say before doing something worthy of praise. Once such an act is done, others will praise such a person.

כז:ג כֹּבֶד־אֶבֶן וְנֵטֶל הַחוֹל וְכַעַס אֱוִיל כָּבֵד מִשְּׁנֵיהֶם:

27:3 A STONE IS HEAVY AND SAND IS WEIGHTY, BUT THE
ANGER OF A FOOL IS HEAVIER THAN BOTH.

The word *kaas*, "anger," can mean either the anger that a fool incites in others or the anger that rises up in a foolish person. If it is the former meaning, then a fool's effect on others is more burdensome than carrying heavy weights would be. If it is the latter, others have to worry about the effect of a fool's anger, which would lack all means of moderation. Rashi takes the word in the former sense. He feels that the "anger of a fool" could have cosmic consequences because a fool can even provoke God.

כז:ד אַכְזְרִיּוּת חֵמָה וְשֶׁטֶף אָף וּמִי יַעֲמֹד לִפְנֵי קִנְאָה:

27:4 WRATH IS CRUEL AND ANGER IS OVERWHELMING, BUT WHO CAN WITHSTAND JEALOUSY?

Gersonides explains why jealousy is more powerful than wrath or anger: A person filled with wrath might show no mercy, and an angry person might want to destroy everyone and everything. Only a jealous person would be pained by good happening to someone else. Only a jealous person would hope that something terrible would happen to someone else, even if that meant that it also had to happen to oneself. Similarly, the jealous person would not want something good to happen to oneself if it meant that it would also have to happen to someone else.

כז:ה טוֹבָה תּוֹכַחַת מְגֻלָּה מֵאַהֲבָה מְסֻתָּרֶת:

27:5 BETTER TO HAVE AN OPEN REBUKE THAN ONE THAT IS CONCEALED BECAUSE OF LOVE.

This translation follows Ibn Ezra, who takes *tochachat* (literally, "reproach of") to refer to the words *m'gulah* (revealed) and *m'sutaret* (concealed). However, a matter of meaning must be raised. Did the writer intend to say that it is better to reprove someone, even openly, than not reprove that person at all out of friendship or love? Gersonides takes that exact meaning. Ibn Ezra is not willing to go that far in his interpretation of this verse. He thinks that a public rebuke is better than a private one, even though friendship might surprisingly suggest a public rebuke, because the resulting embarrassment of such a rebuke may be more efficacious in moving the person to repent and improve.

כז:ו נֶאֱמָנִים פִּצְעֵי אוֹהֵב וְנַעְתָּרוֹת נְשִׁיקוֹת שׂוֹנֵא:

27:6 DEPENDABLE ARE THE WOUNDS OF A FRIEND, BUT DECEPTIVE ARE THE KISSES OF AN ENEMY.

The difficulty in understanding this verse lies in the word *v'natarot*. Although the root *atar* is found elsewhere in the Bible, the sense that is required here is not. On the basis of a similar word in Arabic, some scholars translate this word as "deceptive." The *Targum* translates it as *uvishan* (bad, evil). Rashi understands it as "great, many," while Ibn Ezra interprets the word to mean "thick" or "strong." In line with his understanding of the previous verse, Ibn Ezra thinks that although the words of a friend may seem to hurt when they call for repentance, that friend believes that the person to whom the rebuke is directed can repent and change. An enemy, on the other hand, by manifesting false affection, keeps a person from the kind of repentance that eliminates sin and its consequences. Gersonides understands "the kisses of an enemy" as the enticements of relatives to get involved with transgressions.

Perhaps the author suggests that one can depend on a person as a friend who has suffered on one's behalf ("the wounds of a friend"). One cannot depend on that person who merely manifests affection ("the kisses"), for even an enemy could falsely do so.

כז:ז נֶפֶשׁ שְׂבֵעָה תָּבוּס נֹפֶת וְנֶפֶשׁ רְעֵבָה כָּל־מַר מָתוֹק:

27:7 A SATED PERSON WOULD TREAD ON A HONEYCOMB, BUT FOR A HUNGRY PERSON EVERYTHING THAT IS BITTER IS SWEET.

In this verse is an echo of the old proverb that hunger is the best sauce. Ibn Ezra connects this verse with the next to explain why people wander, something that his own life experience had taught him well. Gersonides understands the verse as a suggestion that the content person will not pursue wealth, while the poor person will do anything to achieve it.

כז:ח כְּצִפּוֹר נוֹדֶדֶת מִן־קִנָּהּ כֵּן־אִישׁ נוֹדֵד מִמְּקוֹמוֹ:

27:8 AS A BIRD WANDERS FROM ITS NEST, SO A PERSON WANDERS FROM HOME.

Rashi applies the verse to scholars who have strayed away from their studies because they have not reviewed what they have learned. Gersonides suggests that the verse may have two different meanings. First, just as a bird must have a good reason to leave its nest, so a person should have a good reason to leave home. Second, having left the nest, it is difficult for the bird to build a new nest in a strange place. Similarly, it is difficult for a person to build a new home in a strange location.

כז:ט שֶׁמֶן וּקְטֹרֶת יְשַׂמַּח־לֵב וּמֶתֶק רֵעֵהוּ מֵעֲצַת־נָפֶשׁ:

27:9 OIL AND INCENSE MAY MAKE THE HEART GLAD, BUT GENUINE ADVICE IS SWEETNESS FOR A FRIEND.

It is difficult to translate both the first clause and the last clause in this verse. With regard to the first clause, Rashi and Ibn Ezra differ as to the "oil." Rashi takes it as persimmon oil, some kind of perfume. Ibn Ezra, on the other hand, understands it as olive oil for anointing. The last two words of the verse are the most difficult to understand: *mei-atzat nafesh* (literally, "advice of the soul). Rashi takes the two words to mean that the person who convinces another by the sweetness of language is better than the one whose soul gives advice. Rashi combines both meanings of *nafesh* ("soul" and "desire") in his alternative comment on the verse: "sweet is the friend" means that it is better to have a friend who declares that a person's acts are acceptable—even sweet to God—than to proceed only with the desires of one's heart. Basing himself on the phrase *namtik sod* (literally, "let us sweeten a secret") from Psalm 55:15, Ibn Ezra takes *metek rei-eihu* (sweetness for a friend) to mean "the secret of a friend." He then understands the clause to mean that receiving a secret is better than getting the most heartfelt advice. Gersonides also understands *metek rei-eihu* as "the secret of a friend." He explains the entire verse as follows: just as perfume and incense (which come from outside a person) can make an individual rejoice, so a secret coming from a friend (who is also on the outside) is better than the advice that an individual's own soul could give (which emerges from the inside). Perhaps if we take the second meaning for *nafesh*, we can translate the verse as "Just as perfume and incense make the heart glad, so is the advice of desire sweeter than a friend."

כז:י רֵעֲךָ ורעה וְרֵעַ אָבִיךָ אַל־תַּעֲזֹב וּבֵית אָחִיךָ אַל־תָּבוֹא בְּיוֹם אֵידֶךָ
טוֹב שָׁכֵן קָרוֹב מֵאָח רָחוֹק:

27:10 DON'T FORSAKE YOUR FRIEND OR YOUR PARENT'S FRIEND, AND DON'T GO INTO YOUR SIBLING'S HOUSE ON THE DAY OF YOUR CALAMITY; BETTER IS A NEIGHBOR WHO IS CLOSE THAN A SIBLING WHO IS FAR.

The parts of this verse seem disjointed. The first clause is clear, but its relation to the second and third clause is not. Rashi takes the "friend" to refer to God and the "sibling" (literally, "brother") to refer to the descendants of Ishmael or the descendants of Esau to provide for assistance when disaster strikes, since past experience with them suggests that one will be harmed rather than helped. Both Rashi and Ibn Ezra understand "neighbor" to refer to a relative, that is, another Jew who will provide the assistance that a far-off relative cannot. Gersonides sees "friend" as another human being.

כז:יא חֲכַם בְּנִי וְשַׂמַּח לִבִּי וְאָשִׁיבָה חֹרְפִי דָבָר:

27:11 MY YOUNG FRIEND, GET SMART AND MAKE ME HAPPY, AND I WILL KNOW HOW TO RESPOND TO THE ONE WHO ANNOYS ME.

It is difficult to ascertain the relationship between the first clause and the last clause. Perhaps the writer feels that someone is denigrating him for having an unintelligent (we may even say "average") child or an underachieving student.

כז:יב עָרוּם רָאָה רָעָה נִסְתָּר פְּתָאיִם עָבְרוּ נֶעֱנָשׁוּ:

27:12 A CLEVER PERSON SEES HIDDEN EVIL; FOOLS PASS BY
AND ARE PUNISHED.

Since this book deals with folk wisdom, there is no need to stretch in order to translate *arum* as "prudent." Being clever (or cunning) is an aptitude of mind and is not necessarily an aspect of virtue. Folk wisdom is filled with heroes who show themselves to be clever and not virtuous. Remember Isaac's response to Esau when he discovers that Jacob has stolen Esau's blessing: "Your brother came *b'mirmah* [with cunning]" (Genesis 27:35). Rashi takes the *arum* to mean "prudent": someone who refrains from sin though the potential punishment the person foresees is hidden from immediate sight. Simply put, fools sin and are punished. Gersonides relates the *arum* as the wise person who controls his or her passions and is rewarded, while fools are given over to their passions and will be punished as a result. This verse is almost the same as 22:3. Like the verse that follows, this text raises questions as to the pattern of editing.

כז:יג קַח־בִּגְדוֹ כִּי־עָרַב זָר וּבְעַד נָכְרִיָּה חַבְלֵהוּ:

27:13 TAKE THE GARMENT FROM THE ONE WHO IS SURETY
FOR A STRANGER, AND HOLD IN PLEDGE THE ONE WHO
IS SURETY FOR A FOREIGN WOMAN.

This verse is quoted from 20:16. Some will argue that this represents an error or even sloppiness in editing. Perhaps the author took the text from a common folk saying that represented the idea for this verse better than any other. Or maybe the author wanted to emphasize a lesson with a familiar teaching.

כז:יד מְבָרֵךְ רֵעֵהוּ בְּקוֹל גָּדוֹל בַּבֹּקֶר הַשְׁכֵּים קְלָלָה תֵּחָשֶׁב לוֹ:

27:14 THE ONE WHO GREETS A NEIGHBOR EARLY IN THE
MORNING WITH A LOUD VOICE, A CURSE WILL BE
ATTRIBUTED TO THAT PERSON.

The author uses *m'vareich* here as it is used in Genesis 47:7, as to "greet" rather than to "bless." However, there is some play on the word in *k'lalah* (the curse), which is directed at the person shouting a greeting early in the morning and waking others. Rashi quotes the midrash that applied this verse to wicked Balaam's blessing Israel instead of cursing it. Gersonides thinks that anyone who would constantly bless a person every morning, day after day, would ultimately be seen by others as pretending to serve some divine function.

כז:טו דֶּלֶף טוֹרֵד בְּיוֹם סַגְרִיר וְאֵשֶׁת מדונים מִדְיָנִים נִשְׁתָּוָה:

27:15 JUST LIKE THE DRIP, DRIP ON A RAINY DAY, SO IS A BICKERING WOMAN.

City life gave new freedom to women. Some men accepted such women and lauded those who operated in the city. Others were threatened by that freedom and upset by those who exercised it. This verse reflects the view of those who opposed such freedom. The end of the Book of Proverbs and its praise of the woman of valor ultimately show support for women who seized the limited freedoms that society offered. Gersonides plaintively explains this verse from the viewpoint of a man who wishes to have quiet at home but who has an unforgiving spouse who disturbs such peace, as does rain dripping in the house through the roof.

כז:טז צֹפְנֶיהָ צָפַן־רוּחַ וְשֶׁמֶן יְמִינוֹ יִקְרָא:

27:16 THE ONE WHO WOULD CONCEAL HER WOULD CONCEAL THE WIND, AND THE OIL OF ONE'S RIGHT HAND CALLS OUT.

This is a difficult verse to translate and understand. The *Targum* takes *tzofneha* (conceals her) as if it were *tzafonah* (north) and translates the first clause as *rucha garvaita kashya* (the north), that is, "the scouring wind is strong." It translates the last clause as *bishma dimina mitkarya*, "the perfume of the right hand." The meaning of both clauses together is unclear. Rashi takes *tzofneha* to mean "conceal her" and explains that it is impossible to conceal a contentious spouse, as it is impossible to conceal the wind. The "oil of one's right hand" is symbolic of purification from leprosy. For Rashi, to have such a spouse is tantamount to having leprosy. The only solution is divorce. For Ibn Ezra, the difficult spouse can neither be concealed nor corrected, so it is a foolish waste of time to try to do so. For him, the "right hand" is a symbol of being prepared for everything. Even so, were the difficult spouse to anoint her husband's right hand (perhaps as an act of affection), he would end up crying out. Gersonides agrees with Rashi's understanding of the first clause. His explanation of the second verse: had the beleaguered husband placed perfume on his right hand, people would know about it because of the lingering aroma. Similarly, people will know about a difficult spouse no matter what a husband does.

כז:יז בַּרְזֶל בְּבַרְזֶל יָחַד וְאִישׁ יַחַד פְּנֵי־רֵעֵהוּ:

27:17 AS IRON SHARPENS IRON, SO A PERSON SHARPENS THE PRESENCE OF ONE'S NEIGHBOR.

Rashi takes the first clause to mean that scholars sharpen their understanding of the halachah through their discussions of it. Gersonides follows Rashi's understanding of the first clause but substitutes *iyun* (philosophical investigation) for halachah. Neither dealt with the problematic last verse. *Panim* can mean "face," so *p'nei* might mean "face of." However, it would be difficult to explain how one "sharpens" the face of one's friend. Rather, we have translated it as "presence," since the presence of another person has an impact on the consciousness of a friend or neighbor.

כז:יח נֹצֵר תְּאֵנָה יֹאכַל פִּרְיָהּ וְשֹׁמֵר אֲדֹנָיו יְכֻבָּד׃

27:18 ONE WHO WATCHES THE FIG TREE WILL EAT ITS FRUIT, SO ONE WHO GUARDS ONE'S MASTER WILL BE HONORED.

Faithful service of one kind is rewarded, just as faithful service of another is as well. Gersonides understands the intellect as "the master."

כז:יט כַּמַּיִם הַפָּנִים לַפָּנִים כֵּן לֵב־הָאָדָם לָאָדָם׃

27:19 AS IN WATER, THE FACE SHOWS THE FACE, SO A PERSON'S MIND TO ANOTHER.

This verse requires a great many assumptions (or additions) in order to make sense of it. The *Targum* recalls the use of the word *kamayim* (like water) in the phrase "unstable as water" when Jacob denounced his son Reuben (Genesis 49:4) and uses it as a symbol of instability. Water is unstable. Faces do not resemble one another, and the hearts (minds) of people are different. Rashi uses *kamayim* to suggest the reflecting quality of water: the face you show to the water is the face that you see in the water. According to Rashi, the second clause follows the sense of the first. If you show affection to your friend, that friend will respond in kind. For Gersonides, as one sees oneself reflected in the water, so one can understand oneself by self-reflection and gain insight into the essence of the human form by such reflection.

כז:כ שְׁאוֹל ואבדה וַאֲבַדּוֹ לֹא תִשְׂבַּעְנָה וְעֵינֵי הָאָדָם לֹא תִשְׂבַּעְנָה׃

27:20 HELL AND DESTRUCTION ARE NEVER SATISFIED, NOR ARE THE EYES OF A HUMAN BEING.

The phrase "hell and destruction" appears in 15:11. Rashi suggests that just as hell and destruction are always ready to receive sinners, so the eyes of sinners are always eager to follow the evil inclination and to pursue what they lust after. Gersonides explains that "hell and destruction" refer to matter as the cause of corruption, which by its nature must be joined to a succession of forms. For him, the second clause presents a profound philosophical notion: the human mind is not satiated by ideas, because the human intellect, itself bereft of ideas, has the constant capacity to absorb more and more ideas. It then becomes the acquired intellect and so comes into conjunction with the ultimate source of ideas, the active intellect.

כז:כא מַצְרֵף לַכֶּסֶף וְכוּר לַזָּהָב וְאִישׁ לְפִי מַהֲלָלוֹ:

27:21 As a refining pot is for silver and a furnace is for gold, so is a person by whom one praises.

Mahalalo (literally, "he praises him") is ambiguous. Rashi takes it to mean "by the one who praises him," that is, a person's worth is measured by those who praise that person. Ibn Ezra takes it to mean "by whom he praises," that is, a person's worth is measured by the kind of person one would praise. We have followed Ibn Ezra in our translation and understanding.

כז:כב אִם תִּכְתּוֹשׁ־אֶת־הָאֱוִיל בַּמַּכְתֵּשׁ בְּתוֹךְ הָרִיפוֹת בַּעֲלִי לֹא־תָסוּר מֵעָלָיו אִוַּלְתּוֹ:

27:22 Were you to grind fine a fool in a mortar with a pestle amidst groats, that person's folly would still not depart.

This is a difficult verse. Some translators simply delete the last three words of the first clause, *b'toch harifot ba-eli* (amidst groats with a pestle), which seem to add little and would make the verse read more smoothly. But the sense of the verse is clear. Groats are hulled and crumbled grain, fragmentary bits. Once groats are ground, they are usable; they are food for humans and animals. A fool, however, is beyond improvement. No matter what you do to or for a fool, the fool remains a fool. Gersonides explains that a fool is a fool because he or she takes things at face value and does not look beyond appearances.

כז:כג יָדֹעַ תֵּדַע פְּנֵי צֹאנֶךָ שִׁית לִבְּךָ לַעֲדָרִים:

27:23 Know your flocks well; pay attention to your herds.

Why would a pastoral notion be contained in the midst of a book written for city dwellers? Perhaps the author collected proverbs of all types. Gersonides, the most city-bound commentator of them all, provides his readers with a philosophical (read: urban) interpretation. The first clause ("know your flocks well") means that if you derive ideas from sense impression, know well the nature of the senses that provide those impressions. The second clause ("pay attention to your herds") means that you should make sure that your sense impressions are in agreement so that you may derive those notions that will lead to universal ideas.

כז:כד כִּי לֹא לְעוֹלָם חֹסֶן וְאִם־נֵזֶר לְדוֹר דּוֹר וָדוֹר:

27:24 WEALTH DOES NOT LAST FOREVER, NOR DOES THE
CROWN ENDURE FOR ALL GENERATIONS.

Perhaps this is another example of a city dweller who yearns for the tranquility of country life, as we have also seen in Ecclesiastes (5:8): "The advantage of the land is paramount. Even a sovereign ruler is subject to the soil." As might be expected, Gersonides reads this verse in a philosophical sense: A person should pursue the acquisition of sense perceptions from which ideas are derived while still alive. With the death of the body, there can be no sense perceptions and hence no more ideas. For Gersonides, the "crown" is the intellect, whose survival after death is dependent on the acquisition of universal ideas and ultimate conjunction with the active intellect.

כז:כה גָּלָה חָצִיר וְנִרְאָה־דֶשֶׁא וְנֶאֶסְפוּ עִשְּׂבוֹת הָרִים:

27:25 WHEN THE GRASS IS FOUND AND THE TENDER GRASS
IS VISIBLE AND THE HERBS OF THE MOUNTAINS ARE
GATHERED IN

This verse suggests a bountiful harvest and is linked to the next verse. Gersonides seems to force his interpretation that these different kinds of grass represent different aspects of sensation.

כז:כו כְּבָשִׂים לִלְבוּשֶׁךָ וּמְחִיר שָׂדֶה עַתּוּדִים:

27:26 THE LAMBS WILL BE YOUR CLOTHING, AND THE GOATS
WILL BE THE PRICE OF A FIELD.

In joining this verse to the previous one, Rashi sees them together as a parable of a teacher who clarifies the tradition that Torah may increase, and one's students ("the lambs," "the goats") will gain fame and honor. He also explains why goats are worth the price of a field: they provide both meat and milk.

כז:כז וְדֵי חֲלֵב עִזִּים לְלַחְמְךָ לְלֶחֶם בֵּיתֶךָ וְחַיִּים לְנַעֲרוֹתֶיךָ:

27:27 THERE WILL BE ENOUGH GOAT'S MILK FOR YOUR FOOD
AND YOUR HOUSEHOLD'S FOOD AND SUSTENANCE FOR
YOUR YOUNG WOMEN.

The last clause suggests that there will be enough goat's milk to sell so that the young women of the household will be able to buy what they need and what they want.

The Active Intellect

Aristotle's discussion of the human intellect in his book *On the Soul* raised the question of how that intellect was activated. Two traditions of interpretation arose, that of Themistius (fourth century C.E.), who held that the intellect activated itself, and that of Alexander Aphrodisius (second century C.E.), who held that it was activated by God or, according to some of his followers, by a separate spiritual entity. When the notion of emanation emerged, with the ten separate spiritual entities proceeding eternally from God, the followers of Alexander developed the notion that the Tenth Emanation was the Active Intellect, which activated the human intellect and contained all universal ideas in an order. Thus the Active Intellect was the source and the goal of Thought.

Tocheichah *(Rebuke)*

The principle of *tocheichah* (rebuke) stems from the name given two sections of the Torah (Leviticus 26 and Deuteronomy 28) that prophesy a series of drastic punishments that Israel will receive should they make the mistake of forsaking the Torah and its commandments. In many synagogues, it is customary for the Torah reader to recite these verses quickly, softly, and without stopping. From these sections emerges the principle of rebuke that a person is obligated to offer friends so that persons will not be "punished" for their actions.

GLEANINGS

Consolation

The true *nechama* is to face reality. We address ourselves to eternity. We have an enduring faith. We have no choice; for this were we created. The bodies consumed in Auschwitz may yet light up a world that lives in darkness. "Our ancestors received the law on Sinai's mount amidst thunder and lightning and cloud and flame, and amidst thunder and lightning and cloud and flame we will keep it." Our prophetic exhortations are the last and best hope of humanity. If we raise but a handful of disciples who treasure our ideals, we will survive. We are an *Am Olam,* an eternal people; the world can never, never destroy all of us. And in that fateful moment when the earth begins to shatter, when the very heavens tremble, when the sun, moon, and the stars turn dark, when the last bomb falls, and the last mushroom cloud evaporates, we will emerge erect, undaunted, dedicated to the hope that a day will yet come when "they shall not hurt or destroy in all my Holy Mountain, for the earth shall be full of the knowledge of the Lord as the waters cover the sea" (Isa. 11:9).

Jacob Rader Marcus, "Shabbat Sermon," *CCAR Yearbook* 99 (1989): 114

CHAPTER TWENTY-EIGHT

כח:א נָסוּ וְאֵין־רֹדֵף רָשָׁע וְצַדִּיקִים כִּכְפִיר יִבְטָח:

28:1 THE GUILTY FLEE THOUGH NO ONE PURSUES, BUT THE
INNOCENT ARE AS CONFIDENT AS A YOUNG LION.

Rashi explains that the *rasha* ("guilty" or "wicked") flee when their day of calamity comes. The innocent do not have to worry and hence are as "confident as a young lion." Ibn Ezra quotes Leviticus 26:36 regarding how the wicked will flee at the sound of a driven leaf. Gersonides explains that the wicked—lacking both intellectual and moral virtues—will be given over to all kinds of accidents and will be constantly terrified. Anything—even nothing—will be enough to get them to run. The righteous, on the other hand, will be serene and confident, as a result of their moral and intellectual virtues.

כח:ב בְּפֶשַׁע אֶרֶץ רַבִּים שָׂרֶיהָ וּבְאָדָם מֵבִין יֹדֵעַ כֵּן יַאֲרִיךְ:

28:2 WHEN THERE IS WRONGDOING IN A LAND, ITS RULERS
WILL BE MANY, BUT WITH A PERSON WHO HAS
UNDERSTANDING AND KNOWLEDGE [THE LAND] WILL
INDEED ENDURE.

The problem in translating this verse is in two words, both of which have two meanings: *kein* and *yaarich*. *Kein* can mean "yes" or "position" (as in Genesis 41:13, where it is an inflected form). However, none of the three primary commentators that we have consulted for this volume take *kein* to mean "position." *Yaarich* can mean either "he causes to endure" or "he endures." Rashi understands the first clause to mean that the land is punished because of its wickedness by having many rulers. He understands the second clause to mean that a wise ruler can enable a people to endure by moving them to repentance. Gersonides adds that by reason of the wise ruler's understanding, the people will achieve a modicum of providence and thus endure.

כח:ג גֶּבֶר רָשׁ וְעֹשֵׁק דַּלִּים מָטָר סֹחֵף וְאֵין לָחֶם:

28:3 A POOR PERSON WHO OPPRESSES THOSE EVEN POORER
IS LIKE A TORRENTIAL RAIN THAT LEAVES NO FOOD.

The comparison between the two clauses is problematic. What is meant by *v'ein lechem* (and no bread)? The *Targum* translates the two words as *d'leit bei yitran* (there is nothing left). Rashi explains the verse and the oppressor's poverty: the oppressor is poor in the knowledge of halachah, a judge who is an irresponsible ignoramus. The legal decisions of such a person are like "torrential rain" that sweeps away topsoil, preventing the land from providing crops. Gersonides picks up the comparison of the poor robbing the poor, something that seems to be a kind of contradiction. So is the rain, which one looks to for the growth of vegetation and sustenance that comes with it, but torrential rain that ruins the ground is similarly a kind of contradiction.

כח:ד עֹזְבֵי תוֹרָה יְהַלְלוּ רָשָׁע וְשֹׁמְרֵי תוֹרָה יִתְגָּרוּ בָם:

28:4 THOSE WHO FORSAKE INSTRUCTION WILL PRAISE THE
WICKED, BUT THOSE WHO KEEP SUCH INSTRUCTION
WILL CONTEND WITH THEM.

The author uses *torah* in this verse to mean moral instruction rather than revealed divine law. The author's point is clear: Those who will not follow the teaching of morality will declare any act moral or will refuse to declare any act immoral. In so doing, they praise the wicked. For Gersonides, the contention with the wicked is to show them their philosophical errors.

כח:ה אַנְשֵׁי־רָע לֹא־יָבִינוּ מִשְׁפָּט וּמְבַקְשֵׁי יְהוָֹה יָבִינוּ כֹל:

28:5 EVIL PERSONS DO NOT UNDERSTAND JUSTICE, BUT
THOSE WHO SEEK GOD UNDERSTAND EVERYTHING.

Rashi translates *mishpat* with the Old French *justicia*. He explains that evil people do not understand that there will be punishment, something that "those who seek God" do know.

כח:ו טוֹב־רָשׁ הוֹלֵךְ בְּתֻמּוֹ מֵעִקֵּשׁ דְּרָכַיִם וְהוּא עָשִׁיר:

28:6 IT IS BETTER TO BE POOR BUT WALK WITH INTEGRITY
THAN BE RICH AND MOVE IN PERVERSE WAYS.

As might be expected, Rashi takes "poor" to mean poor in the knowledge of Torah. Gersonides interprets "poor" as poor in the knowledge of philosophy. This proverb reflects common folk wisdom. Those who are economically poor should feel rich if they are decent human beings.

כח:ז נוֹצֵר תּוֹרָה בֵּן מֵבִין וְרֹעֶה זוֹלְלִים יַכְלִים אָבִיו:

28:7 THE ONE WHO MAINTAINS INSTRUCTION IS AN
UNDERSTANDING CHILD, BUT THE COMPANION OF
GLUTTONS WILL SHAME ONE'S PARENT.

While the author of Proverbs used the word *torah* in a broad sense, Gersonides (and other commentators) understood it as the fundamental document in Judaism. Gersonides explains that the "understanding child" has derived both the intellectual and moral virtues from it. People who have not devoted themselves to the Torah will become fools. As a result, they will become susceptible to the attractions of matter in its most vulgar form: gluttony. Such children will shame their parents.

כח:ח מַרְבֶּה הוֹנוֹ בְּנֶשֶׁךְ ובתרבית וְתַרְבִּית לְחוֹנֵן דַּלִּים יִקְבְּצֶנּוּ:

28:8 THE ONE WHO INCREASES WEALTH BY ADVANCE OR
ACCRUED INTEREST WILL BE GATHERING IT FOR THE
ONE WHO IS GRACIOUS TO THE POOR.

We have followed what is called the "new JPS translation" of the terms *neshech* and *marbit* found in Leviticus 25:37. It takes the former to mean "advance interest" and the latter to mean "accrued interest." Although the latter appears in this verse as *tarbit,* it is clear from the context that *marbit* and *tarbit* have the same meaning. Rashi thinks that the government will hear about greedy people's ill-gotten gains and will take away their money to use it to build bridges and repair roads. This would be a beneficial act for the poor. Gersonides thinks that God will cause the wealth of greedy people to be delivered to gracious people, who will take care of the poor.

כח:ט מֵסִיר אָזְנוֹ מִשְּׁמֹעַ תּוֹרָה גַּם־תְּפִלָּתוֹ תּוֹעֵבָה:

28:9 THE ONE WHO WOULD TURN HIS [OR HER] EAR FROM
HEARKENING TO MORAL INSTRUCTION, THAT PERSON'S
PRAYER WILL ALSO BE AN ABOMINATION.

Since the author uses the word "prayer" rather than "sacrifice," it is possible that this proverb comes from a later period of time, and *torah* may indeed refer to *the* Torah (the product of revelation, and not moral instruction, as we have translated the term). Regardless of the specific meaning of the terms, the idea is insightful and important: proper prayer requires proper behavior.

כח:י מַשְׁגֶּה יְשָׁרִים בְּדֶרֶךְ רָע בִּשְׁחוּתוֹ הוּא־יִפּוֹל וּתְמִימִים יִנְחֲלוּ־
טוֹב:

28:10 THE ONE WHO CAUSES THE UPRIGHT TO GO ASTRAY
ON AN EVIL WAY WILL FALL IN ONE'S OWN PIT, WHILE
THE BLAMELESS WILL INHERIT GOOD.

The "evil way," as Gersonides understands it, is the pit that the evil person has
placed in the path of the upright, hoping that they will fall into it. The sense of the
verse is not that the "upright" perceive the way that they go as evil; instead, it is evil
because it conceals a trap. Hopefully, the one who planned such evil will fall into his
or her own trap.

כח:יא חָכָם בְּעֵינָיו אִישׁ עָשִׁיר וְדַל מֵבִין יַחְקְרֶנּוּ:

28:11 A RICH PERSON IS WISE IN HIS [OR HER] OWN EYES; THE
POOR PERSON WHO COMPREHENDS WILL INVESTIGATE
THE OTHER.

It is a common assumption in most cultures that the achievement of great wealth,
even by inheritance, is a measure of great intelligence. The writer hopes that the
intelligent poor person will be able to match and even overtake the wealthy person
who may not be so wise. Sometimes the rich person is smart enough to hire the wise
person who is not so rich. As might be expected, Rashi takes the "rich" and "poor" to
refer to "teacher" and "student." The former is "rich" in learning, but the latter is
not. Gersonides picks up on the word *yachk'renu* (will investigate him). He thinks that
the intelligent poor person will be able to see what deficiencies the rich person may
have and will be able to capitalize on them.

כח:יב בַּעֲלֹץ צַדִּיקִים רַבָּה תִפְאָרֶת וּבְקוּם רְשָׁעִים יְחֻפַּשׂ אָדָם:

28:12 WHEN THE RIGHTEOUS EXULT, THERE IS GREAT HONOR,
BUT WHEN THE WICKED ARISE, EVERY PERSON IS TO BE
SOUGHT OUT.

As a result of the last verb *y'chupas* (be sought), the last clause makes for a difficult
translation of the entire verse. The *Targum* translates it by *mivtzei* (shall be searched,
found out). Rashi follows the *Targum* with the *hitpalel* (reflexive form) of the root
yitchapas (shall be sought). Ibn Ezra understands the verb to refer to what the wicked
do: they seek out a person's wealth to steal it. For him, the sense of the verse should
be that when the wicked are in the ascendancy, they have the power to expropriate
the wealth of the righteous. This is evidenced in Jewish history of the Middle Ages. For
Gersonides, who takes *y'chupas* to mean "to search for," the meaning of the last
clause is clear: when the wicked take over, the righteous have to hide, and thus each
one of them has to be "searched for."

כח:יג מְכַסֶּה פְשָׁעָיו לֹא יַצְלִיחַ וּמוֹדֶה וְעֹזֵב יְרֻחָם:

28:13 THE ONE WHO HIDES ONE'S SINS WILL NOT SUCCEED,
BUT THE ONE WHO ACKNOWLEDGES [THEM] AND GIVES
THEM UP WILL GAIN MERCY.

The writer presents two aspects of repentance: you do not hide your sins but acknowledge them and then give them up. In *Hilchot T'shuvah*, Maimonides offers the classic example of true repentance: the one who engaged in illicit sex with a particular person and has repented now has the opportunity, desire, and ability to do the same thing again but this time refrains from doing so.

כח:יד אַשְׁרֵי אָדָם מְפַחֵד תָּמִיד וּמַקְשֶׁה לִבּוֹ יִפּוֹל בְּרָעָה:

28:14 HAPPY IS THE ONE WHO CONTINUALLY IS AFRAID, BUT
THE ONE WHO IS HARD-HEARTED WILL FALL INTO EVIL.

"Afraid" of sin seems to be the intent of the writer. "Hardening of the heart" happened to Pharaoh prior to the Exodus of the Israelites from Egypt. Because of it, Pharaoh brought the Ten Plagues on himself and his people. Rashi takes *m'facheid* as being "afraid" of the consequence of sin, that is, the actual punishment. Ibn Ezra takes the word to refer to being "afraid" of God so that one would not sin in the first place. He takes the last clause to refer to the potential sinner who is unwilling to pay attention to reproach and ends up sinning as a result.

כח:טו אֲרִי־נֹהֵם וְדֹב שׁוֹקֵק מֹשֵׁל רָשָׁע עַל עַם־דָּל:

28:15 [LIKE] A LION THAT ROARS AND A BEAR ABOUT TO
ATTACK, SO IS A WICKED RULER OVER A POOR PEOPLE.

The lion and the bear threaten a disaster that is about to occur. Similar to this is a wicked ruler whose power is such that people cannot resist. The *Targum* translates *shokeik* (about to attack) by *matzriach* (screeching). Ibn Ezra derives the word from *shok* (thigh) and thereby takes it to mean "crushing."

כח:טז נָגִיד חֲסַר תְּבוּנוֹת וְרַב מַעֲשַׁקּוֹת שׂנֵאי שֶׁנֶא בֶצַע יַאֲרִיךְ יָמִים:

28:16 THE PRINCE WHO LACKS UNDERSTANDING WILL BE
A GREAT OPPRESSOR; THOSE WHO HATE GAIN WILL
LONG ENDURE.

The example of Solomon's son Rehoboam comes to mind when reading this verse. Following the death of his father, people implored him to make their tax burdens lighter. But the counselors who advised his father told him, "If you will be a servant unto this people and will serve them . . . and speak good words to them, then they will be your servants forever" (I Kings 12:7). However, Rehoboam lacked understanding and threatened the people with even higher taxes: ". . . My father loaded you with a heavy yoke. I will make your yoke even heavier . . ." (I Kings 12:11). As a result, the northern tribes revolted and the kingdom was divided. Both Ibn Ezra and Gersonides join this verse to the previous one.

כח:יז אָדָם עָשֻׁק בְּדַם־נָפֶשׁ עַד־בּוֹר יָנוּס אַל־יִתְמְכוּ־בוֹ:

28:17 A PERSON BURDENED BY THE SHEDDING OF BLOOD, THOUGH HE [OR SHE] FLEES TO THE PIT, NONE WILL SUPPORT HIM [OR HER].

This difficult verse may require the insertion of words into the translation for it to make sense. *Ashuk b'dam nafesh* (literally, "burdened by the blood of the soul," that is, the blood to sustain life, vital blood) requires the addition of "the shedding" to make sense. What the author seems to describe is the plight of one who has killed another and now must flee so that *go-eil hadam*, "the blood avenger" (see Numbers 35:19), cannot catch up and kill him or her. For Rashi, the first clause describes that person who caused another person to sin and, hence, caused the other to lose one's soul. Such a person to the day of death ("flees to the pit") must try to find the other and seek atonement. Ibn Ezra takes *ashuk* as equivalent to *oshek* (the active sense of the verb) and understands it to mean "oppresses." Therefore, he takes the first clause to describe a murderer whose sin is a self-destructive act ("the pit," the place of self-destruction). None will prevent such a person from going there. Gersonides takes the first clause to refer to the God-imposed guilt that the murderer bears. Moreover, wherever the murderer goes, he or she has to fear the vengeance that the blood avengers may seek to exact. Only going to the grave ("the pit") will allay that fear.

כח:יח הוֹלֵךְ תָּמִים יִוָּשֵׁעַ וְנֶעְקַשׁ דְּרָכַיִם יִפּוֹל בְּאֶחָת:

28:18 THE ONE WHO WALKS WITH INTEGRITY WILL BE SAVED, BUT THE ONE PERVERSE IN ONE'S WAYS WILL FALL AT ONCE.

The last word in the Hebrew, *b'echat*, is ambiguous. It may mean "at once," or it may mean "at one." In contrast, our three classic commentators take it to mean "in one." Rashi makes it clear: in one evil brought on by one's perverse ways.

כח:יט עֹבֵד אַדְמָתוֹ יִשְׂבַּע־לָחֶם וּמְרַדֵּף רֵיקִים יִשְׂבַּע־רִישׁ:

28:19 THE ONE WHO TILLS ONE'S OWN GROUND WILL HAVE
PLENTY OF FOOD, WHILE THE ONE WHO PURSUES VAIN
THINGS WILL HAVE POVERTY APLENTY.

Except for the last two words, this verse is a repetition of 12:11: *chasar lev* (lacks
sense) rather than *yisba rish* (will have poverty aplenty). Either the author adapted a
common proverb, these two proverbs were common, or the author culled material
from a variety of collections.

כח:כ אִישׁ אֱמוּנוֹת רַב־בְּרָכוֹת וְאָץ לְהַעֲשִׁיר לֹא יִנָּקֶה:

28:20 A TRUSTWORTHY PERSON WILL HAVE MANY BLESSINGS,
BUT ONE HASTY TO BECOME WEALTHY WILL NOT BE
CONSIDERED INNOCENT.

What seems to be contrasted here is the person who can be depended on with the
one who cannot because the latter is eager to become wealthy regardless of the cost.
Gersonides describes the former person as one who faithfully deals with political and
intellectual ideas and will therefore be blessed. The person who is in pursuit of wealth
does not deal with such ideas. As a result, that person will suffer the consequences of
such a lack of knowledge.

כח:כא הַכֵּר־פָּנִים לֹא־טוֹב וְעַל־פַּת־לֶחֶם יִפְשַׁע־גָּבֶר:

28:21 FAVORITISM IS NOT GOOD, FOR A PERSON WILL COMMIT
A TRANSGRESSION FOR A PIECE OF BREAD.

The author included a variant of the first clause of this verse in 24:23. In both places,
the editor's method requires examination. Since Gersonides adds *b'mishpat*, "in
judgment" or "in court," following the words *hakeir panim*, literally "respecting of
persons," or "favoritism" as in 24:23, he may have had a different text in front of him
when penning his commentary.

כח:כב נִבְהָל לַהוֹן אִישׁ רַע עָיִן וְלֹא־יֵדַע כִּי־חֶסֶר יְבֹאֶנּוּ:

28:22 THE ONE WHO HAS AN EVIL EYE RUSHES AFTER RICHES;
THAT PERSON DOES NOT KNOW THAT A WANT WILL
COME TO HIM [OR HER].

In the Bible, an "evil eye" denotes envy. Seeing what others have, such a person may
plunge headlong into the pursuit of wealth without regard for consequences. The
author suggests one kind of consequence: a lack of planning will bring financial
disaster. Rashi explains the consequence of "a want" as the punishment for the

covetous individual's holding back on the payment of one's religious requirements. Ibn Ezra takes the threatened "want" as fit punishment for that envious person's refusal to provide for the poor. Gersonides suggests that such a person not only will lack money but will also lack friends.

כח:כג מוֹכִיחַ אָדָם אַחֲרַי חֵן יִמְצָא מִמַּחֲלִיק לָשׁוֹן:

28:23 THE ONE WHO REPROVES A PERSON WILL FIND FAVOR IN THE END, MORE THAN ONE WHO FLATTERS WITH WORDS.

The use of the word *acharai* presents us with a difficulty in translating this verse. Although it seems to be the inflected form of *achar* (after me), such a translation would make no sense. Since Ibn Ezra takes the author of Proverbs to be the same as the author of Ecclesiastes (Jewish tradition attributes both books to Solomon), he calls Ecclesiastes 2:18 to the attention of the reader. Ecclesiastes 2:18 ends with the words "...that I should leave it to a person who will be *acharai* [after me]." Ibn Ezra thereby interprets our verse as "The one who reproves a person after me." Rashi interprets the whole phrase *acharai chein* (afterwards), explaining that after a person is reproved, that person will repent and be grateful to the one who moved away from transgression and toward repentance. Rashi also applies the verse to Moses, who reproved Israel, and to Balaam, who flattered Israel. The former tried to move the people of Israel away from sin; the latter wanted to keep them in the clutches of it. Gersonides adds that the reproved one will be grateful to the one who gave reproof for having delivered him or her from danger.

כח:כד גּוֹזֵל אָבִיו וְאִמּוֹ וְאֹמֵר אֵין־פָּשַׁע חָבֵר הוּא לְאִישׁ מַשְׁחִית:

28:24 THE ONE WHO ROBS ONE'S FATHER AND MOTHER AND THEN SAYS, "IT IS NOT SIN" IS A COMPANION OF THE ONE WHO WOULD DESTROY.

It does not seem like the author has to say anything beyond describing a person who would rob his or her parents and see nothing wrong with it. What is unclear, however, is what is meant by the last phrase. According to Rashi, "father" means God, and "mother" refers to the people of Israel. For Rashi, "rob" means "moving others to sin," and "the one who would destroy" is "Jeroboam." According to Ibn Ezra, "father and mother" refer to real parents who are robbed by a child who thinks that he or she ultimately has a right to their possessions, since they will inherit them in any case. Such a child's contempt for his or her parents will eventually "destroy" what would have been inherited. While Gersonides agrees with what Ibn Ezra wrote about "father and mother," he suggests that such heartlessness will carry over in such a despicable person's murdering of others. Thus, that person becomes one "who would destroy."

כח:כה רְחַב־נֶפֶשׁ יְגָרֶה מָדוֹן וּבוֹטֵחַ עַל־יְהוָה יְדֻשָּׁן:

28:25 ONE WITH OVERWHELMING DESIRE WILL STIR UP
STRIFE, BUT ONE WHO TRUSTS IN GOD WILL BE
TOTALLY SATISFIED.

We have translated *y'dushan* (literally, "will be made fat") as "will be totally satisfied."
Ibn Ezra notes that a person with such desire will fear nothing or no one, not even
God. As Gersonides sees it, the person in the first clause can never be satisfied. The
person in the second clause, in control of one's passions, can easily be satisfied.

כח:כו בּוֹטֵחַ בְּלִבּוֹ הוּא כְסִיל וְהוֹלֵךְ בְּחָכְמָה הוּא יִמָּלֵט:

28:26 THE FOOL IS CERTAIN IN HIS [OR HER] OWN MIND,
BUT THE ONE WHO WALKS WITH WISDOM WILL BE
DELIVERED.

The person who is always certain about what he or she thinks is indeed a fool. The
person who would "walk with wisdom" attempts to learn what others have taught.
The latter person will be delivered from his or her problems. For Gersonides, "the one
who walks with wisdom" is the one who has evaluated all manner of causes that
impact on his or her life.

כח:כז נוֹתֵן לָרָשׁ אֵין מַחְסוֹר וּמַעְלִים עֵינָיו רַב־מְאֵרוֹת:

28:27 THE ONE WHO GIVES TO THE POOR WILL NOT LACK
[ANYTHING], AND THE ONE WHO HIDES ONE'S EYES
WILL HAVE MANY CURSES.

The first clause deals with the giving of *tzedakah*, which the author promises will be
rewarded. The second clause focuses on the person who averts one's eyes to avoid
looking at the poor, which the author reminds us will result in punishment. By giving a
specific example of reward and punishment that is measure for measure, Gersonides
tells us that God will reward the one who gives to the poor and will punish the one
who will not do so.

כח:כח בְּקוּם רְשָׁעִים יִסָּתֵר אָדָם וּבְאָבְדָם יִרְבּוּ צַדִּיקִים:

28:28 WHEN THE WICKED RISE, PEOPLE HIDE, AND WHEN
THEY PERISH, THE RIGHTEOUS INCREASE.

According to Ibn Ezra, the "people" who "hide" are those trying to act justly.

Hilchot T'shuvah

Hilchot T'shuvah is part of the *Mishneh Torah*, prepared by Moses Maimonides (1135–1204). This section of the *Mishneh Torah* focuses on the laws of *T'shuvah* (repentance), as its name implies. The goal of the *Mishneh Torah* was to define the law as it stood in the most concise way possible. The *Mishneh Torah* became the standard work on which future law codes were based.

Blood Avenger and Blood Redeemer

The Torah gives permission for family members to seek revenge over the murder of one of its members. The pursuer is called the "blood avenger" or "blood redeemer." In the Bible, the person who sheds innocent blood cannot go unexpiated. Thus, the Torah says, "Whoever sheds a person's blood, by human shall that person's blood be shed, for in the divine image did God make the human" (Genesis 9:6). The blood of the victim is actually portrayed as "crying out from the ground" (Genesis 4:10). The one who is pursued can seek asylum only in one of the designated cities of refuge (see Numbers 35:12, 24–25).

GLEANINGS

Charging Interest

Jewish law forbade the taking of interest from Jews. [See Lev. 25:37.] In an essentially rural community the spread of a money-based economy was discouraged, for it would inevitably lead to channeling farm assets to absentee urban owners (as it has done in many countries since then). In international dealings, however, in foreign exchange, in import and export, which depended on loans and interest charges, the law did not apply; and since the foreign merchant was a non-Jew, the Torah simply permitted interest-taking from non-Israelites (Deut. 23:21). During the Middle Ages, the Church applied this law to Christians and, through a series of restrictive ordinances, forced the Jew into the money-lending trade—thus using him for the necessities of state and at the same time holding him up to obloquy and contempt.

W. Gunther Plaut, *The Book of Proverbs: A Commentary* (New York: UAHC Press, 1961), 283

T'shuvah

This expectation that we must strive *la-alot,* "to go up" toward God not only means that we must strive to talk about God more often and in a more open manner; it also means that we should actively seek God's presence through all we know. The knowledge of our world brought to us by science and technology must be viewed through a filter of awe and wonder. The small, daily acts of kindness and goodness observed must be connected to a sense of the Holy. The love we extend to others and the love that is returned must be seen as an experience that connects us with the Divine. The text states, "Let us by all means go up." We must go beyond intellectualizing our relationship with God and instead begin to feel it within the experiences of our daily lives.

Sally Finestone, "What Should We Expect of Ourselves as Jews? Spying into the Future,"
CCAR Yearbook 99 (1989): 96

CHAPTER TWENTY-NINE

כט:א אִישׁ תּוֹכָחוֹת מַקְשֶׁה־עֹרֶף פֶּתַע יִשָּׁבֵר וְאֵין מַרְפֵּא:

29:1 THE NECK OF SOMEONE MUCH REPROVED WILL STIFFEN.
IT WILL SUDDENLY BE BROKEN AND WITHOUT HEALING.

The first clause suggests that constant reproof ceases to have an effect. The antecedent in the second clause is somewhat unclear: what is it that "will suddenly be broken"? If it is the reproved person's neck that will be broken, literally or figuratively, then the writer wants to remind us that obstinacy can bring on disaster. According to Gersonides, if a person sins and has received divine punishment and still has not learned from one's intellectual and ethical errors, further punishment—from which the punished person will not recover—will come rapidly.

כט:ב בִּרְבוֹת צַדִּיקִים יִשְׂמַח הָעָם וּבִמְשֹׁל רָשָׁע יֵאָנַח עָם:

29:2 WHEN THE RIGHTEOUS BECOME MANY, THE PEOPLE
REJOICE, BUT WHEN THE WICKED RULE, THE PEOPLE
GROAN.

The end of Gersonides' comment may sum up the meaning of the verse: *v'ha-inyan m'vuar* (the matter is clear). This verse is a political truism, and the verse that follows is a moral truism.

כט:ג אִישׁ־אֹהֵב חָכְמָה יְשַׂמַּח אָבִיו וְרֹעֶה זוֹנוֹת יְאַבֶּד־הוֹן:

29:3 THE PERSON WHO LOVES WISDOM WILL MAKE ONE'S
PARENT GLAD, BUT THE ONE WHO SUPPORTS
PROSTITUTES WASTES ONE'S WEALTH.

This statement condemns—as it acknowledges—the attraction of illicit sex. It is not clear whose wealth is being wasted. According to Ibn Ezra, it is the son's wealth that is being wasted. According to Gersonides, it is the father's money that is being spent on prostitutes by the son.

כט:ד מֶלֶךְ בְּמִשְׁפָּט יַעֲמִיד אָרֶץ וְאִישׁ תְּרוּמוֹת יֶהֶרְסֶנָּה:

29:4 A RULER ESTABLISHES A LAND BY JUSTICE, BUT A PERSON
WHO DEMANDS CONTRIBUTIONS WILL DESTROY IT.

The difficulty in this verse is in *t'rumot* (contributions), which usually refers to what is given to priests. The term *ish t'rumot* in the second clause literally means "a person of contributions." Both clauses seem to refer to a monarch. Such a ruler would unjustly take what is due the priests. This is the same kind of ruler who would destroy the land. Rashi refers the entire verse to judges. If one is a true judge, one will establish the land. If one, as a judge, requires "contributions," that judge will destroy the land. Ibn Ezra refers the second clause to a king who would take more than his due. Such a king destroys his own land. Gersonides understands the second clause to refer to that kind of ruler whose exactions affect the civil order to such an extent that all law begins to be affected and none can trust ruler or judge.

כט:ה גֶּבֶר מַחֲלִיק עַל־רֵעֵהוּ רֶשֶׁת פּוֹרֵשׂ עַל־פְּעָמָיו:

29:5 THE PERSON WHO FLATTERS HIS [OR HER] NEIGHBORS
SPREADS A NET FOR HIS [OR HER] STEPS.

To whose steps is the author referring, even if we translate the clause literally, as written, as "his steps"? According to Ibn Ezra, who connects this verse with the one that follows and is in agreement with Gersonides, it is the steps of the one who flatters. However, this verse can refer to the neighbor who is trapped by the charm of the flatterer.

כט:ו בְּפֶשַׁע אִישׁ רָע מוֹקֵשׁ וְצַדִּיק יָרוּן וְשָׂמֵחַ:

29:6 THERE IS A SNARE IN THE TRANSGRESSION OF THE EVIL
PERSON, WHILE THE RIGHTEOUS SING AND REJOICE.

Ibn Ezra and Gersonides agree that the "snare" traps the evil person. Furthermore, according to Ibn Ezra, on seeing the evil person entrapped, the righteous begin to sing. Quoting 11:10, "There is joy [*rinah*] when the wicked perish," Gersonides explains that the righteous rejoice and sing when they see evil people caught in their own snares. *Rinah* can mean both "joy" and "singing."

כט:ז יֹדֵעַ צַדִּיק דִּין דַּלִּים רָשָׁע לֹא־יָבִין דָּעַת:

29:7 A RIGHTEOUS PERSON KNOWS THE CASE OF THE POOR,
BUT A WICKED PERSON DOES NOT UNDERSTAND
"KNOWING."

The sense of the second clause is that a wicked person pretends not to "know" anything about the problems of the poor. Rashi explains in the first clause that the righteous know what the poor need. Referring to the second clause, Ibn Ezra explains that the wicked have neither any information about the poor nor any sense of justice about their plight.

כט:ח אַנְשֵׁי לָצוֹן יָפִיחוּ קִרְיָה וַחֲכָמִים יָשִׁיבוּ אָף:

29:8 MOCKING PEOPLE INFLAME A CITY, BUT THE WISE TURN
AWAY WRATH.

Yafichu (inflame) literally means "breathe out" or "blow on," as in "to fan a flame." Gersonides explains that people who mock others encourage controversy among them. Wise people work for peace. Civil peace is an important notion for all, particularly those for whom the Book of Proverbs was written.

כט:ט אִישׁ־חָכָם נִשְׁפָּט אֶת־אִישׁ אֱוִיל וְרָגַז וְשָׂחַק וְאֵין נָחַת:

29:9 IF A WISE PERSON HAS A LAWSUIT WITH A FOOL,
WHETHER THE PERSON RAGES OR LAUGHS, THERE WILL
BE NO REST.

Rashi takes *nishpat* as "contend." Ibn Ezra, whom we follow in our translation, takes it to mean "has a lawsuit." Gersonides also takes the word to mean "to go to the law." He thinks that the fool will prevent a wise person from presenting one's case, either becoming enraged when the wise person speaks or mocking and laughing at that person if the person is indeed given the opportunity to speak. On reflection, the "fool" is not a fool at all. That person is devious, even crooked, but totally aware of what he or she is doing.

כט:י אַנְשֵׁי דָמִים יִשְׂנְאוּ־תָם וִישָׁרִים יְבַקְשׁוּ נַפְשׁוֹ:

29:10 PEOPLE OF BLOOD HATE AN HONEST PERSON, AND
THOSE WHO ARE UPRIGHT SEEK THAT PERSON'S LIFE.

The second clause makes the verse difficult to understand. One would hardly expect those who are upright to seek the life of an honest person. Some scholars emend *y'sharim* (upright) to *r'sha-im* (wicked), which would make more sense. The *Targum* translates *tam* (honest) in the first clause by *t'mimuta* (honesty, integrity) and translates the second clause as *ut'ritzei bayan la* (and those who are upright desire it). Rashi tries to avoid the problem by suggesting that the verb *y'vakshu* (seek) can mean "care for." He offers as an example the phrase *y'vakeish et nafshi y'vakeish et nafshecha* in I Samuel 22:23. Rashi's forced interpretation is evident by reading the verse from Samuel in context, where it makes more sense: "one who will seek my life and will seek yours." Ibn Ezra seems to be no more successful in resolving the problem of the verse. He explains that the "life" that the "upright seek" is the life of people of blood—as revenge for taking the life of "an honest person." This is a possible interpretation, but it seems similarly forced. Gersonides avoids the problem by interpreting the verse as a philosophical parable: "People of blood" are those given over to their lusts. The *tam* is the appetitive faculty that seeks simplicity and perfection. The upright are those who seek after what the intellect desires. (*Nefesh* can mean "desire," as it does in Genesis 23:8.)

כט:יא כָּל־רוּחוֹ יוֹצִיא כְסִיל וְחָכָם בְּאָחוֹר יְשַׁבְּחֶנָּה:

29:11 A FOOL LETS OUT ALL HIS [OR HER] ANGER, BUT A WISE
PERSON CALMS IT IN THE END.

B'achor is the problematic word in the verse. It can mean "behind," "backwards," or "after." Rashi takes it to mean "afterwards" and understands the verse to mean that first the "fool" speaks and then "afterwards" the wise person responds. Ibn Ezra takes it to mean "behind" and sees it as a veiled reference to the mind that is "behind" the tongue. Thus, the "fool" speaks, and the "wise person" answers, using one's mind. Gersonides combines the views of both Rashi and Ibn Ezra. He understands *b'achor* as a kind of mental delay. The fool acts immediately on impulse. The wise person mulls matters over and only on reflection acts.

כט:יב מֹשֵׁל מַקְשִׁיב עַל־דְּבַר־שָׁקֶר כָּל־מְשָׁרְתָיו רְשָׁעִים:

29:12 THE RULER WHO LISTENS TO LIES WILL HAVE WICKED
PERSONS AS SERVANTS.

Gersonides suggests that the "ruler" is the appetitive faculty that might be subservient to bodily desires and that will mislead the intellect.

כט:יג רָשׁ וְאִישׁ תְּכָכִים נִפְגָּשׁוּ מֵאִיר־עֵינֵי שְׁנֵיהֶם יְהֹוָה:

29:13 THE POOR PERSON AND THE OPPRESSOR MEET;
GOD ILLUMINES THE EYES OF BOTH.

The Septuagint and the Vulgate take *ish t'chachim* (oppressor) to mean "creditor." The Greek takes *rash* (poor person) to mean "debtor." Rashi relates the first clause to the study of Torah. *Rash* refers to the student, and *ish t'chachim* is the clever teacher of Torah. As might be expected, Gersonides relates the first clause to the study of philosophy and like Rashi understands *rash* and *ish t'chachim* as student and teacher. Ibn Ezra takes *t'chachim* as if it were the *hofal* form of the root *nachah* (to smite), as in Deuteronomy 33:3, *v'heim tuku l'raglecha,* "and they were smitten at Your feet." He thus understands the phrase to be the parallel of *rash,* that is, "a person beaten down by poverty," a pauper. Therefore, for Ibn Ezra, the meaning of the entire verse is "The poor person and the pauper meet, and God will illumine the darkness of their poverty."

כט:יד מֶלֶךְ שׁוֹפֵט בֶּאֱמֶת דַּלִּים כִּסְאוֹ לָעַד יִכּוֹן:

29:14 THE RULER WHO TRULY JUDGES THE POOR WILL HAVE HIS [OR HER] THRONE ESTABLISHED FOREVER.

Gersonides observes that just as the ruler who carefully investigates the situation of the poor will get plaudits from the people, so the intellect (the "ruler") that carefully investigates matters will gain ultimate perfection.

כט:טו שֵׁבֶט וְתוֹכַחַת יִתֵּן חָכְמָה וְנַעַר מְשֻׁלָּח מֵבִישׁ אִמּוֹ:

29:15 ROD AND REPROOF GIVE WISDOM; THE YOUNG PERSON LEFT ALONE WILL EMBARRASS HIS [OR HER] PARENT.

This verse comes from the "spare the rod and spoil the child" genre. Both control and self-control are important topics in wisdom literature. Rashi presents the case of wayward Ishmael embarrassing Sarah, who adopted him, as a case that affirms the truth of the verse, a case that we may see differently than Rashi did (see Genesis 16:2). Gersonides notes that control of the passions, which may be aided by the administration of the "rod," is a necessary precursor to the achievement of true wisdom. The person bereft of *musar* (ethical behavior) and *chochmah* (philosophical understanding) would embarrass even his or her own parents.

כט:טז בִּרְבוֹת רְשָׁעִים יִרְבֶּה־פָּשַׁע וְצַדִּיקִים בְּמַפַּלְתָּם יִרְאוּ:

29:16 WHEN THE WICKED INCREASE THERE IS NO MORE TRANSGRESSION, BUT THE RIGHTEOUS WILL SEE THEIR DOWNFALL.

Ibn Ezra thinks that "the righteous" not only will "see" the downfall of the wicked, but will rejoice in it as well.

כט:יז יַסֵּר בִּנְךָ וִינִיחֶךָ וְיִתֵּן מַעֲדַנִּים לְנַפְשֶׁךָ:

29:17 DISCIPLINE YOUR CHILDREN AND THEY WILL SET YOU AT EASE; THEY WILL PROVIDE DELIGHT TO YOUR LIFE.

In order to avoid gender specificity, we have translated this verse in the plural. We have translated *maadanim* (dainties) as "delight." For Gersonides, this verse continues the ideas set forth by the author in verse 15. Having provided discipline for a child by one means or another, the parents now reap the benefit of their children's achievements in philosophy. They are the "delight" of a parent's life.

כט:יח בְּאֵין חָזוֹן יִפָּרַע עָם וְשֹׁמֵר תּוֹרָה אַשְׁרֵהוּ:

29:18 WHEN THERE IS NO VISION, THE PEOPLE RUN WILD;
HAPPY IS THE ONE WHO KEEPS MORAL INSTRUCTION.

As we have seen before, *torah* in this verse means "moral instruction." Rashi explains that the loss of "vision" occurred when the people of Israel complained about the prophets. As a result, prophecy departed from their midst. Ibn Ezra points out that exile was the punishment for being uncontrolled. By taking *torah* to mean *the* Torah, Gersonides explains that only the Torah can meet the needs of all elements of the population to provide both political and intellectual instruction.

כט:יט בִּדְבָרִים לֹא־יִוָּסֶר עָבֶד כִּי־יָבִין וְאֵין מַעֲנֶה:

29:19 WORDS WILL NOT DISCIPLINE A SLAVE; ALTHOUGH THE
SLAVE MAY UNDERSTAND, THERE WILL BE NO ANSWER.

This is neither a politically correct verse nor a politically correct explanation. Rashi suggests that as force is required to control slaves, so force is required to control those who will not obey the decisions of judges.

כט:כ חָזִיתָ אִישׁ אָץ בִּדְבָרָיו תִּקְוָה לִכְסִיל מִמֶּנּוּ:

29:20 IF YOU HAVE SEEN A PERSON QUICK TO ANSWER,
A FOOL HAS MORE HOPE THAN THAT PERSON.

The author used the second clause of this verse in 26:12. Perhaps the author wanted to emphasize the notion that one should think before speaking. A fool has little hope. To have less hope than a fool is a powerful warning to readers of Proverbs.

כט:כא מְפַנֵּק מִנֹּעַר עַבְדּוֹ וְאַחֲרִיתוֹ יִהְיֶה מָנוֹן:

29:21 THE ONE WHO SPOILS ONE'S SLAVE FROM CHILDHOOD
WILL HAVE AT THE END ONE WHO IS ARROGANT.

The last word, *manon*, poses a problem. It occurs nowhere else in the Bible; to find its correct derivation is therefore problematic. Seeing some parallel to *yinon* in Psalm 72:17, Rashi translates the word as "ruler." However, he takes the verse as a parable: *avdo* (literally, "his slave") refers to the *yetzer hara* (evil inclination). Ibn Ezra relates *manon* to *nin* (grandson). Thus, he interprets the verse to mean that if you spoil a young slave, that slave will consider oneself as a grandchild when he or she becomes an adult. Gersonides also takes *manon* to be "ruler" but relates it to the appetitive capacity of the soul.

כט:כב אִישׁ־אַף יְגָרֶה מָדוֹן וּבַעַל חֵמָה רַב־פָּשַׁע:

29:22 AN ANGRY PERSON STIRS UP STRIFE, AND A WRATHFUL
PERSON IS FULL OF TRANSGRESSION.

The first clause in this verse already appeared (with a slight variation) in 15:18, where we translated it as "a hothead picks a fight." Self-control is knowing when, how, and against whom to be angry. Anger and impulsiveness may lead to the loss of self-control.

כט:כג גַּאֲוַת אָדָם תַּשְׁפִּילֶנּוּ וּשְׁפַל־רוּחַ יִתְמֹךְ כָּבוֹד:

29:23 A PERSON'S PRIDE WILL CAST HIM [OR HER] DOWN; ONE
OF LOWLY SPIRIT WILL GRASP GLORY.

"Pride goes before a fall," another warning for those for whom the book was written.

כט:כד חוֹלֵק עִם־גַּנָּב שׂוֹנֵא נַפְשׁוֹ אָלָה יִשְׁמַע וְלֹא יַגִּיד:

29:24 THE ONE WHO WOULD DIVVY UP WITH A THIEF HATES
ONESELF; THAT PERSON HEARS A CURSE BUT SAYS
NOTHING.

Rashi explains the verse as a reference to a person who hears that something has been stolen and knows the thief but does not tell. These kind of people do not tell because they intend to blackmail the thief in order to share the ill-gotten gain. Although Rashi does not say it, such a course of action would be exceedingly dangerous, because the thief may feel that he has nothing to lose by killing the blackmailer. Ibn Ezra thinks that a curse publicly pronounced may itself kill the person who knows but does not tell (see Leviticus 5:1).

כט:כה חֶרְדַּת אָדָם יִתֵּן מוֹקֵשׁ וּבוֹטֵחַ בַּיהוָה יְשֻׂגָּב:

29:25 HUMAN FEAR SETS A SNARE, BUT TRUSTING IN GOD
BRINGS ONE TO HEIGHTS.

Rashi inverts the first clause and interprets it to mean that the snare of sins will cause an individual to fear. Ibn Ezra explains the second clause as meaning that God will elevate those who trust in God.

כט:כו רַבִּים מְבַקְשִׁים פְּנֵי־מוֹשֵׁל וּמֵיְהֹוָה מִשְׁפַּט־אִישׁ:

29:26 MANY MAY SEEK THE FAVOR OF A RULER, BUT
JUDGMENT COMES FROM GOD.

Ibn Ezra explains that giving bribes is a means of seeking "favor." Hence, God—who cannot be bribed—is the One who provides true judgment. The issue of true judgment relates to the next verse.

כט:כז תּוֹעֲבַת צַדִּיקִים אִישׁ עָוֶל וְתוֹעֲבַת רָשָׁע יְשַׁר־דָּרֶךְ:

29:27 A CORRUPT PERSON IS THE ABOMINATION OF THE
INNOCENT; THE ONE WHO IS UPRIGHT IN THE WAY IS
THE ABOMINATION OF THE GUILTY.

Because of the context, we translated *tzaddikim* as "innocent" and *rasha* as "guilty." Gersonides understands the verse to refer to the reputations of judges. Those who are corrupt would misjudge the innocent. Those who are upright would condemn the guilty, as the guilty should be condemned.

Musar

Musar is a term that refers in general to ethical behavior. It was specifically used by Rabbi Israel Salanter (1810–1883), who founded the Musar movement in Germany and Eastern Europe. The idea behind this movement was to teach people to act in an ethical manner as part of their daily activity, even as they mastered the sacred literature. Some of Salanter's writings are collected in *Or Yisrael*. Sometimes, Musar is spoken of as a movement of ethical piety. It was considered by some as a response of the *Mitnagdim* (opponents of Chasidism) to the various weaknesses of Lithuanian Jewry.

GLEANINGS

Me First

Nowhere in the sacred literature of our people do I find justification for "me-first-ism" as a positive value for individuals. Nowhere in our sacred history since Mt. Sinai can I find buttressing for unfettered greed as a good thing for human society. Nowhere in our communal experience can I find a basis for believing that government is by nature an enemy of the people, except when our institutions are feeding at the public trough for our projects. Nowhere in the annals of Jewish history can I find extolled the erosion of the rights of all citizens, vengeful incarceration and the civil murder called capital punishment, the closing of borders to politically persecuted people. Nowhere

Mishlei: A Modern Commentary on Proverbs

in the commands of my *Metsaveh* can I find a mandate to continue discrimination against racial, ethnic, and other minorities in education, in housing, in employment. Nowhere in our writings about human relationships can I find approved the amassing of huge fortunes by a few while millions of individuals and families live on the streets, in automobiles, in hideous public shelters. Nowhere does my God command the establishment of a permanent class of poor people doomed to leave the *yerusha* of their poverty to their children and to their children. Nowhere. I am a liberal because I am a religious Jew...bound to the Covenant we all swore to uphold at *Ma-amad Har Sinai*.

Eugene Lipman, "President's Address," CCAR Yearbook 99 (1989): 17

Dignity of the Poor

The concern for the inherent value and equality of each person led to the requirement that, whenever possible, help must be given to the needy in such a way as to enhance the dignity of the recipient. Better no giving at all than the giving that humiliates, the Talmud says. The concern resulted in policies that distinguish the Jewish tradition from some of the more demeaning aspects of our own social welfare system today. For example, those who claim that they were poor were given relief immediately and investigation of the claim was done afterwards. The reverse is done in our society. It can often be a very humbling and humiliating process. Now, the Rabbis knew that some freeloaders would sneak in to such a system, but with a sense of frustration and irony, the Talmud found a use even for the freeloaders, noting, "Be good to the impostors. Without them our stinginess would lack its chief excuse." More importantly, since *Tsedaka* is an individual as well as communal obligation, the communal authorities taxed every person in the community. Even the poor who are the recipients of welfare funds were taxed. This helped each person fulfill the mitzvah of *Tsedaka* and prevented the stratification of society into two classes. Every person was a giver. Each person helped the poor....

David Saperstein, "Economic Justice and the Jewish Community, A Response,"
CCAR Yearbook 96 (1986): 71

292

CHAPTER THIRTY

לֹ:א דִּבְרֵי אָגוּר בִּן־יָקֶה הַמַּשָּׂא נְאֻם הַגֶּבֶר לְאִיתִיאֵל לְאִיתִיאֵל
וְאֻכָל:

30:1 THE WORDS OF AGUR, SON OF YAKEH: THE BURDEN.
THE PERSON SAYS TO ITHIEL, ITHIEL AND UCAL.

This section of the Book of Proverbs begins with a superscription that assigns it to someone besides Solomon, namely Agur ben Yakeh. It should be noted that the style of the portion that follows is reminiscent of the Book of Job and is different from the style of the rest of Proverbs. Following the tradition that links the entire book to Solomon, Rashi feels compelled to interpret the name as somehow applying to Solomon. He does so by taking Agur from the root *agar* (to bind up) and Yakeh from the root *hikeh* (to vomit) and explains that Solomon gathered up understanding and spewed it forth. Ibn Ezra explains that Agur was a learned and ethical person who lived in the time of Solomon and whose wise words were incorporated into Solomon's book. Gersonides thinks that Agur is Solomon and just as Solomon had called himself Kohelet, a term that suggests some kind of collection, so Solomon called himself Agur, which also suggests some kind of collection. Yakeh, according to Gersonides, suggests that Solomon intended to cast off, as if by vomiting, what was boring and incorrect, so that the correct ideas would remain.

לֹ:ב כִּי בַעַר אָנֹכִי מֵאִישׁ וְלֹא־בִינַת אָדָם לִי:

30:2 I AM MORE BRUTISH THAN A GENTLEMAN, AND I DO
NOT HAVE THE UNDERSTANDING OF A COMMON MAN.

We have left this verse gender specific, since the author, identified in verse 1, is referring to himself. Throughout wisdom literature, there is a distinction between *ish* and *adam*. Since this distinction may reflect class, we have chosen to translate *ish* as "gentleman" and *adam* as "common man." Rashi explains the first clause as the confession of someone who depends on his or her own wisdom rather than depending on what might concern God. Both Ibn Ezra and Gersonides connect this verse with what follows.

לֹא־לָמַדְתִּי חָכְמָה וְדַעַת קְדֹשִׁים אֵדָע: **ל:ג**

30:3 I HAVE NOT LEARNED WISDOM, BUT I HAVE THE
KNOWLEDGE OF ALL [THAT IS] HOLY.

This is a difficult verse. There is a problem with the negative particle *lo* (not) in the first
clause. Although the context does not require it, Ibn Ezra takes it to apply to the verb
eida in the second clause. The second clause could be translated—as we have chosen
to do—as a positive statement. It is unclear to what *k'doshim* (holy things) refers. We
have seen the phrase *daat k'doshim* in Proverbs 9:10, where the term *k'doshim* seems
to be a plural of "majesty," referring to God. Rashi takes the *lo* of the first clause to
refer to the knowledge in the second clause and interprets *k'doshim* as referring to the
teaching of Moses. Thus Rashi indicates that the verse has Solomon regretting that he
thought he could add to or subtract from the teaching of Moses. Gersonides also takes
the *lo* to negate the knowing of the second clause. For him, as he has suggested in his
comment on the previous verse, *k'doshim* refers to the movers of the heavenly
bodies, that is, the separate intelligences.

מִי עָלָה־שָׁמַיִם וַיֵּרַד מִי אָסַף־רוּחַ בְּחָפְנָיו מִי צָרַר־מַיִם בַּשִּׂמְלָה **ל:ד**
מִי הֵקִים כָּל־אַפְסֵי־אָרֶץ מַה־שְּׁמוֹ וּמַה־שֶּׁם־בְּנוֹ כִּי תֵדָע:

30:4 WHO HAS GONE UP TO HEAVEN AND COME DOWN?
WHO HAS GATHERED THE WIND IN ONE'S FISTS? WHO
HAS BOUND UP THE WATERS IN ONE'S GARMENT? WHO
HAS ESTABLISHED THE ENDS OF THE EARTH? WHAT IS
THAT ONE'S NAME? AND WHAT IS THE CHILD'S NAME,
IF YOU KNOW IT?

This passage is reminiscent of the speech from the whirlwind in Job 38. Rashi
attributes the entire passage as a reference to Moses. It was he who ascended to the
heavens to receive the Torah, gathering the soot of the furnace that he might cast into
the wind and bring on the plague of boils. It was Moses who caused the waters to part
at the Re(e)d Sea, and it was he who established the ends of the earth by establishing
the desert Tabernacle. Ibn Ezra understands the passage as a reference to God. It is
God who can ascend to the heavens and descend to the earth. "One's fists" are
metaphors for the Divine Will and the Divine Intellect. It is God who gathers the
waters in the clouds, and it is God who establishes the ends of the earth. Ibn Ezra
deals with the problematic "What is that one's name [literally, 'his name']? And what
is the child's name [literally, 'his son's name']?" by referring the words to those who
might attempt to understand the works of God, thereby putting themselves on the
same level as God. Gersonides understands the verse to refer to the linkage between
the upper and lower worlds: Which beings are corruptible and which incorruptible?
How does the process of emanation proceed, and where does the emanated soul

come from? For the answers to these complicated philosophical questions, Gersonides refers the reader to his work *The Wars of the Lord,* as well as his commentaries on the various writings of Aristotle.

ל:ה כָּל־אִמְרַת אֱלוֹהַ צְרוּפָה מָגֵן הוּא לַחֹסִים בּוֹ:

30:5 EACH WORD OF GOD IS PURE; GOD IS A SHIELD TO ALL WHO TRUST IN GOD.

Tz'rufah (pure) suggests the action of the silversmith removing any possible impurity to mix with the silver being refined. For Rashi, the first clause indicates that each word of the Torah has a meaning. For Ibn Ezra, it indicates that each word provides the kind of instruction that will bring true wisdom. For Gersonides, the ''word'' will provide the individual with the guidance that will assure that person true success. Understanding the first clause in their various ways, the commentators affirm that God is a shield to those who trust in God. This verse suggests a reason for the verse that follows.

ל:ו אַל־תּוֹסְףְּ עַל־דְּבָרָיו פֶּן־יוֹכִיחַ בְּךָ וְנִכְזָבְתָּ:

30:6 DON'T ADD TO GOD'S WORDS, LEST GOD REPROVE YOU AND YOU BECOME A LIAR.

If God's words are perfect, then one cannot add to them or subtract from them. Based upon this, Rashi suggests that if adding to the divine words causes transgressions, how much the more would subtracting from them. Ibn Ezra takes this section as a reference to Solomon acting under different guises. He sees this verse as reproving Solomon for his actions in marrying more women than prescribed and attempting to judge people without the requisite witnesses. Gersonides thinks that if a person sees some excess (in other words, things that should not be added) in the divine words, that person may come to take all of God's words lightly.

ל:ז שְׁתַּיִם שָׁאַלְתִּי מֵאִתָּךְ אַל־תִּמְנַע מִמֶּנִּי בְּטֶרֶם אָמוּת:

30:7 I HAVE ASKED YOU FOR TWO THINGS; DON'T KEEP THEM FROM ME BEFORE I DIE.

In his usual manner, Gersonides explains the last words of the verse: after death one cannot add on to one's philosophical knowledge. The two things requested are given in the next verse. However, the text lists three things.

ל:ח שָׁוְא וּדְבַר־כָּזָב הַרְחֵק מִמֶּנִּי רֵאשׁ* וָעֹשֶׁר אַל־תִּתֶּן־לִי הַטְרִיפֵנִי
לֶחֶם חֻקִּי : יא' במקום י'

30:8 KEEP DECEIT AND LIES FAR FROM ME; GIVE ME NEITHER
POVERTY NOR WEALTH; FEED ME MY DAILY BREAD

None of the commentators seem troubled by the discrepancy in the numbers. For
Gersonides, "deceit and lies," either due to the action of the imagination or to
erroneous information, impedes the philosopher's understanding of reality. "Neither
poverty nor wealth" suggests the proper kind of information that the intellect can
digest: not too little that ideas cannot be formed nor too much that ideas beyond
comprehension are formed. The literal meaning of the second clause seems to suggest
what philosophers mean by the "golden mean."

ל:ט פֶּן אֶשְׂבַּע וְכִחַשְׁתִּי וְאָמַרְתִּי מִי יְהֹוָה וּפֶן־אִוָּרֵשׁ וְגָנַבְתִּי וְתָפַשְׂתִּי
שֵׁם אֱלֹהָי :

30:9 LEST I BE SATIATED AND DENY AND SAY, "WHO IS GOD?"
OR LEST I BE IMPOVERISHED AND STEAL AND CATCH
THE NAME OF GOD

A word in the last clause presents us with a problem for understanding. *V'tafasti* (and I
will catch) makes more sense if applied to a thief than to the name of God. The verbal
root *tafas* is often used to mean "arrest." The *Targum* translates it as *vaachaleil* (and I
will profane). Rashi interprets *v'tafasti* to mean "I will become accustomed to
swearing falsely." Gersonides interprets the entire verse as a philosophical warning:
"Lest I be satiated" with incorrect ideas and "deny," thereby inventing a nonexistent
deity who will lead me to total apostasy, or "lest I be impoverished" and not conclude
my studies and go as far as is possible for a person to investigate. This would lead me
not to establish the necessity of there being a Deity who is the Cause of all existing
things. Such a deficiency on the thinker's part would be akin to "stealing" from God
all existing things. I would then think, as did Epicurus and those who followed him,
that there is no God. This would be "snatching" God's name by denying that there is
any reality behind it. This would be the worst thing of all. The simple meaning of the
verse seems to be making a kind of theological statement to those who have all things
and may feel that they don't need God. In their attempt to get something, those who
lack all things may act in such a manner that they "profane God," that is, they deny
their deepest commitments.

לﹴי אַל־תַּלְשֵׁן עֶבֶד אֶל־אדנו אֲדֹנָיו פֶּן־יְקַלֶּלְךָ וְאָשָׁמְתָּ:

30:10 DON'T SLANDER A SLAVE TO A MASTER, LEST HE CURSE
YOU AND YOU BE FOUND GUILTY.

Rashi explains that one should not pervert justice even against a wicked person lest that person cry out to God (the Master) and you be found guilty. Ibn Ezra relates the verse to informing on a runaway slave. In particular, he applies it to the non-Jewish slave who is escaping a master and wants to go to the Land of Israel and convert to Judaism. Gersonides explains that the "slave" refers to the Torah and "master" refers to God. One should not make a mistake in one's philosophical studies. Nor should one ascribe mistaken ideas as the result of the words of Torah, the "slave" of the Divine Master. To do so would be to "slander" the slave and to curse and be cursed by the Master.

לﹴיא דּוֹר אָבִיו יְקַלֵּל וְאֶת־אִמּוֹ לֹא יְבָרֵךְ:

30:11 THERE IS A GENERATION THAT CURSES ITS FATHER AND
DOES NOT BLESS ITS MOTHER.

This verse, as well as the next three verses, tells of four wicked generations. This may reflect the rubric employed by people to remember the proverbs. The generation described in this verse is particularly wicked, since they transgress the commandment of Exodus 21:17, which refers to the act of cursing one's father as a capital crime.

לﹴיב דּוֹר טָהוֹר בְּעֵינָיו וּמִצֹּאָתוֹ לֹא רֻחָץ:

30:12 THERE IS A GENERATION THAT IS PURE IN ITS OWN
EYES, BUT ITS FILTHINESS IS NOT WASHED AWAY.

Gersonides takes this verse as a philosophical parable: no matter what an investigator may think, if one proceeds on erroneous premises, one will inevitably be led to erroneous conclusions.

לﹴיג דּוֹר מָה־רָמוּ עֵינָיו וְעַפְעַפָּיו יִנָּשֵׂאוּ:

30:13 THERE IS A GENERATION: HOW LOFTY ARE THEIR EYES
AND HOW THEIR EYELIDS ARE ELEVATED.

The message is simple and straightforward: the author decries pride.

לֹ:יד דּוֹר חֲרָבוֹת שִׁנָּיו וּמַאֲכָלוֹת מְתַלְּעֹתָיו לֶאֱכֹל עֲנִיִּים מֵאֶרֶץ
וְאֶבְיוֹנִים מֵאָדָם:

30:14 THERE IS A GENERATION WHOSE TEETH ARE LIKE
SWORDS AND WHOSE JAWS ARE KNIVES TO DEVOUR
THE POOR FROM THE EARTH AND THE NEEDS FROM
THE PEOPLE.

This is a striking image of greed, something akin to the prophetic denunciation of
those "... who sold the righteous for silver and the needy for a pair of shoes" (Amos
2:6). Rashi says that *m'talotav* (jaws) refers to molar teeth. Adding to his assertion that
these verses are philosophical parables, Gersonides refers "teeth" and "jaws" to those
mistaken conclusions that do as much damage as gnawing teeth might.

לֹ:טו לַעֲלוּקָה שְׁתֵּי בָנוֹת הַב הַב שָׁלוֹשׁ הֵנָּה לֹא תִשְׂבַּעְנָה אַרְבַּע
לֹא־אָמְרוּ הוֹן:

30:15 THE LEECH HAS TWO DAUGHTERS, "GIVE," "GIVE";
THERE ARE THREE THINGS THAT ARE NEVER SATISFIED;
FOUR THAT NEVER SAY "ENOUGH."

The image of an insatiable insect drinking the blood of the animals with which it
comes in contact links this clause both with the verse that preceded it and with the
clauses that follow. Those who take advantage of the poor are "bloodsuckers" as
much as any insect or animal that drains the lifeblood of other living things. Rashi
takes "the leech" to refer to the netherworld and the two daughters to be *Gan Eden*
(paradise) and *Geihinom* (hell). Gersonides explains that "the leech" is a worm that
drinks a person's blood and is never satisfied.

לֹ:טז שְׁאוֹל וְעֹצֶר רָחַם אֶרֶץ לֹא־שָׂבְעָה מַּיִם וְאֵשׁ לֹא־אָמְרָה הוֹן:

30:16 THE NETHERWORLD, THE BARREN WOMB, A LAND
LACKING WATER, AND FIRE, IT SAYS NOT "ENOUGH."

Whether *Sheol* should be translated as "the grave" or "the netherworld" is difficult to
decide, as the context may not be altogether definitive. It may well be that the author
intended both meanings, for the one is the entrance to the other. Ibn Ezra takes *Sheol*
as "the grave" into which those who are punished by dying are cast before their time.
Gersonides' comment seems forced: he explains *Sheol* as the lowest kind of existing
things, as prime matter always and insatiably taking on one form after another. Ibn
Ezra explains "a land lacking water" as a land without rain, the lack of which causes
the famine that punishes the proud. He explains the "fire" as what comes down from
heaven to consume those who devour the poor.

ל:יז עַיִן תִּלְעַג לְאָב וְתָבֻז לִיקְּהַת־אֵם יִקְּרוּהָ עֹרְבֵי־נַחַל וְיֹאכְלוּהָ בְנֵי־נָשֶׁר:

30:17 THAT EYE THAT MOCKS A FATHER AND DESPISES A
MOTHER WILL BE PLUCKED OUT BY THE RAVENS OF
THE VALLEY, AND THE YOUNG EAGLES WILL EAT IT.

This is a chilling picture of punishment. It suggests an ancient concern for the feelings and values of parents by children. Rashi explains the last part of the verse: Cruel ravens will pluck out the eye from the unburied corpse, but they will neither eat it nor give it to their young. Kind eagles will not eat the eye, but will give it to their young.

ל:יח שְׁלֹשָׁה הֵמָּה נִפְלְאוּ מִמֶּנִּי וארבע וְאַרְבָּעָה לֹא יְדַעְתִּים:

30:18 THERE ARE THREE THINGS THAT ARE TOO WONDERFUL
FOR ME AND FOUR THINGS THAT I DO NOT KNOW:

Rashi understands *nifl'u* (too wonderful) as those things that are hidden from view as they pass by. Ibn Ezra takes the word simply as "hidden." Gersonides understands the first clause to refer to things that leave no impression and the last clause to those things that do.

ל:יט דֶּרֶךְ הַנֶּשֶׁר בַּשָּׁמַיִם דֶּרֶךְ נָחָשׁ עֲלֵי צוּר דֶּרֶךְ־אֲנִיָּה בְלֶב־יָם וְדֶרֶךְ גֶּבֶר בְּעַלְמָה:

30:19 THE WAY OF THE EAGLE IN THE HEAVENS; THE WAY OF A
SNAKE ON A ROCK; THE WAY OF A SHIP OUT INTO THE
SEA; THE WAY OF A MAN WITH A YOUNG WOMAN.

Gersonides thinks that knowing about these four things may be counterintuitive with one's sensibilities. When we watch any of these things, we may not be anticipating the action that is to follow. Watching an eagle fly is to know that the bird is seeking prey. Watching the snake is to know that the creature is about to strike and kill. Watching the ship as it moves further into the sea is to be aware of the possibility of its sinking. And watching the *almah* ("young woman," not *b'tulah*, "virgin") is to know that illicit sex is intended.

לב: כֵּן דֶּרֶךְ אִשָּׁה מְנָאָפֶת אָכְלָה וּמָחֲתָה פִיהָ וְאָמְרָה לֹא־פָעַלְתִּי אָוֶן:

30:20 THIS IS WHAT AN ADULTEROUS WOMAN DOES: SHE EATS, WIPES HER MOUTH, AND SAYS, "I HAVE DONE NOTHING WRONG."

While the author casts this verse as a woman, reflecting the male-centered culture of the time, the same might also be applied to adulterous men. Rashi understands "eating" as a euphemism for sexual intercourse. He and Ibn Ezra connect this verse to the last clause of the previous verse. Gersonides suggests that as a man should not get involved with an adulterous woman, so a person should not get involved with false ideas. As adultery affects the body, so error affects the mind.

לכא: תַּחַת שָׁלוֹשׁ רָגְזָה אֶרֶץ וְתַחַת אַרְבַּע לֹא־תוּכַל שְׂאֵת:

30:21 FOR THREE THINGS THE EARTH SHAKES, AND THERE ARE FOUR THAT IT CANNOT ENDURE:

The writer now uses a different word to establish a pattern of numbers. Previously, the author used the word *derech* (way). Now the author uses the words *tachat* (beneath, for). Following the same pattern that we have already seen, the next verse tells the reader what the "three" and "four" are.

לכב: תַּחַת־עֶבֶד כִּי יִמְלוֹךְ וְנָבָל כִּי יִשְׂבַּע־לָחֶם:

30:22 A SLAVE WHO BECOMES A RULER; A FOOL WHO HAS PLENTY OF BREAD.

The author seems to suggest that there are things that are what they are by nature. A slave should always be a slave. A fool should starve. What has seemed to be natural for some may not be natural for others. But kings have been brought down and those who are not fit for the job have been raised to power. Fools have eaten well, and wise persons have starved. But the world goes on as it has.

לכג: תַּחַת שְׂנוּאָה כִּי תִבָּעֵל וְשִׁפְחָה כִּי־תִירַשׁ גְּבִרְתָּהּ:

30:23 A WOMAN WHO IS HATED AND YET GETS MARRIED; A SERVANT GIRL WHO DISINHERITS HER MISTRESS.

This verse continues both the focus on women and the notion that some things are by nature the way they are and are troubling when they are not. In this context, the word *s'nuah* (hated) presents a problem, as does the word *tiba-eil* (married). It would seem that marriage should be about love. Therefore, why should one who is hated be married? It may be that here, *tiba-eil* has its original meaning of "having sex." If so, the same kind of reversal of expectations is present. One would expect that sex and love would go together. However, *s'nuah* has the same meaning here as it had in Genesis 29:31, where the condition of Leah is described as "hated," at least in comparison to Rachel. Perhaps if *tiba-eil* refers to marriage, then at a time when marriages were arranged and monetary considerations were an element of marriage, a woman might be "married" for reasons other than love. If *tiba-eil* refers to sex, then the author is suggesting that—as much of the human experience attests—love is only one reason for sex. We have seen the fear that the *sifchah* (maidservant) might disinherit her mistress in the response of mother Sarah to Hagar and Hagar's child Ishmael (Genesis 16:4ff. and Genesis 21:9, 10).

ל:כד אַרְבָּעָה הֵם קְטַנֵּי־אָרֶץ וְהֵמָּה חֲכָמִים מְחֻכָּמִים:

30:24 THERE ARE FOUR THINGS ON EARTH THAT, WHILE
SMALL, REFLECT GREAT WISDOM:

Our translation follows Ibn Ezra's interpretation of *chachamim m'chukamim* (of great wisdom) as reflecting the great wisdom of God. Gersonides takes the word "small" as a moral precept: the would-be philosopher should be modest, "small" in one's own eyes.

ל:כה הַנְּמָלִים עַם לֹא־עָז וַיָּכִינוּ בַקַּיִץ לַחְמָם:

30:25 THE ANTS AS A GROUP ARE NOT STRONG, YET THEY
PREPARE THEIR FOOD IN THE SUMMER.

Ants anticipate the rigors of winter while it is yet summer, preparing for what they will need while they can. Gersonides takes this verse and the next two verses as philosophical parables. From the ants, the would-be philosopher should learn to prepare oneself before beginning one's studies. From the rock-badgers, one should learn to investigate what one has the stamina and training to attempt. And from the locusts, one should learn to gain knowledge of ideas at the proper time.

ל:כו שְׁפַנִּים עַם לֹא־עָצוּם וַיָּשִׂימוּ בַסֶּלַע בֵּיתָם:

30:26 THE ROCK-BADGERS ARE NOT A POWERFUL GROUP,
YET THEY MAKE THEIR HOME IN A ROCK.

Ibn Ezra points out what is obvious: the rock-badgers make their homes in places where they can hide.

לֹ:כז מֶלֶךְ אֵין לָאַרְבֶּה וַיֵּצֵא חֹצֵץ כֻּלּוֹ:

30:27 LOCUSTS HAVE NO RULER, YET THEY ALL GO OUT
IN FORMATION.

The author sees the locusts as an insect army. Perhaps *melech* ("ruler"; literally, "king") should be translated here as "general." Locusts are presented as the host of the army in the midrashic parallel of the Ten Plagues to the "tactics of kings" (*Tanchuma, Bo* 4).

לֹ:כח שְׂמָמִית בְּיָדַיִם תְּתַפֵּשׂ וְהִיא בְּהֵיכְלֵי מֶלֶךְ:

30:28 YOU CAN PICK UP A GECKO WITH YOUR HANDS, YET IT
IS IN THE PALACE OF RULERS.

The word *s'mamit,* which we have translated as "gecko" (a kind of lizard), has been previously translated by others (including Rashi and Ibn Ezra) as "spider." Whether gecko or spider, the sense of the verse is the same: something that is common and available to everyone has the ability to travel in royal circles.

לֹ:כט שְׁלֹשָׁה הֵמָּה מֵיטִיבֵי צָעַד וְאַרְבָּעָה מֵיטִבֵי לָכֶת:

30:29 THERE ARE THREE THAT STRIDE WELL; THERE ARE FOUR
THAT WALK WELL:

With this verse, we return to the pattern of "three and four." Ibn Ezra explains *meitivei tzaad* (stride well) and *meitivei lachet* (walk well) as parallel statements that mean "walking with ease."

לֹ:ל לַיִשׁ גִּבּוֹר בַּבְּהֵמָה וְלֹא־יָשׁוּב מִפְּנֵי־כֹל:

30:30 THE LION IS THE STRONGEST BEAST AND TURNS AWAY
FROM NOTHING.

Rashi reads this verse and the next one as historical parables. The lion in this verse is Nebuchadnezzar. In verse 31, the *zarzir motnayim* is Persia, the goat is Greece, and the king is the king of Aram. Ibn Ezra takes the "lion" literally: the king of beasts is stronger than all other animals and therefore need not fear any of them.

לֹ:לא זַרְזִיר מָתְנַיִם אוֹ־תָיִשׁ וּמֶלֶךְ אַלְקוּם עִמּוֹ:

30:31 THE ROOSTER OR THE GOAT OR THE KING, AGAINST
WHOM THERE CAN BE NO UPRISING.

This is a difficult verse. The meaning of *zarzir motnayim* is not clear. *Motnayim* means "loins." What *zarzir* means, however, is uncertain. Some take it from the root *zaraz* (to be quick, hurry). Thus, the two words together would mean "with girded loins." What that might mean in context is unclear. According to the *Targum* and some modern scholars, the two words mean "rooster." Some others suggest "greyhound." To these options, Ibn Ezra adds "bees" and "the eagle." What is common to the last three definitions, as Ibn Ezra explains, is speed. He explains "the goat" as a matter of herding. Cattle will not pass in front of a goat. The "king" is explained by Ibn Ezra as being so righteous that no adversary can stand in front of him. Gersonides carries on the notion of speed in his explanation of the verse. The *zarzir* is the greyhound. The "goat" is one so quick that it can successfully attack animals stronger than itself. And the king who cannot be withstood is he who attacks with such speed that victory is always his.

לֹב אִם־נָבַלְתָּ בְהִתְנַשֵּׂא וְאִם־זַמּוֹתָ יָד לְפֶה:

30:32 IF YOU HAVE BEEN A FOOL TRYING TO PLAY THE PRINCE,
IF YOU SCHEMED, PUT YOUR HAND IN YOUR MOUTH.

This verse is a warning about moving beyond one's station in life. It is unclear whether *v'hitnasei*, "play the prince," is meant literally or as a metaphor to relate any attempt to move upward in status without reason. In any case, the writer's advice is "shut up!" The wrong words are dangerous, particularly to the wrong people. Rashi takes the first clause to mean that if you have used blasphemous language, you will undoubtedly be "picked up" for it. He takes the second clause to mean that if in your mind you intend to continue with such speech, "put your hand in your mouth" and shut up. Ibn Ezra takes the first clause to mean that if you acted badly when you ascended to royal rule and you have planned to continue with such behavior, just don't do it. Gersonides takes the entire verse to be a philosophical parable. If you have acted foolishly out of pride and depended on your own wisdom without reflecting on whether you are capable of reaching the truth in your investigation, then hold off and investigate still further.

לֹג כִּי מִיץ חָלָב יוֹצִיא חֶמְאָה וּמִיץ־אַף יוֹצִיא דָם וּמִיץ אַפַּיִם יוֹצִיא רִיב:

30:33 AS CHURNING MILK PRODUCES BUTTER, AND PUTTING
PRESSURE ON A NOSE PRODUCES BLOOD, SQUEEZING
ANGER PRODUCES A QUARREL.

Mitz in different contexts means "churning," "pressing," or "squeezing." The author makes the point that the same kind of action can have beneficial or deleterious effects. Pressure can be good or bad. The last clause contains a truth: there are people who are angry without reason. They are simply looking for an outlet for their anger. Such people "squeeze" their own anger, holding it within themselves until they find an excuse to release it. They are "just looking for a fight."

The Separate Intelligences (or Intellects)

"Separate intelligences" or "intellects" play a particular role in the *Guide for the Perplexed* of Maimonides. The way he uses the term in the *Guide* suggests a number of principles for the reader to understand. Maimonides (*Guide* 2:6) calls "angels" what Aristotle called "separate intellects." However, he says, in the time of Aristotle, while the number of spheres was not clear, the movement of the spheres was explained by separate intellects (*Guide* 2:4). Later philosophers limited the number of spheres to ten and concluded that there were ten separate intellects. The last separate intellect was the active intellect; it was the impetus to thought and its ultimate content (*Guide* 2:4). Ever active, the active intellect would always have an effect on those properly prepared (*Guide* 2:18). If this is the case, then it is also a source of prophecy (*Guide* 2:36). What remains unanswered is how God withholds prophecy (*Guide* 2:32).

For Gersonides, Maimonides' successor, the active intellect was the impetus and source of thought. Moreover, it knew all things in an order and endowed sublunar nature with intelligence and purpose. In his commentary to the Torah (on Genesis 48:16), Gersonides notes that it was "the Angel who redeems me from all evil!"

Emanation

Emanation, as a theory, sought to explain how, from an immaterial Deity, a material world arose. This theory was first fully developed in the thought of Plotinus (205–270 C.E.). For him, being flows of necessity from a simple and ineffable source, the One, to an idea structure, intelligence *(nous)*, to the universal soul, to unformed matter, which then receives forms. Proclus (410–485 C.E.) further developed the four steps of Plotinus by subdividing them to make the process more continuous. Though Plotinus used the image of light illuminating darkness, others who followed him used the image of water cascading down a fountain, or of an "overflow."

Emanationism passed into the thinking of some of the religious philosophers of the medieval period, partly due to the erroneous identification of one of Plotinus's books as *The Theology of Aristotle*. Hence, some notions that were accepted as Aristotelian were really those of Plotinus and his followers. The notion of "separate intellects" as emanating from God in an eternal chain is one of them.

For a discussion of emanationism among the mystics, readers can refer to the *Sephirot of the Zohar* (see Gershom Scholem, *Major Trends in Jewish Mysticism* [New York: Schocken Books, 1974], 216).

Epicurus

Epicurus, whose school of thought became known as Epicureanism, was born on the island of Samos in 341 B.C.E. to Athenian parents. He was a prolific writer whose works became synonymous with hedonistic ethics. According to Epicurus, the aim of philosophy is for humans to lead a happy life. Sciences like music, geometry, arithmetic, and astronomy are without value. Some knowledge of logic is necessary to furnish us with a criterion of knowledge. We require physics in order to understand the natural causes of things. Such knowledge is useful because it frees us from the fear of gods, natural phenomena, and death. A study of human nature will teach us what to desire and what to avoid. However, the main thing, according to Epicurus, is to understand that all things are produced by natural—and not supernatural—causes.

Nebuchadnezzar

Sometimes referred to as Nebuchadrezzar, Nebuchadnezzar was king of Babylon and lived from 605 to 562 B.C.E. He captured Jerusalem, destroyed the Temple, and exiled the masses.

Agur, the Son of Jakeh

Both are non-Jewish names which do not elsewhere occur in the Bible. Ibn Ezra, therefore, suggests that Agur was a sage who lived in Solomon's time, a non-Israelite similar to Balaam or Job, neither of whom was identified as a Jew. The Midrash, however, wanting to claim the unified authorship of Solomon for the whole Book, has recourse to an ingenious, if unconvincing etymology: Agur is really Solomon because the latter girt his loins *(ogar)* with wisdom; he is called Bin Jakeh because he was free *(noki)* from all sin; and the words, the burden, are added because he bore the yoke of God.

W. Gunther Plaut, *The Book of Proverbs: A Commentary* (New York: UAHC Press, 1961), 299

Gan Eden *(Paradise) and* Geihinom *(Hell)*

The Jewish version of "hell," *Geihinom,* literally refers to a valley south of Jerusalem on one of the borders between the territories of Judah and Benjamin. (Cf. Josh. 15:8; 18:16.) During the time of the monarchy it was a site associated with a cult that burned children. Jeremiah condemned the practice. In the rabbinic period, the name is used to refer to the place of torment reserved for the wicked after death. It stands in contradistinction to *Gan Eden,* the "Garden of Eden," which, in rabbinic literature, became known as the place of reward for the righteous. In the Bible, these two names never connote the abode of souls after death. Yet, in rabbinic literature, such references abound: in *Pesachim* 54a, *Geihinom* and *Gan Eden* existed even before the world was created; *Geihinom* is at the left hand of God and *Gan Eden* at God's right in the *midrash* to Psalms 50:12.

Leonard Kravitz and Kerry M. Olitzky, *Pirke Avot: A Modern Commentary on Jewish Ethics* (New York: UAHC Press, 1993), 91

GLEANINGS

From Spiritual to Ethical

Now that the hunger of soul of our people is more and more evident, we need to resist the false dichotomy of the spiritual and the ethical. More than resist, we need to build the bridge for our people between Jewish spirituality (which I prefer to call Jewish soulfulness) and the life of mitzvot with its heavy emphasis on Jewish ethics. In the tradition of Leo Baeck we need to teach our people that Jewishly experienced mystery is inseparable from commandment. God's embrace returns us to our duties in the world. In the lives of our prophets religious experience and a passion for justice went hand in hand. Amos had the religious experience of a vision of God, but that vision was of God standing with a plumb line to measure whether his society was just or unjust.

God's presence in our time comes not in a vision, but most significantly, rather, in an inner experience of both stillness and voice. The stillness steadies and affirms us; reassured by God's love we are enabled to care again about others and their rights. The voice with quiet certainty may direct us to a specific task or sometimes it convulsively breaks forth from a depth deeper than ourselves, commanding us that despite everything we live a life that counts for good. In God's inner presence as stillness and voice we are affirmed, we are commanded, we are sent back to our duties as persons and society. To experience God and to hate injustice are, Jewishly speaking, linked experiences. We need to perform the marriage of Jewish spirituality and social action. Jewish soulfulness offers us no escape from responsibility. God's embrace returns us to our duties in the world.

Norman D. Hirsch, "Contemporary Challenges to Liberal Judaism I," *CCAR Yearbook* 100 (1990): 41

The Spirituality of Experience

Spirituality is a mode of living in the awareness of the divine presence, the sacred. It is a recognition of the transcendent, an apprehension of life as a web of interconnections. It doesn't explain the mystery of life; it makes us aware of it. The spiritual life is rooted in experience, encounters with the self, with others and the world. We don't acquire spirituality. We don't go after it; we dwell on it. Spirituality isn't a goal; it's a path. It is a realization that where we are is no coincidence—that we are in the places we inhabit, with the people we meet, not by mere accident, but to redeem the holy sparks that reside there.

Sandy E. Sasso, "The Spark and the Fire," in *Living Words III: Best High Holiday Sermons of 5761*
(Newton Upper Falls, Mass.: Jewish Family and Life, 2001), 145

CHAPTER THIRTY-ONE

לא:א דִּבְרֵי לְמוּאֵל מֶלֶךְ מַשָּׂא אֲשֶׁר־יִסְּרַתּוּ אִמּוֹ:

31:1 THE WORDS OF LEMUEL THE KING, WITH WHICH HIS
MOTHER CORRECTED HIM.

This verse presents us with a number of problems. First, it is not clear who King
Lemuel is. Rashi brings clarification from Jewish tradition: Lemuel is another name for
King Solomon. For Rashi, Lemuel is interpreted as *l'mu* (toward) and *El* (God). Thus,
King Solomon directed himself toward God, in a manner pleasing to God. Perhaps the
author of the Book of Proverbs may be an additional individual, even if Solomon is
somehow related to the content. Perhaps the book was edited by a group nominally
related to Solomon. Since the book is part of the wider genre of wisdom literature, it
is probable that it was composed later than the period of Solomon—though individual
texts may relate to the period of his life. Like the case with other books, perhaps
Proverbs was attributed to Solomon for it to gain immediate acceptance. The use of
bar (son) and *b'ri* (my son) in verse 2 shows the influence of Aramaic and therefore
suggests its composition from a later period of time. Ibn Ezra, whom we might have
expected to take a more critical approach to the book's authorship, suggests that
"mother" refers to Solomon's mother Bathsheba, who wanted her son to study
wisdom and to distance himself from wine and women, which—according to classic
Judaism—are the causes of sin and transgression. Like Rashi, Gersonides also takes
Lemuel as a reference to Solomon. Gersonides understands Solomon's mother to
have instructed him to learn the notions that he himself had developed.

לא:ב מַה־בְּרִי וּמַה־בַּר־בִּטְנִי וּמֶה בַּר־נְדָרָי:

31:2 WHAT, MY CHILD? WHAT, CHILD OF MY WOMB? WHAT,
CHILD OF MY VOWS?

Rashi relates this verse to the time of Solomon's marriage to the daughter of Pharaoh
(I Kings 3:1). He reports the midrash that suggests the marriage was conducted at the
same time as was the dedication of the Temple (I Kings 8:65). At the time, Solomon's
wife brought all kinds of musical instruments into the Temple, which disturbed
Solomon's sleep. This caused him to oversleep the following day, which consequently
delayed the morning sacrifice. In Rashi's narration of the story, Solomon's mother,
Bathsheba, complained to him that since everyone knew that David had been
righteous, if Solomon did not turn out well, people would blame her. Moreover,

Bathsheba claimed to have taken extraordinary measures, even in the last days of her pregnancy, to insure that her son would be active and handsome. Unlike the other wives of David, who wished that their children be fit to rule as a king, she had wished that her unborn child would become a great Torah scholar. Such instruction will assist her warning in the next verse.

לא:ג אַל־תִּתֵּן לַנָּשִׁים חֵילֶךָ וּדְרָכֶיךָ לַמְחוֹת מְלָכִין:

31:3 DON'T GIVE YOUR STRENGTH TO WOMEN NOR YOUR
WAYS TO THAT WHICH WIPES OUT KINGS.

The last word *melachin* (kings) has an Aramaic ending. This again suggests a date of composition considerably later than the period of Solomon. However, the message of the first clause is clear. The intent of the second clause becomes clear as well when we remember that *derech* (way) has a sexual meaning, as noted in the phrase "the way of a man with a young woman" (30:19). Sex is always a temptation.

לא:ד אַל לַמְלָכִים לְמוֹאֵל אַל לַמְלָכִים שְׁתוֹ־יָיִן וּלְרוֹזְנִים אוֹ אֵי שֵׁכָר:

31:4 KINGS, O LEMUEL, KINGS SHOULD NOT DRINK
WINE, AND PRINCES SHOULD NOT SAY, "WHERE IS
STRONG DRINK?"

The advice given to those in the royal family should be taken by all readers. The use of liquor impairs judgment. This is a particularly important caution for those who are in positions to make decisions that influence the life of others.

לא:ה פֶּן־יִשְׁתֶּה וְיִשְׁכַּח מְחֻקָּק וִישַׁנֶּה דִּין כָּל־בְּנֵי־עֹנִי:

31:5 LEST ONE DRINK AND FORGET THE LAW AND SUBVERT
THE CASE OF ANY WHO ARE AFFLICTED.

The prophet Amos, in his condemnation of the sins of those leaders who took advantage of the poor, made a connection between drinking and the lack of moral sense when he cried out against those who "...lay themselves down upon clothes laid in pledge by every altar, and they drink the wine of the condemned in the House of God" (Amos 2:8). We have learned that power itself is a sufficient intoxicant to obliterate the moral sense of those in power.

לא:ו תְּנוּ־שֵׁכָר לְאוֹבֵד וְיַיִן לְמָרֵי נָפֶשׁ׃

31:6 Give strong drink to those about to perish and wine to those who have become embittered.

Far better it would be for those who, as Rashi suggests, are "about to perish" at the hands of the wicked and for those for whom wine dulls the pain of their poverty to have a fair share of the wealth of their society. Justice is better than wine or whiskey.

לא:ז יִשְׁתֶּה וְיִשְׁכַּח רִישׁוֹ וַעֲמָלוֹ לֹא יִזְכָּר־עוֹד׃

31:7 Let them drink and forget their poverty and remember their misery no more.

In order to be sensitive to gender specificity, we have translated the verse in the plural. Waking up from a drunken sleep, the poor person will be as poor as before. Nothing will be changed. Were these two verses to stand alone, we might think that all the problem of poverty requires is some means of distracting the poor from their poverty. It is precisely because the author included the following two verses that we may say that the author of Proverbs affirms the teaching of the Torah and the prophets.

לא:ח פְּתַח־פִּיךָ לְאִלֵּם אֶל־דִּין כָּל־בְּנֵי חֲלוֹף׃

31:8 Open your mouth for those who can't speak, for the case of everyone who is destined for destruction.

Our translation of *b'nei chalof* as "destined for destruction" follows Ibn Ezra. Rashi takes the words to refer to orphans bereft of help. Gersonides takes the words to refer to litigants unable to present their case properly.

לא:ט פְּתַח־פִּיךָ שְׁפָט־צֶדֶק וְדִין עָנִי וְאֶבְיוֹן׃

31:9 Open your mouth, judge righteously, and present the case of the poor and the needy.

This verse continues the notions set forth in the previous verse: the writer asks the reader to speak for those who are unable to do so, for the poor and downtrodden who are unable to present their case in court. Since the writer repeats the first two words of the prior verse, the reader can assume that "the poor and the needy" are those meant by the *b'nei chalof* of that verse.

לא:י אֵשֶׁת־חַיִל מִי יִמְצָא וְרָחֹק מִפְּנִינִים מִכְרָהּ:

31:10 A WORTHY WOMAN WHO CAN FIND? HER VALUE IS FAR
BEYOND THAT OF PEARLS OF CORAL.

This verse and those that follow to the end of the chapter have become the traditional text spoken by a husband to his wife on the Sabbath eve. *P'ninim* (pearls of coral) was translated as rubies in the past. Ibn Ezra's understanding of the verse seems somewhat crass: he takes *eishet chayil* (a worthy woman) as that woman who can acquire men by her wisdom. Gersonides continues Plato's designation of "Matter of female and Form as the male" (*Guide for the Perplexed* 1:17) in his interpretation of the verse: the *eishet chayil* is that matter that properly serves the intellect so that it can achieve perfection. This midrash is somewhat forced and also demeaning to women.

לא:יא בָּטַח בָּהּ לֵב בַּעְלָהּ וְשָׁלָל לֹא יֶחְסָר:

31:11 HER HUSBAND'S MIND IS SET AT EASE; HE DOES NOT
LACK FOR GAIN.

What is striking about this verse and the verses that follow is the portrayal of the wife as involved in manifold activities. It almost seems as if she is the one who conducts all the business. One might say that the city has given this woman the kind of freedom and opportunity that she could not have had in rural areas. Ibn Ezra makes the point that because this exemplary wife has been able to acquire so much, "her husband's mind is set at ease." Gersonides continues his philosophical midrash: the "wife" is that sense perception that will provide proper material for the intellect.

לא:יב גְּמָלַתְהוּ טוֹב וְלֹא־רָע כֹּל יְמֵי חַיֶּיהָ:

31:12 SHE TREATS HIM WELL AND NOT BADLY ALL THE DAYS
OF HER LIFE.

Reflecting on the image of woman commonly found in the Book of Proverbs, we can better understand why the author, before concluding the volume, felt it necessary to praise a wife who consistently acted properly.

לא:יג דָּרְשָׁה צֶמֶר וּפִשְׁתִּים וַתַּעַשׂ בְּחֵפֶץ כַּפֶּיהָ:

31:13 SHE SEEKS OUT WOOL AND FLAX AND WORKS WILLINGLY
WITH HER HANDS.

One wonders whether the writer is contrasting this wondrous woman with those spouses who may be unwilling to do physical labor. Ibn Ezra understands the second clause to suggest that this woman is so eager to work that it is as if her very hands have a mind of their own and desire to be employed. "Wool and flax" are understood by Gersonides to be aspects of sense perceptions as they are interpreted by the intellect.

לא:יד הָיְתָה כָּאֳנִיּוֹת סוֹחֵר מִמֶּרְחָק תָּבִיא לַחְמָהּ:

31:14 SHE IS LIKE THE MERCHANT SHIPS, BRINGING HER
BREAD FROM AFAR.

We have an unintended picture of commerce as it functioned during the life of the writer or, at least, from the time period from which this collection of verses emerges. This is maritime commerce: ships are coming from various ports of the Mediterranean to bring goods to and from the Land of Israel. This kind of commerce must have been so common that the writer is able to use it as a simile for the behavior of the idealized spouse.

לא:טו וַתָּקָם בְּעוֹד לַיְלָה וַתִּתֵּן טֶרֶף לְבֵיתָהּ וְחֹק לְנַעֲרֹתֶיהָ:

31:15 SHE GETS UP WHILE IT IS STILL DARK AND GIVES FOOD
TO HER HOUSEHOLD AND A PORTION TO HER MAIDS.

Rashi explains *chok* (portion) as a designated amount. Our translation of *lailah* (literally, "night") as "while it is still dark" follows Ibn Ezra's view that the woman under discussion arises before dawn. One gets the feeling while reading this verse that while this female paragon of virtue gets up early in the morning to do her work, her husband remains in bed snoring! Gersonides takes the early rising as a metaphor for that bodily preparation that ought to precede intellectual preparation. He refers the reader to *Sefer Hachush v'Hamuchash* (Sense and Sensation), one of Aritstotle's smaller psychological treatises, commented on by Averroës. The text and the commentary were translated by Moses ibn Tibbon. Thus, a book written by an ancient Greek philosopher, commented on in Arabic by a Muslim, translated into Hebrew by a Jew—along with the commentary—was recommended by someone commenting on an ancient Hebrew book of wisdom. Few other statements could encapsulate the cultural world of Gersonides.

לא:טז זָמְמָה שָׂדֶה וַתִּקָּחֵהוּ מִפְּרִי כַפֶּיהָ נטע נָטְעָה כָּרֶם:

31:16 SHE CONSIDERS A FIELD AND BUYS IT, AND FROM THE
FRUIT OF HER HANDS, SHE PLANTS A VINEYARD.

We should once again take note of the woman as a person who engages in legal activity, who is able to plan and buy, and to use the money that she has accumulated ("the fruit of her hands") to buy and plant a vineyard. The power of a woman that is manifest in this set of verses became diminished over time. However, we must note again that the social organization of the city gave both freedom and power to women. *Zam'mah* (she considers) is an interesting word. It often has the meaning of planning something for evil (see Deuteronomy 19:19).

לא:יז חָגְרָה בְעוֹז מָתְנֶיהָ וַתְּאַמֵּץ זְרֹעוֹתֶיהָ:

31:17 SHE GIRDS HER LOINS WITH STRENGTH AND TOUGHENS HER ARMS.

The woman under discussion prepares herself for future business activities, as if she were preparing for combat, putting on armor and exercising her arms.

לא:יח טָעֲמָה כִּי־טוֹב סַחְרָהּ לֹא־יִכְבֶּה בליל בַלַּיְלָה נֵרָהּ:

31:18 SHE KNOWS THAT HER MERCHANDISE IS GOOD, AND HER LAMP DOES NOT GO OUT AT NIGHT.

Taamah (literally, "tastes") is translated here as "knows." This suggests that she "knows" her merchandise, like any good merchant. If she were selling fruit, she would have tasted it. Ibn Ezra suggests that since she constantly checks her merchandise, "her lamp does not go out at night."

לא:יט יָדֶיהָ שִׁלְּחָה בַכִּישׁוֹר וְכַפֶּיהָ תָּמְכוּ פָלֶךְ:

31:19 SHE SENDS HER HANDS TO THE DISTAFF, AND HER HANDS HOLD THE SPINDLE.

The words *kishor* and *pelech* (which occurs here as *falech* for grammatical reasons) are technical terms for parts of the spinning wheel. The first is the small disk at the lower end of the distaff. This causes it to spin and hence is translated here as "distaff." The second is the spindle itself. Rashi translates the words into Old French, which suggests his readers knew the language and the devices described. The author's point is that such a woman is always busy; she wastes no time. And this is to be considered virtuous.

לא:כ כַּפָּהּ פָּרְשָׂה לֶעָנִי וְיָדֶיהָ שִׁלְּחָה לָאֶבְיוֹן:

31:20 SHE STRETCHES OUT HER PALM TO THE POOR AND HER HANDS TO THE NEEDY.

Not only does this woman work all the time, but she also has heart: she gives alms to the poor and sustains the needy. She looks out for those outside the house as she cares for those within.

לא:כא לֹא־תִירָא לְבֵיתָהּ מִשָּׁלֶג כִּי כָל־בֵּיתָהּ לָבֻשׁ שָׁנִים:

31:21 SHE DOES NOT FEAR THE SNOW FOR HER HOUSEHOLD,
FOR ALL OF THEM ARE CLOTHED IN SCARLET.

Rashi understands "scarlet" as dyed garments. Ibn Ezra specifies "household" to mean all of its members. As might be expected, Gersonides understands the garments described as metaphors for proper ethical qualities.

לא:כב מַרְבַדִּים עָשְׂתָה־לָּהּ שֵׁשׁ וְאַרְגָּמָן לְבוּשָׁהּ:

31:22 SHE MADE COVERLETS FOR HERSELF; HER CLOTHING IS
FINE LINEN AND PURPLE.

This woman is well dressed. Such a focus on dress is an aspect of the city life that she enjoys.

לא:כג נוֹדָע בַּשְּׁעָרִים בַּעְלָהּ בְּשִׁבְתּוֹ עִם־זִקְנֵי־אָרֶץ:

31:23 HER HUSBAND IS KNOWN IN THE GATES WHEN HE SITS
WITH THE ELDERS OF THE LAND.

We would interpret this verse as an affirmation of the woman. Her husband becomes well-known as a result of her actions. However, according to Rashi, her husband gains acclaim by virtue of the clothes that his wife has made for him. For Gersonides, humans gain acclaim by virtue of the knowledge that they have accumulated.

לא:כד סָדִין עָשְׂתָה וַתִּמְכֹּר וַחֲגוֹר נָתְנָה לַכְּנַעֲנִי:

31:24 SHE MAKES A CHEMISE AND SELLS IT, AND DELIVERS
GIRDLES TO THE MERCHANT.

Sadin was some kind of vest or undergarment worn by women. We have translated it as "chemise." It may even have been that this ideal woman was an entrepreneur who owned a lingerie business.

לא:כה עֹז־וְהָדָר לְבוּשָׁהּ וַתִּשְׂחַק לְיוֹם אַחֲרוֹן:

31:25 STRENGTH AND HONOR ARE HER GARMENT, AND SHE
WILL LAUGH AT A FUTURE DAY.

For Rashi, the words *yom acharon* (literally, "last day") refer to the woman's day of death. She will die happy, since she knows that she leaves behind a good name. For Ibn Ezra, the words refer to the woman's old age, in which she will be able to laugh, since she lacked nothing, having planned well for it. For Gersonides, the words refer to the day of death, which the intellect need not fear, having achieved perfection. Unwilling to decide among the commentators, we have translated *yom acharon* as "future day."

לא:כו פִּיהָ פָּתְחָה בְחָכְמָה וְתוֹרַת־חֶסֶד עַל־לְשׁוֹנָהּ:

31:26 SHE OPENS HER MOUTH WITH WISDOM, AND THE INSTRUCTION OF CONTINUOUS LOVE IS ON HER TONGUE.

Gersonides suggests that from "wisdom," the intellect can derive the principles and the "instruction of continuous love" by which God directs all existing things.

לא:כז צוֹפִיָּה הֲלִיכוֹת בֵּיתָהּ וְלֶחֶם עַצְלוּת לֹא תֹאכֵל:

31:27 SHE LOOKS WELL TO THE WAYS OF HER HOUSEHOLD AND HAS NEVER EATEN THE BREAD OF IDLENESS.

From what has been described, this ideal woman has never had a moment to be idle. Rashi explains that *tzofiyah* (looks well) means that the woman has paid attention to the needs of the members of the household, instructing them to act with care and with modesty.

לא:כח קָמוּ בָנֶיהָ וַיְאַשְּׁרוּהָ בַּעְלָהּ וַיְהַלְלָהּ:

31:28 HER CHILDREN ARISE AND MAKE HER HAPPY, AND HER HUSBAND PRAISES HER.

The *Targum* translates *va-y'ashruha* (make her happy) as *vihavun lah tuva* (give her good, ascribe good to her). This may underlie the familiar translation of the word as "call her blessed." Ibn Ezra notes that her children have even awakened early to praise their mother, because she has spent the night at work. The next verse contains the praise of husband and children.

לא:כט רַבּוֹת בָּנוֹת עָשׂוּ חָיִל וְאַתְּ עָלִית עַל־כֻּלָּנָה:

31:29 [THEY SAY,] "MANY WOMEN HAVE DONE WELL, BUT YOU HAVE SURPASSED THEM ALL."

The term *banot* (daughters) is used here rather than *nashim* (women). Perhaps it is more of a term of endearment.

לא:ל שֶׁקֶר הַחֵן וְהֶבֶל הַיֹּפִי אִשָּׁה יִרְאַת־יְהוָה הִיא תִתְהַלָּל:

31:30 GRACE IS DECEITFUL AND BEAUTY IS VAIN, BUT A
WOMAN WHO FEARS GOD IS TO BE PRAISED.

Since physical beauty is often praised, the author feels that it is necessary to praise
moral beauty. Although Rashi suggests that physical beauty is not to be praised, such
beauty was praised in the troubadour poetry of his time and place. The poetry of the
Spanish Jewish poets is replete with praise of women's beauty. According to a strange
passage in *Midrash Taanit* 4:8, on the fifteenth of Av and on the Day of Atonement,
"the daughters of Jerusalem would go forth to dance in the vineyards" to attract
potential husbands, and they would quote this verse.

לא:לא תְּנוּ־לָהּ מִפְּרִי יָדֶיהָ וִיהַלְלוּהָ בַשְּׁעָרִים מַעֲשֶׂיהָ:

31:31 GIVE HER THE FRUIT OF HER HANDS, AND LET HER
DEED PRAISE HER IN THE GATES.

At the end of his commentary, Rashi presents a midrash on the verses dealing with the
eishet chayil (woman of valor). The woman stands for Torah. Happy is the person who
is worthy of finding her/it. "He does not lack for gain" either in this world or in the
next. "She seeks out wool and flax" means one who studies the Torah, Mishnah, and
the midrash and repeats what one studies. "She is like the merchant ships": the Torah
brings blessing and sustenance to its students. "She gets up while it is still dark": those
who study Torah arise early in the morning. "Gives food to her household": the
teacher apportions what students should learn. "She considers a field and buys it":
the Torah, with design, controls Esau, the man of the field. "And buys it" (literally,
"takes it") refers to taking Esau from the world to destroy him. "She plants a
vineyard": the Torah plants Israel in the world-to-come. "She knows" (literally,
"tastes"): the Torah knows its word. "Her lamp does not go out at night" refers in this
interpretation to the final plague in Egypt; the firstborn Egyptians were smitten and
Israel was protected during the night visit of the Angel of Death. "She does not fear
the snow": the Torah protects from the snow and from the fire with which the wicked
will be punished. "All of them are clothed in scarlet" refers to the blood of the
covenant of circumcision. "She looks well to the ways of her household" means that
the Torah teaches the correct way to keep far from transgression. "Her children
arise": these are the students of Torah. "Her husband" is the Holy One of Blessing.
"Grace is deceitful and beauty is vain" refers to idolatry and what is associated with it.
"Give her" refers to the world-to-come. "The fruit of her hands" means the glory,
greatness, power, and dominion due to the Torah.

315

Aramaic

Aramaic is a Semitic language known since the ninth century B.C.E. as the speech of the Aramaeans and adopted as speech by various non-Aramaean peoples, including the Jews after the Babylonian captivity. The Talmud is written in Aramaic and Hebrew. The *Kaddish* is written in Aramaic as well. Aramaic is found in several other places in the *Tanach,* including the Book of Daniel.

Averroës (Ibn Rushd)

Averroës or Ibn Rushd (1126–1198) was the foremost figure in the Islamic philosophical world. He was born in Cordoba to the *qadi* (or chief judge) of the area. Averroës mastered vast areas of knowledge and became a *qadi,* a physician, a scientist, and a philosopher. It is as a defender of the rational approach to religion and as a commentator on Aristotle that he is best known as a philosopher. Ibn Rushd's *The Incoherence of the Incoherence,* a response to Al-Ghazali's *The Incoherence of the Philosophers,* passed throughout the medieval world and was familiar to the Jewish commentators on Maimonides' *Guide for the Perplexed.* Averroës' commentaries in Latin translation provided the texts for Christian scholastic philosophy and gained him the title of "the Commentator." Averroës also wrote a commentary on Plato's *Republic.* Averroës played the same role in Islam as did Maimonides in Judaism and Thomas Aquinas in Christianity. Perhaps Maimonides was influenced by his fellow Cordoban. It is clear that he saw some of Averroës' commentaries on Aristotle. It is also clear that the two had much in common, including having their philosophic work subject to condemnation.

Moses ibn Tibbon

Born in Grenada in 1150, Moses ibn Tibbon settled in Lunel and died in Marseilles in 1230. A physician as well as a philosopher, Moses ibn Tibbon translated Maimonides' *Guide for the Perplexed* from Arabic to Hebrew. He consulted with Maimonides on the translation, which he completed in 1190. He also translated "The Essay of Resurrection" and "The Commentary on *Avot,*" as well as its introduction, "The Eight Chapters." Ibn Tibbon wrote commentaries on the entire Bible, of which only some portions are extant: a philosophical treatise on Genesis 1:9 called *Maamar Yikavu HaMayim* (an essay on "Let the waters be gathered"); a philosophical commentary on Ecclesiastes; and a philosophical commentary on Song of Songs. Ibn Tibbon was an enthusiastic follower of Maimonides' allegorical method, seeing the biblical narratives as *m'shalim* (proverbs) and the mitzvot as *hanhagot* (directions for behavior). His translation of the *Guide for the Perplexed* was "blamed" for spreading the ideas of Maimonides.

GLEANINGS

A Woman of Valor

A good wife / who can find her
she is worth far more than rubies
she brings good and not harm
all the days of her life
she girds herself with strength
and finds her trades profitable
wise counsel is on her tongue
and her home never suffers for warmth
she stretches her hands to the poor
reaches her arms to the needy
all her friends praise her
her family blesses her
she is known at the gates
as she sits with the elders
dignity, honor are her garb
she smiles at the future.

Susan Grossman, "eshet chayil—A Woman of Valor," in Ron H. Isaacs and Kerry M. Olitzky,
A Jewish Mourner's Handbook (Hoboken, N.J.: KTAV Publishing House, 1991), 78

The following translation takes the same text from Proverbs and modifies it for use by
a woman in praise of her husband. It is also by Rabbi Susan Grossman.

A good man who can find him
he is worth far more than rubies
all who trust in him
never lack for gain
he shares the household duties
and sets a goodly example
he seeks a satisfying job
and braces his arms for work
he opens his mouth with wisdom
he speaks with love and kindness
his justice brings him praises
he raises the poor, lowers the haughty.

Ibid.

Sometimes, their children are invited to add:

These two indeed do worthily
true leaders in Zion
give them their due credit
let their works praise them at the gates.

Ibid., 79

The Feminist Challenge

What makes feminism a compelling question for all varieties of Judaism is that it provides a paradigm for illustrating the interrelation of the chronic problems of Judaism in modernity. What makes it a gift and an opportunity, rather than simply a challenge, is that the question is posed, not by people who wish to destroy or abandon Judaism, but by people of good will who are committed to re-forming authentic Jewish answers. What, then, does Reform Judaism stand to gain from feminism? First of all, it gains feminist values—an emphasis on empowerment and competence for everyone, as opposed to hierarchies of knowledge and power—and, hence, a better education for every Jew. Second, it gains an ethics of caring based upon relation and its obligations that integrates public and private and communal and personal, and extends also to obligations to the larger society and the natural environment. An illustration of this world would be the predominant work ethic of women rabbis that sees small as beautiful, and that refuses to sacrifice the needs of family to the needs of the congregation.... Third, it gains a reverence for the body and, hence, inclusion of our body-experience in our religious expression. Examples of these would be the new life-cycle rituals that women have been creating—rituals that sanctify birth and pregnancy, that sanctify sad experiences such as miscarriage, and that sanctify the experiences of aging.

The second category of things that Reform Judaism stands to gain from feminism, I've called feminist Torah. And one of those would be an extended canon. My friend, Lynn Gotlieb, says that if there are what we call *bubbe meises* and that those are traditional stories of women, we ought to recognize that most of what we're studying are *zeide meises*. So what I would like to do is to add the *bubbe meises* to the *zeide meises*. A second thing that I think we would gain would be a new concern with hermeneutics. We would have to ask all over again how we can have a conversation with texts from whose world we are alienated or absent. And, third, is a renewed interest in theology. Are there ways to talk about God and our relationship with God that do not mirror a patriarchal social structure? Are there ways to understand holiness that do not locate the antithesis of holiness in woman and the qualities associated with her?

Rachel Adler, "Contemporary Challenges to Liberal Judaism II," *CCAR Yearbook* 100 (1990): 45–46

Performing Rituals

There is a combination of domesticity and danger when one thinks of performing rituals. My childhood kitchen and dining room were the locales of the first ceremonies I witnessed. Over the dining room table the Sabbath candles would be lit by mother and grandmothers. Each had her own candlesticks, brought, in my grandmothers' case, from Russia. The tabletop would be flickering with flame. The women closed their eyes with the traditional prayer, then made three concentric circles, the first fanning the face, the next reaching out, the third a wide encompassing movement. My mother's movement was different, a bringing in of the circle, closer and closer. I could hear whispering as private wishes were added to the traditional prayers.

If I asked what they wished my mother, shy in her life, would simply say it was for the family. Then, at a later time, she would add, "I'm bringing in the light." My Big Baba, the taller of my two grandmothers, would say, *fon mir, tsu dir, tsu di ganze velt*—from me, to you, to the whole world. Both sets of circles ordered my life for a long time.

E. M. Broner, *Bringing Home the Light: A Jewish Woman's Handbook of Rituals*
(San Francisco: Council Oak Books, 1999), 1

Gefilte Fishing

There is no fish called gefilte. Carp, tuna, salmon, bass, but no gefilte. Fishing for gefilte fish is foolish. It betrays an ignorance about fish and about life. It is like mistaking the moon's reflection for the moon itself. It is like eating the menu and imagining it to be the meal. We may become full, but we are never nourished.

Gefilte fish is stuffed fish. Fishing for gefilte fish is stuffing oneself full of nonsense. And we do it all the time.

Gefilte fishing is a metaphor of the spiritual quest. We are seeking that which cannot be sought. If we seek outward, we find that it is inward. If we seek inward, we find that it is outward. Why? Because the gefilte fish is smarter than we are. It sees us coming and flees.

True spirituality is not inward or outward. God is not inside us or outside us. From God's perspective, there is no in or out. In and out only make sense from the point of view of the self that defines them.

God and gefilte know no self. God and gefilte have no point of view, no perspective. God and gefilte are all views and all perspectives simultaneously. Good and evil, right and wrong, war and peace—all this comes from God (Isaiah 45:7). We need not seek God amidst the stuff of everyday life; we need only recognize God as the stuff of everyday life.

Rami M. Shapiro, *Gefilte Fishing: A Guide to Spiritual Awakening*
(Miami: Light House Books, 1994), 11

The Journey

The journey that we all make through life is guided by forces far beyond our conscious knowledge. We are like travelers who innocently buy our tickets for a trip, never quite knowing where the journey will end or how. The destinations of our lives and their meanings are revealed only later on. Only after we arrive at our stop, shake off the dust, and look back at the distance may we say, "Of course! This makes perfect sense."

Tirzah Firestone, *With Roots in Heaven: One Woman's Passionate Journey into the Heart of her Faith* (New York: Plume, 1998), 338

Biographies

Dr. Rachel Adler holds a joint faculty position at the University of Southern California and Hebrew Union College–Jewish Institute of Religion in Los Angeles.

Rose Haas Altschuler was a community leader in Chicago who helped to establish the North Shore Congregation Israel (now in Glencoe) and its Sunday school.

Rabbi Terry Bookman is the senior rabbi of Temple Beth Am in Miami, Florida. He pioneered the notion of a spiritual checkup with his congregants and was among the first to place daily spiritual workouts on his congregation's website.

Rabbi Eugene B. Borowitz is the leading liberal Jewish theologian in North America, known for his articulation of the covenental relationship and his championing of personal autonomy, which permeate his writings. A senior member of the faculty of Hebrew Union College–Jewish Institute of Religion, he is the Sigmund L. Falk Distinguished Service Professor of Modern Jewish Thought and was formerly the director of education at the Union of American Hebrew Congregations.

E. M. Broner is professor emerita at Wayne State University and the author of nine books, including *A Weave of Women* and *Mornings and Mourning: A Kaddish Journal*. She is also co-author of *The Women's Haggadah*.

Rabbi Wayne Dosick is one of the leading teachers of Jewish spirituality in North America. He is the spiritual leader of the Elijah Minyan in San Diego, a member of the faculty of San Diego University, and the author of numerous works that reclaim the spiritual dimension of Jewish religious practice and belief.

Dr. Jean Bethke Elshtain is on the faculty of the University of Chicago. Following the receipt of her Ph.D. from Brandeis University, she joined the faculty of the University of Massachusetts and then Vanderbilt University where she was the first woman to hold an endowed professorship at that institution. While she is the author of numerous books and articles, particularly in the area of feminism and feminist politics, her latest books are *The King is Dead* and *Political Mothers*. She also writes a regular column in *The New Republic*.

Rabbi Edward Feinstein serves Valley Beth Shalom in Encino, California.

Rabbi Sally Finestone is assistant director at Harvard University Hillel.

Rabbi Tirzah Firestone is an author, psychotherapist, and founding rabbi of the Jewish Renewal Congregation in Boulder, Colorado.

Ray Frank (1864–1948) was a schoolteacher, writer, and popular lecturer who came close to being the first female rabbi.

Rabbi Irving (Yitz) Greenberg is the president of the Jewish Life Network and the founding president emeritus of CLAL: National Jewish Center for Learning and Leadership. He is also the chairperson of the U.S. Holocaust Memorial Commission.

Joel Lurie Grishaver is the creative chairperson of Torah Aura Productions, an educational products and textbook company. Joel is a prolific writer and trend-setting educator.

Rabbi Susan Grossman is the rabbi of Beth Shalom Congregation of Howard County, Maryland.

Rabbi Joshua Hammerman is the spiritual leader of Temple Beth El in Stamford, Connecticut. He writes a regular column for the (New York) *Jewish Week*.

Lee Meyerhoff Hendler is a lecturer on leadership, Jewish identity, and intergenerational philanthropy. She is president of Chizuk Amuno Congregation in Baltimore, Maryland.

Rabbi Norman D. Hirsch is rabbi of Temple Beth Am in Seattle, Washington.

Rabbi Richard Israel was the director of the Hillel Council of Greater Boston and author of *The Kosher Pig*.

Rodger Kamenetz is best known as the author of *The Jew in the Lotus,* which was made into a documentary film. He is Professor of English and Religious Studies at Louisiana State University. He is also a poet, whose works include *Terra Infirma* and *The Missing Jew*.

Rabbi Harold S. Kushner is the rabbi emeritus of Temple Israel in Natick, Massachusetts, and the author of numerous books, including *When Bad Things Happen to Good People.*

Rabbi Lawrence Kushner, formerly the spiritual leader of Temple Beth El of the Sudbury River Valley in Sudbury, Massachusetts, is on the faculty of Hebrew Union College–Jewish Institute of Religion. He is among the leading Jewish spiritual teachers in North America and the author of numerous books.

Rabbi Shoni Labowitz is the codirector of Living Waters, a holistic spa and retreat center in Florida.

Rabbi Steven Z. Leder has served the Wilshire Boulevard Temple in Los Angeles since 1986.

Tehilla Lichtenstein was the cofounder with her husband, Rabbi Morris Lichtenstein, of the Society of Jewish Science. Following his death, she continued as the first woman to occupy a Jewish pulpit in North America.

Rabbi Eugene Lipman (1919–1994) was a social activist who served as rabbi of Temple Sinai in Washington, D.C.

Rabbi Jane Rachel Litman is on the faculty of California State University, Northridge, and serves Congregation Kol Simcha of Orange County, California.

Rabbi Mark Joel Mahler is rabbi of Temple Emanuel of South Hills in Pittsburgh, Pennsylvania.

Dr. Jacob Rader Marcus was director of the American Jewish Archives and Distinguished Service Professor of American Jewish History at Hebrew Union College–Jewish Institute of Religion in Cincinnati.

Rabbi Gunther Plaut is the Senior Scholar of Holy Blossom Temple in Toronto, Ontario, Canada, where he served as rabbi for many years. He is the author/editor of many books, including the seminal *The Torah: A Modern Commentary*, the standard liberal commentary on the Torah.

Rabbi Bernard S. Raskas is the rabbi emeritus of Temple of Aaron Synagogue in St. Paul, Minnesota.

Melinda Ribner, C.S.W., is the founder and director of the Jewish Meditation Circle and author of *Everyday Kabbalah: A Practical Guide for Meditation, Healing and Personal Growth*. She has also taught at the New York Kollel.

Rabbi Jeffrey Salkin is the spiritual leader of the Community Synagogue in Port Washington, New York, and the author of several books, including *Putting God on the Guest List* and *Searching for My Brothers*.

Rabbi David Saperstein is the director of the Religious Action Center in Washington, D.C.

Rabbi Sandy Eisenberg Sasso, author of the award-winning *God Said Amen, God's Paintbrush, In God's Name, But God Remembered, A Prayer for Heaven's Sake*, and *God in Between*, is rabbi of Congregation Beth-El Zedeck in Indianapolis, IN. She is active in the interfaith community and has written and lectured on the renewal of spirituality and the discovery of religious imagination in children of all faiths. She is the second woman to be ordained a rabbi (1974) and the first rabbi to become a mother.

Rabbi Zalman Schachter-Shalomi is considered by many to be the father of the Jewish Renewal Movement in North America and is the force behind Aleph, the consortium of Renewal organizations, as well as the Pnai Or synagogues, the original of which he founded in Philadelphia. Originally trained as a Lubavitch rabbi, he also holds a D.H.L. in Human Relations from Hebrew Union College–Jewish Institute of Religion. He coined the term "spiritual eldering" and is the author of a book by the same name.

Rabbi Alexander M. Schindler (1926–2000) was the president of the Union of American Hebrew Congregations from 1973–1996.

Rabbi Harold Schulweis is the senior rabbi of Valley Beth Shalom in Encino, California, where he pioneered many innovative synagogue models including para-rabbis. Rabbi Schulweis is the author of numerous books and articles, including *Finding Each Other in Judaism: Meditations on the Life Passages*.

Francine Weinman Schwartz is an author and teacher of adult Jewish education and Holocaust studies.

Dr. Kenneth Seeskin is Professor and Chair of the Department of Philosophy at Northwestern University and holds the position of Director of the Jewish Studies Program.

Dr. Alice Shalvi is the former director of the Conservative Yeshiva in Jerusalem.

Rabbi Rami Shapiro is director of Metivta in Los Angeles. He is the author of numerous books, including *Wisdom of the Jewish Sages, Minyan*, and *The Way of Splendor*.

Biographies

Rabbi Byron L. Sherwin, Ph.D., is the academic vice president of the Spertus Institute in Chicago, Illinois, and the author of numerous books, monographs, and articles.

Gloria Steinem is a writer, activist, and feminist organizer who is the consulting editor of *Ms.*, the magazine she cofounded in 1972. She is president of Voters for Choice and author of several books, including *Moving Beyond Words* (New York: Simon and Schuster, 1995).

Rabbi Jack Stern is rabbi emeritus of Westchester Reform Temple in Scarsdale, New York, and past president of the Central Conference of American Rabbis.

Rabbi Michael Stroh is rabbi of Temple Har Zion in Thornhill, Ontario, Canada.

Rabbi Joseph Telushkin is an associate at CLAL: National Center for Jewish Learning and Leadership and has been on the faculty of the Wexner Heritage Foundation. He also serves as rabbi of the Synagogue for the Performing Arts in Los Angeles, California.

Rabbi Allan C. Tuffs is rabbi of Temple Shalom in Levittown, Pennsylvania.

Dr. Ellen Umansky is Abrams Professor of Jewish Thought at Fairfield University in Fairfield, Connecticut.

Rabbi Arnold Jacob Wolf is the rabbi emeritus of KAM–Isaiah Israel Congregation in Highland Park, Illinois.

Rabbi Samuel Wolk was rabbi of Temple Beth Emeth in Albany, New York.

Rabbi David Wolpe, author and scholar, is the rabbi of Sinai Temple in Los Angeles, California.

Rabbi Eric H. Yoffie is the president of the Union of American Hebrew Congregations.

Dr. Edward Zerin is a rabbi and codirector of the Westlake Center for Marital and Family Counseling in Westlake Village, California.